ARNOLD WOLFERS, Sterling Professor Emeritus of International Relations, Yale University, is presently Special Advisor (formerly Director) of the Washington Center of Foreign Policy Research, The Johns Hopkins School of Advanced International Studies. Professor Wolfers was born in Switzerland in 1892. He holds a Doctor of Law degree from the University of Zurich, a Ph.D. from the University of Giessen, and honorary degrees from Mt. Holyoke College and the University of Rochester. He practiced law in Switzerland, and from 1930 to 1933 he was the Director of the Hochschule für Politik in Berlin.

Professor Wolfers came to the United States in 1933 to teach at Yale, where he remained until his retirement in 1957. He has been a Consultant to the Office of the Provost Marshal General (1942–44); Office of Strategic Services (1944–45); National War College (1947–1951); Institute of Defense Analyses (1960–); Department of State (1960–); and Civilian Advisory Group of the Army War College (1962–). His books include *Britain and France between Two Wars* (1940); *The Anglo-American Tradition,* as co-editor with L. Martin (1956); *Alliance Policy in the Cold War,* as editor and co-author (1959); and *Discord and Collaboration* (1962).

Britain and France between Two Wars

CONFLICTING STRATEGIES OF PEACE FROM VERSAILLES TO WORLD WAR II

ARNOLD WOLFERS

The Norton Library NEW YORK

W · W · NORTON & COMPANY · INC ·

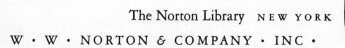

First published in the Norton Library 1966 by arrangement with Harcourt, Brace & World, Inc.

Published simultaneously in Canada by George J. McLeod Limited, Toronto

PRINTED IN THE UNITED STATES OF AMERICA
2 3 4 5 6 7 8 9 0

ACKNOWLEDGMENTS

I wish to acknowledge the aid and counsel which I have received from my colleagues at Yale University. To my friend, Mr. Nicholas J. Spykman, I owe a debt of warm gratitude for his penetrating and careful criticism of the entire manuscript, for his unfailing advice, and valuable suggestions.

To Mr. Robert Blum, my research assistant, I cannot hope to give all the credit he deserves. I am deeply indebted to him for his untiring and self-effacing assistance, his devotion and his grasp of the intricacies of the subject. Without his help, it would have been impossible to work through the mass of material which forms the background of this study and which includes among other documents the French and British parliamentary debates between 1918 and 1939, and all the discussions in the League that dealt with European affairs. His advice and his many contributions have been invaluable.

My sincere thanks go to Miss Evelyn Whelden for her helpful criticism of the language and style, and to her and the members of the Institute staff for all their work of typing, checking, and proof-reading.

ARNOLD WOLFERS

CONTENTS

PART TWO: BRITAIN

Britain and France between Two Wars

CONFLICTING STRATEGIES OF PEACE
FROM VERSAILLES TO WORLD WAR II

Introduction

ONLY twenty years after peace had been concluded with Germany at Versailles, Britain and France were again at war with her. Long before that, the new order of Europe which had been instituted at the close of the World War had begun to disintegrate, and vanquished Germany had gradually taken the political initiative away from the victors of 1918. The decay of a peace settlement as radical and rapid as this needs to be explained, but the complexity of the problem is such that no single explanation can be found.

To what extent, if any, the terms of the Treaty of Versailles must bear responsibility for what followed will long remain a favorite topic of controversy. Economic policies—erection of new and higher tariff walls, unsound international capital movements, debt payments, and the manipulation of currencies—are very generally credited with a part of the blame. And everyone will admit that the foreign policies of the Great Powers subsequent to the signing of the treaties were an important, if not a decisive, factor.

There is no great power inside or outside of Europe that did not add to the troubles with which that Continent was beset: the Soviet Union by its efforts to undermine the social order of Western Europe, Japan by starting a new era of imperialistic expansion, the United States by a sudden reversal of policy from active participation in the World War and in the treaty-making of Versailles to political isolation, and finally each of the European states in countless fashions.

Once the Peace Conference was over, Europe was left to face its own problems. Whereas the Conference, like the World War itself, had been more than a purely European matter, in the twenty years to follow the policies of the great European powers, victors and vanquished, dominated the European scene. The fate of the new order came to rest almost exclusively on the course of action which they decided to pursue. In recent years Germany, with her sensational return to political prominence, may have seemed the sole dynamic force influencing the trend of events in Europe. Long before Hitler came upon the scene and took to himself all the credit for freeing his people from the "shackles of Versailles," German policy had been leading up to this result. Determined to overthrow the "system of Versailles," she had been from the beginning a potent agent of change. At the same time, Britain and France, the two main beneficiaries of the treaty among the Great Powers, were at no stage of the proceedings to be classed as mere passive onlookers. Even when the preponderance and unquestioned leadership with which they had started had begun to vanish, and their interests and ideas ceased to dominate the councils of Europe, the eyes of the world still turned to London and Paris whenever Europe was confronted with any new crisis. When the post-war settlements collapsed and Europe was again plunged into war it was British and French policies, more than any others, that went down to defeat.

The Conference of Versailles left to Britain and France a difficult heritage. In the Conference itself the striking difference in interest and outlook that separated the two countries had been revealed. The Treaty of Versailles represented a compromise between widely divergent views. Although both countries did, to be sure, concur in a desire to preserve the newly established peace, each set out to follow the strategy of peace which it believed was in its best interests. The conflict between their policies was to become a major source of their misfortunes.

Every "strategy" implies a choice of means to an end. The two countries saw eye to eye as far as the ultimate goal was concerned, not merely because they both wished to preserve peace, but because they both realized that a possible revolt of those who were dissatisfied and embittered by the peace settlements was the main threat to peace with which they would have to cope. They disagreed, however, in regard to the means by which this danger could best be averted.

Traditional European diplomacy offered a choice of two types of peace policy. One consisted in building up unquestioned preponderance of power on the side of the defenders of the established order, and in equipping them with the means of coercion necessary to prevent a successful revolt. This meant holding the lid down on the boiling kettle of European unrest and dissatisfaction. It was this conception, as we shall see, which, on the whole, appealed to the French as best fitted to meet the requirements of their security. The other strategy called for a removal of the causes of revolt in order to eliminate the chances of an explosion. This meant taking the new order merely as a starting point in a process of continuous adjustment, intended eventually to produce a new and more generally satisfactory settlement. Britain, by virtue of her geographic position, her interests, and her outlook on European affairs, was drawn toward this alternative, although not without certain important reservations. There was obviously little hope of reconciling two such divergent courses.

But these were not the only solutions proposed for the problems of post-Versailles Europe. Two other policies found powerful advocates, one emanating from Washington, the other from Moscow, the two centers of strongest external influence on Europe. Lenin called upon Europe to unite under the banner of Communism and to escape from imperialist rivalry by merging into the one and universal Bolshevist union. Woodrow Wilson, on the other hand, stirred Europe with a program that was hardly less revolutionary, in which he invited the peoples of Central Europe, against whom the United States were then fighting, to set up democratic régimes, and called upon all nations to form a "steadfast concert of peace," a league of the democratic countries which, by "common agreement for a common object," would give security and justice to all.

The Russians struggled hard for many years after peace had been established to gain influence on the Continent and to promote world revolution, while the United States turned its back on Europe immediately after the Peace Conference. Nevertheless, the Wilsonian concepts and promises remained an element to be reckoned with long after the influence of Lenin on European affairs had receded. Governments which were democratic, in form at least, were set up all over Central Europe, largely because of the hopes raised by Wilson. The League of Nations was erected and the Covenant, on Wilson's insistence, was incorporated into the Versailles Treaty. "Wilsonian" ideas remained a powerful factor in the shaping of European party programs, particularly in Britain. It is hardly an exaggeration to say that a third type of peace strategy, later centering on collective security, accompanied the traditional French and British foreign policies throughout the post-war era. It complicated the situation by turning the Franco-British dispute into a triangular one. This third or "Wilsonian" factor went down to defeat together with the other two. When democracy was abandoned in Germany in 1933 and when, only a few years later, the League lost nearly all political significance, the disintegration of the Versailles order in general was well under way.

The success of the British and French, as well as of the "Wilsonian," peace policies depended to a large extent on the degree of harmony and agreement between the three schools, for every conflict between them offered an opportunity to the "other side." It should not be forgotten that there was another side, to all intents another world, always potentially if not actually in revolt against the newly established order of 1919. The picture of Europe between the two wars would be gravely distorted if a discussion of British and French foreign policy were to relegate the moves of the opposing forces entirely to the background. For a short time, it is true, from 1924 to 1929, it looked as if that other world, willingly or under pressure, had resigned itself to its fate and that Europe was on the threshold of a long period of tranquillity. This was the "era of prosperity," when vast capital exports from the United States and other centers of capital wealth were giving temporary relief to many countries. It was a period when neither Germany, Japan, nor Italy had gained enough strength to challenge the control over the affairs of the world enjoyed by the nations then predominant, or else were still hoping that their objectives might be realized through a gradual process of peaceful adjustment. Liberal opinion in all countries believed in those days that a "new era" of universal peace and international co-operation was at hand and that the new peace machinery had effectively outlawed aggression and war. That this was a sad delusion was soon to become manifest.

In 1929, the reign of prosperity came abruptly to an end, and soon afterwards peace was disrupted. Economic disaster undermined the strength of the satiated powers, while it increased the discontent of the others. The forces of rebellion against the existing distribution of power and wealth that had long been smoldering below the surface broke out openly, first in the Far East, then in the Mediterranean, and finally in the heart of Europe. The movement gained in momentum from many factors—from the power of faith in a just cause as well as from bitter resentment, from the pressure of economic adversity as well as from unsatiated ambition and dreams of empire. Revolutionary forces mingled with nationalistic passions to help undermine the established order.

The threat of this eruption threw its shadow over the policies of Britain and France from the very start. Would the defenders of the peace and of the *status quo* be strong and united enough to keep the forces of revolt under control, or would they be able to reach new agreements with their opponents by which to appease them before the revolt flamed out into war? The answer is obviously in the negative. Peace was not preserved. Our analysis, first of French and then of British foreign policy in the period from Versailles to the outbreak of the new war in Europe, will concern two peace strategies which were almost continually in conflict and ended in failure.

PART ONE: FRANCE

I. The Policy of "*Sécurité*"

EVER since the World War "*sécurité*" has been the keynote of French foreign policy. At least, this is what her statesmen have unanimously and consistently proclaimed. This term, taken by itself, does not throw much light on the particular character of French policy. After all, almost every government in the world professes to be seeking peace, safety, and security. The specific meaning of the term becomes more apparent when the French speak of their desire for "*garanties de sécurité contre une agression de l'Allemagne.*"[1] France was obsessed by the fear of a new war with Germany. At Versailles, she was almost exclusively occupied with efforts to obtain protection from the menace of future German aggression. But the settlements reached at the Peace Conference did not allay her fears; she continued ever after to seek new guarantees. This psychological background has to be remembered in order to understand a policy of security such as France came to pursue. It was a policy directed not merely toward the defense and enforcement of the Treaty of Versailles (which was regarded as the minimum requirement for French security), but also toward the erection of still more safeguards against Germany.

At first sight it seems astonishing to find France already hypnotized by the "German menace," at a time when Germany was

[1] A collection of diplomatic documents published by the Ministère des Affaires Etrangères in 1924 and covering the security negotiations from the close of the World War to 1923 bore the title: *Documents Diplomatiques: Documents relatifs aux négociations concernant les garanties de sécurité contre une agression de l'Allemagne (10 janvier 1919–7 décembre 1923).*

prostrate, exhausted, and internally disrupted. Many British observers considered this French preoccupation as evidencing an almost hysterical nervousness, "a sort of pathological obsession,"[2] if not, in fact, a cloak for imperialist designs for conquest and revenge. But the French were not concerned about the near future; they were convinced that the advantages France had gained, great although they might be at the time, were only temporary and precarious. "*Les années dangereuses ne sont pas surtout les années présentes; ce sont celles qui viendront après,*" said Paul-Boncour in 1924.[3] "*Le temps,*" complained Poincaré in 1922, "*a déjà, en passant, travaillé contre nous.*"[4] That France's view was not too pessimistic the following chapters should help to make plain. Because the dangers that threatened the *status quo* were still remote, there was all the more reason to fear lest countries which were less vitally concerned and more prone to optimism, like Britain, fail to take the threats with proper seriousness and refuse to prepare in time the means with which to meet them.

Overshadowing all other considerations was the knowledge that Germany was potentially far stronger than France. A country of forty million inhabitants was facing one of seventy million. Add to this the French belief that the Germans were a particularly aggressive and military nation, which had been the cause of all previous encounters and which would seek revenge if given an opportunity, and the conclusions are obvious. On the basis of these assumptions, France could feel secure only if two conditions were

[2] Comte Wladimir d'Ormesson, *France* (1939), p. 10, when speaking of British opinion about the French policy of security.

[3] Joseph Paul-Boncour, August 23, 1924; France, *Journal Officiel, Débats Parlementaires,* Chambre des Députés, 1924, p. 3103; hereinafter cited: Chambre, *Débats.*

[4] Raymond Poincaré, President of the Council of Ministers, June 29, 1922; France, *Journal Officiel, Débats Parlementaires,* Sénat, 1922, p. 984; hereinafter cited: Sénat, *Débats.*

fulfilled. She and the countries on whose assistance she could rely would have to be made capable of holding Germany permanently in a state of "artificial inferiority." In addition, France would have to possess sufficient military superiority of her own to ward off German invasion until her allies could come to her support. This was a program calling for a reversal of the natural order of power on the Rhine. It was a difficult and, in any event, a precarious undertaking.

It is only fair to add that the French insisted that they were seeking not superiority or hegemony, but merely trying to equalize Germany's natural advantages. But this is only a matter of terminology. What France wanted to equal was not Germany's actual power, but her potential strength. She justified her demand for relatively larger armaments for herself and for military control of German territory by contending that Germany would be able to make up for the difference by a superior "*potentiel de guerre.*" "*Nous avons le droit,*" said Fabry in 1933, "*quand on cherche l'égalité de sécurité, de demander une supériorité de moyens, sans quoi nous acceptons délibérément l'hégémonie militaire de l'Allemagne. . . . Il faudra toujours qu'une des deux puissances soit plus forte que l'autre. Les traités ont voulu que ce soit la France. C'était juste et nécessaire.*"[5]

A policy such as France set out to pursue was in danger of becoming involved in a vicious circle. If Germany was regarded as so dangerous and potentially so powerful that the free development of her forces would have to be permanently crippled and parts of her territory taken away or put under military control, it was inevitable that her resentment would be aroused and her "aggressiveness" heightened. The British, as we shall see, never ceased to emphasize this fact. Was not the danger intensified by

[5] Jean Fabry, November 14, 1933; Chambre, *Débats*, 1933, p. 4108. See also Alexander Werth, *The Destiny of France* (1937), pp. 223-224.

the very means which were designed to remove it? But the French believed that they had no alternative, since they could see no other way of eliminating the German menace. This accounts for the demands which they presented at Versailles and afterwards, the object of which was to defeat in advance even the most violent future German revolt.

The French Government did not propose the extreme program that some Frenchmen advocated. This would have consisted in breaking up Germany into small states and putting an end to the existence of an overpowering neighbor. Instead, France demanded that her strategic frontier be on the Rhine. "*Quand on est maître du Rhin, on est maître de tout le pays* [meaning the Rhineland]. *Quand on n'est pas sur le Rhin, on a tout perdu,*" declared Foch in May, 1919.[6] This was an age-old French credo. "*Sécurité totale*" for France, and, if the French were right, for the Anglo-Saxon democracies, required that the German territory on the left bank of the Rhine, as well as the Rhine bridges, be placed permanently under French or Allied military control. The Anglo-Saxon countries refused to accept this thesis. Instead, the treaty provided for the permanent demilitarization of the Rhineland and for its temporary military occupation by allied troops. To this, however, were added pacts of guarantee in which the United States and Great Britain promised to assist France in the case of unprovoked German aggression.[7] These pacts and the provisions

[6] Marshal Foch, declaration to the Peace Conference, May 6, 1919; *Documents Diplomatiques, op. cit.*, p. 54.

[7] On March 14, 1919, during the negotiations regarding the guarantees of security, President Wilson and Lloyd George, confronted by France's demands for the permanent occupation of the left bank of the Rhine, offered to Clemenceau in exchange the promise of American and British assistance to France in the event of German aggression. The French, as may be seen in Clemenceau's note of March 17, and particularly in the attitude adopted by Marshal Foch and Raymond Poincaré, then President of the Republic, were reluctant to barter tangible physical guarantees of security for promises of future assistance. The

concerning the Rhineland were together considered by France's allies to be a satisfactory substitute for the establishment of the Rhine as a military frontier. The intention was to remove the danger of a sudden invasion of French soil by the demilitarization provisions and thus to give the Anglo-Saxon allies or guarantors

treaties were signed in almost identical terms at Versailles on June 28, 1919. Article 1 of both treaties provided for immediate assistance to France "in the event of any unprovoked movement of aggression against her being made by Germany."

The preamble to the British treaty contained a formula that was to symbolize to the French the humiliation of having accepted treatment as a "*nation protégée*":

"Whereas there is a danger that the stipulations relating to the Left Bank of the Rhine contained in the Treaty of Peace signed this day at Versailles may not at first provide adequate security and protection to the French Republic; and

"Whereas His Britannic Majesty is willing, subject to the consent of His Parliament and provided that a similar obligation is entered into by the United States of America, to undertake to support the French Government in the case of an unprovoked movement of aggression being made against France by Germany; . . ."

The preamble to the treaty with the United States, on the other hand, explained that German aggression against France would not only result in "exposing France anew to the intolerable burdens of an unprovoked war, but that such aggression on the part of Germany would be and is so regarded by the Treaty of Versailles as a hostile act against all the Powers signatory to that Treaty and as calculated to disturb the Peace of the world by involving inevitably and directly the States of Europe and indirectly, as experience has amply and unfortunately demonstrated, the world at large; . . ." The third paragraph of the preamble, corresponding to the first paragraph in the British treaty quoted above, declared that both "the United States of America and the French Republic" fear that the Versailles Treaty might not provide security "to France, on the one hand and the United States of America, as one of the signatories of the Treaty of Versailles, on the other: . . ."

The British treaty was approved in the House of Commons on July 21, 1919, and in the House of Lords on July 24, 1919; ratifications were exchanged with France on November 20, 1919. However, as the result of the failure of the United States to ratify its treaty with France, the agreement with Great Britain did not come into force. Texts of the treaties: *Cmd. 221* (The Command papers are listed in numerical order in the Bibliography); French text in *Documents Diplomatiques, op. cit.*, Nos. 14, 15. See also Documents Nos. 4-13 for the negotiations, and the account given by André Tardieu, *La Paix* (1921), Chapters V and VI.

time to come to France's assistance if Germany should nevertheless try to attack her. The French, not without bitterness and disappointment, bowed to this compromise, rather than lose the friendship and future support of their great allies. What made them feel that they had "lost the peace" was the failure of these treaties to become effective, thereby destroying what France had even then regarded as only a second-best solution to her problem. Not only was the strategic superiority of France now brought far below her expectations, but the most effective promises of assistance for which France could hope had vanished. At the same time Germany's dissatisfaction was by no means removed.

At Versailles, France wavered between two methods by which Germany might be kept in check. Either she could try to rely largely on making herself superior in power and thus become less dependent on outside help, or she could put her faith primarily in the military assistance which she could obtain from others. At no stage of the negotiations, however, was the French Government ready to drop the demand for what she came to call *"la solidarité des alliés."*[8] Even the strategic frontier on the Rhine was, Marshal Foch argued, to be a part of *"l'organisation défensive de la Coalition."*[9] A coalition comprising all of the Great Powers with the exception of the two Central European Empires had been necessary to defeat Germany. The *"caractère interallié de sa victoire,"* as Tardieu put it,[10] was not forgotten by France. It convinced the French that Germany could be held in check only with the help of allies. *"L'idée dominante, on serait tenté de dire la hantise des gouvernements français,"* says a French writer, *"fut de chercher des alliés contre tout retour offensif de la puissance alle-*

[8] Georges Clemenceau, President of the Council of Ministers, September 25, 1919; Chambre, *Débats,* 1919, p. 4580.

[9] Memorandum, January 10, 1919; *Documents Diplomatiques, op. cit.,* p. 13.

[10] André Tardieu, President of the Council of Ministers, November 8, 1929; Chambre, *Débats,* 1929, p. 3065.

mande."[11] In some form or other the grand coalition of the World War would have to be carried over into peace-time.

This accounts for the intense dismay of the French when, even before the adjournment of the Versailles Conference, they found themselves deserted by almost all of their great allies. Some of them were never to be recovered. Russia was struggling in the throes of the Bolshevist Revolution, and was for a long time considered as an enemy rather than as a friend. More than once during the post-war years she was on the verge of alignment with Germany. Next, the United States turned her back on Europe and refused even to ratify the Versailles Treaty. Not only did the pact of guarantee which Wilson had negotiated with Clemenceau fail to materialize, but the pledges of assistance contained in the League Covenant did not become binding on the United States. Two other Great Powers on the side of the victors, Japan and Italy, left the conference so dissatisfied that they could not be relied upon to defend the new order. As a result, Britain was the only Great Power from which any semblance of "allied solidarity" could be expected.

Relations with Britain therefore became one of France's major preoccupations. But even there she had to cope not merely with resistance in minor matters, but with a complete lack of agreement on what was for France the crux of the whole matter, namely, the necessity of enforcing the treaties upon Germany and of supplementing the guarantees of security which they contained.

While it may not be hard to understand why French demands for security against a German attack from across the Rhine should have been so extensive, there is another and more perplexing aspect of her policy, with which we shall deal in detail as we go along. France, despite her fear, did not limit herself to preparations for

[11] H. Beuve-Méry, *Vers la plus grande Allemagne* (Centre d'Etudes de Politique Etrangère, Section d'Information, Publication No. 14, 1939), p. 67.

the protection of her own soil, but left no doubt that she was determined to enforce the Peace Treaties in their entirety and to defend the whole new continental *status quo*. She wished to be regarded not merely as "*la garde du Rhin*"; her army was also to be "*la garantie de la stabilité politique de l'Europe,*"[12] the defender not only of her own frontiers, "*mais . . . de toutes les frontières, . . . de tous les peuples.*"[13] It would seem that this was greatly multiplying the dangers by which she was threatened. Was she not entangling herself unnecessarily in Germany's quarrels in remote regions and drawing the wrath of the revisionist powers upon herself? If by nature she was as much weaker than Germany as she claimed, could she afford to take on responsibilities of a continental scale? There seems at first sight to be such incongruity in this attitude that some people have doubted the sincerity of French fears and have believed that her clamor for more security was but a façade hiding a desire to enjoy supremacy or hegemony on the Continent. More flattering to France, and more in line with many declarations by her statesmen, would be the supposition that, apart from considerations of her own security, she was genuinely and generously concerned in the fate of the new Slavic states in Central Europe which she, as a defender of the small powers, sought to protect from German aggression.

While we cannot hope to penetrate into the real and decisive motives behind French policy—and they probably varied from period to period and from statesman to statesman—it seems most likely that France was again involved in the same vicious circle. She had two obvious reasons for pledging assistance to countries like Poland or Czechoslovakia. She feared, for one thing, that Germany, if she were able to expand in the East, would become so powerful that she could turn around and attack France successfully.

[12] André Tardieu, May 23, 1922; Chambre, *Débats,* 1922, p. 1545.

[13] Aristide Briand, President of the Council of Ministers, October 27, 1921; Sénat, *Débats,* 1921, p. 1811.

Also, she wished to assure herself of the assistance of those countries, whose military strength was by no means negligible as long as Germany was held to the provisions of the Versailles Treaty in regard to armaments. They were substitutes for France's prewar ally, Czarist Russia.

But, while France was acquiring the support from them which she had not been able to obtain from the Great Powers, she was at the same time incurring grave new risks. The defenses in the East might prove to be not only inadequate but a source of German exasperation and a major cause of conflict. French entanglement, in that case, might be the surest means of bringing about the new war on the Rhine against which she was seeking to protect herself. Not until the French policy had met with serious setbacks did some Frenchmen, after 1936, come to express the opinion that the far-flung commitments were a mistake and that France should seek security by entrenching herself behind the Maginot Line.

By making the sanctity of treaties and the strict enforcement of the *status quo* the fundamental principle of her foreign policy, France became involved in the same contradictions which had afflicted her commitments in the East. She believed it necessary for her security not to allow any provisions of the Peace Treaties to be violated with impunity or changed in favor of Germany. A precedent (the "*redoutable précédent*" of which Poincaré expressed his fear) [14] might otherwise be created. "*Une fois le premier détail de l'architecture tombé,*" exclaimed Herriot, "*tout l'édifice tomberait lui-même.*" [15] But in order to prevent any precedent from serving as a wedge by which Germany might start a general assault on the order of Versailles, France made herself the

[14] Raymond Poincaré to the British Ambassador in Paris, August 20, 1923; Ministère des Affaires Etrangères, *Documents Diplomatiques: Réponse du Gouvernement français à la lettre du Gouvernement britannique du 11 août 1923 sur les Réparations (20 août 1923)*, p. 7.

[15] Edouard Herriot, President of the Council of Ministers, July 11, 1924; Sénat, *Débats,* 1924, p. 1055.

target for all revisionist attacks. If she was to adhere to her purpose consistently, she had to oppose changes of the post-war settlements, even though they might conceivably have satisfied the Germans and thus have removed the dangers which she was trying to avert.

The specific connotation of the term "*sécurité*" as it was used by the French to explain their objective now becomes clearer. It referred to a state of things in which not only was the danger of a German invasion of French soil to be eliminated—security in the narrow sense of the word—but in which the entire new *status quo* as established in the Peace Treaties would be firmly protected by the superiority of the powers which were ready to defend it. "Security" came to play such an important role in post-war diplomacy that it is worth keeping this original French meaning in mind. Committees on "security" were established; pacts of "security" were negotiated; the relation of disarmament to "security" was debated at length. Later, interest came to center on "collective security." But even then something of the original French connotation was attached to the term. It was still an attempt to lay the specter of a German revisionist "explosion" against the established order by assigning superior force to the defenders of the "law."

If it seems unworthy of a Great Power to be motivated so exclusively by fear, and to think of itself as "*le seul grand peuple au monde qui soit menacé dans sa vie,*"[16] it should be remembered that, while France may initially have acted only from fear of another German invasion, her policy of security had led her to become the champion of the *status quo* and of the entire order of Central as well as of Western Europe. Her anxiety was, therefore, that of a nation with responsibilities and ambitions truly continental in character and extent.

[16] Paul Reynaud, December 27, 1935; Chambre, *Débats*, 1935, p. 2813.

II. Guarantees of Security

THE French quest for "security" had an amazingly broad scope in that it took into account the whole scale of threats to which France believed herself to be exposed.

She very naturally feared above all else lest she become the victim of another invasion, the battleground of another war. Her arguments at Versailles stressed the fact that German armies had crossed into France four times in a hundred years. (She glossed over the possibility that her own statesmen might have had some part in bringing about these invasions, three of which were directed against the Napoleons.) It was not astonishing that France should seek to avoid a repetition of what had been for her the greatest disaster of the last war. There was sympathy, therefore, in many quarters for her desire to ward off the danger of a new invasion, which was referred to as "direct attack" or "*agression directe*."

But France was not content with guarantees against direct attack, however elaborate they might be. She felt that such guarantees would not stand the test if Germany were allowed to gain mastery over Central and Eastern Europe. There existed, therefore, a second type of threat which was called "indirect attack" or "*agression indirecte*"; it would consist of an attack by Germany on one or more of her eastern or southeastern neighbors.[1] Preventive measures had to be taken against this contingency. Indirect aggres-

[1] For the distinction between "*agression directe*" and "*indirecte*" see France, Ministère des Affaires Etrangères, *Documents Diplomatiques: Documents relatifs aux négociations concernant les garanties de sécurité contre une agression de l'Allemagne (10 janvier 1919–7 décembre 1923)*, p. 92.

sion covered a wide realm of possibilities, which France had little desire to define or delimit with precision. By a slight stretch of the imagination, indeed, any effort to change the new *status quo* in the East or Southeast could be said to render France less secure or even to threaten her indirectly with invasion in the more or less remote future. The more unlikely it seemed that Germany would be capable or desirous of attacking France on the Rhine, the more decisive a role did "*agression indirecte*" come to play in European affairs, involving the whole controversial issue of the territorial, economic, and national problems of Central and Eastern Europe. The entanglement of France in the conflicts of that part of Europe became a matter of grave concern to the British.

France pushed her claims still further. It was not enough to set up barriers around Germany which would keep her from sending troops across her borders. Who could hope to stop Germany on those borders, particularly in the East and Southeast where her neighbors were relatively weak and unconsolidated, if she were free to develop the strength of which she was capable and attain a political position which would allow her to risk such an attack? Precautionary measures of security would therefore have to reach back into what might be called the preliminary stages of German aggression. It was necessary to prevent the Germans from preparing an attack. Her armaments had to be kept at a low level, her troops prohibited from approaching the French border (occupation or demilitarization of the Rhineland). It has even been suggested that reparations were used to reduce Germany's economic *potentiel de guerre*.

In a country where statesmen were turning their attention almost exclusively to the problem of security, there was bound to be a display of ingenuity in the discovery of means to guarantee this security. In fact, the French developed a most elaborate theory of guarantees. A distinction was drawn between "*garanties physiques*" and the other types of guarantees, mainly contractual in nature, which were spoken of as "*garanties supplémentaires.*" [2] An important section of French public opinion on the Right, headed by men like Marshal Foch, Poincaré, then President of the Republic, Franklin-Bouillon, and Louis Marin, was profoundly dissatisfied with the outcome of the Peace Conference, and some even opposed France's ratification of the treaty because the Allies had refused to grant France the ideal "*garantie physique*" of her security, that is, a strategic border on the Rhine. "*La nature,*" wrote Marshal Foch, in a note submitted to the Peace Conference on January 10, 1919, "*n'a disposé qu'une barrière sur la route de l'invasion: le Rhin.*" Any other guarantee, according to him, would be "*d'un effet lointain et inconnu.*" The French Government, in a memorandum of February 25, 1919, "*sur la fixation au Rhin de la frontiere occidentale de l'Allemagne et l'occupation interalliée des ponts du fleuve*"—a document that reveals many of the basic conceptions by which French post-war policy was to be guided—tried to convince the Anglo-Saxon countries that they, too, would profit by the "*garantie physique*" of the Rhine, "*la protection minima des démocraties occidentales et d'outre-mer,*" [3] which would give the maritime powers "*la possibilité de débarquer sur le Continent et de s'y battre.*" The Anglo-Saxon powers were deaf to the French argument that there might

[2] For this distinction see *ibid.*, p. 26 (French memorandum of February 25, 1919); André Tardieu, government representative for the debate on the Peace Treaty, September 2, 1919, Chambre, *Débats*, 1919, p. 4092; Georges Clemenceau, President of the Council of Ministers, December 29, 1918, Chambre, *Débats*, 1918, p. 3733.

[3] Marshal Foch's memorandum of January 10, 1919, and the French Government memorandum of February 25, 1919, are printed in *Cmd. 2169*, Nos. 9, 10 and in the *Documents Diplomatiques*, *op. cit.*, Nos. 1, 2. These publications also contain most of the other important documents relating to the negotiations regarding security from 1919 to 1923, particularly with reference to the Anglo-French alliance.

be equally valid reasons for France to establish a "*zone de sécurité*" on German soil and to separate the Rhineland militarily from the rest of Germany, as for them to keep the oceans under the control of their great fleets. When British statesmen later proclaimed that Britain's frontier was on the Rhine, they did not use the phrase literally. All they meant was that Great Britain was interested in the protection of France's eastern boundary, part of which in the Alsatian sector actually ran along the Rhine. France, having been denied the only "*garantie physique*" which nature provided, later replaced it, in a sense, by the Maginot Line of fortifications. All along, however, her efforts were directed toward the substitution of other guarantees for the unattainable "physical guarantee." Whether or not she would have tried to obtain them anyway to supplement the protection which the Rhine would have offered cannot be conjectured.

The character of these other guarantees—the "*garanties supplémentaires*" which France tried to obtain from other countries—significantly influenced French peace strategy and helps to explain many of the most striking French moves both at Geneva and elsewhere. The purpose of all of the guarantees was to add to the strength of French national armaments, her first line of defense. The "*garanties supplémentaires*" therefore consisted in bringing the armies of other nations to the support of France in case she should become involved in another war with Germany. They were secondary lines of defense, and part of a comprehensive system of security that could be measured in quantitative terms by being compared with the number of French army corps to which it was equivalent in the opinion of the general staff. To perform this function the guarantee had to consist either of a reliable promise of military assistance, or, if that could not be obtained, of promises of such economic or financial aid as would help the French to win a war. Greater importance was attached, naturally, to promises of military assistance. If reliable, such promises might decrease the strain on the first line of defense, the national armaments, but they could be counted as substitutes only if they implied "immediate and automatic assistance" based on "pre-arranged military plans" and providing for prompt "technical execution." A "*garantie supplémentaire*" was of no value unless it contained these basic provisions, and they became the criteria by which the French judged all proposals brought forth in conferences on disarmament and security.[4]

The simplest form of a promise of military assistance was the old-fashioned alliance, and it was, therefore, hardly surprising that France should set out to build up a whole system of such alliances and pacts of mutual assistance. A large part of her foreign policy centered around the negotiation of such agreements. Indeed, they provided the key to her relations with most countries. But these pacts were frowned upon in some circles because they conflicted with the new theories of international diplomacy which had spread from the Anglo-Saxon countries to the Continent. While France did not on this account abandon her alliance policy, she did attempt, as we shall see, to give it a new form and to supplement the alliances by "international guarantees" or collective agreements. The League of Nations naturally presented itself as the most important and most promising guarantee of this nature. Even French statesmen who were skeptical about the League in the beginning supported it when it was recognized as possibly offering an additional "international guarantee" which might develop into a general alliance providing for reliable assistance to France by all the members of the League in case of a German attack. Since the League was too cumbersome to offer aid rapidly and could not save France from invasion, it was classified as a "guarantee of vic-

[4] See below, pp. 167 ff.

tory" rather than as a "guarantee against invasion." Its function would in any case be that of a last line of defense in a whole hierarchy of defense measures called *"l'organisation de la paix,"* ranging from national armaments through alliances and multilateral agreements to general pacts and covenants.

France was often criticized, particularly in the days of Poincaré, for being over-pedantic about the legal aspects of international affairs and for insisting with such vehemence on the "sanctity" of the Peace Treaties. Actually, her attitude was a natural consequence of her policy of security. Even the so-called "physical guarantees" depended for their success to some extent upon the fulfillment of legal obligations and the acknowledgment of legal rights. Of what use was the Rhine as a barrier unless France had the right to station her troops on the bridges and could depend on being assisted in the defense of her rights? The non-physical guarantees were based even more conspicuously on legal grounds. Since they consisted in promises of assistance, their reliability depended entirely on the way in which nations would live up to their legal obligations, and on the interpretation they would give to the law by which they were committed. Therefore, to uphold the principle of the sanctity of treaties meant, above all, being sure that her allies as well as the members of the League would honor their signatures.

A similar "legalistic" attitude was adopted toward Germany. By treaty after treaty, by signature after signature, France sought to chain her to the *status quo* and to make any move of liberation by which she might seek to free herself of the *"liens dans lesquels on a essayé de l'enfermer"* [5] not merely illegal, but a breach of promise to a large group of nations. The more France could rely on public opinion throughout the world to react vigorously against

[5] Jean Fabry, March 1, 1929; Chambre, *Débats,* 1929, p. 775.

violations of the law, the more she could hope for action against a lawbreaker. She dug herself in, not only behind walls of mortar but also behind a closely knit network of legal trenches, and made her security depend to not a slight degree on the reliance she could place on international law. It was an unfortunate result of this policy that the Germans came to consider the acceptance of obligations under international law as identical with acquiescence to the French defense of the *status quo* of Versailles. This emphasis on legality also made it doubly important for France to live up to her own treaty obligations. "*Toute notre défense contre l'Allemagne,*" said Herriot, "*. . . a consisté à nous placer toujours sur le terrain des contrats.*"[6] When she defaulted on her war debts, when she was hesitant—to say the least—to undertake strong League action against Italy, critics at home were quick to point out the dangers of such examples.

In a world of sovereign states every country is concerned with safeguarding itself from external attack. There is nothing unusual, therefore, in a policy the objective of which is to obtain greater security. The exceptional character of France's policy lay in a difference of degree rather than of direction. It was not "normal" for the policy of a great power, especially a victorious power, to be based so openly on the fear of future attack by its vanquished opponent and so exclusively focused on guarantees of safety. Just as in legal phraseology one speaks of the limits of "legitimate defense," one might be tempted to define the limits of "legitimate security." Certainly, from the point of view of stability and of "moral disarmament," a situation which called for so elaborate a "system of guarantees" was beset with dangers. The more the strategy of peace after the World War reflected the French idea

[6] Edouard Herriot, President of the Council of Ministers, December 12, 1932 (during the debate on war debts); Chambre, *Débats*, 1932, p. 3530.

of the need for "guarantees of security," the more it was led to emphasize force, even though it were "collective force," arrayed against the "potential aggressor." Acceptance of the French thesis meant establishing coercion against the "lawbreaker" as the basic principle of international efforts for peace.

III. Party Differences on Foreign Policy: Rightists and Leftists

THUS far the question has not been raised whether French foreign policy can be discussed as if it were based on conceptions and attitudes representative of the whole French nation. Yet in no country has the government changed more frequently, nor the pendulum of political power swung back and forth between groups of parties in such quick succession. French parliamentary debates, with their countless passionate controversies on both foreign and domestic issues, confirm the accepted picture of internal dissension. There may be found under the surface, however, a surprising degree of unity in matters of foreign policy. The Germans, particularly, must have been struck by the fact that none of the many changes of ministry distracted the French from their monotonous insistence on the necessity for more guarantees of security, and from their unswerving faith in the sanctity of the Peace Treaties and the *status quo*.[1]

Unity and passionate controversy, although superficially contradictory, are not incompatible. While the relentless efforts of every cabinet were directed toward keeping Germany in the

[1] Pierre Cot was able to say in 1935: "*Depuis 1919, la France a été dirigée par des hommes appartenant à différents partis politiques. Mais, depuis 1919, nous avons connu, sur un point essentiel, la continuité de notre politique extérieure. MM. Poincaré, Briand, Tardieu, Herriot, Paul-Boncour ou Daladier, M. Barthou lui-même, tous nos ministres des affaires étrangères ont estimé que la France devait être intransigeante sur un seul point: l'organisation des sanctions et de la sécurité collective.*" December 13, 1935; Chambre, *Débats*, 1935, p. 2482.

place assigned to her at Versailles, parties and statesmen were far from agreeing as to the best means of attaining this end, although even in regard to the means there was more harmony than might be expected from the general internal dissension. The Rightist parties, for instance, although skeptical about the League, were not entirely hostile once they discovered its potential value as a supplementary line of defense. The Leftist group, for their part, raised little objection in principle to alliances and opposed them more in name than in substance. The most violent controversies, accompanied by heated debate, fiery press campaigns, and bitter personal attacks, however, dealt with the relative merits of the different devices for security. Was it wiser to seek assistance in London or in Rome? Was it better to take refuge with the League or to act alone? Was it safer to use "*la méthode de la contrainte*" or to put faith in "*la méthode de la persuasion*"[2] and a policy of "*rapprochement*," which its opponents called "*la politique d'illusions*"?[3] The nature of the attacks which every French cabinet had to endure from its critics tended, nevertheless, to reveal a fundamental unity. While the opposition of the day accused the government of having failed to acquire or to maintain a certain guarantee of security—for instance, for not having strengthened the League or for not having maintained intimate relations with this or that country—the same charge would in due time be lodged against the accusers when they in turn came into power.

Several reasons can be given to explain why a nation which was more deeply at odds on domestic issues than Great Britain should have been less clearly divided into schools of thought on international affairs. In the first place, while in Britain the new theories built up around the League and collective security ran counter to traditional concepts of national policy, the French idea of an "or-

[2] Raymond Poincaré, July 10, 1924; Sénat, *Débats*, 1924, p. 1029.

[3] Henry Franklin-Bouillon, March 3, 1931; Chambre, *Débats*, 1931, p. 1521.

ganisation de la paix" fitted in perfectly with conservative conceptions of a policy of security. In the second place, once having made guarantees of security the cornerstone of her foreign policy, France had but few allies from which to choose. Whether or not the parties supporting the government liked to have the country dependent on British support, there was no guarantee equal to that which Britain could offer. Most of the time, therefore, "British orientation" prevailed, accompanied as the case might be by enthusiasm and bright hope, or by resignation and even resentment. Finally, the relative unity and constancy in the direction of French foreign policy can be accounted for by the way in which all French post-war governments were composed. Through almost all the changes, which by their frequency convey a false impression of instability, there runs an uninterrupted thread of Radical-Socialist domination in nearly every cabinet. The shift back and forth between Left and Right swung the political pendulum for the most part from one wing of the Radical-Socialist party to the other, leaving a relatively stable power in the center, to be influenced alternately by Left and Right.

On some occasions, when the transition from one party coalition to another and, therefore, from one type of influence to another was more abrupt or more radical than usual, the consequences were felt throughout Europe. They became visible in changes in the temper, if not in the direction, of French foreign policy. This happened, for instance, when Poincare replaced Briand in 1922 during the Cannes Conference, and even more conspicuously when in 1924 Poincaré's government, clearly Rightist in tendency, was followed by the Herriot government of the *Cartel des Gauches*. The shift to the Left in 1932 after a long period of coalition government and the even sharper swing to the Right in 1934 with the short-lived Rightist government of Doumergue and Barthou gave marked new turns to French foreign policy. Barthou's successors, Laval and Flandin, continued more or less the course laid out by him. In 1936, there occurred a very decided swing to the Left, extremely significant from the domestic angle, when Léon Blum's *Front populaire* government came into power. In 1937 and 1938, the pendulum swung back. But by 1936, France had lost so much of her freedom of choice and action that internal changes were not mirrored with equal strength in the course of her foreign policy.[4]

In view of this situation, it seems justifiable to discuss French foreign policy as a whole rather than to deal separately with the policies of opposing schools of thought. Since this may overemphasize what unity and stability there was, it will be necessary to refer constantly to the conflict of interests and philosophy dividing the Left and the Right. In the discussion of some of the crucial stages of the period the effects of this internal conflict will receive a prominent place.

[4] See below, pp. 391-415, for the Chronology, 1919-1939, which includes all important changes of government for both France and Great Britain and indicates significant conferences, treaties, diplomatic visits and negotiations, and other outstanding events during the period from 1919 to the outbreak of the war in September, 1939.

IV. Flaws in France's Legal Armor

FOR twenty years France struggled to retain the superiority over Germany which the Peace Treaties had assigned to her. It was a losing battle. One by one the guarantees which she had obtained were destroyed or became inoperative. Gradually military predominance and political initiative shifted from victorious France to vanquished Germany. The reasons for this dramatic reversal were manifold. The flood was too strong for the dikes, and the dikes were not as powerful as they appeared to be.

The French were fully aware of Germany's military and economic potentialities. They were facing a country with a growing population, that was already nearly double that of France, a nation not, perhaps, richer in natural resources, but with an industrial equipment if not a technological skill superior to hers. The military prestige of the German armies was unequaled; it had never been higher than at the close of the World War. If, therefore, Germany should ever succeed in throwing off the fetters of Versailles, her rebound would be formidable. A French Senate report of 1920 put it in these words: *"L'Allemagne de Versailles, c'est sans doute l'Allemagne vaincue, mais c'est aussi l'Allemagne restée compacte, conservant, renforçant même son unité; c'est l'Allemagne impuissante aujourd'hui mais capable de devenir à nouveau redoutable demain; . . ."*[1]

[1] Senate Foreign Affairs Committee Report of June 23, 1920, on the Treaty of St. Germain; Rapporteur, Imbart de La Tour; France, *Journal Officiel, Documents Parlementaires,* Sénat, 1920, Session ordinaire, Annexe No. 266, p. 257; hereinafter cited: Sénat, *Documents.*

To the threat of Germany's material potentialities dangers of a less tangible nature had to be added. Was not Germany the land of "Prussian militarism"? Could any superficial change in the form of government be trusted to bring about a change in spirit? And last but not least, Germany after Versailles was going to be a dissatisfied country, a country in revolt, whatever the French might choose to do. For apart from her losses on the Continent, she had suffered, according to Clemenceau, the greater blow of no longer being a "world Power." [2] Her colonial, her naval, and her commercial stakes outside of Europe were gone. Germany was not the country to forget that. A spirit of revenge would hold the German people in its grip and direct its energies toward a future reckoning with the countries that had defeated it.

The French feared that they, more than any other of the victorious powers, would become the target of Germany's wrath, not so much because France was Germany's "hereditary enemy," but because the ungrateful task of executing the Treaty of Versailles fell mainly upon her. Many of the principal provisions of the treaty, it must be remembered, contained obligations which Germany could discharge only over long periods of time. She could not pay reparations in less than sixty odd years; disarmament would take some years to complete. Because of her geographical position and her particular interest in Germany's prompt and complete compliance with the treaty, France became its chief executor. *"La guerre nous a laissés avec un traité, dont les difficultés d'application et d'exécution sont énormes,"* exclaimed Briand.[3] France was bound, therefore, to reap unpopularity in Germany, and to be accused in other countries of keeping the war spirit alive

[2] Memorandum to Lloyd George, March 31, 1919; *Cmd. 2169*, p. 89.

[3] Aristide Briand, President of the Council of Ministers, April 24, 1921; Chambre, *Débats*, p. 2358.

and of delaying the return to normal conditions. *"C'est nous qui resterons ainsi pour l'Allemagne le symbole toujours présent de la défaite, et c'est sur nous que se concentreront ses désirs de revanche,"* said Léon Bourgeois in 1919.[4]

The French, as we have mentioned earlier, sought to equip themselves with a powerful armor of legal guarantees and rights of enforcement. Had they been willing to trust the sheer force of the military superiority which they possessed in 1919, they would not have been so much worried by legal considerations. But once they became convinced that in the long run they would have to be assured of British support, their freedom to employ what coercive means they possessed was greatly curtailed. Since it was Britain's policy to curb as much as possible any rigid or harsh enforcement of the Versailles Treaty, she would not merely hold France strictly to the rights she held under the treaty and under international law, but would tend to interpret them as narrowly as possible. France, once she wanted to have British consent or British cooperation for coercive action against Germany, had to bow to the British interpretation of the law. What narrow limitations this put on French freedom of action can be gathered from the fact that, according to the British, France had no right under the Versailles Treaty to take any coercive action without previous agreement with her allies. After the occupation of the Ruhr, which was undertaken in spite of British protests, all French parties submitted to this rule. Poincaré bemoaned the fact that *"l'inconvénient des mesures communes telles qu'elles dérivent du traité lui-même c'est que, comme elles exigent finalement l'unanimité des alliés, c'est presque toujours, fatalement, la politique de la*

[4] Léon Bourgeois, Rapporteur on the Treaty of Versailles for the Senate Foreign Affairs Committee, October 3, 1919; in his *Le Traité de Paix de Versailles* (2nd ed., 1919), p. 153; also in Sénat, *Documents*, 1919, Session ordinaire, Annexe No. 562, pp. 569 ff.

moindre action qui l'emporte." [5] Briand was expressing the same sentiment when he said:

> *Le traité subordonne, en matière de coercition, toute possibilité d'action à une solidarité constante entre tous gouvernements alliés intéressés.*
>
> *Si l'on a pu croire, à un moment donné, qu'il en était autrement et que l'on pouvait s'engager isolément dans une action coercitive, on a bien été obligé de reconnaître que ce n'était pas la bonne voie, et il a bien fallu, en fin de compte, s'engager formellement à ne commettre aucun acte de coercition qui n'ait été délibéré et accepté par tous les alliés.* [6]

When, under these circumstances, Herriot suggested that "*le meilleur moyen pour la France d'assurer sa sécurité est de se placer partout dans son droit,*" [7] he was pleading for a course of action which placed France virtually under British supervision.

On the face of things, it seems hard to believe that the Treaty of Versailles, criticized so sharply—and rightly, we believe—for its severity and many injustices, should not have given France sufficient guarantees to prevent Germany from becoming powerful enough to challenge and overthrow French superiority. But French pessimism and dissatisfaction proved not unfounded. With the

[5] Raymond Poincaré, President of the Council of Ministers, November 23, 1923; Chambre, *Débats*, p. 3683. On another occasion he said, "*Exiger l'adhésion unanime de tous les alliés pour garantir les droits que nous tenons du traité, c'était, en réalité, nous mettre à la merci de puissances moins interessées que nous à l'exécution. . . . Et ce traité, dont l'exécution reposait essentiellement sur l'entente des alliés, a été faussé et vicié, dès le début, d'abord par l'éloignement des Etats-Unis, . . . puis, hélas! par le refus que l'Angleterre a presque constamment opposé à toute idée d'action énergique concertée.*" January 18, 1924; Chambre, *Débats*, pp. 155-156.

[6] Aristide Briand, Foreign Minister, December 20, 1929; Sénat, *Débats*, 1929, p. 1310. Briand was referring to the French occupation of Frankfort and other German towns on April 6, 1920. See below, p. 43 n. 19.

[7] Edouard Herriot, President of the Council of Ministers, August 23, 1924; Chambre, *Débats*, p. 3081.

political conditions what they were and with Britain's policy and interpretation of the treaty what it was, none of the guarantees was to prove unassailable. This was true for the occupation of the Rhenish provinces, for Germany's disarmament, for the demilitarization of the Rhineland, and for at least one of the territorial stipulations.

THE OCCUPATION OF THE RHINELAND

The occupation of "the German territory situated to the west of the Rhine, together with the bridgeheads," was the only "guarantee for the execution" of the Versailles Treaty explicitly mentioned as such in the text.[8] But this occupation was definitely limited in time; it was to last for five years for the first zone, ten for the second, and fifteen for the third.[9] It could therefore be of no real help in enforcing any of the permanent restrictions on Germany's freedom, such as her disarmament or the demilitarization of the

[8] Part XIV of the treaty, containing Articles 428 to 432 on occupation, and Article 433 regarding the withdrawal of German troops from Russia and the Baltic countries, is entitled "Guarantees."

[9] The evacuation of the first zone (Cologne) which would normally have been effected January 10, 1925, was postponed by the Conference of Ambassadors because of Germany's failure to carry out satisfactorily certain of the treaty provisions regarding her armed forces. However, the withdrawal of troops began on December 1, 1925, and was officially completed January 31, 1926, three and a half months after the conclusion of the Locarno agreements. The Germans looked to early evacuation of the remaining zones as a natural consequence of the "spirit of Locarno," but the French did not regard themselves as bound in this respect. The British favored early withdrawal. On September 16, 1928, agreement was reached at Geneva, opening negotiations for evacuation as well as for a definite settlement regarding reparations. The creation of the Young Committee and the meeting of the Hague Conference resulted from this agreement. The troops left the second zone (Coblenz) on November 30, 1929, after the first session of the Hague Conference, and evacuated the third and final zone (Mainz) on June 30, 1930, after the Young Plan had been brought into effect. Royal Institute of International Affairs, *Survey of International Affairs, 1925*, II, pp. 172-193; *1927*, pp. 101-114; *1929*, pp. 167-188.

Rhineland.[10] It was, as the treaty says, merely a guarantee of "execution," that is, of the temporary process by which Germany would disarm and pay reparations. That the enforcement of reparations, even more than of disarmament, was the main purpose of this guarantee can be gathered from the fact that reoccupation of the zones after they had once been evacuated was permitted only if Germany refused to observe her obligations in regard to reparations (Article 430).[11] As long as it lasted, this guarantee was important and powerful; it enabled the French to be "*les*

[10] It was provided, it is true, that the evacuation might be prolonged beyond the fifteen years, but only "if at that date the guarantees against unprovoked aggression by Germany are not considered sufficient by the Allied and Associated Governments" (Article 429). This provision was inserted as a protection for France against the possible non-ratification of the treaties of guarantee with the United States and Great Britain, which were intended to replace the original French demands for permanent occupation. "*En un mot,*" wrote Tardieu, "*pas de traités de garantie, pas d'évacuation en 1935.*" *La Paix* (1921), pp. 233-236. The British insisted that the Allies, and not France alone, had the right to decide on the prolongation of the period of occupation, and since the Anglo-Saxon countries objected even to an occupation as long as fifteen years, there was little chance that this provision would ever be applied. Indeed, discussion long before 1935 centered exclusively on Article 431, which allowed for the withdrawal of the troops before the expiration of the period of fifteen years in case Germany had complied "with all the undertakings resulting from the present treaty."

[11] It was doubtful whether reoccupation was practicable anyway. As Poincaré, then President of the Republic, wrote to Clemenceau, April 28, 1918; "*Comme, en réalité, ce sont nos troupes qui rentreront sur le territoire allemand, nous passerons aisément, en effet, pour des envahisseurs.*" *Le Temps*, September 12, 1921, p. 1.

Another provision of the treaty (paragraph 18 of Annex II to Part VIII) which gave the Allied Powers the right to take action which might include "economic and financial prohibitions and reprisals and in general such other measures as the respective Governments may determine to be necessary" was also limited to the case of default on reparations. On the occasion of the occupation of the Ruhr in 1923 the British denied the legality under this paragraph of French military occupation of German territory outside the treaty zones, even in case of default on reparations. However, they appeared to assume that the Allies had always had the right jointly to threaten Germany with the occupation of further territory and even "with a renewal of war" in case of the failure to perform her Versailles obligations. To this the French replied that the British

maîtres de la paix," as one Frenchman put it,[12] and its disappearance in 1930 was regarded by Marin as "*la perte de tous les contrôles, de tous les gages, de toutes les garanties que nous avions.*" [13] But it was never intended as a protection for France in a later period when Germany might have recovered and become dangerous once more.

GERMAN DISARMAMENT

The reduction and limitation of Germany's armaments were not to be temporary. Yet here, too, time worked against France. The treaty provided that the military, naval, and air clauses should be "executed by Germany under control of Inter-Allied Commissions" (Article 203). But once these commissions were satisfied that the process of disarmament had been completed, and that Germany had disarmed according to the treaty, they were to be dissolved and all further control over German compliance with this part of the treaty left to the Council of the League of Nations. This was done in 1927.

Germany, said the Versailles Treaty in Article 213, was obliged to "give every facility for any investigation which the Council of the League of Nations, acting if need be by a majority vote, may consider necessary." [14] It can hardly be contended that this stipu-

themselves had previously regarded military occupation of German territory in case of default of reparation payments as legitimate and that, "*si l'Angleterre a, comme elle le dit, songé à recommencer la guerre, la France, elle, n'a jamais eu une idée pareille.*" Curzon's note of August 11, 1923, and Poincaré's reply of August 20, 1923; France, Ministère des Affaires Etrangères, *Documents Diplomatiques: Réponse du Gouvernement français à la lettre du Gouvernement britannique du 11 août 1923 sur les réparations* (*20 août 1923*), pp. 13-18, 40, 61-62.

[12] Edouard Soulier, Rapporteur on the Hague Accords for the Foreign Affairs Committee, March 27, 1930; Chambre, *Débats*, 1930, p. 1341.

[13] Louis Marin, March 27, 1930; Chambre, *Débats*, 1930, p. 1318.

[14] On the activities of the Inter-Allied Commission of Control and the negotiations regarding its dissolution, see Royal Institute of International Affairs, *Survey of International Affairs, 1927*, pp. 83-101.

lation guaranteed France against future German rearmament. Would the League ever vote an investigation? Would the League or the Allies take action if an investigation proved that Germany was violating the clauses on disarmament? Would France be regarded as having the right to act alone, possibly to use military force against Germany, if collective action was not available? Whatever the answer to this last question might be under international law (and nothing is more controversial than the problem of reprisals and self-defense), France, as we have said before, was not willing to risk acting alone, particularly if such action might cause her to be blamed for the illegal or aggressive use of force. *"S'il fallait recourir à l'article 213,"* said Paul-Boncour, *"je ne voudrais pas que la France fût seule."* He thought it advisable for France *"d'y préparer d'abord l'esprit de ses amis."* [15] He and other French statesmen realized that no country was irrevocably committed to help France enforce the military provisions; therefore they favored a general disarmament convention which would provide for guarantees of execution and for *"l'engagement solidaire des Etats signataires pour la faire respecter."* [16] But here France faced another grave dilemma. She could not hope to get other countries, particularly Germany, to sign such a general disarmament convention unless she herself agreed to reduce her own armaments. She would therefore have to sacrifice an important part of her military superiority in order to acquire guarantees for the remainder. If she refused to do this and insisted on the continued

[15] Joseph Paul-Boncour, Foreign Minister, January 16, 1934; Sénat, *Débats*, 1934, p. 41. In spite of repeated affirmations of the existence of a *dossier* proving German secret rearmament the French Government never produced this evidence and never requested a League inquiry under Article 213. The Rightists demanded repeatedly that it be done. Political reasons, among which respect for Britain's wishes was the most important, explain the hesitation of the government; see the Chambre, *Débats* for November 9, 10 and 14, 1933.

[16] Joseph Paul-Boncour, Foreign Minister, November 14, 1933; Chambre, *Débats*, 1933, p. 4101.

unilateral disarmament of Germany, she was threatened with moral condemnation. According to British opinion at least, the Allies were morally, if not legally, committed by the preamble to Part V of the Versailles Treaty, which declared that Germany undertook to disarm "in order to render possible the initiation of a general limitation of the armaments of all nations." Viscount Grey, for example, in speaking of Germany's disarmament, declared that "you cannot make control of a great nation's armaments permanent in that way, and sooner or later, unless there be some reduction of armaments in other countries, you will find it impossible to prevent Germany from beginning again to increase her armaments."[17] Unilateral disarmament by Germany, although not German disarmament as such, was therefore, according to this thesis, also regarded as only temporary, and no sanctions were provided in case Germany should some day decide to rearm. When she did rearm in 1935, the League condemned the violation of the treaty stipulations on armaments, but the Council's resolution of April 17 merely said that unilateral repudiation of treaty obligations "should, in the event of its having relation to undertakings concerning the security of peoples and the maintenance of peace in Europe, call into play all appropriate measures on the part of Members of the League and within the framework of the Covenant." The resolution then went on to request a committee "to

[17] July 24, 1924; Great Britain, House of Lords, *Parliamentary Debates*, Vol. 58, col. 959.

The French never accepted the argument that the preamble to Part V obligated the powers other than Germany to disarm. They declared that they stood by Article 8 of the Covenant, which speaks of reduction of armaments "to the lowest point consistent with national safety and the enforcement by common action of international obligations," and which requires the taking into account of "the geographical situation and circumstances of each State." This excluded any mathematical ratio. "*Il y a, d'un côté*," said Tardieu, "*les obligations imposées aux pays ex-ennemis par le traité de paix et, de l'autre, le désir spontané des pays ex-alliés d'arriver à une réduction générale des armements.*" President of the Council of Ministers, November 13, 1930; Chambre, *Débats*, 1930, p. 3387.

propose for this purpose measures to render the Covenant more effective in the organisation of collective security and to define in particular the economic and financial measures which might be applied, should in the future a State, whether a Member of the League of Nations or not, endanger peace by the unilateral repudiation of its international obligations."[18]

THE DEMILITARIZED ZONE

This brings us to the outstanding guarantee, one that was to be permanent without qualification. The provisions of the Treaty of Versailles concerning the demilitarized zone read as follows:

ARTICLE 42

Germany is forbidden to maintain or construct any fortifications either on the left bank of the Rhine or on the right bank to the west of a line drawn 50 kilometers to the East of the Rhine.

ARTICLE 43

In the area defined above the maintenance and the assembly of armed forces, either permanently or temporarily, and military manoeuvres of any kind, as well as the upkeep of all permanent works for mobilization, are in the same way forbidden.

ARTICLE 44

In case Germany violates in any manner whatever the provisions of Articles 42 and 43, she shall be regarded as committing a hostile act against the Powers signatory of the present Treaty and as calculated to disturb the peace of the world.

[18] League of Nations, *Official Journal*, XVI (May, 1935), pp. 551-552.
For documents concerning the activity of the Committee of Thirteen created by this resolution, including the special French memoranda on sanctions in case of treaty violations, see Georg von Gretschaninow, ed., *Materialien zur Entwicklung der Sicherheitsfrage im Rahmen des Völkerbundes*, Zweiter Teil, *1928-1935* (Volume II, Part 2 of Viktor Bruns, ed., *Politische Verträge: eine Sammlung von Urkunden*), pp. 701 ff.

Together with the guarantee pacts with Great Britain and the United States, which never materialized, the demilitarized zone was to be the main substitute for the strategic frontier on the Rhine. From a military point of view it was of tremendous importance. When Germany remilitarized the Rhineland in 1936, the superiority of France and much of her power and influence vanished. It is therefore of the greatest interest to discover whether in this case, also, weaknesses in the legal armor help to explain the collapse of so essential a guarantee.

The French were not satisfied with the provisions of the Versailles Treaty because they set up no permanent control over the demilitarized zone and did not oblige any country to aid France in preventing or suppressing remilitarization, which the treaty declared to be a "hostile act."[19] Effort after effort was made by the French to supplement the treaty in this respect. The first attempt in 1919 to introduce a pledge for the protection of the demili-

[19] France, according to the British, was not allowed, even against this type of "hostile act," to take action, or what in international law would be called "reprisals," except with the consent of her Allies.

Britain protested vigorously when, on April 6, 1920, Millerand, then President of the Council, ordered French troops to occupy the German towns of Frankfort, Darmstadt, Hanau, Dieburg, and Homburg, all outside of the territory occupied under the terms of the treaty. The French took this action after Germany, in order to quell Communist disturbances in the Ruhr, had sent troops in excess of the number which the French considered necessary into a part of the demilitarized zone. The British Government instructed its ambassador in Paris to abstain from further participation in the Conference of Ambassadors until the French gave adequate assurances that "*en aucune circonstance un des alliés n'agira dans des questions si importantes sans que les autres alliés n'en soient informés et n'y aient donné leur consentement.*" The French Government gave these assurances and withdrew the troops on May 17. See Millerand's statement to the Chamber of Deputies, April 13, 1920: Chambre, *Débats*, 1920, p. 916; and Briand's statement to the Chamber of Deputies, November 8, 1929: Chambre, *Débats*, 1929, p. 3052. Briand quoted from the Franco-British correspondence of 1920 to justify his own policy with regard to the evacuation of the Rhineland. See above, p. 36.

tarized zone into the pacts of guarantee failed. Britain and also the United States limited their promises of assistance to "the event of any unprovoked movement of aggression" against France (Article 1).

After that the French again tried to fill the gap in their legal defenses during the negotiations for a treaty with Britain in 1922. But although they sought to have a violation of the provisions on demilitarization defined as an *"agression directe contre la sécurité de la France, au même titre que l'agression contre le territoire français,"* [20] Lloyd George was willing to have Britain guarantee France only in case of "unprovoked aggression against the soil of France." [21] Curzon, in a note of February 17, 1922, declared, "I am clear in my own mind that in so far as British public opinion will endorse our guarantee, it will be in the belief that it can only become operative in the event of a German army actually crossing the French frontier and invading French soil." [22]

No agreement was reached in 1922, and the matter came up again in the negotiations for the Geneva Protocol. "Violation of the rules laid down for a demilitarized zone" were declared to be "equivalent to resort to war" (Article 10). The Protocol, however, was not ratified.[23]

Finally, at Locarno, the guarantee seemed to be obtained, and Briand could stress this as one of the main benefits of the Locarno Treaty to France: *"Dorénavant, la violation par le Reich de la*

[20] Memorandum of January 8, 1922, from Briand to Lloyd George; *Cmd. 2169,* p. 122. See also Poincaré's memorandum submitted February 2, 1922; *ibid.,* pp. 138-140.

[21] British draft treaty, January 12, 1922; *ibid.,* p. 127.

[22] *Ibid.,* p. 155.

[23] References to demilitarized zones in League discussions and proposals are reviewed in Major-General J. H. Marshall-Cornwall, *Geographic Disarmament: a study of regional demilitarization* (1935), Chapter XI. "The Problem of the Rhineland" is discussed in Chapter XII.

zone rhénane démilitarisée doit suffire à déclencher l'action anglaise et italienne."[24]

The events of 1936 proved him to have been unduly optimistic about his achievements. The Locarno Treaty drew a distinction between two kinds of breaches of Articles 42 and 43: flagrant and non-flagrant. Only in the first of the two was France given the right of immediate and independent action and provided with a promise of immediate assistance by Britain and Italy. League action would follow, but did not have to be awaited. In non-flagrant cases the matter was referred to the Council of the League.[25]

[24] Statement to the *Petit Parisien*, Paris, February 26, 1927; *Société des Nations*, IX (1927), p. 214.

[25] Articles 2 and 4 of the treaty read as follows:

ART. 2. Germany and Belgium, and also Germany and France, mutually undertake that they will in no case attack or invade each other or resort to war against each other.

This stipulation shall not, however, apply in the case of:

(1) The exercise of the right of legitimate defence, that is to say, resistance to a violation of the undertaking contained in the previous paragraph or to a flagrant breach of articles 42 or 43 of the said Treaty of Versailles, if such breach constitutes an unprovoked act of aggression and by reason of the assembly of armed forces in the demilitarised zone immediate action is necessary;

(2) Action in pursuance of article 16 of the Covenant of the League of Nations;

(3) Action as the result of a decision taken by the Assembly or by the Council of the League of Nations or in pursuance of article 15, paragraph 7, of the Covenant of the League of Nations, provided that in this last event the action is directed against a State which was the first to attack.

ART. 4. (1) If one of the high contracting parties alleges that a violation of article 2 of the present treaty or a breach of articles 42 or 43 of the Treaty of Versailles has been or is being committed, it shall bring the question at once before the Council of the League of Nations.

(2) As soon as the Council of the League of Nations is satisfied that such violation or breach has been committed, it will notify its finding without delay to the Powers signatory of the present treaty, who severally agree that in such case they will each of them come immediately to the assistance of the Power against whom the act complained of is directed.

(3) In case of a flagrant violation of article 2 of the present treaty or of a flagrant breach of articles 42 or 43 of the Treaty of Versailles by one of the high contracting parties, each of the other contracting parties hereby undertakes

Since action by the League was expected at best to be slow, if it was going to be effective at all, the enforcement of demilitarization depended in the main on the definition of what constituted a flagrant violation. In fact, in 1936, both France and Britain acted as if Germany's breach of the treaty did not come under this heading, and the consequences are known. Here, then, the interpretation given to the treaty came to be of utmost significance. Many writers had pointed out that according to Articles 2 and 4 a breach was flagrant only if it fulfilled two conditions, namely, that it was, first, "an unprovoked act of aggression," and, second, that "immediate action is necessary."[26] In view of all the controversy over the nature of "aggression," it was very uncertain how these terms would be interpreted. What really mattered was the way in which the British Government would construe them and under what conditions Britain would feel bound to assist France against a German violation of this provision of the Locarno Treaty.

immediately to come to the help of the party against whom such a violation or breach has been directed as soon as the said Power has been able to satisfy itself that this violation constitutes an unprovoked act of aggression and that by reason either of the crossing of the frontier or of the outbreak of hostilities or of the assembly of armed forces in the demilitarised zone immediate action is necessary. Nevertheless, the Council of the League of Nations, which will be seized of the question in accordance with the first paragraph of this article, will issue its findings, and the high contracting parties undertake to act in accordance with the recommendations of the Council provided that they are concurred in by all the members other than the representatives of the parties which have engaged in hostilities.

[26] See Otto Brück, *Les sanctions en droit international public* (1933), p. 155; Karl Strupp, *Das Werk von Locarno: eine völkerrechtlich-politische Studie* (1926), pp. 65 ff.; Paul Barandon, *Das System der politischen Staatsverträge seit 1918* (1937), p. 147; Jacques Bardoux, *L'Ile et l'Europe: la politique anglaise, 1930-1932* (1933), p. 198. In *State Security and the League of Nations* (1927), Bruce Williams, on the contrary, identifies the guarantee of the demilitarized zone with that of territorial integrity. Evidences of unprovoked aggression are "the crossing of the frontier; the outbreak of hostilities; or the assembly of armed forces in the demilitarized zone," he says, and assumes that in each of these cases the remedies are the same (p. 221).

The British Government made no explicit statement interpreting its obligations, but the declarations of Anthony Eden, then Foreign Secretary, leave no doubt as to its attitude.

He stated on March 9, 1936, that in case of an "actual attack" on France or Belgium, the British "would regard themselves as in honour bound to come . . . to the assistance of the country attacked."[27] Later he expressed Britain's interest in the "integrity of France and Belgium" and hence in seeing that "no hostile force should cross their frontiers."[28] But since nobody even suggested that Germany was intending to attack France or to violate the integrity of her soil, these assurances only underlined the unwillingness of Britain to assist France against the action of remilitarization itself.[29] What, then, had the Locarno Treaty added to the pledges which Britain had previously offered for the defense of French soil and which the French believed had been supplemented by a guarantee of the demilitarized zone? The answer is not difficult to give. A breach of Articles 42 and 43 was flagrant only if German troops entered the demilitarized zone for the purpose of marching on to the French border and invading French soil. In this case there was certainly a threat of aggression, even if not an actual act of aggression, and "immediate action" was necessary, because if Britain and France were to await League action the Germans might already have reached French territory before being stopped. All, then, that Britain had done at Locarno was to promise that, instead of waiting for an actual invasion of

[27] Great Britain, House of Commons, *Parliamentary Debates*, Vol. 309, col. 1812. A complete collection of documents and speeches relating to the Locarno accords, including their origins, their interpretation, and their breakdown is contained in Fritz Berber, ed., *Locarno: a collection of documents* (1936).

[28] Great Britain, House of Commons, *Parliamentary Debates*, March 26, 1936; Vol. 310, col. 1443.

[29] There was "no reason," Eden also said, "to suppose that the present German action implies a threat of hostilities." March 9, 1936; *ibid.*, Vol. 309, col. 1812.

France, her assistance would be brought into action as soon as an attacking army entered the treaty zone. This was not worthless as long as the Rhineland was demilitarized, and all German troops were stationed beyond the right bank of the Rhine. But it was no guarantee of demilitarization as such.

This being the case, since Britain's interpretation had to be accepted in practice, it was even more important for France to discover what were her guarantees against non-flagrant violations. But here there was even more subject for controversy and conflicting interpretations. One thing was certain. Nothing was allowed to happen until the Council of the League had decided that a breach of the treaty had taken place and until it had so notified the Locarno signatories (Article 4, paragraph 2). But whether, after this had been done, France alone or the Locarno Powers or even the League itself could threaten or undertake military action for the purpose of driving the German troops back over the Rhine was not only controversial but highly doubtful according to the interpretation of the Covenant prevalent at Geneva as well as in Britain. The question was not clearly answered, since the League postponed taking any decision aside from fulfilling its role under Article 4, paragraph 2; it then dropped the matter altogether.

The following legal considerations may help to clarify the issue. In a case of non-flagrant violation, such as was supposed to have taken place in 1936, legal rights for three types of coercive action have to be discussed, namely, action by France alone or by the Locarno Powers or by the League.

Could France act alone since the Council had decided that a breach had taken place? It had been maintained by the French on various occasions that nothing in the Treaty of Versailles or in the Covenant deprived her of the rights of reprisal under international law. But Article 2 of the Locarno Treaty permitted French action against Germany, apart from the case of a flagrant breach of the demilitarized zone, only if Germany resorted to war (Articles 15, paragraph 7, and 16, of the Covenant) or "as the result of a decision taken by the Assembly or by the Council . . ." That put the matter clearly up to the League and deprived France of the rights she might otherwise have had.

Could the Locarno Powers or the signatories of the Versailles Treaty decide to take action without a specific recommendation of the Council? The Locarno Treaty provided that once the guarantors were notified by the Council of a breach having been committed "they will each of them come immediately to the assistance of the Power against whom the act complained of is directed." But how could they assist France if France herself in cases of non-flagrant violation had no right to act? And did they have any right under international law or under the Covenant to take military action against a country that had not resorted to war or committed an act of aggression against them? Did the fact that the Versailles Treaty had called this breach a "hostile act" give them any special rights of military intervention after the Locarno Treaty had established the difference between flagrant and non-flagrant violations? These questions were never officially answered.

Could the League Council recommend or even permit the Locarno Powers to take military action? When the matter came before the Council in 1936, the Locarno Powers suggested League action under Article 11 of the Covenant. This, according to the prevailing interpretation of the Covenant, was the only article that permitted the League to apply coercive measures against a country that had violated a treaty without having resorted to war. But it was controversial whether even under this article action could be taken against a non-member or any country not participating in the vote, which had to be unanimous. Furthermore, it was doubtful whether measures under Article 11 could have a military character. This was illustrated by the resolution of the

League Council in 1935, quoted above, which referred to Germany's breach of another part of the Versailles Treaty, namely, the disarmament clauses. The maximum the Council could apparently do, again in 1936, according to this interpretation, would have been to recommend economic or financial measures.

The conclusions that follow from this review of the legal position as interpreted by the British, the League, and by the French Government in 1936 are perplexing after all that the Locarno Treaty was supposed to have done to guarantee the demilitarized zone. France was not protected, at least not by any right of military action, against even such a complete remilitarization and refortification of the Rhineland as began in 1936, unless the Germans should enter the Rhineland for the purpose of opening hostilities against France. Only in this case was France free to act alone and assured of British assistance and of support by the League. In all other cases the best she could hope for under the prevailing interpretation was a decision by the League inviting its members or the Locarno Powers to take economic or financial action. Actually, in 1936, even this was not forthcoming.

Legal considerations were, of course, not the only factor in the situation. All depended on how at a given moment Britain and the League would interpret the law. Whether they would have interpreted it the way they did if the French Government had decided to take action or had insisted on an interpretation more favorable to France, nobody can tell. The French Government, when submitting the matter to the Council, did not specify whether it regarded the breach of Articles 42 and 43 as flagrant or not. It did not officially ask for immediate British assistance, and declared that it would be content with whatever action the Council of the League would recommend. But Flandin stated, on the other hand, "If it were only a question of rights, the text of the Locarno Treaty would authorise the French Government to take strong and decisive measures forthwith."[30] Therefore, it remains an open question whether the French actually doubted their own rights of action or were merely submitting to British pressure. According to Flandin, the restoration of the demilitarized zone, as France would have preferred, "*pouvait être atteint si les puissances signataires du traité de Locarno s'étaient trouvées d'accord pour exercer à Berlin la pression suffisament énergique. J'ai pu rapidement me convaincre que cet accord ne pouvait être réalisé.*"[31] It has been suggested, however, that internal difficulties of a financial nature impressed themselves on the government. Some have attributed France's inaction to a mere lack of courage or to pro-Fascist leanings. Certainly the legal situation, whatever other influence it may or may not have had, did facilitate British evasion, and enabled the French Government to shift the responsibility first to the Locarno Powers and thence to the League. It might also be added that this legal argumentation reflected a deep-seated aversion of the British to take military action in a case where no attack on another nation had taken place, and possibly a feeling among the French that this was not a "good case" on which to base action involving the danger of war. The permanent maintenance of a state of unilateral demilitarization proved difficult for legal and political as well as for psychological reasons, even though its abolition constituted in all but German eyes a grave violation of a solemn treaty.

THE TERRITORIAL SETTLEMENT

This brings us, finally, to the territorial provisions of the Treaty of Versailles. They, at least, it would seem, should have been unassailable. If it was right to expect that every violation of the

[30] Pierre-Etienne Flandin, Foreign Minister, League of Nations Council, March 14, 1936; *Official Journal*, XVII (April, 1936, Part I), p. 313.

[31] March 20, 1936; Chambre, *Débats*, 1936, p. 1063.

territorial stipulations would take the form of a military attack or invasion of another country's territory, both international law in general and the League Covenant provided the necessary protective weapons. Countries were not only permitted to defend their soil by military action, but also to assist one another in so doing. Therefore, France was eager to negotiate further pacts and treaties bearing on the problem of aggression not because she lacked the right to take action against an aggressor, but because she wanted to obtain more reliable promises of assistance, and expected that promises of non-aggression would put a check on would-be aggressors.

And yet one loophole existed even in this realm; it was the one through which territorial revision started on its course. This was the *Anschluss* of Austria with Germany. It was prohibited both by the Treaty of Versailles and by the Treaty of St. Germain, except with the unanimous consent of the League Council.[32] Since such consent was not given in 1938, the *Anschluss* constituted a clear-cut breach of the treaties. It is likely that nothing short of the threat or use of military force could at that time have prevented it. It is, however, a matter for debate whether military intervention on the part of other nations was permissible under international law. Italy and Austria's other neighbors might, to be sure, have pleaded that they were acting in self-defense. Whether world opinion would have been on their side if they had invaded Austrian or German territory and thereby started a war cannot be determined with certainty. If France had decided to attack Germany on the Rhine, her position under international law would have been still more debatable. That leaves the problem unsolved as to whether the League, if the matter had been referred to it, would have had the right to recommend military action. The answer apparently would be in the affirmative if the

[32] See below, p. 112 n. 29.

League had felt entitled to decide that Germany had compelled Austria to accept the *Anschluss* by the use of military force and invasion. If the *Anschluss* was considered to be merely a violation of a treaty, and not a "resort to war," the League again had no legal grounds, if our earlier interpretation of the Covenant is right, on which to set military intervention in motion or to permit military action by its members.

It should not, we repeat, be concluded from this summary of flaws in the legal machinery set up by France and her allies to keep Germany tied to the provisions of the Peace Treaties that France's failure to act rested solely on legal grounds. If the political situation at home and abroad had been different, she might very well have been able to discover means of interpreting the law in such a way as to fit her purpose, and might have acted without even the semblance of illegality. Whether any French government would have been willing, if it had not been for the dependency on Britain, to go further and to discard considerations of legality altogether cannot, of course, be answered. What we have tried to show is merely that international law, the Versailles Treaty, the League Covenant, and the subsequent agreements, at least as interpreted by Britain, did not give France freedom to enforce even the most essential provisions of the treaty with what was at the crucial moment the only effective means, namely, military action. In some cases the guarantees were definitely limited in time and scope and specifically drawn up so as to prevent isolated action by any one country.

Ironically enough, the elaborate structure erected under French leadership to stop aggression and make it illegal not only left loopholes for treaty violation short of aggression, but rendered military intervention against "law breakers" and "treaty violators" that were not guilty of war-like aggression more difficult than it had been before. The Germans profited by this situation in full recognition of the opportunities which it offered and freed themselves of Versailles by skillfully attacking the points of least legal resistance. Germany first strengthened her position by two sensational violations of the treaty that involved her in no military action outside of her own borders, rearmament first, remilitarization of the Rhineland afterwards. This enabled her to take the more dangerous step of violating the prohibitions regarding the *Anschluss* and to march her troops into Austria. This in turn put her in so powerful a strategic position that she was able without too much risk to threaten Czechoslovakia with armed intervention of a kind which might very well have brought upon her League sanctions or military action by other nations. If there is any doubt, therefore, about the influence of law on the actions of countries claiming to be its defenders, it should at least be evident that the weaknesses which are inevitable in any set of legal guarantees help direct the course of those countries which wish to change or to break the law. At the same time, experience in this case shows that revisionist forces in revolt against a *status quo* which they deem patently unjust are likely to acquire the skill and also the disregard for the established law that enable them to achieve their objectives, however carefully their opponents may seek to build up legal defenses against them.

V. French Policy toward Germany

THE many weak spots in the legal scaffolding with which France was provided by the Treaty of Versailles and the post-war pacts and agreements cannot suffice to explain her inability to maintain her superiority over Germany. If she had actually possessed the hegemony with which she was so often credited, she might, if necessary, have gone beyond her legal rights with as much impunity as Germany has done since then. Proof of her fundamental weakness came when, after trying one course of action after another, she failed to attain her objective and had to resign herself and watch Germany resume her liberty of action. All groups in France had agreed that the main objective was to insure Germany's respect for the *status quo* of Versailles. The collapse of this policy was therefore a defeat for all French parties. The difference of opinion between the Right and Left as to the methods best suited to make Germany accept her position was a contributing cause to French failure. The controversy raged over two issues: should Germany be forced or should she be persuaded to conform, and should France act according to her own ideas or make her actions contingent upon British consent and support.[1]

The Rightists and Nationalists all took a very pessimistic view of Germany and of her future intentions. They were constantly accusing their political opponents of blindness to the German danger and of deluding the public with the "*optimisme à la mode,*

[1] With the latter question we shall deal in the next chapter; with the former, here. Franco-German relations will, of course, enter into the discussion directly or indirectly throughout all the following chapters.

fait d'insouciance et de crédulité."[2] It impressed them little that Germany was now in form a democratic republic. They were convinced that the Germans, whatever their form of government, would never voluntarily accept the position assigned to them at Versailles. Germany, it was said, understood no language save that of force. Any admission of weakness by France or any concession would simply encourage Germany to make new demands and to violate still more of the obligations she had undertaken. "*L'Allemagne en tant que nation,*" wrote Poincaré, "*ne se résigne à tenir sa parole que sous l'empire de la nécessité.*"[3] Germany would have to be kept in a position where she would have no freedom of choice.

Since France, no less than her allies, was determined not to give up any of her essential war spoils, it followed logically from this French view that the Treaty of Versailles, if it were to remain the law of Europe, would have to be executed with "*rigueur inexorable.*"[4] It was France's duty, according to Poincaré, to inspire Germany with respect for "*la volonté française.*"[5] If it was correct to expect that Germany would eventually revolt no matter how considerately France and her allies treated her, there was no need to be concerned whether stern action and enforcement would exasperate the Germans. They would have to be kept in check by the threat or use of preponderant power in any case. If constant pressure and punitive action were to lead to the dissolution of the Reich or to the alienation of the Rhenish provinces, no harm

[2] Henry Lémery, March 28, 1931; Sénat, *Débats,* 1931, p. 689.

[3] Raymond Poincaré, President of the Council of Ministers, to the French Ambassador in London, June 29, 1923; France, Ministère des Affaires Etrangères, *Documents Diplomatiques: Documents relatifs aux notes allemandes des 2 mai et 5 juin sur les réparations* (*2 mai–3 août 1923*), p. 50.

[4] Louis Barthou, general rapporteur for the Committee on the Peace, September 2, 1919; Chambre, *Débats,* 1919, p. 4102.

[5] Raymond Poincaré, President of the Council of Ministers, December 21, 1923; Chambre, *Débats,* p. 4354.

would have been done, to say the least. This point of view of the Right may sound brutal; nevertheless, as far as Germany was concerned, it is doubtful whether in the long run harsh treatment caused any more resentment than the universally accepted objective of French policy—the maintenance *ad infinitum* of the new *status quo* of Versailles.

It should also be mentioned that many opponents of the "big stick" in France and elsewhere were not so much concerned about the justice of enforcing the treaty as they were desirous of replacing national enforcement by international action, national sanctions by those of the League. The Rightists had no objection to international sanctions if they pledged others to participate with France in the risks and burdens of executing and defending the treaty. In fact, they had always been very eager to supplement national sanctions by League assistance. But they disliked admitting that France, to whom a policy of enforcement was regarded as vitally necessary, should refrain from action until she was assured of the co-operation of others. The Right, therefore, emphasized the need for strong independent French action, or what their opponents described as a "*politique d'isolement et de force.*"[6]

In the period before 1924 the Rightists had their best opportunity to conduct French foreign policy in full accord with their views. In 1923 Poincaré ordered French troops to occupy the Ruhr, Germany's great mining and industrial center. No active step of French post-war policy had more far-reaching and important consequences. "*La politique de la Ruhr*" became not only the symbol of French Rightist policy but also its crucial test. The opportunity was offered by German defaults on her reparation obligations. The immediate purpose was therefore the enforcement of German obligations under the Treaty of Versailles. But France's

[6] Edouard Herriot, President of the Council of Ministers, ministerial declaration, June 17, 1924; Chambre, *Débats*, 1924, p. 2307.

action had deeper implications. Sanctions similar in character had previously been applied by the Allies, when German cities outside of the occupied zone were brought under military control.[7] What gave the invasion of the Ruhr its special significance was the fact that it was intended as a showdown. Germany was to be taught a lesson and to be made to realize once and for all that she had no chance to resist France's superior power. At the same time, France was demonstrating to Britain that she could act alone if need be and that she was prepared to take independent action. "*Nous y sommes, en réalité,*" said Dubois, "*parce qu'il n'y avait plus d'autre moyen d'en imposer à l'Allemagne, et je me permettrai d'ajouter: d'agir sur nos alliés eux-mêmes.*"[8] Had this venture been successful, France might have gained the power to enforce the treaty according to her own wishes and attained hegemony on the Continent. Britain's strong protests did not stop Poincaré's invasion of the Ruhr, and Germany was forced to capitulate. Yet the episode ended with the defeat of Poincaré and of Rightist foreign policy in France. The Rightists never fully recovered from this setback. Majority opinion in France reacted violently against both military adventures and "*actions isolées.*" "*Nous sommes hostiles à la politique d'isolement et de force qui conduit à des occupations et à des prises de gages territoriaux,*"

[7] On March 8, 1921, the Allies occupied the towns of Düsseldorf, Duisburg, and Ruhrort. This action was taken as a result of Germany's failure to give a satisfactory reply to the Allied ultimatum of March 3rd calling for acceptance of the Paris memorandum of January 28th which laid down a series of demands regarding German disarmament and reparation payments. France, Ministère des Affaires Etrangères, *Documents relatifs aux Réparations*, Tome Premier, 1922, Nos. 11, 13. The Allied troops were withdrawn from the three towns on August 25, 1925, less than a month after the evacuation of the Ruhr by French troops.

Previously, on April 6, 1920, the French had occupied German towns outside of the treaty zones, but withdrew after British protests. See above, p. 43 n. 19.

[8] Louis Dubois, former French delegate to and chairman of the Reparation Commission, January 18, 1924; Chambre, *Débats*, 1924, p. 165.

declared Herriot, who succeeded Poincaré.[9] Later he said, "*Il fallait choisir entre le rétablissement de l'entente interalliée et le maintien de l'action isolée.*"[10]

Germany's "passive resistance" in the Ruhr was an important contributing factor. It deprived France of most of the material advantages which she might otherwise have gained. It helped arouse public opinion in the world and heightened the isolation of France. Because of this resistance, the "pacific" occupation became a violent international conflict threatening the economic stability of the world. Another influential factor was the economic repercussions in France. The sudden drop in the external value of the French franc was the turning point which started the downfall of Poincaré at home. But what counted most was the specter of British hostility.

Probably few people at the time realized how decisive a crisis had been reached in Franco-German relations. The policy of enforcing the Treaty of Versailles by the use of military power was never to be used again. The first serious attempt had ended in failure. If Germany proposed and signed the Locarno Treaty to guard against new French invasions, as was maintained, she was unnecessarily cautious. No government in France after 1924 was prepared to risk independent military action. After the occupation of the Ruhr, Germany, despite her military inferiority, was therefore actually safe from direct military pressure except on the left bank of the Rhine.

The French Rightists were bitter but resigned. For nearly ten long and decisive years they confined themselves to protests and criticism. They were able to help defeat the policy of their oppo-

[9] Edouard Herriot, President of the Council of Ministers, ministerial declaration, June 17, 1924; Chambre, *Débats*, 1924, p. 2307.

[10] August 21, 1924; Chambre, *Débats*, 1924, p. 2958. The most decisive influence in producing this result of the Ruhr occupation on French policy, the reaction of Great Britain, will be treated later.

nents, but they could offer no constructive alternative. Most of their leaders, when pressed in debate, confessed that independent military action was out of the question. For success Britain's consent and co-operation would have been necessary, but that was not obtainable. France's position, both externally and internally, was not strong enough for any French government to dare undertake the risks of another adventure like the Ruhr occupation. The events of 1933 and 1934, of which more will be said later, bear out this thesis. When at that time it was rumored that France might consider a preventive war to stop Germany, Rightist leaders in the Chamber flatly disclaimed support of any such action. "*La guerre préventive,*" exclaimed Lémery, "*mais nul n'y songe et le mot seul nous fait horreur.*" [11]

If the Rightist theory about Germany was correct, the only alternative to "*une politique de force*" would have been for France to stop trying to maintain the *status quo* of Versailles. The Leftists refused to accept this conclusion. When they came into power in 1924, they embarked upon a new course in foreign policy, which they proclaimed would replace the use of force without impairing France's security or the *status quo*. They were convinced that it was the Rightists who by their "sabre-rattling" had endangered France's position. Had not the world—particularly the Anglo-Saxon world—come to suspect France of military and imperialistic aims and turned away from her? The Germans were being driven into the arms of the Soviet Union, and the latent state of war between France and Germany made impossible any lasting peace and prosperity. It was madness, they argued, to attempt the "*compression à perpétuité d'un peuple de 60 millions d'habitants.*" [12]

Furthermore, the entire policy of threats and sanctions was re-

[11] Henry Lémery, January 12, 1934; Sénat, *Débats*, 1934, p. 24.

[12] Aristide Briand, Foreign Minister, December 26, 1929; Chambre, *Débats*, 1929, p. 4678.

garded as not only dangerous, but unnecessary as well. The Rightist assumption of German aggressiveness and future revolt was entirely too pessimistic. France was dealing with "*deux Allemagnes*"[13] and must learn to differentiate between them, lest they otherwise unite in a spirit of nationalistic resistance.[14] The "new Germany" of the Republic, which was directed "*vers la paix*," had to be distinguished from the remnants of the old military and reactionary Germany. Briand and his friends set out to help consolidate this "new Germany." "*Rapprochement*" with her was the cornerstone of Briand's policy and the basis of his and Stresemann's common efforts from 1925 to 1929.

According to the French theory of the two Germanys, nationalist Germany wanted revenge, while republican Germany wanted peace and prosperity. It was assumed that the former was conspiring against the essential clauses of the Versailles Treaty, while the dissatisfaction of the latter was directed only against the "ephemeral clauses," that is, those concerning the execution of the treaty, and against the treatment which Germany had been receiving from her former enemies. To appease and satisfy the new democratic Germany required only that the Rightist policy of force, humiliation, and threats be replaced by a spirit of friendly co-operation and negotiation. Briand liked to emphasize, for instance, the salutary effect it would have on the Germans to be welcomed back into the community of nations, to be given a place on the Council of the League of Nations, and to be permitted in general to participate in the discussions of the affairs of the world.

France was now willing to show moderation in the methods of execution. The occupation of the Rhineland was to be made less visible. Germany, in matters of disarmament and reparations, was

[13] Léon Blum, January 11, 1923; Chambre, *Débats*, 1923, p. 22.
[14] Edouard Herriot, June 2, 1922; Chambre, *Débats*, 1922, p. 1668.

to be trusted to fulfill her obligations rather than controlled and supervised. The emphasis, therefore, was on a change of form and of spirit, rather than on a change of substance. It was in no sense a revisionist program; its sole purpose was to make the *status quo* of Versailles more acceptable to the Germans.

The policy of *rapprochement* ended in failure. The new Germany was only temporarily consolidated, and the Germans, even before Hitler came to power, showed no signs of abandoning their claims for revision of the essential clauses of the Treaty of Versailles. The Leftists in France and elsewhere tried to blame the Rightist opposition at home for the failure of the new policy. The French Rightists, it is true, accused Briand of misplaced confidence in Germany, undue optimism, and dangerous weakness, and did try to put obstacles in the way of his policy. They were not comforted by the reminder that France's concessions were to be only in matters of execution, such as the termination of the occupation of the Rhineland. Since they were convinced that Germany could not be trusted and that the rights of enforcement embodied in the treaty were already too limited in time and scope, every modification in favor of Germany appeared to them as a sacrifice of French security, already too poorly protected. French nationalist attacks on Germany were also used by the nationalist opponents of Stresemann in Germany to prove the futility of his policy and the continued hostility of France. That too helped to shorten the period of reconciliation. Yet there is every reason to believe that the policy was doomed, even without Rightist opposition in both countries. It was based on a fundamental misunderstanding between the French and the Germans.

Briand's ideas did not lack ingenuity. If by extending better treatment to the Germans, he could have succeeded in persuading them not only to fulfill their treaty obligations voluntarily, but also to give up any desire to revise the treaty, France would no longer have had to insist on provisions, the sole purpose of which was to guarantee Germany's obedience and permanent submission to the treaty. Briand was proposing a bargain by which the Germans would waive their claims for future revision in return for immediate relief from pressure and economic discomfort. He was, therefore, hoping that a spirit of resignation might come to prevail in Germany. Unfortunately for him, the Germans did not understand this to be the sense of the new policy, and no German government could have remained in power if it had lent its ear to such a suggestion.

The theory of the "*deux Allemagnes*" was bound to cause misunderstanding when applied to foreign policy. To be sure, there were two—and perhaps three or four—Germanys as far as internal loyalties and ideologies, or economic, political, and social interests were concerned. In domestic affairs there was hardly any unity between Communists, Republicans, Nationalists, and National Socialists. But in foreign affairs, as in France, the situation was quite different. Just as the French parties, with all their controversies, agreed on a policy of security based on the maintenance of the *status quo* of Versailles, so did all German parties and statesmen with any influence on foreign policy take it for granted that the Treaty of Versailles required drastic revision.

Differences of opinion in Germany on foreign affairs did not bear upon this fundamental and ultimate objective, but upon the best ways and means thereto, that is, on questions of timing and aggressiveness. Stresemann and Briand were agreed on one thing: they both wanted to put an end to acute conflict between the two countries, since it was shattering their economic life and even endangering the existence of the German Republic. But while the French wanted to settle down once and for all on the basis of the new order of Europe, Germany was struggling only for a breathing spell. She would have to be patient, moderate, and reasonable,

Stresemann insisted, if she were ever to regain enough strength to be able to put forward her claims with any hope of success.

Stresemann has been accused of having deceived Briand. Was he not simply advising Germany to "lie low" so that she might gain time to prepare for the great attack on the treaty? However, it is unnecessary to postulate an interpretation so unfavorable to Stresemann's sincerity in his dealings with Briand. Germany inaugurated the policy of *rapprochement* with what she regarded as great sacrifices. By the treaty signed at Locarno she waived her claims to Alsace and Lorraine; she put her signature to an agreement that provided for the permanent demilitarization of the Rhineland; she promised not to use force to change the boundaries of Germany in the east. Stresemann assumed that this, together with a willingness on the part of Germany to fulfill her current treaty obligations, should be enough gradually to allay France's fears and suspicions of her neighbor. Once she learned to feel secure at the side of Germany, France would come to realize that it was to her own advantage and to that of her continental allies to accept the German point of view and promote revision of some of the most unjust and untenable provisions of the Versailles settlement. Reconciliation was thus to pave the way toward peaceful change.

It is hard to believe that so shrewd a statesman as Briand could have been under any illusions as to the German feelings about Versailles, at least at the time the policy of *rapprochement* was inaugurated. But what he apparently hoped for was that time would work in favor of France. If the German Republic were given time to consolidate, and if the German people regained prosperity through economic collaboration with France, would they not realize that they could live and prosper without changing the order of Versailles? Would they not then prefer to abide by the *status quo* rather than risk their own welfare by creating new trouble and perhaps plunging Europe into a new war? Briand's plans for European confederation and economic agreements, proposed during the same period, would lessen the importance of boundaries and thus eliminate the main incentive for territorial revision. *Rapprochement* would reconcile Germany with the *status quo*.

The effects of this basic Franco-German misunderstanding, the "*équivoque*" of Locarno (as Millerand, one of Briand's ardent opponents, repeatedly called it),[15] were bound in time to make themselves felt. Impatience grew on both sides and in both countries strengthened the nationalists, who were hostile to the Locarno policy and who were soon able to declare triumphantly that the promises were not being fulfilled. Germany was waiting for evidence that her "good behavior" and her voluntary acceptance of certain essential clauses of the Treaty of Versailles were going to bear fruit in the form of substantial concessions. The French, meanwhile, were waiting for Germany to show her gratitude for having been spared further threats and intimidations and to cease raising new claims every time one had been satisfied. It is not surprising that under these circumstances *rapprochement* should have ended in dismal failure.

When France ordered the last of her troops of occupation to evacuate the Rhineland on June 30, 1930, five years before the date set by the treaty, she was in the eyes of her Rightists making an unforgivable concession and forfeiting the only remaining instrument of pressure by which Germany might be forced to obey the treaty. But the German response was hardly one of gratitude. Immediately following the liberation of the occupied area, there was a sudden surge of violent nationalism in Germany, which induced the German Government to inaugurate an active revisionist foreign policy. The French gesture of confidence, it was said in Germany, had come too late, and after all was only the response to Germany's concessions under the Young Plan, which exacted from

[15] Alexandre Millerand, June 3, 1926; Sénat, *Débats*, p. 1120.

her the payment of vast sums for the lifetime of two generations. Since Germany's policy was steadily fixed on the future revision of many of the permanent provisions of the treaty, French concessions affecting merely the execution of the treaty, even if better timed and more willingly granted, could not have solved the difficulties.

In 1930, the policy of *rapprochement* came to an end. If the policy of force pursued by the Rightists had failed, the new policy of persuasion and conciliation had fared no better. Briand was still a member of the government, although most of his power and prestige had vanished, when, less than a year after the evacuation of the Rhineland, Germany and Austria in a surprise move negotiated a protocol for the establishment of a customs union, interpreted by the French as the beginning of active "revisionism." They were forced by France to drop the proposal, for she was still in possession of superior power and could threaten Germany into compliance with her wishes now that "cooperation" had failed. But both force and persuasion only postponed the day when Germany's claims for revision would have to be heard. In 1932, reparations were canceled; after that came German rearmament and then the rapid succession of moves by which the Hitler government revised the treaty.

Once German rearmament and the remilitarization of the Rhineland had taken away France's most important advantages and had destroyed her hope that Germany might resign herself to a relatively modest place on the Continent, the issue for France became a different one. It was now a question of whether she would have to resign herself to accepting any changes of the *status quo* which Germany would demand or undertake, or whether she could risk resistance at this late stage and find sufficient support from other powers. France made some efforts to stem the tide, which will be discussed later. But she lost the initiative to Britain, whose policy of "appeasement" was not likely to reverse the course of events in favor of France. By 1938 there were definite signs of resignation in both the Leftist and Rightist camps.

When men on the Left like Léon Blum and other leaders of the *Front populaire* declared themselves ready to discuss disarmament and other means of conciliation with the National Socialist government, they were no longer motivated by the former hope of strengthening the "new Germany." They were advocating what seemed to them the lesser evil as compared to an open clash with a powerful and dreaded neighbor. They were less willing now to oppose Hitler than the British Leftists, who were becoming increasingly militant and calling upon the government to stop the dictators at practically any cost.

On the Right the change was even more striking, if not sensational. After having proclaimed for twenty years that French security depended on the maintenance of the *status quo* in Central as well as in Western Europe, prominent leaders on the Right suddenly discovered that France and her empire could after all be safely defended from behind the Maginot Line. The policy to be followed, recommended Montigny, was to "*distendre des engagements trop lourds, engager la France dans une politique réaliste où elle serait sûre de n'affronter la guerre que pour la défense de ses intérêts vitaux.*"[16] If the French Government had followed earlier this policy that was now being recommended, the course of European history after the World War would have been radically different.

Opposition to the new policy of retrenchment was voiced, however, by members of both the Left and Right. Its exponents were accused of pro-Fascism, of shameful compliance with the wishes of the British Conservative government, or of blindness to the consequences which such a course would entail for France. Could France

[16] Jean Montigny, June 23, 1936; Chambre, *Débats*, 1936, p. 1535.

with impunity betray her allies in Central Europe? Could a great power give up her right and duty to interfere beyond her frontiers? What if Germany should become an "*empire gigantesque*" and turn around and demand from France the return of Alsace, the iron ore of Lorraine, and France's colonial possessions? [17]

In the days of the Czechoslovak crisis of 1938, the fight between the two schools, now called the "*pacifistes*" and the "*bellicistes,*" the exponents of retrenchment and of resistance, respectively, reached its climax. Retrenchment, or what the British called appeasement, won the day. The Munich agreement was more willingly accepted in France than in Britain, although her acquiescence in the face of sweeping territorial revision spelled a complete collapse of her whole traditional policy and although she, not Britain, was committed by an alliance to assist Czechoslovakia. It seemed, therefore, that France had at that point definitely resigned herself to the role of a "little France," limiting her defenses to her own soil and her own colonial possessions.

But resignation was not permanent. The development of a new sense of internal strength and unity, and the influence of two external factors helped France regain a feeling of strength. Even though this did not permit her to take the initiative in calling a halt to Germany, it allowed her to follow the lead of Britain when the latter chose this course. One external factor was the reversal in Britain's policy itself, which took place in the spring of 1939, when Britain committed herself to defend Poland. This suddenly removed that which ever since the days of the Ruhr had been the one insuperable obstacle to a "*politique de force*" on the part of France, and a main reason for the spread of a spirit of resignation. Even though some French statesmen might still have preferred to remain passive, France could hardly do so when Brit-

[17] Paul Reynaud, January 26, 1937, Chambre, *Débats,* 1937, p. 168; February 26, 1938, Chambre, *Débats,* 1938, p. 648.

ain entered upon a course for which the French had pleaded for over twenty years.[18] It was not without irony that Britain turned to the one-time French point of view just at the moment when some prominent French statesmen were recommending its abandonment, and after France had lost most of the defenses which she had sought to build up for the purpose of pressing this policy effectively.

The other external factor was provided by Italy. Shortly after the Munich Conference, the Italian Government allowed territorial claims on France to be voiced in the Italian Chamber. French pride and resentment at being treated as potentially a second Czechoslovakia aroused a new spirit of resistance against the partners of the Rome-Berlin axis.

Little more will be said about France's attitude toward Hitler's policy during the days of the Czechoslovak crisis and the British and French pledge to Poland, because the lead had come to lie entirely in the hands of the British.[19]

[18] After Germany's occupation of Bohemia and Moravia, Jean Ybarnégaray said that only "*les partisans de l'entente avec l'Allemagne, à tout prix, même au prix de la lâcheté, même au prix de l'abdication*" could continue to urge France to "*laisser les mains complètement libres à l'Allemagne.*" March 17, 1939; Chambre, *Débats*, 1939, p. 1035.

[19] In fact, France's new pledge to Poland was first made known by Neville Chamberlain in a statement to the House of Commons, March 31, 1939; Great Britain, House of Commons, *Parliamentary Debates*, Vol. 345, col. 2415. See below, p. 293.

VI. National Armaments

BEFORE treating the various French efforts to obtain pledges of military assistance from other countries, a brief account must be presented of the development of her own military forces, that is, of her first line of defense. It has never been an easy task for a government to burden its country with long military service and heavy military budgets, but the French post-war situation in regard to armaments was peculiar in that the main objection was not domestic but international. A nation that stood for strong armaments in the early post-war years and all through the twenties was certain to be conspicuous and attract the disapproval of world opinion. Today the situation is reversed, and countries like Great Britain are being blamed for having neglected their armaments too long. There were, of course, people in France who were hostile to the idea of strong French armaments, Communists who were not concerned about French national interests or even about the existence of an independent France, pacifists who believed in the uselessness of military preparations, adherents to the "new doctrine" which proclaimed "peace through disarmament." But while in the Anglo-Saxon countries not only public opinion but also governments were committed to general limitation and reduction of land armaments, in France successive ministries and the great majority of the people insisted on the necessity of strong armed forces. The task they had set for themselves, execution cf the Treaty of Versailles and permanent enforcement of the new order against Germany, could not be carried out except with considerable military strength. No country could expect to borrow this strength from others or obtain pledges of assistance from others unless it were strong itself and willing to make the necessary sacrifices to defend its own interests. Still less could other countries, the French felt, require France to reduce her armaments except in so far as they were willing to shift the burden onto their own military forces.

How much this view differed from that of Great Britain and the United States was revealed dramatically during the Washington Conference of 1921-1922. The clash between the French and other delegations typified the atmosphere of estrangement and mutual recrimination which for years rendered co-operation difficult. To the French it appeared that the Anglo-Saxon countries were proposing to place between themselves and Germany the superiority of their fleets while condemning France to a status of inferiority on the seas, inviting her to reduce her armaments on land, and forcing her to defend herself against charges of "*arrière-pensées*"[1] and "*le spectre truqué de la France impérialiste.*"[2] They were bitter to find that countries which were unwilling to take "*une part des charges et des périls qu'elle doit supporter*" should assume "*le droit de fixer une limite à ses armements.*"[3] Once the basic premises of French post-war foreign policy are accepted, that for the sake of her security she had to maintain the *status quo* against a rebellious Germany and that force was needed for the purpose, her attitude toward armaments is entirely logical. The Anglo-Saxon point of view must, therefore, have seemed

[1] Aristide Briand, President of the Council of Ministers, November 21, 1921, Third Plenary Session; United States, *Conference on the Limitation of Armament, Washington, November 12, 1921–February 6, 1922*, p. 119.

[2] Albert Sarraut, Minister of Colonies, February 1, 1922, Fifth Plenary Session; *ibid.*, p. 255.

[3] Aristide Briand, President of the Council of Ministers, November 23, 1921, Committee on Limitation of Armament; *ibid.*, p. 429.

to the French either blind or deliberately hostile toward their country.

As the French saw it, France was burdened with a task which might at any moment require the use of force either for sanctions or for war. She had to be prepared to carry out this military action successfully. The opponent was known. Her military experts alone would be capable of fixing the amount of military equipment necessary for this purpose; it was within their normal duties to do so. Once, therefore, the total amount of troops and armaments which would have to be ready on her side was established, the only matter which was still open for discussion was the question of how large a proportion of these military forces should be French, and what part would be supplied by allied troops pledged to the support of France. During the entire period, from the Washington Conference to the end of the Geneva Disarmament Conference, France offered to reduce her own armaments in exact proportion to the supplementary allied or international military assistance promised. "*Il nous faudrait des garanties aussi efficaces au point de vue de la sécurité que celles que nous assure notre armée même.*"[4] The more assistance, the less French armaments; and vice versa.

This did not mean that the size of these potential "allied armies" was once and for all fixed at an absolute figure. It varied of course with the size and strength of the potential opposing forces, that is, with the extent of German armaments. There is no reason, therefore, to disbelieve the French contention that she had reduced her war-time armaments one-third by the time of the conference at Washington, and that they were still further reduced before the

[4] M. Jusserand, Ambassador in Washington, to M. Briand, July 15, 1921, reporting a statement made by him to Secretary of State Hughes; France, Ministère des Affaires Etrangères, *Documents Diplomatiques: Conférence de Washington, juillet 1921–février 1922*, p. 6.

Disarmament Conference met at Geneva. Maginot went so far as to say that "*de toutes les nations, la France est incontestablement celle qui, depuis dix ans, s'est engagée le plus résolument, le plus hardiment et, je dirai même, le plus courageusement dans la voie de la limitation des armements.*" [5] Since Germany's armaments had been much more drastically cut, French reductions did not destroy her tremendous relative advantage. It was only when she was asked to reduce still further or to wipe out entirely this relative advantage that her resistance stiffened and became insurmountable.

The French, it should be pointed out, regarded the idea of parity of arms with Germany as unjust, since it would give Germany the full benefit of her superior "*potentiel de guerre.*" Equality of armaments meant inequality of security. Furthermore, they insisted, it would be a mistake to treat a possible aggressor on equal terms with a country "which may be forced to defend itself from . . . aggression" [6] and dangerous to agree on general disarmament

[5] André Maginot, War Minister, February 24, 1931; Chambre, *Débats*, 1931, p. 1124.

"*Pourquoi,*" asked M. Herriot, President of the Council of Ministers, speaking at Gramat, September 25, 1932, "*laissons-nous dire que nous n'avons rien fait dans l'ordre du désarmement?*" And he proceeded to demonstrate France's case: "*En 1921, la loi militaire en vigueur dans notre pays est la loi de trois ans. Dès le 1er avril 1923, tenant compte des engagements pris et des garanties de sécurité résultant de l'occupation rhénane, le Parlement français abaisse les effectifs en ramenant la durée du service à dix-huit mois. En 1928, après les accords de Locarno et la résolution prise en 1927 par l'assemblée de la Société des nations, la loi du 31 mars abaisse de nouveau les effectifs en fixant la durée du service à douze mois. Et, chez nous, il s'agit non d'effectifs théoriques, mais d'effectifs réels. Tout récemment, citoyens, notre gouvernement a réduit les budgets de défense nationale de dix pour cent par rapport à ceux de 1932. . . . En dix ans, n'est-ce pas là un effort considérable?*" *Le Temps*, September 26, 1932, p. 6.

[6] André Tardieu, President of the Council of Ministers, April 12, 1932, Disarmament Conference, General Commission; League of Nations, *Records of the Conference for the Reduction and Limitation of Armaments*, Series B, *Minutes of the General Commission*, Vol. I (1932. IX. 64), p. 53.

when only the "*nations de bonne foi*" could be trusted to carry it out.[7] Léon Blum was nearly alone in taking exception to the arguments of his colleagues in the Chamber, when he proclaimed that "*le désarmement général est nécessaire.*" [8]

It therefore was hardly fair to accuse France of militarism, since her armaments were the only means by which a policy such as she was pursuing could be carried out with any chance of success. If criticism was due, it should have concerned the policy, not the instrument. Many critics, however, shared the curious (but widespread) delusion of the post-war period that in the "new era" military force was no longer necessary to make countries submit to a state of things which they disliked or resented to the point of revolt.

How effective French armaments were we do not intend to judge. That is a matter for military appreciation. Certainly France cannot be accused of failing to keep her armaments up to the requirements of the task or of underestimating, as the British did, the extent of the preparations on the opposing side. There seem, however, to have been conflicting purposes within her military policy that go back to a contradiction in general foreign policy of which more will be said later. To fortify the Franco-German border by establishing the Maginot Line was a defensive policy in the narrowest sense of the word.[9] It protected France from in-

[7] Aristide Briand, Foreign Minister, November 30, 1927; Chambre, *Débats*, 1927, p. 3404.

[8] Léon Blum, January 19, 1932; Chambre, *Débats*, 1932, p. 51. See also his *Les Problèmes de la Paix* (1931); English edition, *Peace and Disarmament* (1932).

[9] The first special credits for the "*Organisation défensive de la frontière*"—later known as the Maginot Line—were voted by the Chamber of Deputies and Senate on December 28, 1929, one month after the evacuation of the second Rhineland zone, six months before the evacuation of the third and final zone. Presenting to the Chamber of Deputies his arguments for the defensive plans to which detailed study over a considerable period of time had already been

vasion; it looked toward the defense of French soil and territorial integrity. Certainly it indicated no intention on the part of France of going to the assistance of allies in Central Europe, although not to do so would have contradicted the French Central European policy. As long as the Rhineland was demilitarized and Belgium was a military ally of France, the Maginot Line did not necessarily prevent an offensive strategy. At that time a march on Berlin was popularly regarded as a mere "walk-over." But, psychologically, fortifications of such importance did not favor the development of an offensive spirit. Moreover, if the critics of French armaments are right, this policy was coupled with neglect of the kind of *troupes de choc* which the modern offensive requires. The result was to leave France unprepared for a military situation in which the German border would be defended by a German line of fortifications and in which the passage of troops across Belgium would be prevented by Belgium's resumption of a policy of independence or neutrality. France's military policy tends to prove that, notwithstanding her far-flung commitments on the Vistula and the Danube, she was more concerned about receiving than about giving support, more preoccupied with the defense of her own soil than with the protection of small countries.

devoted, André Maginot, War Minister, referred to the evacuation of the Rhineland and declared:

"Il n'est pas douteux que le jour où, par suite du retrait de nos troupes, notre frontière du Nord-Est se trouvera privée de la protection que lui assure la barrière du Rhin, il sera indispensable que cette frontière, qui demeurera ouverte, soit, au moyen d'une forte organisation défensive, assurée d'une protection nouvelle.

"Personne en France ne comprendrait que l'évacuation anticipée de la Rhénanie n'eût pas comme contre-partie immédiate la mise en état de défense de notre frontière du Nord-Est."

The projected defensive arrangements would be a protection against invasion, and would compensate *"l'infériorité numérique de notre couverture du temps de paix."* They should be completed by 1935, *"c'est-à-dire avant que nous entrions dans la période des classes de la guerre, celles qu'on appelle les classes creuses."* December 28, 1929; Chambre, *Débats*, 1929, pp. 4774-4775.

VII. The Quest for British Assistance

IF there was one conviction which all Frenchmen shared, it was the belief that outside of their own military preparedness an *entente* with Britain must become the cornerstone of France's system of security. Not that British support would be enough—it had to be supplemented by many other measures of security. But it was the *conditio sine qua non*, the French insisted, of the safety of their country and of the peace of Europe. *"C'est leur intime union qui assure la paix du monde,"* said Briand in 1921.[1] And his Rightist opponent, Franklin-Bouillon, exclaimed in 1934, *"Ai-je besoin de répéter que tant que l'Angleterre ne se rangera pas, fermement et pour toujours aux côtés de la France, jamais la paix ne sera assurée dans le monde?"*[2] France needed Britain as an ally, or so at least she firmly believed. Her entire post-war foreign policy might therefore be characterized not only as an effort to keep Germany in her place but also as a continuous struggle to get Britain to pledge her support against Germany.

A Franco-British alliance did not become an accomplished fact until 1936. After Germany tore up the Locarno Treaty, Britain promised that she would "immediately come to the assistance of your [the French] Government, in accordance with the Treaty of Locarno, in respect of any measures which shall be jointly decided upon," and would, "in return for reciprocal assurances from your

[1] Aristide Briand, President of the Council of Ministers, January 20, 1921; Chambre, *Débats,* 1921, p. 51.

[2] Henry Franklin-Bouillon, November 30, 1934; Chambre, *Débats,* 1934, p. 2843.

Government, take, in consultation with your Government, all practical measures available to His Majesty's Government for the purpose of ensuring the security of your country against unprovoked aggression."[3] Staff conversations were begun and military agreements prepared. In December, 1936, M. Delbos declared for the French Government, "*Je tiens à déclarer, au nom du Gouvernement, que de même toutes les forces de la France, sur terre, sur mer et dans les airs, seraient spontanément, immédiatement utilisées pour la défense de la Grande-Bretagne, dans le cas d'une agression non provoquée.*"[4]

From 1919 down to 1936 France was, for the most part, unsuccessful in her dealings with Great Britain. For all her military superiority on the Continent at the close of the World War, she could not force Britain's hand. Her very conviction that she needed British support put her in a weak bargaining position. She became dependent because she could not afford to antagonize Britain. This does not imply that Britain herself did not in turn suffer from this conflict of views on the German issue. By the time France submitted to British leadership and acknowledged her dependency, the evil which Britain had been trying to forestall, that is, the revolt of Germany against the Treaty of Versailles and its protagonists, had already taken place. This revolt, when it came, forced Britain into a direction which came more and more to coincide with that which France had sought to follow in the earlier period. The two countries defeated each other.

[3] This declaration was contained in a letter drafted in London, March 19, 1936, in conjunction with the proposals drawn up by the Locarno Powers (*Cmd. 5134*, p. 7). The letter was, in the event of the failure of these proposals, to be addressed by Great Britain and Italy to Belgium and France. On April 1, 1936, the British Government transmitted the letter of March 19th to the Belgian and French Governments (*Cmd. 5149*); the declaration contained therein came into effect, and staff conversations began on April 15th.

[4] Yvon Delbos, Foreign Minister, December 4, 1936; Chambre, *Débats*, 1936, p. 3328.

The troubles between France and Britain, as we have mentioned earlier, had already started at Versailles. France, not having been allowed to move her strategic frontier to the Rhine, had made her security dependent upon Anglo-Saxon pacts of guarantee which never went into effect. Being left with neither the Rhine nor the British guarantee, France was under constant pressure to make further sacrifices if she wished to gain a new promise of British assistance.

Under these circumstances, the Treaty of Versailles was a bad starting point for a policy of "allied solidarity." France was bitter; her statesmen complained that she had "lost the peace" after having won the war. The World War alliance was not continued in a sense that would offer France the assurance of British assistance in case the war on the Rhine should break out again, and France soon lost much of her good reputation with the Anglo-Saxon countries as the result of her demands for a military frontier on the Rhine and for the severe treatment of Germany after the war. She who had been "*la grande victime*" was soon defending herself against Anglo-Saxon accusations of militarism and imperialism. "*On ne cesse de lui attribuer des arrière-pensées absurdes, des ambitions secrètes, des accès périodiques de mégalomanie,*" exclaimed Poincaré in 1923.[5] The early years after Versailles saw acute conflict with Great Britain, and as early as 1920 Millerand was objecting to the talk of a "*crise des alliances.*"[6]

Under Millerand in 1920 and under Poincaré in 1922 and 1923 dissatisfaction with Britain was freely voiced by the government. Poincaré turned down an offer for a pact of guarantee by Britain because it did not contain the requirements of a reliable and effec-

[5] Raymond Poincaré, President of the Council of Ministers, November 23, 1923; Chambre, *Débats*, 1923, p. 3691.

[6] Alexandre Millerand, President of the Council of Ministers, March 26, 1920; Chambre, *Débats*, 1920, p. 742.

tive alliance.[7] It was later in the same period that France invaded the Ruhr, a procedure which the British regarded as illegal and highly undesirable. But when in 1924 the French swung away from Poincaré's policy of the "strong hand" and promised to withdraw their troops from the Ruhr, a trend was already setting in which was to lead eventually to France's complete submission to British leadership.

[7] The negotiations for an Anglo-French alliance were initiated by the French Ambassador in London during the course of an interview with Lord Curzon, British Foreign Secretary, on December 5, 1921. They were continued by Lloyd George and Briand in London on December 21st, when Briand said that the treaty would be the nucleus of a more general agreement which might even include Germany. During the Cannes Conference in January, 1922, the two statesmen exchanged memoranda outlining the positions of their respective countries, and Lloyd George submitted a draft treaty to the French. At this point M. Briand was forced out of office, partly because it was suspected that he was too ready to accept the British point of view in the negotiations. He was replaced by M. Poincaré, who, in a memorandum of January 29th, rejected the British draft and submitted counter-proposals. The British then took a less active interest and insisted that such outstanding matters as European economic recovery, the status of Tangier, and peace with Turkey had to be settled first. Poincaré is then reported to have said that "he attached no importance whatever" to the alliance in the form presented him, and that "France was absolutely indifferent as to whether there was a Pact or not." The negotiations came to an end, although mention of the problem was occasionally revived. After the French had entered the Ruhr in January, 1923, they refused to allow the suggested renewal of security negotiations to be used as pressure on their Ruhr policy. The British professed their continued readiness to resume discussions, and Lord Curzon maliciously explained that if he had refrained from pushing the matter it was "because it seemed to me somewhat invidious to suggest to the greatest military Power in Europe that her frontiers required some additional defence to that which her own armies could provide."

During the active stage of negotiations the French point of view had centered around several distinct problems. The French insisted on reciprocity in the new alliance, having in mind the unilateral character of the guarantee pact of 1919 which was "*humiliante dans la forme parce qu'étant unilatérale, elle ne place pas la France sur un pied d'égalité avec l'Angleterre.*" Furthermore, the simple guarantee of France by Britain was useless, because in case of German aggression "*le salut de l'Angleterre exigerait évidemment son intervention immédiate, et cette intervention devrait se produire automatiquement avec ou sans garantie.*"

Poincaré objected to the duration of the treaty which, according to the draft

France, of course, was far too powerful at that time to become merely a tool in the hands of the British. One way of escaping British tutelage was to find substitutes for British assistance. Another was to take advantage of any British need for French support and to force the British to compromise. If there had been any adequate substitute, the French would have been in a much stronger position. However, a continental power equal in strength to Great Britain did not exist. Independence from her World War ally could be achieved only if the need for aid itself could be diminished. In the days of Briand and Franco-German *rapproche-*

presented by Lloyd George, was to be ten years. It meant that the treaty would end at the very moment when, as a result of the evacuation of the Rhineland, "*la France perdrait une des plus sérieuses garanties de sécurité pour sa frontière.*" "*L'Allemagne,*" asked M. Poincaré, "*ne serait-elle pas, dans dix ans, plus à redouter qu'à l'heure présente?*"

In order to make the projected alliance effective it was "*indispensable,*" the French argued, "*de maintenir un étroit contact entre les Etats-Majors des deux pays,*" because in their opinion, it was "*impossible de prévoir une coopération éventuelle des forces militaires, navales et aériennes des deux pays sans que des dispositions soient prises pour rendre cette coopération effective.*"

The French insistence on a guarantee of the demilitarized zone has already been discussed. They also insisted that the assistance should not be limited to the case of attack "against the soil of France," on the ground that if only actual penetration of French territory would bring the alliance into operation, the invasion would have begun by the time British assistance could become effective. They were also of the opinion that a treaty "*serait complètement inutile s'il restait limité au cas d'agression directe par l'Allemagne,*" but since Britain was unwilling to undertake commitments in Eastern Europe, the French agreed that the two countries should merely consult in case of a threat to peace in the East. An "*étroite entente politique*" would develop, and the British would realize that "*son étroit accord avec nous assurera mieux que tout autre moyen la paix de l'Europe . . .*"

The relevant documents are contained in the British Blue Book, *Papers respecting Negotiations for an Anglo-French Pact*, France, No. 1 (1924), Cmd. 2169, and in the French Yellow Book, *Documents Diplomatiques: Documents relatifs aux négociations concernant les garanties de sécurité contre une agression de l'Allemagne (10 janvier–7 décembre 1923)*. See also J. Paul Selsam, *The Attempts to Form an Anglo-French Alliance, 1919-1924* (1936); and the observations of Briand and Poincaré in the French Chamber of Deputies, April 1, 1922; Chambre, *Débats*, 1922, pp. 1347 ff.

ment it appeared as if such a possibility of loosening French dependency on Britain had been discovered. *Rapprochement* with Germany, it is true, was in line with British wishes for appeasement, but at the same time it lessened France's fear of Germany and her desire for British pledges of assistance. Perhaps the British disliked a really close collaboration between France and Germany because they might lose control over France and Western Europe if their assistance and mediation were no longer required. That Briand's plan for a European confederation did not meet with much sympathy across the Channel tends to confirm this suspicion. However, the dreams of intimate Franco-German co-operation were short-lived.

Some French statesmen who were particularly opposed to Britain's views and were resentful of her attitude called for a "*politique continentale*," that is, continental alliances, instead of a British alliance. The small Central European allies, Poland and Czechoslovakia, were not strong enough to serve as a substitute. It looked, however, as if France might free herself from Britain when Barthou, and after him Laval, set out in 1934 and 1935 to negotiate first with the Soviet Union and then with Italy. By that time, however, Germany had already become so strong that no French government, whatever its feelings toward Britain may have been, dared to antagonize her and run the risk that she might remain neutral in a new war. For this reason the Franco-Soviet alliance was so worded as to obviate any danger that France would have to go to Russia's assistance without having first assured herself of Britain's consent. The Laval-Mussolini agreements of January, 1935, were sacrificed by France before the year was over, when it became necessary to choose between the friendship of Italy and that of Great Britain. There was no country that could really take the place of Britain in France's scheme of security. In 1919, Tardieu defied anyone to show him "*une politique continentale qui puisse apporter à la France autre chose qu'un appoint; une politique continentale dont la valeur numérique et mondiale puisse se comparer à celle de la politique que nous vous apportons."* [8]

As a result, France was constantly driven to make concessions, both by the need of pleasing Britain and by the pressure of Germany's resistance. She had to pursue a policy which was weaker and more conciliatory than most of her statesmen actually desired and which many regarded as calamitous. Even so it was far from satisfactory to either the British or the Germans. Her dilatory tactics and her continual efforts to keep at a minimum the concessions that in the end had to be made brought upon her the blame for defeating Britain's attempts at appeasement as well as for undermining the Republican Government in Germany. The method of military sanctions was abandoned after the Ruhr, primarily because of British dissatisfaction. The evacuation of the Rhineland, which had been occupied by the Allies as one of the provisions of the treaty, was hastened by the knowledge of British impatience. At one moment Britain even applied pressure by threatening to withdraw her troops independently of France. "*Nos amis anglais voulaient s'en aller. Nos amis belges voulaient s'en aller. Nous ne voulions pas nous séparer,*" Briand explained.[9] French consent to the Hoover moratorium in 1931 came only after a delay of several weeks and thereby destroyed any chances of saving the Austrian and German banks from collapse. The principle of German equality in arms was accepted in 1932, only after Germany had withdrawn from the Disarmament Conference. The enumeration could be prolonged. But while in every instance public opinion in Britain became impatient with France, the French—at least the

[8] André Tardieu, government representative for the debate on the Peace Treaty, September 2, 1919; Chambre, *Débats*, 1919, p. 4095.

[9] Aristide Briand, Foreign Minister, November 8, 1929; Chambre, *Débats*, 1929, p. 3055.

Rightists—were disturbed by the "collusion" between Germany and Britain and resented the concessions that had to be made to please Britain. "Whatever points we conceded, we have always conceded them owing to pressure from the United States or from Great Britain," wrote Tardieu.[10] One member of the Chamber even spoke of *"l'hégémonie germano-anglo-saxonne, qui, de plus en plus, nous isole dans le monde."* [11] It seemed to the French that France was sacrificing her security bit by bit only to encourage more audacious demands from Germany.

At times France was in a position to put up resistance. One of the most striking cases in which the British needed French assistance and were therefore willing to make a bargain with her at the expense of Germany may serve as an illustration. In 1928, Great Britain was preparing to discuss naval disarmament with the United States, and wanted France to back her in her views on cruiser tonnage. France agreed to do so in what was called the "Franco-British naval compromise" and received in return a British promise to support the French thesis that trained reserves should not be taken into account in any future convention on land armaments.[12] The details are not of importance here; it is significant merely to note that this was a case in which France was able to strengthen her position in regard to Germany by removing the dangerous possibility that the German view on trained reserves would be adopted by Britain. It was during this period, too, that Lloyd George was demanding for Britain "strict impartiality in

[10] André Tardieu, *France in Danger* (1935), p. 33.

[11] Alfred Margaine, January 19, 1932; Chambre, *Débats*, 1932, p. 52.

[12] The correspondence regarding the Anglo-French naval compromise is contained in the British White Paper, *Papers regarding the Limitation of Naval Armament*, Miscellaneous No. 6 (1928), Cmd. 3211; and in the French Blue Book, *Limitation des Armements navals. Trente-cinq pièces relatives aux travaux préparatoires du désarmement et à la limitation des armements navals (21 mars 1927–6 octobre 1928)*.

our relations with European Powers," and complaining that she was "tied to the apron-strings of France." [13]

France was not able to make many such bargains, since Britain was rarely in need of support against other countries. When in 1935, during League sanctions against Italy, the British feared Italian reprisals against their navy in the Mediterranean and sought French support, the French were either not skillful or not powerful enough to exact from Britain the pledge they most needed—an unequivocal British commitment to defend the demilitarized zone on the Rhine—in return for a promise to stand by Britain in the Mediterranean.[14]

It is interesting to compare two periods in which the French felt themselves to be in a strong position and acted independently. The first was in 1922 and 1923 and has already been discussed; the other came in 1931 and 1932. History does not generally repeat itself, but the policies pursued by France during these two periods, separated from one another by eight eventful years, offer an interesting parallel. She was again hoping that the use of a policy of "*la main forte*" would enable her to stop an imminent revolt of German nationalism; yet at the same time she shrank from the specter of French isolation which might follow upon the application of a policy of which Britain disapproved. The external circumstances were in many respects strikingly similar on the two occasions. In 1922 and 1923, the murder of Rathenau, the abortive *Putsch* of Hitler, and other events were evidence of a rising wave of nationalism in Germany. In 1930, National Socialist representation in the Reichstag jumped from 14 to 107, and Brüning, seeking to stem the rise of National Socialism, embarked on what

[13] David Lloyd George, speech in Manchester, December 8, 1928; *Société des Nations,* XI (1929), p. 341.

[14] See the British White Paper, *Dispute between Ethiopia and Italy, Correspondence in connexion with the application of Article 16 of the Covenant of the League of Nations,* Ethiopia No. 2 (1936), Cmd. 5072.

was called an "active foreign policy," vigorously pushing German claims for the cancellation of reparations, for general disarmament, and for a customs union with Austria. In France, in both periods, Rightist influence was great and the government believed that a resolute stand, rather than further concessions, could check the Germans. On both occasions France was strong financially, while both Britain and Germany were in the throes of serious economic and financial troubles.

If, therefore, there ever was a situation comparable to that of the earlier days of Poincaré it was in 1931 and 1932. But France's actions on this occasion were far less spectacular than in the days of the Ruhr. While the French Government did show a spirit of resistance to British pressure and to German demands, no use of force was made or even suggested. Germany and Austria were forced to drop their proposed customs union and it was rumored that the withdrawal of French funds had brought about the collapse of the *Kreditanstalt* in Vienna and that the same procedure was being used to subject Britain to pressure. In the Disarmament Conference, which opened early in 1932, Tardieu blocked progress toward disarmament by submitting ambitious plans for security. More important still, in April of 1932, plans for an embracing agreement on armaments with Germany that would have been acceptable to Great Britain, the United States, and Italy were wrecked in the "April tragedy"[15] by Tardieu's refusal to attend a conference with Brüning, MacDonald, and Stimson. Public opinion in the Anglo-Saxon countries was becoming convinced that French obstinacy was defeating Brüning, the last pillar of the German Republic which was then entering upon its final struggle with the National Socialists.

Once again, as in 1923, there was severe tension, not only be-

[15] John W. Wheeler-Bennett, *The Pipe Dream of Peace: the story of the collapse of disarmament* (1935), Chapter III.

tween France and Germany, but also between France and Britain. It ended in a way which was strikingly similar to that of 1924. A swing to the Left in France once more gave the premiership to Edouard Herriot, who again reversed the direction of French foreign policy and offered to make concessions to Germany for the sake of securing close ties with Britain. In 1924, he promised to liquidate the occupation of the Ruhr; in 1932, at Lausanne, he sacrificed practically all of France's reparations claims. When he came to justify his actions before the Chamber he pointed out the dangers of French isolation as he had done in 1924, and emphasized the need of intimate co-operation with Britain. The parallel can be carried one step farther. While Herriot was able on both occasions to improve Franco-British relations by his willingness to adhere more closely to the British point of view, both the agreement which he and MacDonald negotiated at Geneva in 1924 (the Geneva Protocol), and the so-called "Declaration regarding future European cooperation," signed by Britain and France after the close of the Lausanne Conference in 1932, turned out to have only a temporary character with no binding effects.[16] Herriot was vio-

[16] The "Declaration regarding future European cooperation" of July 13, 1932 (*Cmd. 4131*), summoned the nations to "rally to a new effort in the cause of peace, which can only be complete if it is applied both in the economic and political sphere" and declared the intention of Britain and France "to give the lead" in bringing about these objectives in the spirit of the Lausanne Agreement. Their program was defined as follows:

"1. In accordance with the spirit of the Covenant of the League of Nations they intend to exchange views with one another with complete candour concerning, and to keep each other mutually informed of, any questions coming to their notice similar in origin to that now so happily settled at Lausanne which may affect the European régime. It is their hope that other Governments will join them in adopting this procedure.

"2. They intend to work together and with other Delegations at Geneva to find a solution of the Disarmament question which will be beneficial and equitable for all the Powers concerned.

"3. They will co-operate with each other and other interested Governments

lently attacked by his opponents at home. "*En cédant aux Allemands,*" exclaimed Franklin-Bouillon, "*vous croyez regagner les Anglais.*"[17] "*L'amitié franco-britannique,*" asked Flandin, "*doit-elle, nécessairement, se traduire par l'adoption constante du point de vue britannique?*"[18] Herriot answered, "*Je redoute l'isolement.*"[19]

These quotations, taken from the debates in the Chamber, are but one indication of the never-ceasing and vehement controversy raging between the Leftists and the Rightists in regard to the attitude France should take toward Britain. While, as we have said before, everyone was agreed on the need of British support, particularly in case of war, the two groups disagreed, both on the

in the careful and practical preparation of the World Economic Conference.

"4. Pending the negotiation at a later date of a new commercial treaty between their two countries they will avoid any action of the nature of discrimination by the one country against the interests of the other."

By the French the declaration was regarded as a "revival of the Entente Cordiale"—so M. Herriot is said to have described it—as a promise of future Anglo-French co-operation and as providing for a common front with regard to war debt payments to the United States. The British denied that the declaration possessed any such exclusive character and emphasized those provisions which it was hoped would secure wide acceptance. Seventeen European states, including Germany, accepted the invitation to adhere to the declaration in pursuance of paragraph 1.

[17] Henry Franklin-Bouillon, October 28, 1932; Chambre, *Débats*, 1932, p. 2912.

[18] Pierre-Etienne Flandin, December 29, 1932; Chambre, *Débats*, 1932, p. 3759.

[19] Edouard Herriot, President of the Council of Ministers, December 12, 1932; Chambre, *Débats*, 1932, p. 3530.

André Tardieu's *France in Danger* (1935) reviews the failure of France's policy after the World War and emphasizes what he regards as the critical change when Herriot replaced him as head of the French Government in May, 1932, and proceeded, in his opinion, to abandon all the positions to which he had clung. In the preface to his book *Sur la Pente* (1935), he contends that when he resigned in May "*la doctrine et les titres internationaux de la France étaient intacts,*" but that "*cette doctrine et ces titres, défendus par vingt-six gouvernements, de 1919 à 1932, ont été, sauf le bref redressement de 1934, constamment désertés, de 1932 à 1935*" (pp. viii-ix).

best methods by which to gain British assistance and with regard to the price which France should pay for it.

It can be generally stated that until 1936, when a new phase set in, Franco-British relations increased in intimacy in direct proportion to the influence of the Leftist group in the French Government. The high points were reached with the Herriot ministries of 1924 and 1932 and with the *Front populaire* government under Léon Blum in 1936. Tension between France and Britain, on the other hand, was greatest with Millerand in 1920, Poincaré in 1922 and 1923, and during the ministries of the early thirties, in which Laval, Tardieu, and Barthou controlled French foreign policy.

The Leftists—Socialists and Radical-Socialists—were for the most part ardent exponents of a policy of close Franco-British cooperation. They were bent on improving the atmosphere between the two countries and on bringing French foreign policy as closely as possible into line with British views and wishes. They had particularly cogent reasons for wishing to gain for France the assurance of British support. If it were obtained, they believed, all the force would be taken out of the Rightist arguments for stronger French armaments. With a spreading feeling of security in France, such as they expected to follow British commitments, popular opinion would be more in sympathy with the Leftist policy of conciliation. The Leftists, generally optimistic in their hopes and declarations, insisted that Britain would assume new commitments if only France complied with British suggestions, and that France would thus be amply compensated for her concessions to Germany. High hopes were set on the rise of Leftist influence in Great Britain, particularly after the Leftist groups in the two countries had come in 1924 to agree on the principles of the Geneva Protocol, which provided for a "League with teeth" and therefore for stringent British commitments on the Continent. Strong and isolated French action against Germany, such as the Rightists recommended, was opposed, not only because it was militaristic and might involve France in the horrors of a new war, but because it might endanger the attitude of public opinion in Great Britain toward firm and embracing commitments. There was, too, another reason for the pro-British attitude of the Left. It was to their advantage in their domestic political struggle to be able to point to the sympathies which they alone could command in Great Britain. It followed that if the French people were eager to assure themselves of British assistance, they should vote for the Left.

Since there existed a harmony of views between Britain and the French Leftists with regard to the proper policy toward Germany, both favoring a policy of conciliation and concessions, it is hard to say in any particular case whether a concession to Germany, such as the liquidation of the occupation of the Ruhr or the evacuation of the Rhineland, was made to satisfy Great Britain, or merely justified afterwards as having been necessary to mend or strengthen the ties with Great Britain. Britain over and over again was made to serve as an alibi.

For the Rightists the situation was far more difficult. They faced a dilemma. While they wanted British support, they disapproved violently of the policy which Britain wished France to pursue with regard to Germany. They were bitter about Britain's attitude toward France's demands at Versailles. They were the target for all the British attacks on "French militarism and imperialism." Their opponents at home were morally supported by the British. What wonder then that they would have liked at times to break loose from all ties with Britain? But the more they sought or threatened to do so, the more they became the main obstacle to peace in the eyes of the British. The bitter clash between Lloyd George and Clemenceau at Versailles, in which each accused the other of nationalistic egotism, or that between Lord Curzon and

Poincaré during the occupation of the Ruhr, or again that between Sir John Simon and Barthou in 1934 during the final session of the Disarmament Conference, are all symptomatic of the tension that existed between Britain and the French Rightists from the end of the World War down to the days of the alliance.[20]

[20] In his note to Clemenceau of March 26, 1919, Lloyd George argued that peace would "depend upon there being no causes of exasperation constantly stirring up the spirit of patriotism, of justice or of fair play." He could not "conceive any greater cause of future war than that the German people, who have certainly proved themselves one of the most vigorous and powerful races in the world, should be surrounded by a number of small States, many of them consisting of people who have never previously set up a stable Government for themselves, but each of them containing large masses of Germans clamouring for reunion with their native land." He argued for what he called a "long-sighted peace," and urged that once the peace terms were accepted the Allies should "do everything possible to enable the German people to get upon their legs again." The peace treaties should be drawn up "as if we were impartial arbiters, forgetful of the passions of war." Clemenceau replied to these suggestions in a note of March 31, in which he agreed with the general object "to make a lasting peace, and in order to do so, to make a just peace," but pointed out that "colonial advantages, naval advantages, or advantages connected with commercial expansion" would "appease" Germany and not "territorial advantages in Europe" as suggested by Lloyd George. "Germany," stated M. Clemenceau, "was before the war a great world Power whose 'future was on the water.' It was of this world power that she was proud. It is this world power that she will not console herself for losing." The method proposed by Lloyd George would mean that a "certain number of absolute and definitive guarantees would be acquired by maritime peoples who have not known invasion," whereas, for "the continental countries, on the other hand, that is to say, for those who have suffered most by the war, would be reserved . . . partial and temporary solutions." In a biting reply Lloyd George, on April 2, countered Clemenceau's list of British gains from the draft treaty by listing the advantages derived by France to all of which, he sarcastically wrote, "France seems to attach no importance. . . ." This situation, he playfully remarked, would make possible "a peace with Germany, which will satisfy everybody, especially the Germans." *Cmd. 2169*, Nos. 16, 18, 19.

The encounter between Lord Curzon, British Foreign Secretary, and M. Poincaré is also worthy of mention. There had been a personal meeting of the two in Paris in September, 1922, when Curzon's protests against France's Near Eastern policy were countered by such a biting retort that Curzon is said to have left the room in haste and collapsed. Harold Nicolson, *Curzon: The Last Phase, 1919-1923* (1934), p. 274. Perhaps this incident was still in Curzon's mind when a year later on August 11, 1923, he sent to M. Poincaré a complete state-

The Rightists, it must be admitted, did not seek to justify their attitude solely on the ground that a strong policy toward Germany would produce results more important to France than any future assistance from Great Britain. They contended that there was no need for France to be so concerned over British support, since it

ment of the British attitude toward the situation in the Ruhr. *Cmd. 1943;* also in the French *Documents Diplomatiques: Réponse du Gouvernement français à la lettre du Gouvernement britannique du 11 août 1923 sur les Réparations* (*20 août 1923*), pp. 55-69. He frankly advanced a thesis which could only anger the French:

"His Majesty's Government remain of opinion that an undertaking freely entered into, because acknowledged to be just and reasonable, stands, in practice, on a different footing and offers better prospects of faithful execution, than an engagement subscribed under the compulsion of an ultimatum, and protested against at the very moment of signature as beyond the signatory's capacity to make good." Lord Curzon then developed Britain's legal, political and economic arguments against the Ruhr occupation.

In his reply of August 20, M. Poincaré refuted the entire argument of the British Foreign Secretary and restated fully France's policy. As for Britain's interest in the matter, M. Poincaré suggested that, "*L'intérêt de l'Angleterre est sans doute que l'Allemagne se relève; il n'est certainement pas que la France soit abaissée.*" Aimed directly at the British was the observation: "*C'est la résistance de l'Allemagne qui prolonge une situation douloureuse; tout ce qui peut encourager la résistance de l'Allemagne contribue à cette prolongation, et tout ce qui ne décourage pas cette résistance l'encourage.*"

Another bitter clash between British and French statesmen occurred during the meeting of the General Commission of the Disarmament Conference, May 30, 1934, held after M. Barthou had broken off negotiations in his note of April 17. Sir John Simon refused to admit that negotiations with Germany could break down completely. The conference, he argued, should "introduce some realism into its idealism," and he tacitly approved the "realistic view" of the small neutrals that "the Conference would 'have to take into account in conventional form the situation resulting from a *de facto* rearmament.' " The British, as "bridge builders," insisted that "some method had to be found which would keep her [Germany] in touch in the hope of bringing her back within the ambit of discussion and negotiation with a view to ultimate agreement." The French Foreign Minister, in a speech delivered with an oratorical display of frankness that left its mark in Geneva, attacked the British attitude. France, he contended, had not closed the door to future negotiations, although it could not accept certain British proposals as a basis. They seemed to be a complete surrender to German threats. "Apparently they were expected to abandon any system which did not at once receive the unqualified approval of Germany. Apparently they had arrived—the

would be forthcoming in case of war whatever France did in the meantime. Britain would have to defend France in order to protect herself. The Rightists had always resented any suggestion that Britain had fought in the last war only to save France. "When Great Britain declared war on Germany in 1914," wrote Tardieu, "and when the United States in 1917 declared war, it was because they realized . . . that France's danger was their danger also." [21] All along, the Rightists would have liked to conclude a clear-cut Franco-British military alliance with prearranged military plans, such as that which came into existence after 1936. But when Poincaré's proposal for such an alliance—instead of a mere unilateral pact of guarantee—was turned down they became skeptical of any effort to make Britain undertake new and reliable commitments. French concessions, they claimed, would be the last thing to move the British. Even before that Poincaré had said, "*Ce serait la pire maladresse que de paraître mendier des amitiés et d'oublier ce que nous sommes, ce que nous valons et ce que nous pouvons.*" [22] Only a strong France could hope to impress and attract Britain. It was better, therefore, to act according to their own inspiration and hope that the British would some day awaken from their blindness and realize that France had been right in predicting that only a policy of relentless firmness could save both countries from the German menace.

With the rise of National Socialist Germany and the rearma-

League of Nations, which represented nearly the whole world, had arrived—at such a point that one Power, because it had abruptly, violently, left the Disarmament Conference, could command it and impose its will upon it." After all, "Who was threatening Germany? Certainly not France." League of Nations, *Records of the Conference for the Reduction and Limitation of Armaments*, Series B, *Minutes of the General Commission*, Vol. III (1936. IX. 1), pp. 661 ff.

[21] André Tardieu, "The Policy of France," *Foreign Affairs*, I (September, 1922), p. 23.

[22] Raymond Poincaré, *Histoire Politique: chroniques de quinzaine*, III, p. 164; from the *Revue des deux mondes*, June 15, 1921.

ment that followed, the attitudes of the French parties toward England underwent a metamorphosis. From the time Germany proclaimed her freedom from the disarmament restrictions of Versailles and announced a huge rearmament program, no statesman in either France or Britain could doubt that co-operation between the two countries was necessary for both. Early in 1935, during the discussions for a Western air pact, Britain for the first time welcomed the possibility of military assistance from France. The reciprocal promises of assistance exchanged between the two governments in 1936 ended the long period of vacillation and conflict in their relations. The alliance was a reality.

Soon after that, in 1937, the British Government inaugurated a policy of "realism" and "appeasement." Now it was the Leftist parties in both Britain and France that opposed efforts to conciliate the dictators and were reluctant to make concessions to National Socialist Germany. French Rightists, who previously had rejected concessions, now not only approved of the conciliation policy pursued by the British Conservative government, but wanted France to pattern her policy on the British model. "*Nous n'avons plus une faute à commettre,*" said Flandin in 1937, "*et c'en serait une, à notre sens, que de ne pas adapter strictement notre politique aux réalités, à l'exemple de celle dont s'inspirent nos amis britanniques, dont la collaboration confiante et totale doit rester la base même de notre action diplomatique.*"[23] The difference of opinion was no longer between Britain and France, but along party lines common to both countries. The strongly anti-Fascist groups on the Left in the two nations, which favored collective security and resistance to the dictators, were united in opposition to the conservative elements, which advocated appeasement. If there was any serious disagreement from that time on between the two governments, it was

[23] Pierre-Etienne Flandin, November 19, 1937; Chambre, *Débats*, 1937, p. 2482.

not made public. France seems to have submitted without reservation to British leadership, especially in regard to Germany. The conflict which had previously been the keynote of all their relations and the cause of so much trouble for both countries was over. When "appeasement" reached its climax at Munich there was no sign of dissent between the two governments. When six months later Britain took the lead in a policy of new commitments and firm resistance in the East which ended in war, there appeared to be absolute unity of Franco-British action. But while France had come to follow Britain's lead and initiative, the outcome was certainly more in harmony with French predictions and earlier intentions than with those of Britain.

VIII. Central European Friends and Allies

Rhine, Vistula, and Danube

FOR twenty years after the close of the World War the British hoped that the eastern frontier of France would serve as the continental line of defense for both countries. Never did the French adhere to this view. While the importance of the Rhine as a "*garantie naturelle*" and the function of the Rhineland as a "*zone de sécurité*"[1] necessary for France's security was emphasized—often over-emphasized—the eyes of France were always turned toward Germany's eastern and southeastern borders. Fearing Germany's ambitions in Central Europe and determined to check them, France set up defenses on the Vistula and on the Danube as well as on the Rhine. This would seem to make her clamors for "safety on the Rhine" paradoxical, if not insincere. As a matter of fact, her Rhine policy had a dual nature. It had its narrowly defensive aspect, for the fear of a renewal of the invasion of 1914 was always present with the French. But the government, at least, must have known that this was at the time only a very remote possibility. What mattered in the near future was to prevent Germany from moving against her weaker neighbors in the east or southeast and to keep the way open for France to come to the assistance of these countries. French Rhine policy aimed not only to defend French soil, but also to hold over Germany the threat

[1] France, Ministère des Affaires Etrangères, *Documents Diplomatiques: Documents relatifs aux négociations concernant les garanties de sécurité contre une agression de l'Allemagne (10 janvier 1919–7 décembre 1923)*, pp. 28, 29.

of French military pressure by invasion. "*Les Allemands, en effet, ne se lanceront pas volontiers dans l'aventure d'une guerre tant qu'ils sauront que cette guerre pourra avoir comme premier champ de bataille des territoires qui sont allemands ou qui sont appelés à le devenir*," said Maginot.[2] France's desire to station troops on the bridges of the Rhine or in the Rhineland and to have Germany's western flank unfortified and unprotected arose not merely from her defensive needs in Western Europe but from her wish to be provided with access to her eastern allies. "*Le Rhin*," wrote Poincaré, "*offrirait aux Alliés une excellente ligne de départ pour une démonstration décisive*."[3] And Montigny has spoken of the "*frontière désarmée sur laquelle nous pouvions faire facilement certaines opérations de police*."[4] As long as Germany was defenseless against French military moves across the Rhine, she was paralyzed in every other direction and deprived of her natural advantages over the smaller powers in the East. Thus the demilitarization and defortification of the Rhineland were "*une protection indispensable pour les Etats nouveaux . . . à l'Est et au Sud de l'Allemagne*," as the French declared in 1919.[5] When Germany remilitarized and refortified her western provinces after March, 1936, French territorial security, that is, the safety of her own soil, had long been provided for by the Maginot fortifications. This helps to explain why Great Britain was so little disturbed by the remilitarization of the Rhineland. Since the new situation spelled no immediate danger for France, Britain could see no reason for alarm about a change which at the worst would make it possible for Germany to act more freely in respect to Central Europe, a

[2] André Maginot, March 2, 1926; Chambre, *Débats*, 1926, p. 1136.

[3] Raymond Poincaré, *Histoire Politique: chroniques de quinzaine*, II, p. 137; from the *Revue des deux mondes*, December 1, 1920.

[4] Jean Montigny, July 31, 1936; Chambre, *Débats*, 1936, p. 2327.

[5] Government Memorandum of February 25, 1919; *Documents Diplomatiques*, *op. cit.*, p. 20.

region in which Great Britain still considered herself not vitally interested. Those most affected were Germany's eastern neighbors.

The dual nature of France's policy on the Rhine caused her many difficulties in her relations with Great Britain. She was trying to persuade the Anglo-Saxon powers that the Rhine was an "international frontier," a "*barrière commune*," as Foch called it, protecting the western democracies against future German (or Russian) aggression.[6] "*Vous ne pouvez pas plus admettre l'Allemagne sur le Rhin*," exclaimed Briand in addressing Britain, "*que vous ne pouvez l'admettre à Calais. Si vous songez à votre pays, vous n'avez pas le droit de vous désintéresser de cette frontière du Rhin. Elle est la vôtre comme la nôtre.*"[7] Woodrow Wilson was repeatedly quoted by the French as having called the Rhine the "frontier of freedom"—"*la frontière de la liberté.*"[8] But while many people in the Anglo-Saxon countries might sympathize with the idea of making the Rhine a strategic dividing line between Germany and the western world, France wished it to be a one-way barrier only. She wanted others to protect her on the Rhine, but not to stop her there. She refused to consider any system of security limited to Western Europe which would force her to retreat behind her borders and disinterest herself in Central or Eastern Europe. That, however, is what the British had in mind when they spoke of the Rhine as Britain's frontier. Only much later, in

[6] Memorandum submitted to the Peace Conference, January 10, 1919; *ibid.*, p. 12.

[7] Aristide Briand, President of the Council of Ministers, June 4, 1926; Sénat, *Débats*, 1926, p. 1137.

[8] In his addresses to the French Senate, January 20, 1919, and to the Chamber of Deputies, February 3, 1919, Wilson declared that France had defended the "frontier of freedom"; Ray Stannard Baker, and William E. Dodd, eds., *The Public Papers of Woodrow Wilson: War and Peace*, I, pp. 392, 406.

The French Government in its memorandum of February 25, 1919, used Wilson's expression to support the argument for permanent occupation of the Rhine, and Clemenceau repeated it in his note of March 17, 1919. *Documents Diplomatiques, op. cit.*, pp. 20, 33.

1937 and 1938, did some French statesmen in a mood of despair and resignation espouse the idea of a "little France" entrenched behind the Maginot Line.

The contradiction between the British and the French interpretations of the function of the Rhine was well illustrated at Locarno. Britain welcomed the Locarno Pact precisely because it differentiated between the West and the East and limited Britain's commitments to a guarantee of the frontiers on the Rhine. The French protagonists of Locarno insisted that France's eastern allies gained by the pact, since the new guarantees of the demilitarization of the Rhineland confirmed France's free access to them. On the other hand, the opponents of the pact in France were concerned over the fact that while Germany had promised unequivocally not to seek any change of her western boundaries, she had been allowed in regard to her eastern boundaries to give a much less comprehensive pledge, namely, not to seek change by the use of force. Every such differentiation, either by Britain or Germany, was a blow to the French conception of European affairs. The problem of holding Germany in her place was like that of besieging a fortress. Of what use would it be to stand guard on one exit only? Security against Germany called for an "indivisible" siege. It is significant, however, to note that the term "encirclement" was rarely used by Germany before 1939, when Britain, who for twenty years had opposed France's efforts to link the western defenses with those in the East, at last adopted the French view.

When, therefore, the Senate rapporteur on the Treaty of St. Germain said in 1920, "*La sécurité de la France vis-à-vis de l'Allemagne, elle n'est pas seulement en cause sur le Rhin,*"[9] he gave the clue to France's policy on the Vistula and on the Danube. Eighteen years later Ybarnégaray told the Chamber that "*le jour*

[9] Imbart de La Tour, Rapporteur on the Treaty of St. Germain for the Foreign Affairs Committee, June 30, 1920; Sénat, *Débats*, 1920, p. 1064.

où Hitler aura réalisé la Mitteleuropa, le sort de notre pays . . . sera inexorablement fixé."[10] This then was France's "*cauchemar,*" the main explanation for her active interest in the East.

Whether her fear was justified or not we shall not seek to discover. Her policy in a sense revolved in a vicious circle. Because she wanted to weaken Germany and hedge her in she helped Poland and Czechoslovakia to obtain territory transgressing the German ethnic borders, backed their resistance to German demands for adjustment, and used them as allies in building up defenses against Germany. Thereby she intensified the tension on Germany's eastern borders and hastened the moment when her entanglements in the East would draw her into a struggle that would endanger her security. It is also worth noting that a policy of security which sought to forestall every possible future threat, however remote, was bound to force France to oppose Germany on a most comprehensive scale. Thus in Central Europe any German expansion, spread of influence or economic penetration, or the *rapprochement* of any country with Germany, was pictured as a threat to French security. Any one of these might be a stepping-stone to future political absorption. "*L'équilibre européen*" as it existed after Versailles was said to be at stake.

France claimed that she was defending the new *status quo* in Central Europe against what was variously labeled as a renascence of pre-war pan-Germanism or as a revival of Germany's "*Drang nach dem Osten.*" Germany's desires for *Anschluss* with Austria, for the return of territories inhabited by Germans, or for closer economic ties with the Danubian countries were put into the same category as any actual or assumed plans for conquest or political domination of the non-German peoples in Southeastern Europe. Germany's neighbors in the East served the defense of France proper by being "*contre-poids contre la puissance alle-*

[10] Jean Ybarnégaray, February 25, 1938; Chambre, *Débats*, 1938, p. 595.

mande"[11] and "*forces de résistance nécessaires à notre tranquillité.*"[12] They were bulwarks against a Germany which might take up "*l'éternel rêve pangermanique de la Mitteleuropa, et ses desseins d'hégémonie allemande sur le Danube et sur les routes d'Orient.*"[13]

France thus undertook what Montigny called the "*rôle écrasant du gendarme de l'Europe, en service commandé sur toutes les frontières les plus exposées.*"[14] To bar for all time any designs Germany might have for the redress of her grievances or for a new order in Central Europe and to crush any ambitions that country might have in directions and regions so remote from France was a tremendous task for which France was inadequately equipped.[15]

Inadequate Eastern Defenses

The most conspicuous weakness in France's position was lack of support by other great powers. For twenty long years the British made every effort to avoid entanglement in the affairs of Central Europe. Both their initial attitude and the complete reversal that took place after March, 1939, will be discussed. It is significant to note that the latter came about only after Germany had already carried out two of the plans which France had been most anxious to avert, namely, union with Austria and disruption of the Czecho-

[11] Stéphen Pichon, Foreign Minister, December 29, 1918; Chambre, *Débats*, 1918, p. 3724.

[12] Georges Clemenceau, President of the Council of Ministers, December 23, 1919; Chambre, *Débats*, 1919, p. 5336.

[13] Senate Finance Committee Report of December 7, 1923, on loan to the Kingdom of the Serbs, Croats, and Slovenes; Rapporteur, Henry Bérenger; Sénat, *Documents*, 1923, Session extraordinaire, Annexe, No. 798, p. 144.

[14] Jean Montigny, June 23, 1936; Chambre, *Débats*, 1936, p. 1535.

[15] French policy on the Danube is very ably discussed in H. Beuve-Méry, *Vers la plus grande Allemagne* (Centre d'Etudes de Politique Etrangère, Section d'Information, Publication No. 14, 1939); see particularly pp. 54 ff.

slovak state. Britain apparently was ready to give Germany considerable leeway in the Southeast before trying to put a stop to the revival of German "hegemony on the Danube." We shall find Italy at France's side for a part of the time, but she was mainly interested in defending the Austrian sector of the "Eastern front" which France was trying to establish. The Soviet Union was ready in 1934 to join with France in treaties designed to stem the tide. Her sincerity was never tested. It is claimed that she was prepared to give effective military assistance for the defense of Czechoslovakia. But at that time her access to the borders of Germany was precarious, if not impossible, because by then Poland and Rumania had emphasized their neutrality and were said to have refused to accord free passage to the armies of the Soviet Union

The success of France's policy in Central Europe depended, therefore, on the strength of her own forces and on the assistance which she might expect to obtain from Poland, Czechoslovakia, Yugoslavia, and Rumania. But even with these countries, her most natural friends and allies, full harmony of purpose and policy never came to exist. This is surprising on first sight, because France could claim in all justice that she was not pursuing a narrowly egotistical policy in Central Europe. Her own national interest was of course paramount, but to a large degree it ran parallel with the interests of countries like Poland or Czechoslovakia, who regarded any rise of German power or influence in their direction as a menace to their very existence. Their birth as nations had come about as the result of liberation from Teutonic, Hungarian and, in the case of Poland, also from Russian domination.

France came to regard herself so completely as the guardian of the smaller nations against the Germanic colossus that even former enemies, such as Austria and Hungary, came to be included among those whom she meant to "protect." Much sincere feeling of friendship and responsibility toward the "young nations," particularly toward the Poles and Czechs, who had contributed to the Allied cause during the World War, led the French people to back the policy of their government, which could always count upon a sympathetic response when it stood up for the "*aspirations nationales*" of the smaller Slavic nations in the East.

Yet the road toward effective co-operation between France and these countries was beset with difficulties, which were psychological, strategic, economic and political in character. These account for the eventual failure of French policy in the East.

The psychological problem lay in the fact that these countries were too dependent on France militarily, politically, and financially for their own self-esteem. They resented their dependency. They resented even more the fact that France expected gratitude from them for her generous support. France, as Viénot put it, was misunderstood and was being suspected in Central Europe and in the Anglo-Saxon countries of seeking "*avant tout à s'assurer une clientèle politique, et cela dans un intérêt étroitement égoïste.*"[16] Indebtedness, here as elsewhere, was not a source of sympathy for the creditor. But the psychological strains, which were often enough silenced by feelings of real community of interest and conviction, were not a decisive factor.

The strategic problems were far more serious. As long as Germany was unilaterally disarmed and the Rhineland demilitarized, the French had free access to their eastern friends and allies across German territory. Yet as long as Germany remained in this artificial state of military inferiority, the dangers against which France sought to protect herself and her friends on the Vistula and the Danube were not actually present. Nobody could expect a disarmed Germany with a defenseless flank in the West to open an attack on her eastern neighbors or to start a march down the Danube.

[16] Pierre Viénot, Rapporteur on the Austrian loan for the Foreign Affairs Committee, December 29, 1932; Chambre, *Débats*, 1932, p. 3753.

She might open her markets to those countries; she might attract them as customers. But while this would be disagreeable to France, it involved no threat against which the small states in the East needed protection.

The strategic situation would, however, change completely if France failed to keep Germany disarmed and the Rhine borders open to French military action. When, therefore, after the announcement of German rearmament, France failed to take the preventive action for which Poland is said to have been prepared, and permitted Germany a year later to remilitarize the Rhineland, France's small eastern allies became strategically so remote from her that the possibility of military assistance of an effective kind became highly doubtful. The Maginot line of fortifications, as has been pointed out earlier, was hardly an indication that the French armies were prepared to carry an attack into Germany. Surprisingly enough, the contradiction between a military policy restricted to fortifications and armies equipped for defense and a foreign policy of far-flung commitments and wide zones of interest seemed to dawn on the French only when it was too late for France's Central European friends to seek protection elsewhere. Montigny in 1937 warned the French Government to be cautious about engagements "*que l'on ne pourrait tenir militairement sans une sorte de folie.*" [17] General Maurin asked, as early as 1935, how anybody could expect France to resort to an offensive after having spent billions on establishing a fortified barrier: "*Serions-nous assez fous pour aller, en avant de cette barrière, à je ne sais quelle aventure?*" [18] Although this was not by any means the view taken by all responsible French statesmen, such considera-

[17] Jean Montigny, January 26, 1937; Chambre, *Débats*, 1937, p. 167.

[18] General Louis Maurin, War Minister, March 15, 1935; Chambre, *Débats*, 1935, p. 1045.

tions must none the less have been distressing for France's friends and allies in the East.

Ever since the World War access to the new states in Central Europe for armies coming to their assistance had been a vexatious problem and had played an important role in international discussions. The French were keen to remove any legal obstacles that might bar the way to the "*passage des troupes*" across neutral territory. This problem of the passage of troops was one reason for French appreciation of the existence of the League. It was impossible to get all the nations in Europe to enter into alliances which would commit them to bring assistance to countries in the Central European danger zone; as members of the League, however, they were obliged to allow the passage of troops, providing these were acting on behalf of the League (Article 16, paragraph 3 of the Covenant). It was to France's interest, therefore, that in case she should ever have to come to the assistance of her eastern allies, she should be able to do so not by having to fight an old-time "private" war, but by participating in League sanctions against the country attacking one of the Central European states. But the League collapsed before the actual test in Central Europe came. Several members had already shown their disinclination to live up to the Covenant by declaring that they would not permit the passage of troops acting under League auspices and in execution of Article 16. Poland and Rumania thus cut off the Soviet Union from Czechoslovakia, and Belgium's neutrality barred the way for any French or Franco-British attack on Germany in the north. Switzerland, taking advantage of her privileged position as a neutral state in the League, had forbidden the passage of ammunition from France to Poland as early as 1920, in the days of the Polish-Soviet War. With the development of the Rome-Berlin axis into a military alliance, an iron curtain of hostile armies and navies closed

France's approaches to the East, from the North Sea to the Mediterranean.

Another weakness of the French alignment with the Slavic states of Central Europe which was strongly felt was economic in character. France was unable, due to the structure of her own economy, to help cure the economic ills from which all Danubian countries, victors and vanquished alike, suffered throughout the post-war period. Apart from Czechoslovakia, where industry and agriculture were well balanced, and where economic conditions compared favorably with those of other European countries, the Central European states from the Baltic to the Balkans suffered not merely from monetary instability and unbalanced budgets, but from the more fundamental maladjustments of a predominantly agricultural production. While France was in a better position than any other country to meet their purely financial needs and thus to finance large governmental expenditures on armaments, she was not able to offer an outlet for large agricultural surpluses. She was struggling against the stream when she tried to match the advantages which Germany could offer these countries. French statesmen, particularly those who, like Tardieu and Flandin, had made a special study of the economic woes of the Danubian area, were not blind to this fact.[19] They fully realized that, since the

[19] When on May 18 and 19, 1931, the League of Nations Council debated the procedure to be followed regarding the Austro-German customs union protocol of March 19, the French delegation, led by Briand, submitted a "critical memorandum" attacking the protocol on legal, political, and economic grounds. At the same time, M. Flandin, French Finance Minister, had prepared a "constructive memorandum," entitled "Proposals for Remedying the Present European Crisis," which was submitted on May 16 to the Commission of Enquiry for European Union. *Minutes of the Third Session of the Commission,* 1931. VII. 7, pp. 79 ff. The memorandum suggested that a preferential system for the agricultural products of Central and Eastern Europe should be set up. Separate international agreements were recommended for solving the crisis of over-production, the organization of the industrial market, and the eventual reduction of tariff barriers. The memorandum urged that the powers to which Austria had

very existence of the mass of the people was at stake, economic interest was bound in the long run to gain the upper hand over political or sentimental considerations. In 1931, Germany's star was already rising. She proposed a customs union with Austria, which was to be open to other Danubian countries, and offered preferential treatment and a wide market for their agricultural exports. Even if France had succeeded in inducing her allies of the Little Entente to support her "constructive plan" for Danubian economic confederation and to draw Austria and Hungary into their orbit by sufficient concessions, the authors of the plan knew well enough that such a confederation, to be successful, must still depend upon winning a sufficient market in Germany. France was trying to

pledged her independence should help contribute to her material development, and that Austria's chief customers should grant special facilities to her trade. Finally, financial co-operation was recommended, an agricultural mortgage credit system endorsed, and the facilitating of large government loans urged.

Discussion of the problem of relieving the situation of the Central European countries continued, and on March 5, 1932, the French Government—Tardieu was its head and Flandin its Finance Minister—submitted to the British delegation at Geneva a new plan for Danubian customs preference. This plan, dated March 2, was offered by France with "*le seul souci de servir l'intérêt général européen.*" In view of the failure of credit methods alone to solve the situation, it was held that "*il est temps d'apporter à la situation des remèdes d'ensemble qui, dans l'inefficacité constatée des solutions particulières, peuvent seules permettre d'assainir la situation.*" A tariff agreement based on a reciprocal preferential system among the Danubian countries was recommended, and a conference of the interested states, Austria, Hungary, Czechoslovakia, Yugoslavia, and Rumania, was suggested. Text of the plan, *L'Europe Nouvelle*, XV (April 2, 1932), p. 445. A month later, Tardieu and Flandin went to London where they elaborated their plan before a conference of the four Great Powers which met April 6-8. They recommended that preference be accorded to the products of the Danubian countries and that a loan be raised for their benefit. However, the interests of the states were too divergent, the plan was rejected, and the conference failed. Royal Institute of International Affairs, *Survey of International Affairs, 1932*, pp. 22-23. Five months later, from September 5-20, the Stresa Conference, which had been called by the Lausanne Conference, again tried to solve the economic difficulties of the Danubian region, but its labors left no permanent results. *Ibid.*, *1932*, pp. 23-27, 87-95. Texts relating to the Stresa Conference, *L'Europe Nouvelle*, XV (October 15, 1932), pp. 1230-1240.

"square the circle" in her desire to save those countries both from economic disaster and from an ascendance of German influence. It meant drawing them away from Germany and yet helping them to secure German markets.

Last, but not least, the political obstacles helped to defeat the French purposes. Poland was one of the first countries with which France signed a thorough-going military alliance after the World War (she was preceded only by Belgium). France negotiated a consultative pact with Czechoslovakia in 1924, and followed this by pacts of mutual guarantee with both Poland and Czechoslovakia in 1925. Her relations with Austria, we will find, tended to make France a guarantor of Austria's independence. It was evidently her intention, therefore, to build up an iron ring of defenses around Germany, holding her in bounds in the West, the East, and the Southeast. But she never succeeded in making the chain solid. What were to have been links in the chain remained separate and unconnected units. There was never any treaty of mutual assistance between Poland and Czechoslovakia. Most of the time they were on anything but amicable terms, their latent hostility culminating in Poland's participation in the partition of Czechoslovakia in 1938. Nor was there ever any close co-operation between Czechoslovakia and Austria. All the French attempts to coax the Little Entente powers into establishing a Danubian confederation fell on deaf ears. The fault may have been with Czechoslovakia, with Austria, or with both of them. In any case, the Danubian front against Germany remained "*pulvérisé*." [20]

The only legal basis for common action and mutual assistance on which France might rely in case support was needed for one of the links of the would-be ring around Germany was the Covenant of the League of Nations. It may well be that France would never have developed any real or realistic interest in the League

[20] Jean Molinié, April 7, 1922; Chambre, *Débats*, 1922, p. 1442.

if she had not discovered in it a possible means of integrating her separate and strictly bilateral pacts and agreements with these Central European countries. If Poland, for instance, was unwilling to promise assistance to Czechoslovakia in a bilateral pact in case the latter should become a victim of German aggression, or if Great Britain was unwilling to commit herself on behalf of either Poland or Czechoslovakia, these countries might nevertheless go into action under the League Covenant, which committed them to participate in sanctions against an aggressor. This offers a key to French opposition to Hitler's repeated proposals for bilateral pacts. France had signed more bilateral pacts than any other country, but they were tied together through the League Covenant. Hitler's "bilateralism" was an effort to isolate Germany's neighbors from one another and to eliminate the general alliance represented by the League Covenant. The French could not forget the historical parallel of Bismarck moving "*du Sleswig à Sadowa et de Sadowa à Sedan*" [21] or, as Paul-Boncour put it, "*je me refuse d'oublier que Sadowa a précédé Sedan.*" [22]

Czechoslovakia fully realized the importance and advantage of the Covenant, provided it could be made to work. She and the other members of the Little Entente became the staunchest supporters of the League, or, more exactly, of League sanctions. But neither they nor the French ever regarded the League, in its existing condition, as a sufficient guarantee. To the very last they tried to strengthen the legal provisions for mutual assistance and to "underpin the Covenant," by additional multilateral or so-called regional agreements. These did not materialize; both the "Danubian Pact," for which preparations were made at the Stresa Conference of 1935, and the Eastern Locarno Pact, for which negotia-

[21] Henry de Jouvenel, January 16, 1934; Sénat, *Débats,* 1934, p. 47.

[22] Joseph Paul-Boncour, Rapporteur on the Locarno accords for the Foreign Affairs Committee, February 25, 1926; Chambre, *Débats,* 1926, p. 964.

tions were still under way at the same time, failed. By 1938, the prestige of the League had sunk so low that even the most optimistic laid their faith only in the old-time bilateral military alliances that were in force at the time.

Thus France embarked on a Central European policy which could hardly be called one of pure self-defense. While she was undoubtedly concerned with the possibility of "*une agression indirecte*," that is, with the fear that Germany might some day prepare an attack on France by freeing herself first of possible embarrassments on her eastern borders, she also assumed the far more ambitious role of Europe's guardian against a revival of pan-Germanism and a German drive toward the East. She thus undertook a precarious and costly position of leadership in regions geographically remote where her predominance rested on foundations which were unsound economically, strategically, and politically.

In an area in which, as the French were the first to admit and even to emphasize, the post-war settlements had failed so obviously to create satisfactory conditions of political stability or economic prosperity, France was seeking to eliminate German influence and German "solutions," yet was in no position to offer acceptable substitutes. Nothing, therefore, but her temporary military superiority over Germany allowed her to function as the guardian of the new Slavic states and of the independence of Austria, and this advantage rested, as far as Central Europe was concerned, mainly on her free access into Germany on Germany's unprotected western flank. Once France proved to be too weak, too isolated, or too peace-loving to maintain this superiority and free access, if need be, by force, her entire Central European policy collapsed like a house of cards. Resistance to Germany's "*Drang nach dem Osten*," would therefore have to come from

Great Britain or from the Soviet Union. In any bloc which might set out to save the remnants of the post-war settlements in Central Europe, France could then be no more than an acquiescent partner.

France may perhaps pride herself for her part in the consolidation of the new or aggrandized states on the Vistula and the Danube during the most difficult period of their infancy. But at the same time she rendered impossible any adjustment or change of the *status quo* which might have permitted pre-Hitlerian Germany to play a constructive role in shaping a new economic and political order in the East and Southeast and might have given a sufficient outlet to German energies to save both the German Republic on the one hand, and the new Slavic states on the other. Instead, a policy of resistance based primarily on military force prepared the way for the aggressive methods and demands of Hitler's revisionist policy and thus contributed to the series of circumstances which plunged Europe into a new and disastrous struggle.

Austrian Independence

To stop future German expansion in the East and Southeast by supporting allied nations whose interests, at least as far as Germany was concerned, ran parallel with those of France, was a simple matter compared with the task of making the new Austrian Republic—a former ally of Germany and herself a German-speaking country—serve as a barrier against her great German sister-nation to the north. Yet, such was France's intention. Austria, with six million inhabitants, two million of which were concentrated in the capital of a one-time great empire, had come into existence simultaneously with the rump state of Hungary, after the Czechs, Slovaks, Poles, Rumanians, Yugoslavs, and Italians had carved none too modest slices out of the old Austro-Hungarian Empire. This was not a very impressive bulwark and counterweight against a German Reich which even after Versailles retained the contours of a great power.

The *Anschluss*, as it was called, was thought to menace France directly in that it would permit Germany to recover the man-power of which she had been deprived elsewhere and would thus alter the military ratio between her and France. But there were deeper issues involved. The "*raison d'Europe*," a principle rarely invoked in the twentieth century, was said to require the separation of the two countries.[23] The balance of power, generally regarded as a principle of British foreign policy exclusively, was often mentioned in this connection by the French. An independent Austria, it was said, was "*un élément essentiel de la stabilité et de l'équilibre de l'Europe centrale*"[24] or, as one Frenchman put it, German rule both in Berlin and Vienna would mean German hegemony over Europe.[25] It would turn Czechoslovakia into a "*presqu'île dans un océan germanique*."[26] Also, it was pointed out, the absorption of Austria would bring the Germans into close proximity to Trieste, Belgrade, and Budapest, and would thereby allow German influence to spread unhindered all through the Danubian area and into the Balkans. Experience since 1938 shows that the French were by no means excessively pessimistic as to the effects of the *Anschluss* on a policy which was intended to prevent German intrusion into the Danubian basin.

Unfortunately for French designs, Austria lacked both sufficient will and sufficient power of her own to resist the "*tentations*

[23] Henry Bérenger, Chairman of the Foreign Affairs Committee, December 30, 1932; Sénat, *Débats*, 1932, p. 1543.

[24] Joseph Paul-Boncour, Foreign Minister, November 14, 1933; Chambre, *Débats*, 1933, p. 4103.

[25] Louis de Chappedelaine, May 25, 1934; Chambre, *Débats*, 1934, p. 1250.

[26] Senate Foreign Affairs Committee Report of June 23, 1920, on the Treaty of St. Germain; Rapporteur, Imbart de La Tour; Sénat, *Documents*, 1920, Session ordinaire, Annexe No. 266, p. 261.

presque irrésistibles" which, according to Briand,[27] were attracting her toward Germany. She also failed to receive the external support which might have enabled her successfully to assume the role laid out for her in the French scheme of things.

There was no difficulty in establishing legal barriers to the *Anschluss*. They were first incorporated in the peace treaties of Versailles and St. Germain, which prohibited union between the two countries except by unanimous consent of the Council of the League of Nations. Since France had a vote on the Council and since, as Briand put it, "*tout au moins la voix de la France ferait défaut*," there was no reason to fear a unanimous decision.[28] New and more elaborate prohibitions were included in the protocol of 1922, by which Austria received financial aid from France and others. The protocol was prolonged for another ten years in 1932 as the price Austria had to pay for further financial assistance.[29] But it indicated poor psychology to believe that any temporary gratitude which the Austrians may have felt for having been saved from financial disaster would be able to offset their resentment at having been forced to make political concessions in order to satisfy their creditors. The significance of the additional prohibitions of

[27] Aristide Briand, Foreign Minister, March 28, 1931; Sénat, *Débats*, 1931, p. 691.

[28] Aristide Briand, Foreign Minister, May 8, 1931; Chambre, *Débats*, 1931, p. 2658.

[29] The treaty safeguards against Austro-German union were the following: Article 80 of the Treaty of Versailles, signed June 28, 1919, provided:

"Germany acknowledges and will respect strictly the independence of Austria, within the frontiers which may be fixed in a Treaty between that State and the Principal Allied and Associated Powers; she agrees that this independence shall be inalienable, except with the consent of the Council of the League of Nations."

In Article 88 of the Treaty of St. Germain signed September 10, 1919, it was declared that:

"The independence of Austria is inalienable otherwise than with the consent of the Council of the League of Nations. Consequently Austria undertakes in the absence of the consent of the said Council to abstain from any act which might directly or indirectly or by any means whatever compromise her independence,

the protocol became clear when, in 1931, the judges of the Permanent Court of International Justice, by a majority of one, interpreted them as rendering illegal the customs union protocol which Germany and Austria had negotiated in March, 1931. Actually, however, this decision had no practical importance, as the project had been abandoned as a result of French pressure two days before the decision was rendered.

If international treaty law had been a sufficient guarantee, France could have rested secure. But she was not blind to the dangers threatening a legal status against which, from 1918 on, both Germans and Austrians were in open revolt, and which violated the principles of self-determination on which the whole Central European settlement was supposed to rest. Other guarantees were necessary.

Efforts were made to strengthen the internal forces of resistance to union with Germany. Immediately after the World War the French, with keen political instinct, acquitted the Austrians of their share in the alleged war guilt of the Central Powers. Austria

particularly, and until her admission to membership of the League of Nations, by participation in the affairs of another Power."

In Protocol No. I of the agreements for the restoration of Austria, signed in Geneva, October 4, 1922 (League of Nations, *Treaty Series*, XII, p. 387), Austria, in exchange for the arrangements made for her financial and economic rehabilitation, undertook "in accordance with the terms of Article 88 of the Treaty of St. Germain, not to alienate its independence; it will abstain from any negotiations or from any economic or financial engagement calculated directly or indirectly to compromise this independence."

On July 15, 1932, ten months after the abandonment of the Austro-German customs union project, the League of Nations Council approved the Lausanne Protocol providing for a further loan to Austria by Belgium, Great Britain, France, and Italy. In the preamble to the protocol it was affirmed:

"That the above Governments, including the Austrian Government, declare that such assistance is given on the basis of Protocol No. I signed at Geneva on October 4th, 1922, and of all the undertakings resulting therefrom; the provisions of which Protocol are to be considered as here reproduced"; League of Nations, *Official Journal*, XIII (July, 1932), p. 1461.

was depicted as the victim of pre-war pan-Germanism. French tutelage was to help save her from falling once more under the Prussian yoke. Every sign of a desire for independence was welcomed. Austrian governments which emphasized the traditional "Danubian orientation" as against the "German orientation" were morally, if not financially, supported; even a return of the Hapsburgs would have found favor with some French statesmen, since it appeared the strongest available antidote to German leanings. In 1922, Herriot spoke of the active, intelligent, and generous minority in Austria which had been won to the cause of independence.[30]

In the case of Austria even more than in that of the other countries in Central Europe, the inability of France to put the country on its feet economically was of major importance. The French realized that Austria, with her unbalanced economy, could not prosper, perhaps not even exist, unless she were incorporated into a larger economic unit. If, therefore, no other form of economic union were offered to her, she was bound out of sheer economic desperation sooner or later to fall to Germany.

This raises the question as to why the neighbors of Austria, some of whom were friends and allies of France, were not induced to save Austria from economic and political isolation. The *status quo* in Central Europe which France was protecting with so much energy was apparently not exactly to her taste. The Austro-Hungarian Empire had not dissolved itself into a number of independent states to suit any French purpose or plan. The dissolution occurred in 1918, even before the hostilities of the World War had ended, as the result of a series of revolutionary acts of emancipation on the part of the nationalities which had composed the former Empire. France was faced with the *fait accompli.* She

[30] Edouard Herriot, April 7, 1922; Chambre, *Débats*, 1922, p. 1442.

accepted and sought to make the best of it, although it was anything but satisfactory to her. Some people regret, declared a Foreign Affairs Committee report of 1921, that there was no longer to be any state on the Danube which would be *"vigoureux et puissant, capable de faire échec à l'ambitieuse Allemagne." "Cela aurait été mieux,"* the report goes on to say.[31]

France, after the World War, reverted to her traditional efforts to balance the power of Germany by that of another great power in Central or Eastern Europe. First the Hapsburgs, then Czarist Russia, had for long periods of history served this purpose. Now that Russia was no longer in a position to fulfill her pre-war functions, a Danubian confederation came to be a favorite suggestion of the French. Every *"plan constructif"* which French statesmen offered as a solution for the woes of the Danube was a plan for some form of close co-operation, economic if not political, between the states, victorious and vanquished, which had formed the Austro-Hungarian Empire. But the new or aggrandized states, Czechoslovakia, Rumania, and Yugoslavia, resisted. *"Les a-t-on assez suppliés?"* asked Pezet in 1938.[32] *"Il faut les pousser à se grouper,"* a Foreign Affairs Committee report had suggested in 1920.[33]

Notwithstanding her financial and military hold over her "friends and allies" on the Danube, France did not have her own way. She did not dare to antagonize even these smaller states, for fear of jeopardizing her own security. When the Little Entente was first formed, Briand assured Beneš of French sympathy for a

[31] Senate Foreign Affairs Committee Report of June 30, 1921, on the Treaty of Trianon; Rapporteur, M. Reynald; Sénat, *Documents*, 1921, Session ordinaire, Annexe No. 507, p. 817.

[32] Ernest Pezet, February 25, 1938; Chambre, *Débats*, 1938, p. 575.

[33] Chamber of Deputies Foreign Affairs Committee Report of March 31, 1920, on the Treaty of St. Germain; Rapporteur, Alfred Margaine; Chambre, *Documents*, 1920; Session ordinaire, Annexe No. 660, p. 579.

project, as he said, "*groupant nettement . . . les Etats alliés de l'Europe centrale.*"[34] He raised no objection to the exclusion of the one-time enemies from the new bloc that was to control the Danubian basin, although it should have been evident that the formation of the Little Entente, with its hostility toward Hungary and its clear political separation from Austria, was a deathblow to any plan for Danubian reintegration. As far as France's allies in that region were concerned, what the French called the pulverization or Balkanization of the Danubian area was final. Nor did economic co-operation between the so-called "successor states" fare much better. The tariff policy of the Little Entente states was certainly not calculated to relieve Austria's economic woes.

There was therefore no likelihood that Germany's influence on Austria could be offset by that of the Little Entente. The idea of a union between Austria and Hungary made no headway either, again because of the hostility of the powers of the Little Entente, who regarded it as a stepping-stone to the much-feared restoration of the Hapsburgs. In the early thirties, plans were discussed for a regional pact by which all of Austria's neighbors were to guarantee her independence and enforce it, if necessary. The idea was to prevent what Pezet called the "*Anschluss de guerre*" with Germany as contrasted with a possible future "*Anschluss de paix*" with the Danubian countries.[35] Why Germany should ever have been expected to put her signature to such a pact is hard to understand. Yet at Stresa, in 1935, Britain, France, and Italy decided to call a conference for that purpose. The rift between France and Italy arising out of the Ethiopian War put an end to these plans.

No country ever gave any formal guarantee to Austria other than that contained in Article 10 of the League Covenant for cases

[34] Quoted in Raymond Poincaré, *Histoire Politique: chroniques de quinzaine*, II, p. 231; from the *Revue des deux mondes*, February 1, 1921.

[35] Ernest Pezet, February 25, 1938; Chambre, *Débats*, 1938, p. 575.

of external aggression.[36] Britain was quite unwilling to consider any specific commitment. The Soviet Union was not invited to do so and was too remote, in any case, to be of practical aid. Italy alone, of the Great Powers, was as much interested in the maintenance of Austrian independence as was France, and was, as an immediate neighbor, more capable of giving effective military support to Austria than any other country. This assistance proved its worth in 1934, if it is true that Italian military demonstrations on the Brenner actually prevented the Nazi coup supposedly scheduled to follow the murder of Chancellor Dollfuss. Once France lost her free access to Central Europe, and Germany became so strong that nothing but the threat of immediate military intervention could stop Hitler from marching on Vienna, the fate of Austria's independence rested entirely with Mussolini. When he de-

[36] In Protocol No. I of the agreements for the restoration of Austria, signed at Geneva, October 4, 1922 (League of Nations, *Treaty Series*, XII, p. 398), not only did Austria agree not to alienate her independence, but the other signatories, Great Britain, France, Italy, and Czechoslovakia (Belgium and Spain later adhered to the protocol) agreed, "That they will respect the political independence, the territorial integrity and the sovereignty of Austria," that they would ask no special privileges in Austria or commit any act contrary to the protocol, and that should occasion arise, "with a view to ensuring the respect of these principles by all nations," they would appeal "either individually or collectively, to the Council of the League, in order that the latter may consider what measures should be taken, and that they will conform to the decisions of the said Council."

Protocol No. I of 1922 was specifically reaffirmed in the League Protocol of July 15, 1932, regarding Austria. See above, p. 112 n. 29.

In February, 1934, after six months of continual German interference in her affairs, Austria submitted her case to France, Great Britain, and Italy, who issued a joint communiqué on February 17 in which, after referring to the alleged "German interference in the internal affairs of Austria," they declared that they took "a common view of the necessity of maintaining Austria's independence and integrity in accordance with the relevant treaties." Royal Institute of International Affairs, *Documents on International Affairs, 1933*, p. 395.

The signatories of the February communiqué consulted during the League of Nations Assembly in 1934, which met barely two months after the murder of Chancellor Dollfuss. After reviewing various suggestions for a Central European pact, they contented themselves with declaring on September 27 that they "recog-

cided that the maintenance of friendship with National Socialist Germany was worth more to him than the independence of Austria, France could only look on and watch the one-time "*élément essentiel de l'équilibre*" being washed away.

Poland and Czechoslovakia

France had little luck with her great allies of the World War. Not one of them was willing to regard the maintenance "*de l'ordre créé par les traités*" as a vital interest or to commit itself irrevocably to defend the new *status quo*. She had no such trouble with Poland and Czechoslovakia, the two new states on Germany's eastern borders. Much as they might differ in other respects with each other or with France, they knew that their very existence was bound up with France's success in defending the post-war settlements. Up until the Czech crisis of 1938, therefore, French "*fidélité aux alliances*" in Central Europe and the reliance of Ger-

nize that the Declaration of February 17, 1934, regarding the necessity of maintaining the independence and integrity of Austria in accordance with the Treaties in force, retains its full effect and will continue to inspire their common policy." *Ibid., 1934*, p. 298.

During the Rome discussions of January 4-7, 1935, between Laval and Mussolini, Austria was a principal subject of concern. The French and Italian communiqués of January 8 referred to it, and the latter declared that agreement had been reached on the desirability of concluding a Central European accord for non-intervention. Recognizing the necessity of maintaining Austrian independence and integrity, the Italian communiqué declared that "*au cas où cette indépendance et cette intégrité seraient menacées, les deux gouvernements italien et français se consulteraient entre eux et avec l'Autriche en vue des mesures à prendre. Cette consultation serait, par la suite, étendue par l'Italie et par la France aux autres Etats, afin de s'en assurer le concours.*" *Ibid., 1935*, I, p. 23.

In the Franco-British communiqué of February 3, 1935, it was affirmed that Great Britain, in view of the declarations of February 17 and September 27, 1934, "consider themselves to be among the Powers which will, as provided in the Rome Agreement, consult together if the independence and integrity of Austria are menaced." *Ibid., 1935*, I, p. 26.

many's neighbors in the East on French support were the most stable and unquestioned facts of European politics.[37]

From the French point of view, Poland and Czechoslovakia were of the utmost strategic value. They were "bastion states" projecting as salients deeply into German territory. France had good strategic reasons to support the ambitious territorial aims of the two nations at the close of the World War and to help them gain the boundaries finally agreed upon. As a result, their geographical and strategic position was what Clemenceau called "*singulièrement avantageuse à notre point de vue.*"[38] Also, fortunately for France, they were certain to remain in fear of "*un retour de l'impérialisme germanique,*" as Poincaré remarked.[39]

During all of the pre-Hitlerian era Poland seemed to be in greater danger than Czechoslovakia. The separation of Danzig from the Reich, the establishment of the so-called Polish Corridor, cutting off East Prussia from the rest of the Reich, the partition of the former German province of Upper Silesia, which gave Poland the greater part of the rich mining districts, as well as the methods which the Poles employed to secure the regions which they coveted, exasperated German nationalism and insured broad popular backing for any move directed against Poland. The pre-eminent desire of Hitler's government to obtain military and economic control

[37] There is no way of knowing whether, as some writers and statesmen have suggested, France would have concluded no alliances with continental countries if Britain and the United States had given her satisfactory pledges. "*Laissées ainsi à elles-mêmes,*" writes Raafat, "*les puissances continentales, notamment la France, la Belgique, la Pologne, la Roumanie, la Tchécoslovaquie et la Yougoslavie inquiètes de l'avenir, soucieuses de leur sécurité, cherchaient à assurer celle-ci par leurs propres moyens et en s'unissant par des traités d'alliances et des conventions d'entente; . . .*" *Le Problème de la Sécurité Internationale* (1930), pp. 121-122.

[38] Georges Clemenceau, President of the Council of Ministers, December 23, 1919; Chambre, *Débats*, 1919, p. 5336.

[39] Raymond Poincaré, *Histoire Politique: chroniques de quinzaine*, III, p. 151; from the *Revue des deux mondes*, June 15, 1921.

of *Mitteleuropa,* however, was to make Czechoslovakia rather than Poland the first victim of National Socialist "dynamism" and of Germany's quest for *Lebensraum.*

A Franco-Slavic alignment for the purpose of keeping Germany in check was nothing new. It was in good French tradition. French statesmen liked to quote Bismarck's remark that "*une Pologne libre équivaudrait pour l'Allemagne à une armée française sur la Vistule*" as a proof of the common interest that united Poland and France. In a sense these new Slavic states served as substitutes for Czarist Russia, France's great Slavic ally of pre-war times.

Once the two new states were consolidated (Poland only after having nearly succumbed in 1920 to the Bolshevist armies marching on Warsaw), and once they had, with the aid of French credit, supplied themselves with an impressive military establishment, their position as compared to that of the weak and disarmed Germany of Versailles was very strong. Not only was it enough to make them relatively safe, but also to give them considerable political weight in the affairs of Europe and in their relations with France, their ally and creditor. Poland never made a secret of her aspirations to the position of a great power, to which she felt her size and a population of thirty-five million entitled her. For this reason also she was seriously considered at times as a possible fifth partner to a new European concert, at the side of Great Britain, France, Italy, and Germany. The Four-Power Pact which the other four negotiated in 1933 came as a blow to her and made her suspect France's loyalty. Czechoslovakia, on the other hand, was undeniably a small power. But the establishment of the Little Entente, in which she and her statesmen played a leading role, created a combination of powers which as a unit had practically the status of a great power, with influence in the innermost councils of Europe and the League.

These countries, like other lesser states, were able to take the stage more frequently in post-war days because of the existence of the League of Nations, than would have been the custom before the World War. Woodrow Wilson had hoped to serve the interests of the smaller nations by giving them a position of approximate equality in the new world concert of nations. It was not realized at the time that this meant involving them in responsibilities and entanglements which they had been able previously to avoid. They became partisan in every issue which came before the League. Poland and the Little Entente assumed a most exposed position in the League, often one of leadership, because in the great struggle between the defendants of the post-war *status quo* and the revisionist powers they were the pre-destined leaders of the anti-revisionist forces. They came to be the most ardent, the most dogmatic, the most relentless exponents of "anti-revisionism."

It should not be forgotten that any discussion of "revision," that is, of peaceful change of the established order, including existing territorial provisions, concerned directly the integrity of these countries. Revision was not simply a matter of abstract principles and general peace strategy, as so many pro-League and Leftist intellectuals seem to have believed. Revision, like collective security, when mentioned or debated by European statesmen in responsible positions, had a definite and very concrete political connotation, because, as far as the near and therefore politically pertinent future was concerned, revision ("territorial revision," at least) was directed exclusively against the territorial settlements on the Danube and on the Vistula. Franklin-Bouillon was not exaggerating when he said, "*La revision des traités ne vise qu'une catégorie de puissances: nos alliés*,"[40] by which he meant Poland and the Little Entente powers. When Italy joined the revisionist camp, it is true,

[40] Henry Franklin-Bouillon, April 6, 1933; Chambre, *Débats*, 1933, p. 1941.

territorial arrangements in the Mediterranean were also brought into the discussions.

If, in practice, there ever was any opportunity for revision by peaceful procedure, it could only have been in regions where the existing territorial arrangements manifestly violated the Wilsonian principle of self-determination and where, for this reason, the pressure of public opinion, particularly that of the Anglo-Saxon countries, might induce the *status quo* powers to submit to "peaceful change" rather than risk the dangers of isolation. The Germans realized the limits this set to their "revisionism" and realistically started out with claims that fell within this category. Any discussion of revision, therefore, came to imply a threat either to Poland's possession of the Corridor and to her rights and privileges in Danzig, to the territorial integrity of Czechoslovakia, to the independence of Austria, or to the existing boundaries of countries holding lands inhabited by Hungarians or Bulgarians. This, in turn, led the Central European anti-revisionist powers to discourage even the slightest mention of peaceful change. Since they had the backing of France, they were able to prevent the League from ever laying any emphasis on Article 19, the importance of which had been stressed at the Peace Conference, and which provided for the revision of treaties.

There is no reason to be indignant about the anti-revisionist stand of the Central European powers. They were too weak to dare make concessions to the revisionist countries, lest they bring upon themselves complete distintegration; yet at the same time they were too strong, what with the assistance given them by France and by the League, to feel obliged to accept limited and negotiated change as a lesser evil if compared to the concessions which a powerful neighbor might some day enforce upon them. France, as one Frenchman put it in 1938, deceived them for nineteen years into believing that they were sufficiently protected to dare oppose Germany's demands.[41] She incurred particularly grave responsibilities toward her smaller allies by persisting in this attitude at a time when interests of her own were already drawing her away from her uncompromising anti-revisionist stand, and she no longer contemplated without hesitation military action outside of her borders.

France was torn between her "*fidélité aux alliances*" on the Continent and her growing dependency upon the support of Great Britain and Italy. Both the British and the Italians, when faced with the insistent demands of the Germans, favored "peaceful change" to satisfy Germany, and stressed the injustice and instability of the post-war arrangements in Central Europe. The Four-Power Pact, proposed to the French by Mussolini and MacDonald, reflected the conflict between France's larger friends and her smaller ones. Since the main purpose of the Four-Power Pact, in its original draft, was to provide for a discussion of Germany's revisionist claims by the Great Powers, it was evident that this meant a consideration of territorial changes on the Danube and on the Vistula. Only a violent reaction on the part of Poland and the Little Entente powers, threatening France with the loss of her Central European allies, led that country to resist the combined pressure of Britain and Italy and to insist on a change of the text of the pact. As a result, "revision" was drowned in a sea of safeguards for the *status quo*.[42] In League terms, Articles 10 and 16 won another victory over Article 19. But it was only a Pyrrhic victory, as subsequent events were to prove.

[41] Ernest Pezet, February 25, 1938; Chambre, *Débats*, 1938, p. 575.

[42] See the collection of documents in France, Ministère des Affaires Etrangères, *Pacte d'Entente et de Collaboration paraphé à Rome le 7 juin 1933*. See also the debates in the French Chamber of Deputies and Senate which clearly reveal France's concern over the possible alienation of her small allies due to the Four-Power Pact: Chambre, *Débats*, April 6, May 30, and June 9, 1933; Sénat, *Débats*, May 4, 1933.

Nobody can tell what would have happened if France and the other Great Powers had induced the Central European states to seek to come to terms with Germany, even at the price of great concessions, before it was too late. They might have been drawn inextricably into the German orbit and lost to France as allies. Whether they would have been saved from partition and the destruction of their independence cannot be judged. But since this fate did actually overtake them, it is obvious that they could not have fared worse if they had made an effort to negotiate adjustments rather than to take upon themselves the responsibility for a policy of inflexible resistance to change. Instead of saving them, this policy of fanatical defense of the *status quo* disrupted the League and poisoned relations between the powers of Europe. It is at least conceivable that political and economic negotiations between these countries and their dissatisfied neighbors, particularly before Hitler came onto the scene, might have led to a more stable order in Central Europe than the one established in 1919. In any case, it is surprising that Poland and Czechoslovakia, as well as France, were not more aware of the fundamental weakness of their position.

It may be appropriate in this connection to draw a comparison between these "new states" and certain other small countries in Europe, so as to indicate more clearly the vulnerability of the position of the former. Some small and very weak states have been able to live safely and peacefully in Europe in the midst of the struggles and rivalries of the Great Powers; Switzerland and Holland, for instance, have done so for over a century. This, however, has been possible only because, so far at least, they have been able to satisfy three important requirements, all of which were lacking from the outset in the case of the new Central European states. First, they could count on a relative balance of power and a state of rivalry between their great neighbors which would make their existence as buffer states important. In the second place, they maintained strict neutrality and refused to line up with any one of their neighbors. In the third place, none of their neighbors questioned their boundaries, nor did any minorities within their borders seek to be emancipated.

A comparison of Poland and Czechoslovakia with states of this kind demonstrates easily why the former, although stronger from a military point of view, were more vulnerable to the effects which the rise of Germany's military strength had on power relationships in Europe. Neither on the Polish nor on the Czechoslovak borders did there exist the kind of balance of power and rivalry which would permit a small buffer state to take refuge with one neighbor if the other became a menace. Germany was Czechoslovakia's only powerful neighbor. The Little Entente could not be regarded as a counterweight since it was an alliance against Hungary, not against Germany. Each partner was worried about one of its large neighbors, but about a different one in every case. While Czechoslovakia would have liked to enlist support against Germany, Rumania was interested in assistance only against the Soviet Union, and Yugoslavia, against Italy. Poland was apparently in a better position, since she did have two great neighbors. But she could never feel sure that Germany and the Soviet Union might not join forces against her. The memories of the days of partition and the political implications of the Rapallo Treaty did not soothe her anxieties. In addition, her fears of Bolshevism prevented her from relying on the Soviet Union as a potential ally against Germany.

Neither Poland nor Czechoslovakia started out as "neutral powers." The true neutral states in Europe are characterized by the fact that they are not taken into account in the balancing of rival groups. They enter upon no alliances and cannot be regarded as potential allies in case of war. The Poles and the Czechs, on the contrary, were members of the coalition that had fought Germany in the World War; they became allies of France soon after they had been constituted as independent nations; they weighed heavily in the establishment of the preponderance of the *status quo* powers or in what France called the *"équilibre continental." "Equilibre"* in the French sense of the term called for the unquestioned preponderance of one group of powers, namely, the one which was backing the established order. Poland and Czechoslovakia were therefore important elements in the power relations of the great states, and their friendship was worth gaining. Thus, Poland was to be helped by France because *"l'existence d'une Pologne forte, servant de contre-poids à l'Allemagne, a toujours été considérée comme un des facteurs indispensables de l'équilibre européen."* [43]

If the preponderance of the group to which the smaller states belonged declined, they would be its most vulnerable members. Poland in 1933 came to realize the dangers. It is reliably reported that she was ready on several occasions to take action to stop German rearmament and to prevent the loss of French military superiority. When she found France unwilling she tried to save herself by reverting to neutrality. In 1934, she signed an agreement with Germany which seemed to link the two countries so closely that some even suspected Poland of having become a German ally; she remained however an ally of France and also tried to improve her relations with the Soviet Union. While this new policy of contradictory pacts may have saved her from early disaster, it did not change the inherent weakness in her position. Czechoslovakia, for her part, either did not desire or did not dare to follow in the same path. Even after the Rhineland had been remilitarized she continued to place her faith in the alliance with France, which she had supplemented by a pact of mutual assistance

[43] Senate Finance Committee Report of December 7, 1923, on loan to Poland; Rapporteur, Henry Bérenger; Sénat, *Documents*, 1923, Session extraordinaire, Annexe No. 799, p. 147.

with the Soviet Union. Czechoslovakia could thus expect more military support in case of war, but had become in effect the spearhead of the anti-German coalition and, as such, was exposed to the gravest dangers.

About the justice of the established borders little need be said. It is well-known that Germany was never reconciled to the boundaries that had been mapped out for these new states at the close of the World War, and that the other neighbors were equally unwilling to accept them as permanent. Poland herself contested Czechoslovakia's right to the Teschen district and participated in the partition of 1938. Internally, both countries were threatened by the disaffection of considerable parts of the population, representing ethnic minorities, and as a French Foreign Affairs Committee report of 1920 had pointed out, suffered very much as had the old Austro-Hungarian Empire from the fact that they were "*assemblages disparates.*" [44]

With all of these inherent weaknesses in the position of the two new states, the French policy of "bastion states" on Germany's eastern borders was as vulnerable as her policy in Austria. Poland and Czechoslovakia were useful to her as allies as long as Germany was disarmed and had an open flank in the West. But they were not strong enough to help her keep Germany from refortifying and remilitarizing the Rhineland. Once that was accomplished, they became liabilities rather than assets. Whether France, after her ability to assist her Central European allies had been so drastically reduced, ever urged them to seek a friendly agreement with Germany even at the price of far-reaching concessions is not known.[45]

[44] Chamber of Deputies Foreign Affairs Committee Report of November 23, 1920, on the Treaty of Trianon; Rapporteur, Charles Daniélou; Chambre, *Documents*, 1920, Session extraordinaire, Annexe No. 1649, p. 276.

[45] The change in British and French policy after the Munich Conference and following the German occupation of Bohemia and Moravia in March, 1939, is discussed more fully below, pp. 292 ff.

IX. The Great Continental Powers: Allies or Opponents?

Alliances and Ideologies

GERMANY, by virtue of her geographical position, has been haunted by Bismarck's "*cauchemar des coalitions*," the fear of encircling alliances. France, on the contrary, afraid of a neighbor potentially stronger than herself, gravitates toward alliances and has shown an appetite for promises of assistance against Germany which has not been easily saturated. The "Wilsonian" doctrine which condemned alliances as being a cause of war—an explanation that found most favor in the Anglo-Saxon countries—was in this respect prejudicial to the interests of France, although no serious objection was ever raised to the conclusion by France of her "small alliances." This left the question open as to whether political barriers would be put in the way if France should ever wish to restore the great continental alliances that preceded the war, and thus open the way for a new division of Europe into powerful hostile blocs. The Austro-German alignment had been destroyed beyond repair by the dissolution of the Austro-Hungarian Empire. The prospective partners for the Western states were now the Soviet Union and Italy. Of the two, the Soviet Union was the more important, being potentially the greatest military power on the Continent. Since France was the most alliance-minded and alliance-seeking continental power, it would hardly have been natural to expect that she would have sought an alignment with both Russia,

Bolshevism notwithstanding, and with Italy. But instead France throughout most of the period was on anything but friendly terms with these powers and lived in constant fear of the development of a German-Soviet bloc. This paradox will have to be explained.

Before discussing French policy toward these states in detail, it is worth while to consider the anomalous situation in which Europe as a whole found itself under the "no-great-alliance" system. An undivided and all-embracing concert of powers such as the British would have liked did not evolve. Nor was there, as the French desired, a broad coalition capable and desirous of holding Germany in her place. Instead, a peculiar triangular setup came into existence, out of which any of three different combinations of powers could at any time develop. There were the two democracies in the West, victorious and saturated countries. In the center, there were Germany and Italy dissatisfied, revisionist, and later Fascist. Finally, there was the Bolshevist Soviet Union in the East. The possible alignment of the four Great Powers in the West was dreaded by the Soviets and interpreted as an anti-Soviet coalition. If, instead, the Western Powers drew closer to the Soviet Union, Germany considered herself to be encircled. Finally, any sign of German-Soviet co-operation made France and Britain feel insecure. In the relationship between any two of the groups, therefore, considerations affecting the third participant in this triangular struggle were constantly involved.

As a result of this Europe passed through varying alignments and suffered from a state of unusual political instability. The situation was made vastly more complicated and unsettled by the existence, side by side with the tension between the three groups of states, of a second type of conflict, just as real as the first, a conflict of a social and revolutionary character. Each of the three groups of powers represented not merely the national interests of the British, French, German, or Russian people, but also a specific political, social, and economic régime—democratic, Fascist, or Bolshevist—and the faiths and philosophy of that régime. Each of the three régimes differed in many fundamental ways from the others. Yet any two of them had several features in common, and this quasi-unity could be and was expressed in what came to be known as "ideological fronts."

Whenever there was talk in any European capital of the Bolshevist menace to "Western civilization" or of the need for a common defense of Europe's cherished traditions and economic or social institutions, it was the Soviets who began to fear the formation of a hostile coalition. On the other hand, whenever Paris announced that the Soviet régime was developing into a democratic system or that the "peace-loving nations" were facing the common dangers of an attack by the "aggressor countries," it was for Germany and Italy to suspect that a Soviet alignment with France and possibly with Britain was in the offing. Finally, when statesmen in Berlin or Moscow came to speak of "proletarian countries" being oppressed or exploited by the "imperialist plutocratic democracies," there was every reason to suspect *rapprochement* between the Soviet Union and Germany.

Negative platforms, such as anti-Communism or anti-Fascism, proved particularly effective weapons. Historians may some day be able to discover who first had the ingenious idea of using them, and whether the "common front against Fascism" fostered by Moscow or the "anti-Comintern" plank inspired by Berlin was first to appear on the political horizon of Europe. Very obviously, in a triangular conflict there is nothing as effective as a negative platform for uniting two parties against a third. Both Moscow and Berlin were using slogans likely to find broad popular support in democratic countries. Conservatives in Britain and France were ready, although they disliked Fascism, to join hands with Fascists when they appeared in the role of anti-Communists. Liberals and

Socialists, even though they might hate Communism, were none the less willing to co-operate with Communists disguised as anti-Fascists. The governments of France and Great Britain, democratic states with a free play of party politics, realized the danger to their national unity which this "ideological warfare" involved, and refused to commit their countries to either the anti-Communist or anti-Fascist camp. "*Qui donc, parmi nous, songe à faire dépendre la paix, l'organisation de la paix, de l'identité des régimes?*" asked Daladier.[1] And Flandin declared, "*Non, la solution n'est pas, dans le monde, de dresser l'un contre l'autre deux blocs: bloc des démocraties contre bloc des Etats totalitaires.*"[2]

Since ideologies were not lacking to popularize any one of the three possible alignments, all of the governments involved were free to choose on the basis of their national interests the alignment toward which they wished to direct their efforts and the ideology, if any, of which they desired to make use. The world was least prepared for the combination which emerged in August, 1939, when National Socialist Germany and Communist Russia signed a pact of friendship. Actually, this one may prove to have been the most natural as far as community of ideas and régime is concerned. It may have divided Europe into the two camps which represent the most fundamental cleavage: democracy versus totalitarianism. To be sure, considerations of political expediency may prevent Britain and France from proclaiming any such ideological platform. By silence they may hope to separate the Soviet Union from Germany or to wean Italy farther from the entente with Germany that had been cemented in the Rome-Berlin axis. The conflict between the Great Powers will never express any clear-cut issues

[1] Edouard Daladier, President of the Council of Ministers, June 9, 1933; Chambre, *Débats*, 1933, p. 2825.

[2] Pierre-Etienne Flandin, speech in Bordeaux, February 14, 1938; *Le Temps*, February 14, 1938, p. 6.

in terms of opposing régimes or ideologies such as the crusader for democracy or for some other cause might like. The national interest, as a rule, takes precedence. But it would be a grave mistake to conclude from this that there exists no real social and ideological conflict or that, when a clash between opposing social and political régimes or philosophies occurs and does coincide with the struggle between the powers, it will not have important consequences.

France and the Soviet Union

Franco-Soviet relations after Versailles present three questions: Why did Franco-Soviet co-operation find no place in the original French scheme for Europe? Why and in what stages did the *rapprochement* take place which led to the Franco-Soviet Pact in 1935? Why did France, after the pact was signed, continue to make reservations with regard to this new alignment with the Soviets?

From the days of Versailles down into the early thirties, France's official attitude toward the Soviet Union was one of aloofness, if not of hostility. She took at times a leading role in opposing Soviet influence. It was Clemenceau who suggested a policy of encircling Russia by a "*fil de fer barbelé*."[3] Of French origin, then, was the idea of a "*cordon sanitaire*" around Russia composed of the new small states on the Soviet borders. Open hostility flared up again and again, in later times, and alternated with periods of non-intercourse or diplomatic coolness. One may try to explain this attitude of France either by the supposition that the French *bourgeoisie* was too class-conscious and too resentful of the tremendous financial losses France had suffered through the Bolshevist Revolution to permit any other stand, or by the argument that the

[3] Georges Clemenceau, President of the Council of Ministers, December 23, 1919; Chambre, *Débats*, 1919, p. 5337.

French were too conscientious to have any part in spreading the poison of Bolshevism into Europe. Both these explanations, however, are inadequate, since neither the French upper classes nor the French Government hesitated in 1934 to change its attitude, although no settlement of the debts had been reached, and Stalin's régime had come no nearer to satisfying the standards of "Western civilization."

The truth of the matter is that in the early post-war years an alliance with the Soviet Union was neither necessary nor desirable from the French point of view. As long as Germany was disarmed and had an open flank in the West, the ring of smaller powers which France had formed around her, together with the superior military equipment of France, was sufficient to keep Germany in her place. Much of France's clamor for more security at that time has to be explained not primarily by a sense of insufficient military superiority, but rather by a desire to forestall British pressure in favor of Germany, and to counteract the demands for French disarmament. However, even if France had desired to find more allies, Soviet Russia would not have suited the purpose. As yet she was anything but a strong military power. Her assistance, if it had been obtained, would have antagonized France's other Eastern European allies, whose military value was greater. It was natural, therefore, that throughout this period the only French objective with regard to Soviet Russia was to isolate and remove her as far as possible from the regions in which France had established her preponderance.

A "Chinese Wall" cutting Russia off from any political, economic, or military contacts with powers to the west of her would have been the ideal solution. To this, unfortunately for France, there were several serious obstacles. There was the British desire, forcefully presented by Lloyd George at the Genoa Conference of 1922, to reëstablish economic intercourse with Soviet Russia. The fact that at that conference France put obstacles in the way of the British plans brought the much graver danger of Russo-German co-operation into the picture. From the days of Genoa, when Soviet Russia and Germany signed the Treaty of Rapallo inaugurating a policy of political, economic, and secret military co-operation, down to the present war, the cloud of a possible Russo-German alliance darkened the French political skies. To isolate the Soviet Union it was necessary to keep Germany away from her, an objective which was hard to reconcile with the full execution of the Versailles Treaty.

It may well be that Briand's policy of Franco-German *rapprochement*, which culminated in the signing of the Locarno Treaties, sprang partly, at least, from a desire, shared by Great Britain, to draw Germany away from her new friend in the East. "*Aujourd'hui, que voyons nous?*" asked Briand. "*Une Allemagne résolument tournée vers l'Occident, en dépit de ses accords avec la Russie; une Allemagne qui a choisi, qui a compris enfin que son véritable intérêt était de s'entendre avec les alliés et particulièrement avec la France.*"[4] As a matter of fact, Stresemann's policy was constantly under fire at home because it was said to have had a chilling effect on Germany's relations with the Soviet Union, and to have barred her from taking sides definitely with the East against the West, as some German statesmen and groups had wished to do ever since the end of the World War. In any case, there was always enough Russo-German friendliness to strengthen Germany's position in the councils of Europe, and to keep a bridge open over which Russia could exert influence in Central and Western Europe. The Soviet Union herself had several reasons for not wanting to turn her back on the West, such as her ambition to spread world revolution, her territorial claims against

[4] Declaration to the *Petit Parisien*, February 26, 1927; *Société des Nations*, IX (1927), p. 215.

Poland and Rumania, and her paramount interest in preventing any anti-Bolshevist European coalition.

When the threat of Germany's new power became acute, France could no longer close her eyes to the danger of Soviet hostility and particularly of a common German-Soviet enmity toward Poland. The best way to divert Soviet attention away from Europe was to make her feel more secure on her western borders. France undertook to bring this about after 1930, and not only signed a pact of non-aggression with the Soviet Union, but encouraged the conclusion of similar agreements between the Soviet Union and Poland and Rumania. At the time, the Soviet Union, alarmed by the ascendancy of Japan in the Far East, was equally interested in directing her policy away from Europe and freeing her western flank. "*Par ce pacte,*" exclaimed Paul-Boncour in referring to the non-aggression treaty of 1932, "*la grande Russie est entrée dans le système général de nos accords et de nos ententes.*" [5]

But this was only an intermediary stage in Franco-Soviet relations, foreshadowing a complete reversal of French policy toward the Soviets. The rise of Hitler and the certainty that Germany was going to rearm were undoubtedly prime factors in the change. The French began to remember "*le grand contre-poids qui nous a permis, en rétablissant l'équilibre, de faire face à la puissance impériale germanique.*" [6] It was the good fortune of France in 1933 that the Soviet Union, thanks to National Socialist hostility, was ready for the change. Soviet statesmen remained fearful of German ambitions toward the East, notwithstanding the renewal of the Berlin Treaty of friendship and consultation and the extension of new credits by National Socialist Germany to the Soviet Union.

[5] Joseph Paul-Boncour, Foreign Minister, May 18, 1933; Chambre, *Débats*, 1933, p. 2437.

[6] Henry Bérenger, Chairman of the Foreign Affairs Committee, May 4, 1933; Sénat, *Débats*, 1933, p. 791.

The first year of Hitler's rule was one of preliminaries as far as Franco-Soviet relations were concerned. The Soviet Union, represented by Litvinov, abandoned her former attitude of scorn for the Geneva ideology, and gradually assumed a leading role in advocating and propagandizing those ideas on aggression and security for which France and her friends had so long stood. Her desire to underline this new identity of views and interests became evident in May, 1933, when Radek, then the mouthpiece of the government in the Soviet press, came out with an unqualified denunciation of treaty revision. The Soviet Union thus revealed her willingness to become an ally of the *status quo* powers.

Negotiations for a Franco-Soviet alignment started in November, 1933, on Soviet initiative and centered around a pact of mutual military assistance. They were crowned with success when the Franco-Soviet Pact was signed in May, 1935.[7] More will be said

[7] After the recognition of the Soviet Union by the Herriot government on October 28, 1924, the first decisive step in Franco-Soviet *rapprochement* was the signing of the pact of non-aggression on November 29, 1932 (League of Nations, *Treaty Series*, CLVII, p. 411), negotiations for which had been begun in the summer of 1931. By the French, at least, this agreement was heralded as beginning a period of friendly relations. See the debates on the treaty, May 16 and 18, 1933; Chambre, *Débats*, 1933. The unanimous approval of the treaty by the Chamber of Deputies on May 18, 1933—eight days after Karl Radek had denounced treaty revision in his sensational article in *Pravda*—was the occasion for renewed official expressions of friendship, and when on July 6 M. Litvinov visited MM. Daladier and Paul-Boncour, President of the Council of Ministers and Foreign Minister, respectively, political negotiations of a more intimate character were considered. The atmosphere thus created was favored by M. Herriot's semi-official visit to Soviet Russia in August and September and the visit of a French air delegation, headed by Pierre Cot, Air Minister, in September. After preliminary conversations, definite overtures for the conclusion of a treaty of mutual assistance were made by the Soviet Government in November. The signing of the German-Polish Pact of non-aggression on January 26, 1934, and the appointment of Louis Barthou, an "old-school realist," as Foreign Minister after the February riots in Paris, gave a fresh impetus to these developments. After breaking off the disarmament negotiations on April 17, M. Barthou sought to enlarge the proposed Soviet security agreement into a grand alliance against Germany. With this objective he visited Warsaw and Prague, April 22-27, dis-

about the nature of this pact later.[8] Here we are interested in it as it relates to the new alignment between France and a country which had come once again to be regarded as a great continental military power. The change in the European "*équilibre*" caused by the imminence of German rearmament was sufficient to induce in France a "*retour à l'équilibre traditionnel de notre diplomatie.*" [9]

Since the negotiations with the Soviets in 1934 were conducted by a French Rightist government and lay in the hands of Barthou, it cannot be claimed that bourgeois class-consciousness of the French upper classes was an absolute obstacle to a policy of friendliness to the Soviets when national interests were involved. It is therefore difficult to believe that anti-Bolshevist sentiment could have been primarily responsible for the reluctance with which

cussed the proposed Eastern Pact with M. Litvinov in Geneva on May 18, and visited Bucharest and Belgrade, June 20-26. Finally, on July 8, he went to London where under British pressure he gave to the proposed pact the "reciprocal" character of an "Eastern Locarno," which, however, failed of acceptance due to the opposition of Germany and Poland. M. Barthou proceeded to arrange for the admission of Soviet Russia as a member of the League of Nations (September 18, 1934), and after his assassination less than a month later (October 9), his work was taken up by Pierre Laval. In view of the failure to conclude an Eastern Pact, Laval and Litvinov signed an agreement on December 5, 1934, providing that neither country would negotiate regarding an Eastern Pact independently of the other. During the Franco-British conversations in London, February 1-3, 1935, and during the March and April visits of Sir John Simon and Mr. Eden to Berlin and of Mr. Eden to Warsaw, Moscow, and Prague, attempts were made to reduce the opposition between the German and Polish hostility to provisions for mutual assistance and Soviet and Czechoslovak insistence thereon. The failure of these attempts was followed on April 9, 1935, by the announcement of the French and Russian intention of concluding a treaty for mutual assistance. Less than a month later, on May 2, the Franco-Soviet Pact was signed (League of Nations, *Treaty Series,* CLXVII, p. 395), and was followed on May 16 by the signing of the Czechoslovak-Soviet Pact. *Ibid.,* CLIX, p. 347.

[8] See below, pp. 174, 175 n. 34.

[9] Henry Bérenger, Chairman of the Foreign Affairs Committee, December 18, 1934; Sénat, *Débats,* 1934, p. 1395.

France later on approached the automatic military commitments and staff conversations which the Soviets desired as a supplement to the pact. There were a number of parallel influences that restrained France in her dealings with the Soviet Union, so that it would be sheer guesswork to try to apportion the responsibilities and to try to discover how potent a factor anti-Bolshevist sentiment was. There can be no doubt that it rose to important heights in the years that followed the signing of the Soviet pact, partly under the influence of skillful anti-Communist propaganda from Fascist quarters at home and abroad, and partly in reaction to the growth of Communist power in French domestic politics.

If we turn our attention to the other factors that worked in the same direction, the influence of Great Britain, as so often, takes first place. Great Britain did not at first object to the *rapprochement* between France and the Soviet Union. Even if she had, she would have found it difficult to stop France in 1934, when her influence over that country was at a low ebb. It was at that time that France shattered Britain's hopes for a disarmament convention, and Barthou delivered the most pointed attack on Britain that had ever been heard at Geneva. But while the British viewed favorably the idea of bringing the Soviet Union into the League of Nations and into the network of security pacts which was being considered to compensate France for the impending rise of German military power, she did refuse to countenance an old-time military alliance.[10] Only after Germany refused to join in a regional agreement did France receive Britain's consent to a bilateral pact of mutual assistance between herself and the Soviet Union. Even then, the pact was accompanied by a protocol protecting France from any commitment which might bring her into conflict with Great Britain. It meant in practical terms that French assistance

[10] Britain's influence on the negotiations for an "Eastern Locarno" is discussed below, pp. 273 ff.

to the Soviet Union was conditional on British consent. By a devious path, Great Britain was thus bestowed with the power to make the ultimate decision regarding the *casus foederis* between the Soviet Union and France. "*La France,*" said the rapporteur on the pact, "*devrait, pour rester fidèle, ainsi qu'elle s'y engage par le protocole du traité, aux accords de Locarno, vérifier que les puissances garantes, Grande-Bretagne et Italie, conçoivent comme elle les circonstances de l'agression et en imputent au même Etat la responsabilité entière.*" [11] While the legal refinements might well have been swept aside in a case of emergency, the fact that such provisions were attached to the pact had great political significance. France's right to delay assistance to the Soviet Union until the League or Great Britain had reached a decision was openly applauded by French statesmen who were unfriendly to Russia as a check on the very kind of "automatism" which France, in her earlier negotiations for an alliance with England, had declared to be the criterion of reliability for a pact of mutual assistance. Arrangements for immediate military co-operation between the two general staffs, if they were ever contemplated by the French Government, were rendered difficult and hazardous. "*Dès le début,*" Flandin claimed, "*la conception d'une alliance analogue à celle d'avant la guerre avait été résolument écartée.*" [12] (To Germany the restrictions regarding the *casus foederis* gave far less comfort, since they only shifted the responsibility for the working of the pact from Paris to London.)

This leads to a second factor operating against close Franco-Soviet ties. During the crucial years, between the time the pact was signed in 1935 and the Munich Conference in 1938, Soviet foreign

[11] Henry Torrès, Rapporteur on the Franco-Soviet Pact for the Foreign Affairs Committee, February 11, 1936; Chambre, *Débats,* 1936, p. 353.

[12] Pierre-Etienne Flandin, Foreign Minister, February 25, 1936; Chambre, *Débats,* 1936, p. 580.

policy under Litvinov was bent on strengthening ties with France and the League and on assuming a position of leadership on the "anti-aggressor front." But in France, fear of Germany, now in the full swing of feverish rearmament, militated against any irrevocable commitments to the Soviet Union, lest they preclude an agreement with Germany, which was not deemed impossible. Germany's reaction to the Franco-Soviet Pact and her violent anti-Bolshevist propaganda suggested that Hitler might some day be willing to negotiate a settlement with the Western Powers if he could exclude the Soviet Government from the councils of Europe. His policy was expected to follow the pattern of the Four-Power Pact, which the British Government was also inclined to favor. Thus, French statesmen and parties, whether motivated by anti-Communist feelings, by sympathies for Fascism, by fear of Germany, or by respect for Britain's wishes, sought to keep the door open for solutions in which Russia might not be acceptable as a partner. The French Government did not hesitate to participate in the Munich Conference, although the Soviet Union, an ally both of France and of Czechoslovakia, was not invited and was completely excluded from the negotiations regarding the future of Czechoslovakia.

One last and not unimportant motive tending to strengthen this aversion to any too irrevocable ties with the Soviet Union was the French concern over Poland and, to a lesser degree, over Rumania. All along, a return to the pre-war alliance with Russia had been rendered difficult by the fact that France had begun after Versailles by accepting the lesser Slavic states as substitutes for the great Slavic ally of pre-war days. These countries, with the exception of Czechoslovakia, who had no common border with Russia, never ceased to fear not only the spread of Bolshevist ideology, but future Russian claims to parts of their territory. Any French alignment with the Soviet Union, therefore, tended to push them into the German orbit. It was very doubtful from the point of French security whether promises of Soviet military assistance, even if they could be relied upon, could compensate France for the loss of her lesser military allies in Central Europe to the German camp. Since there was also some question as to whether Poland and Rumania could be persuaded to permit the passage of Soviet troops across their territory, these Central European powers became a serious obstacle to co-operation with the Soviet Union.

The new policy toward the Soviet Union upon which France embarked after 1935 therefore remained half-hearted and ambiguous. While for a short period this new orientation gave the Soviets a position of influence at Geneva and in the councils of Europe, it brought little glory to them, as the unhindered progress of the successive wars in China, Ethiopia, and Spain indicated. At the same time it gave Germany a welcome excuse, if not justification, for violating the Locarno Treaty, and helped cement the alignment between the so-called anti-Comintern powers, without removing the danger for France of renewed German-Soviet co-operation at a later date. In any case, after the Munich Conference decisions regarding future Franco-Soviet co-operation lay with Moscow and London rather than with Paris. France had become dependent on Great Britain; and the Soviets, apparently less afraid of Germany than were the Western Powers, had the stronger bargaining position and the greater freedom of action. French policy toward the Soviet Union resolved itself into a series of unsuccessful attempts to bring Russia and Great Britain together and thus to reconstitute the one-time Triple Entente. Once all hope of a settlement with Hitler was gone, and Great Britain approved such an entente in the spring of 1939, the way was clear, as far as France was concerned, for a straightforward military alliance of the prewar type. That it failed to materialize was not due to any lack of desire on her part but to Stalin's preference for a pact with Hitler.

France and Italy

The relations of France with Italy after 1919 were not dissimilar to those with the Soviet Union. This other Great Power on the Continent, another wartime ally of France, was also allowed to remain outside of the French security system until the days of German rearmament. Here again appears a contradiction between the French obsession with guarantees of security and her apparent indifference or ineptitude in the matter of securing closer bonds with Italy. The latter was a co-member of the League and, therefore, committed under Article 16 to participate in League sanctions; but her influence at Geneva and her interest in the League were not great at any time. She was a guarantor of the Franco-German boundary through the Treaty of Locarno; but nothing speaks more clearly of the difference with which she and Great Britain were regarded in Paris than the almost complete lack of any mention of Italy in the many debates on Locarno which took place in the French Chamber. Relations between France and Italy, which had been strained ever since Italy had left the Versailles Conference dissatisfied and resentful, remained tense all through the pre-Hitlerian era.

There were many reasons, some similar to those existing in the Russian case, why France should have been reserved and cautious in her dealings with Italy and should have held back from any serious effort to make her an ally. For once, however, Great Britain was not the stumbling-block. Friendship between the two countries would have been to her interest, if only because it would have removed one of the most serious obstacles to an agreement on disarmament among all of the naval powers. An alliance might have been a different matter, to be regarded with some suspicion by the British, but the likelihood of that was very remote.

As in the Soviet case, differences of ideology and régime had some influence in keeping the two countries apart, only here the roles of the Left and the Right were reversed. The Rightists frequently accused their opponents on the Left of allowing anti-Fascist feelings to poison the atmosphere between the two countries and to stand in the way of friendly settlements.

Another factor which we have encountered in the Russian case played an even more significant part here: the opposition of the Little Entente to any close ties between France and Italy. This was not simply a question of rivalry between two groups of potential allies of France. Italy's ambitions ran directly counter to the vital interests of the Little Entente states. What Yugoslavia sought from France was protection against Italy, not against Germany. Italian support of Hungarian revisionism, as well as of the Bulgarians and Macedonians, her desire to make the Adriatic an Italian sea, the sympathies which she showed at times for a Hapsburg restoration, and her penetration into Albania were all threats to one or another of the Little Entente powers.

But the decisive obstacle to co-operation between France and Italy lay in the fact that Italy, unlike Poland or the Little Entente, was a dissatisfied country and could not be attracted to France by mere guarantees of the established order.[13] She was out for change, not for the enforcement of the *status quo,* and many of the changes which she desired could be effected only by far-reaching French concessions. This placed France in a most serious quandary. It may have taken her a long time to realize the seriousness of the situation, since the French tended to underestimate the potential military and political value of Italy. But she could not have ignored the menace that might some day arise if a power of the

[13] See Maxwell H. Macartney, and Paul Cremona, *Italy's Foreign and Colonial Policy, 1914-1937* (1938), Chapter X; Muriel Currey, *Italian Foreign Policy, 1918-1932* (1932), Chapters X and XI.

size and energy of Italy were allowed to remain unfriendly and hostile. There could be no question of pushing Italy out of Europe as had been attempted with the Soviet Union. By her geographical position and her interests she belonged in the very heart of European affairs. The danger of an alignment with Germany may have seemed less than in the case of the Soviet Union, since Austria seemed to be an ideal apple of discord. This possibility existed, nevertheless, and it compelled France to choose between making sacrifices to Italy or to risk losing her to the German camp.

A country as eager as France for new guarantees of security would certainly have lined up with Italy if only the price had not appeared too great. But more was involved for France than this or that concession, this or that naval agreement, this or that cession of colonial rights or territory. The whole conception of the preservation of the *status quo* could not be harmonized with Italian or Fascist "dynamism" driving for greater power, broader political influence, and larger colonial possessions. Italy's policy may be called imperialist or laid to the need of a newcomer seeking to make up for the advantages already possessed by longer-established empires; she certainly never made any secret of the fundamental objective of her foreign policy. It was the same substantially before, during, and after the World War. This did not mean that Italy was necessarily bent on gaining advantages only at the expense of France; but the increase of power which Italy desired was bound to have unfavorable consequences for France and her allies however it was achieved. It would affect France's influence on the Danube and in the Balkans, her naval superiority over Italy, her traditional role in the Near East, and, finally, the security, if not the size and extent, of her African possessions. It was certain to weaken some of the allies of France. Finally, it involved the risk that precedents would be established which would constitute a threat to the whole program of enforcement of the existing post-war order and territorial *status quo*. Because Italy's aims were "revisionist" they were hostile to the French system of security.

If any French statesmen doubted the seriousness of Mussolini's revisionist policy on the ground that Italy had also profited by the post-war peace treaties and obviously would not allow any changes prejudicial to herself, they were woefully mistaken as to the workings of a revisionist policy. No revisionist country favors the change of all existing boundaries or settlements. It merely insists that some particular changes which it desires and considers justified shall be given precedence over any comprehensive guarantee of the established order. Once these particular changes have taken place, the former revisionist country may well join the *status quo* group and, having become saturated, desire to see the new order enforced. Mussolini, indeed, if we may believe his own statements, was considering this possibility after the conquest of Ethiopia.

Since France was never willing to sacrifice her *status quo* principles or to make any sweeping concessions to Italy for the sake of her friendship and support, the cordiality of the relations between the two countries came to depend on whether Italy would consider waiving or postponing her claims in order to assure herself of French backing. Such support would be important to Italy only if she anticipated the need of assistance against Germany, a need likely to arise only in connection with the problem of Austro-German *Anschluss*.

French policy toward Italy began to change at the same time as that toward the Soviet Union.[14] The coincidence was no acci-

[14] Without retracing in full the various attempts at Franco-Italian reconciliation made since 1919, it may be useful to indicate the immediate antecedents of the Rome agreements of January 7, 1935. As in the case of Soviet Russia, they coincided with the beginnings of the National Socialist régime. It was M. Paul-Boncour as President of the Council who named Henry de Jouvenel to be Ambassador in Rome with the special mission of bringing about an improvement in Franco-Italian relations. M. de Jouvenel took up his post on January 25, 1933, five days before Adolf Hitler was named German Chancellor. The Four-Power

dent. In face of the rise of Germany's power the French Government looked for new allies. After preliminary attempts to improve relations with Italy and the Soviet Union had been made in 1933, Barthou, in 1934, set out to forge a new and more powerful ring of continental alliances around Germany with which to supplement the now insufficient "small ring" in Central Europe and to balance the effects of Germany's impending rearmament. Why she found the Soviets in a responsive mood, we have explained. Italy

Pact, negotiated during the subsequent months and initialed on June 7, was regarded by the French of importance mainly, if not only, as a contribution to Franco-Italian *rapprochement*. From the Italian side the tone adopted toward France became friendlier, and in the spring and summer of 1934 official and unofficial contacts and exchanges between the two countries were numerous. In May, 1934, it was first suggested that the French Foreign Minister, then Louis Barthou, should visit Rome. Plans in this direction and preparations for a settlement were given a fresh impetus by the Nazi coup in Vienna on July 25, 1934, and the murder of Chancellor Dollfuss.

It was Pierre Laval, who became Foreign Minister after the assassination of M. Barthou, who paid the visit to Italy (January 4-7, 1935) and signed the Rome agreements amidst repeated French and Italian assurances of mutual friendship. In the Joint Declaration, Laval and Mussolini, recognizing that the agreements concluded by them settled the major differences between their two countries, proclaimed the friendship of France and Italy and their intention to co-operate and consult. By a separate treaty the boundaries of the French and Italian colonies in Africa were readjusted through cession by the French of 44,000 square miles on the Libyan border and 309 square miles on the Eritrean frontier. France agreed to transfer to Italy 2,500 shares (approximately 7 per cent) of the Djibouti-Addis Ababa Railway. Finally, a special accord regarding Tunisia provided for the gradual disappearance of the special status of Italian nationals in Tunisia. The two countries recommended the conclusion of a Central European agreement of non-intervention, and agreed in any case to consult each other in the event of a threat to Austrian independence. Finally, they expressed their opposition to any unilateral modification of obligations in regard to armaments and their intention to consult in the event of such a situation arising.

Although the agreements were approved by both houses of the French legislature, the Ethiopian dispute prevented the exchange of ratifications. Simultaneously with the revival of her claims against France, Italy denounced the agreements on December 17, 1938. Text of the agreements: Royal Institute of International Affairs, *Documents on International Affairs, 1935*, I, pp. 18-24; text of Italy's denunciation of the agreements, December 17, 1938, and the French reply, December 25, 1938: *New York Times*, March 30, 1939, pp. 1, 6.

had even more urgent and pressing reasons to fall in with the French plans. The union of Austria and Germany, which Italy had so consistently and vigorously opposed as a threat to her vital interests, seemed to be the first item on Hitler's revisionist program. By July, 1934, with the murder of Dollfuss, a crisis was reached and Italy, it is said, set out to prevent the *Anschluss* by the threat of armed intervention. Here was an opportunity, if ever there was one, for France to draw Italy into her camp.

Laval and Mussolini signed a series of agreements on January 7, 1935—the so-called Rome agreements. The French rejoiced in the belief that the alignment of the two countries had been accomplished. In fact, according to Flandin, the French and Italians, a few months later at the Stresa Conference, exchanged definite promises of military assistance, with an Italian promise to defend the demilitarized zone in the Rhineland and a French promise to defend Austria's independence.[15] The short-lived "Stresa front" represented the height of Italian co-operation with the Western democracies and was supposed to inaugurate complete understanding among the three powers both in regard to general policy and future dealings with National Socialist Germany.[16] French Rightist statesmen, who for years had been extremely critical of French foreign policy, hailed the Stresa front as the "*salut de l'Europe*"[17] and as "*la seule véritable clarté*" since Versailles.[18]

[15] Pierre-Etienne Flandin, February 26, 1938; Chambre, *Débats,* 1938, p. 640.

[16] On March 23, 1935, one week after the promulgation of the new German law regarding the armed forces, and the denunciation of the armament restrictions imposed upon Germany by the Treaty of Versailles, the British, French, and Italian Governments announced their intention of meeting in Stresa on April 11, prior to the session of the League Council called to consider Germany's action. The Stresa Conference lasted from April 11 to 14 and considered principally the questions of German rearmament and Austrian independence. Text of the agreements adopted by the Conference: Royal Institute of International Affairs, *Documents on International Affairs, 1935,* I, pp. 80-82.

[17] Henry Lémery, June 25, 1936; Sénat, *Débats,* 1936, p. 615.

[18] Jean Ybarnégaray, February 25, 1938; Chambre, *Débats,* 1938, p. 596.

This enthusiasm and confidence in the newly acquired security shows the significance attached to Italian support, particularly at a time when the French had every reason to be pessimistic, the Stresa Conference having been called for the purpose of dealing with Hitler's proclamation of unrestricted rearmament.

If the published versions of the Rome agreements contained the whole text, France would appear to have been able to satisfy Italy with a minimum of concessions, no more indeed than a modest fulfillment of her part of the promises made to Italy in 1915 and 1917.[19] The Rome agreements therefore represented no break with France's traditional policies, since the transfer of a stretch of desert land could hardly be interpreted as a precedent for any extensive territorial revision. But Italy's claims for empire and for a position of greater power were left unsatisfied. For this reason it has been contended that Laval must have promised Mussolini more than the published agreements contained, namely, a free hand in Ethiopia. Whether or not this was the case may never be known. If he did, subsequent events proved that France could not break

[19] The Treaty of London of April 26, 1915, which determined the conditions under which Italy agreed to enter the World War on the side of the Allies, provided in Article 13: "In the event of France and Great Britain increasing their colonial territories in Africa at the expense of Germany, those two Powers agree in principle that Italy may claim some equitable compensation, particularly as regards the settlement in her favour of the questions relative to the frontiers of the Italian colonies of Eritrea, Somaliland and Libya and the neighbouring colonies belonging to France and Great Britain."

The agreements concluded at St. Jean de Maurienne, April 19-21, 1917, defined in greater detail Italy's share in Asia Minor and in the anticipated partition of Turkey.

Italy never considered that these promises were lived up to by the Allies, in spite of certain minor frontier rectifications in Africa by France and the cession of Jubaland to Italy by Britain. See René Albrecht-Carrié, *Italy at the Paris Peace Conference* (1938); text of the Treaty of London, Document 3; St. Jean de Maurienne agreement, Document 6. For the various frontier rectifications, see Royal Institute of International Affairs, *Survey of International Affairs, 1920-1923*, pp. 360-361; *1924*, pp. 463-470.

with the past and permit a country to wage a "war of aggression" against another member of the League. If he did not, he was in error in believing that Mussolini could be induced to sacrifice his "dynamic" policy for certain minor concessions and for French support in maintaining the independence of Austria.

While it is of comparatively little importance from the point of view of this discussion whether Laval was guilty of either of these errors in judgment, it is worth mentioning the fact that there are several arguments in support of the assertion that Laval did not give Mussolini a free hand for war on Ethiopia. Laval himself mentioned two. In the first place, France was far too much interested in saving the League from the cataclysm which would follow if Italy were allowed to proceed with a war of conquest. Besides, she was even more interested in preventing Italy from dispatching large armies to Africa when the two countries were just deciding to act jointly in barring German moves in the West and South of Europe. "*J'aurais été imprudent ou coupable,*" Laval said, "*de faciliter ou de provoquer je ne sais quelle entreprise militaire en Ethiopie, précisément parce qu'elle nous priverait de la présence et du concours de l'Italie en Europe.*" [20] There is another argument which Laval did not mention. From the habitual attitude which the French took toward Italy it seems very likely that they underestimated the degree to which Mussolini was committed to a policy of aggrandizement and expansion. It was perhaps too much to expect anyone to foresee that Italy would forfeit her vital defensive or "static" interests on the Brenner for the sake of African conquest. Mussolini did not make it plain until after Stresa that Italy had no intention of keeping her face turned to the Brenner. Laval therefore acted in harmony with current French conceptions if, as he claimed, "*par une formule de désistement éco-*

[20] Pierre Laval, President of the Council of Ministers, December 28, 1935; Chambre, *Débats*, 1935, p. 2865.

nomique" he offered to Italy only "*le droit, à l'exclusion de la France, de demander des concessions dans toute l'Ethiopie, sauf à respecter nos droits acquis.*"[21]

If France was not willing to do more to satisfy Italy, Germany's promises would seem to have gone farther. It seems paradoxical that a "have" country with rich possessions should have been more limited in the concessions it could offer, and therefore find itself in a weaker bargaining position than a "have-not" country. But while France, due to the principles on which her policy rested, could not go beyond the promise of military assistance for the defense of the *status quo* on the Brenner and of certain small concessions, and was not able to fulfill any of Italy's expansionist wishes, Germany needed to have no hesitation in promising Italy compensation for the loss of Austrian independence at the expense of other countries. Italy seems to have believed that German political and military assistance would serve not merely defensive purposes but effectively aid her dreams of empire and expansion. Mussolini in any case chose to risk Italy's position on the Brenner rather than abandon his colonial plans. Possibly he believed that Laval had given his consent, and may have acted under the false impression that Italy would be strong enough to defend Austria even though she engaged herself in Ethiopia and antagonized France. Or he may have decided, on the contrary, that Germany would have her way in Austria anyway, regardless of the steps Paris and Rome might take and may therefore have seen no reason to sacrifice his other plans for a hopeless watch on the Brenner.

At the close of the Ethiopian campaign, it looked for a moment as if Mussolini was ready to listen to French proposals for a resumption of the Stresa policy. Since he had realized his desires for

[21] December 28, 1935; Chambre, *Débats*, 1935, p. 2865. See also his statements of March 22, 1935, Chambre, *Debats*, 1935, p. 1208; and March 26, 1935, Sénat, *Débats*, 1935, p. 395.

imperial conquest, it would no longer have been inconsistent if for a period of time he had consented to regard Italy as a "saturated" country, and concentrated on blocking the *Anschluss* which he continued to dread. If there was such a moment, France let it slip. The *Front populaire* government then in power did not seek any *rapprochement* with Italy, and could not, Delbos argued, independently recognize the conquest of Ethiopia, *"sans manquer à ses obligations envers la Société des Nations."* [22] The clamors of the Rightists that France return to Stresa remained unheard.

For the continued and widening split between France and Italy there was a stronger reason, once the Spanish civil war had started in July, 1936. Italy was now not only the violator of the Covenant and the "aggressor" in Ethiopia, but by actively taking sides with the Fascist insurgents in Spain was interfering with political, strategic, and ideological interests of France in a zone of vital importance to her. Leftist sympathies in France were wholeheartedly on the side of the Spanish Government, and it was as much as the French Government under Léon Blum and his successors could do to keep the country in a position of "neutrality" and "non-intervention." They justified this policy mainly by a *"préoccupation humaine de ne pas laisser s'aggraver et se prolonger les atrocités de la guerre et la volonté de l'empêcher de s'étendre à l'Europe."* [23] Another reason was, as usual, the desire not to antagonize Britain. *"Quelles que soient les conséquences sur d'autres terrains,"* said M. Grumbach, one of the Socialist leaders, *"la France doit considérer la collaboration avec l'Angleterre comme la pièce maîtresse de son effort en faveur de la paix."* [24] It was consequently impos-

[22] Yvon Delbos, Foreign Minister, February 23, 1937; Sénat, *Débats*, 1937, p. 188.

[23] Yvon Delbos, speech to Radical Socialist Congress, Lille, October 30, 1937; *Le Temps*, October 31, 1937, p. 3.

[24] Salomon Grumbach, December 5, 1936; Chambre, *Débats*, 1936, p. 3353. France's policy toward the Spanish civil war is discussed in the Royal Institute

sible to accept either the demands of the Left-wing extremists for intervention, or to satisfy the Rightist insistence on the importance of friendship with Italy.

Any resumption of co-operation with Italy seemed out of the question under these circumstances. According to the Leftists in France, Italy's action also affected vital French interests, since it threatened French communications to Africa, both from the Balearic Islands and on the Spanish peninsula. The Rightists continued, nevertheless, to clamor for a return to the "Stresa front." It would be difficult to say whether the main factor was sympathy for General Franco and the Spanish insurgents, a hope of saving the freedom of French communications with Africa by establishing friendly relations with those whom they expected to be Spain's future rulers, or a desire of drawing Italy away from Germany. "*L'histoire démontrera,*" said Flandin, "*s'il a été sage de subordonner l'amitié italienne à l'affaire espagnole.*" [25]

But once the opportunity for *rapprochement* had gone by, if indeed it ever existed, the factors drawing Italy away from France (fear of Germany, the growing conviction that Germany could not be restrained in Austria anyway, the "ideological" conflict with France in Spain, the rising tide of Italy's colonial appetite, now turning against French rights and possessions) became stronger and induced Mussolini to side with Germany.

of International Affairs, *Survey of International Affairs, 1937,* II, pp. 138-151. See also the Chamber debates of December 4 and 5, 1936, January 15, November 19, 1937; and the Senate debates of January 21, February 23, and December 28, 1937.

[25] Pierre-Etienne Flandin, February 26, 1938; Chambre, *Débats,* 1938, p. 644.

X. "*L'Organisation de la Paix*"

The League of Nations: "Garantie Internationale"

SO far, we have been treating French foreign policy as if it were restricted to national armaments, to alliances and other bilateral agreements. The League of Nations and the other "peace machinery" have been mentioned only incidentally. The time has now come to analyze the Geneva institution as it fitted into French policy.

The League of Nations was not a French conception. The original plans were American and British. It was Woodrow Wilson who had insisted that the Covenant be incorporated into the Peace Treaty. Since the French were obsessed at Versailles by a desire for effective guarantees of security both against another invasion by Germany and against any future German revolt against the treaty, they were interested in the proposed League only so far as it would serve as an additional guarantee against the German menace. The British conception of a League as a kind of new concert of powers primarily for consultative and conciliatory purposes did not suit the French at all. To their way of thinking, the usefulness of a League for security depended on its means of coercion and not on provisions for conciliation likely to lead to a policy of concessions and compromise.[1] The American proposal appeared far more promising. Wilson stressed the importance of guaranteeing the territorial integrity of the member-states against external

[1] See Alfred Zimmern, *The League of Nations and the Rule of Law, 1918-1935* (1936), Part II, Chapter X.

aggression; this was later incorporated in Article 10 of the Covenant. Here was a commitment in defense of the new *status quo* which needed only a *gendarme* capable of applying the sanctions with which to enforce it. From being the most skeptical participant in the negotiations, the French became the most fervent advocates of a powerful and coercive League and wished to equip it immediately with an international police force.[2] The League, not the individual members, was to be the *gendarme*. This would have given the League much of the character of a "super-state."

Although a League such as the French proposed would have been the most powerful collective guarantee of the established order that had ever existed, France, it should be emphasized, never showed the least intention of relinquishing her other guarantees of security, such as armaments and alliances and accepting the League as a substitute. She had perfectly logical arguments with which to justify this attitude. First, even the most strongly worded Covenant might not prove workable and dependable. Secondly, a League with practically universal membership would be cumbersome and slow in its processes, however well organized, and could therefore never be expected to provide security against a sudden attack or invasion. The emphasis from Versailles on, therefore, was on such guarantees as the strategic frontier on the Rhine, superiority in arms, and bilateral pacts or guarantees of military assistance. Only after the "*échecs successifs dans la recherche de sécurité et de garantie interalliées,*" said a Foreign Affairs Committee Report in 1926, did the French Government set out "*de trouver la sécurité française dans une garantie internationale.*"[3]

[2] See below, p. 161 n. 16.

[3] Senate Foreign Affairs Committee Report of March 31, 1926, on the Locarno Accords; Rapporteur, M. Labrousse; Sénat, *Documents*, 1926, Session ordinaire, Annexe No. 194, p. 891.

There is no justification for saying, as Hindmarsh does (*Force in Peace*, p. 115), that "the Three Powers Guarantee Treaty of 1919 between Great Britain, France,

Since the League was to be merely a "*garantie supplémentaire*" of French security and an integral part of a whole system of defenses, its purpose, as far as France was concerned, was obviously the same as that of her armaments and alliances. It was regarded as another instrument to keep Germany in her place and to deter or defeat "*une agression de l'Allemagne.*" But this meant that France was seeking to build up the League against a specific country, not against an unspecified potential aggressor. Her moves at Geneva become meaningful and logical if this is remembered. Her intentions became particularly clear, as we shall see later, whenever there was any question of punitive measures against any country other than Germany. On every such occasion her usual eagerness for League sanctions became lukewarm or ceased to exist. This was often a cause of conflict with other members. Britain and the so-called neutral countries had no intention of allowing the League to be directed specifically against Germany or against any one country. The main value and advantage of the League, as compared to the old-time alliances, in their opinion, lay in the fact that it could not be regarded as provocative by any country.

The issue never came completely into the open, since the French, like the other members, discussed League matters only "*en termes généraux et en termes imprécis,*" as Lémery put it.[4] The French, like everyone else, spoke of "potential aggressors," not of Germany, of "security," not of the security of the *status quo* powers. The farthest they went in making their intentions plain was to refer to "*nations de bonne foi*" who were to protect themselves

and the United States was intended to compensate France for her failure to secure positive guarantees in the Covenant." Tardieu, in defending the Treaty of Versailles in the Chamber of Deputies, September 2, 1919, clearly stated that the alliances were offered "*au lieu de la fixation au Rhin de la frontière occidentale de l'Allemagne, ou de l'occupation indéfinie par les forces alliées de la région rhénane, . . .*" Chambre, *Débats*, 1919, p. 4091. See also Tardieu's book, *La Paix* (1921), Chapters V and VI, for a first-hand account of the negotiations.

[4] Henry Lémery, June 25, 1936; Sénat, *Débats*, 1936, p. 615.

against *"nations de mauvaise foi,"* or to mention the *"éventuels défenseurs de la paix,"* [5] who had to deal with *"les pays qui ont été les agresseurs."* [6]

The use of abstract phraseology on the part of France has two possible explanations. The French may have realized that they would have to adapt themselves, in language at least, to the views of those members who took the general and impartial purpose of the League literally. *"L'ennemi, on ne peut pas le nommer,"* said Lémery with regret, and declared, *"C'est cela qui a toujours empêché de faire de la sécurité collective autre chose qu'une fiction."* [7] The disadvantages which France was to suffer from the contradiction between her concrete political objective and the abstract goal pursued by others will be seen later.

The other explanation is that the French were not aware of the conflict because they naïvely identified their security with that of the world, and the particular "potential aggressor" whom they dreaded with the country against which all "peace-loving nations" were seeking to build up means of protection. Once the preservation of peace in general was identified with the *status quo* of Versailles, and the establishment of the rule of law among nations with the rigid enforcement of the peace treaties, the countries vitally interested in defending the *status quo* and in maintaining the treaties unchanged were inevitably led to identify their national interest with the general cause of peace. France was such a country. She was therefore never troubled by any conflict of principle, such as the British came to face, between her traditional national policy and the requirements of a new League policy. Her goal was the same whether she was seeking to strengthen her own armaments

[5] Pierre-Etienne Flandin, President of the Council of Ministers, radio broadcast, February 4, 1935; *Le Temps,* February 6, 1935, p. 1.

[6] André Maginot, War Minister, February 24, 1931; Chambre, *Débats,* 1931, p. 1125.

[7] Henry Lémery, June 25, 1936; Sénat, *Débats,* 1936, p. 615.

and alliances or to reinforce the Covenant. In both cases she was working for *"l'organisation de la paix."*

Since both Rightists and Leftists in France were in agreement as to the fundamental purpose of the League, discussions between them centered around the relative merits of alliances as compared with the League. There was ample opportunity for differences of opinion concerning the place that should be given to each of the various means of defense in the hierarchy of guarantees forming the total organization of peace.

Ever since the time when the Anglo-Saxon scheme for a League of Nations was first presented and received with skepticism by men like Clemenceau, the Rightists in France had remained cool, or hostile, to the League. They had many reasons for this attitude. We need hardly be reminded that they had no sympathy for the *"idéologie périlleuse du président Wilson"* [8] which advocated the League not simply as a new and useful instrument of national foreign policy but as the forerunner of a new era of international peace and good will. These to them were Utopian dreams, if not, as some suspected, merely devices of Anglo-Saxon hypocrisy to distract France from her real interests. If the League was to be of any use, it would have to prove itself as a workable "general alliance." They made no secret of the fact that they regarded this as the essential function of the League. Pichon, referring to the Covenant in 1919, declared that it constituted *"en somme, si on l'examine de près, une sorte de traité d'alliance générale entre les différentes nations dont il porte la signature,"* adding, however, that *"elle n'interdit pas d'ailleurs les alliances particulières."* [9] *"Pourquoi ne pas parler clair? La Société des Nations a été conçue*

[8] Louis Marin, December 12, 1932; Chambre, *Débats*, 1932, p. 3543.

[9] Stéphen Pichon, Foreign Minister, September 24, 1919; Chambre, *Débats*, 1919, pp. 4545-4546.

comme une vaste alliance," said Lémery.[10] Even Briand once spoke of the Covenant as "*un pacte d'alliance générale.*"[11]

If the League was to be an alliance, was it an effective and hence a valuable one, or were its deficiencies too great to make it worth while for France to shape her policy in accord with its requirements? The answer the Rightists gave was not complimentary to the League. The pledges of the Covenant were couched in terms that left room for evasion. The definition of the *casus foederis* was vague and too narrowly restricted. The operation of common action was left unprepared and would therefore lack the necessary military precision. If France could induce her fellow members to transform the League into a genuine coalition, the situation would be different; but the Rightists doubted her ability to do so. If she failed, the League might become an obstacle rather than an effective supplement to France's other lines of defense. Would not some countries, notably Great Britain, refuse to enter any new bilateral defensive alliances on the ground that they were sufficiently committed by the Covenant? Would not objections be raised to French armaments and to alliances with other countries as injurious to the new peace machinery at Geneva or to the spirit of the League? The French themselves might be lulled into a false sense of security and put undue faith in the League, meanwhile neglecting more reliable defenses. The efforts devoted to the work at Geneva would in any case detract dangerously from the energy with which the government pursued more important tasks. "*Poursuivez-vous donc l'illusion que c'est là que vous allez résoudre ces problèmes et allez-vous y abriter la sécurité de votre pays?*" asked Ybarnégaray.[12]

When we consider how profoundly the Rightists feared the risks

[10] Henry Lémery, June 25, 1936; Sénat, *Débats*, 1936, p. 615.

[11] Aristide Briand, Foreign Minister, April 21, 1925; Chambre, *Débats*, 1925, p. 2235.

[12] Jean Ybarnégaray, March 9, 1933; Chambre, *Débats*, 1933, p. 1218.

France would incur if she supported the League, it is surprising that they not only rendered lip service to the Geneva institution, but when they were in control of the French government sent staunch supporters of the League as delegates to Geneva. In view of the frequent changes of ministry that took place in Paris, the continuity in the French delegation is rather astonishing. Some men, like Paul-Boncour, held a seemingly permanent seat. The Rightists apparently realized that, however much they might dislike the League, a vigorous French pro-League attitude was expedient. Furthermore, some of the arguments which prompted the Leftists to favor an active French League policy could not be entirely refuted. Was it not better to have nations committed under the League Covenant than not to have them committed at all? Was it not better to co-operate with other countries through the League than to risk isolation?

After 1936 there was no longer any need for lip service to the League or for an opportunist policy directed at making the best of the institution. France had just suffered acutely from the conflict between her policy of alliance with Italy and her obligations under the Covenant which had forced her to participate in sanctions against Italy. The British Government turned away from the League and, in accordance with French wishes, entered into an alliance with France. Now the French Rightists could come out openly against the League, without having to fear that their attitude would deprive France of British friendship or otherwise harm her. Others, like Flandin, who had not been hostile to the League now turned their backs on it. "*Aucun de nous, certes,*" Flandin declared in 1937, "*ne songe à abdiquer l'idéal de la sécurité collective et de l'assistance mutuelle garantie par une Société des nations, . . . Malheureusement, pour le moment, tout cela n'est qu'un rêve dans une église désertée.*"[13]

[13] Pierre-Etienne Flandin, November 19, 1937; Chambre, *Débats*, 1937, p. 2482.

Leftists and moderates like Briand, Herriot, Paul-Boncour, and Blum encountered none of the difficulties in working out a French League policy which troubled their opponents. Whatever disadvantages France might suffer through the League would in their eyes be many times balanced by the benefits to be derived, particularly if France successfully molded the League according to her own conceptions. One of the reasons why they favored the League was negative; they did not want to see France return to the old alliance system pure and simple. Some agreed with Woodrow Wilson that alliances of the traditional type were a potential cause of war. Like the British, they emphasized the danger of possible counter-alliances, which would again divide Europe into hostile blocs. Others, although they privately believed that alliances were still the best path to security, thought that France would harm herself, under the circumstances, if she tried to restore the pre-war system. They feared the effect on public opinion in the Anglo-Saxon and neutral countries, which they knew to be extremely hostile to the policy of alliances. France, they said, could not afford to lose the moral support of "world opinion," on which depended so much of the assistance which she might need in time of war.

But while the Leftists were warm supporters of the League, they had no more intention than their opponents of contenting themselves with the Covenant as it was. "*Il y a une idée qui, je crois, fait l'accord de tous les partis en France,*" said de Jouvenel. "*C'est que la Société des Nations n'existera que quand elle aura la force d'appliquer des sanctions.*"[14] It was necessary, said Paul-Boncour, "*qu'on empêche la Société des nations de tourner en une académie émettant des voeux platoniques, ou formulant une morale sans obligation ni sanction, . . .*"[15] An active League pol-

[14] Henry de Jouvenel, January 11, 1934; Sénat, *Débats*, 1934, p. 49.

[15] Joseph Paul-Boncour, Chairman of the Foreign Affairs Committee, March 28, 1930; Chambre, *Débats*, 1930, p. 1366.

icy meant for France continual efforts to strengthen the coercive machinery of the Geneva institution. There was no question of maintaining the "*status quo*" of the Covenant. Instead, France from the outset made suggestions which were truly revolutionary in the light of European tradition. The idea of providing the League with an international police force recurred in every French proposal from Versailles to the French peace plan of 1936.[16]

[16] The principal plans which France put forward may be briefly summarized: To the Commission on the League of Nations which sat during the 1919 Peace Conference, the French delegation submitted a plan adopted June 8, 1918, by the *Commission ministérielle française de la Société des Nations*. David H. Miller, *The Drafting of the Covenant* (1928), II, pp. 238-246 (English), pp. 403-411 (French). The nature of the diplomatic, juridical, economic, and military sanctions to be employed under the direction of a Council was defined. The military sanction which would be employed to ensure the execution of the decisions of the Council and of the tribunal and to oppose any hostile armed force "*est confiée soit à un effectif international, soit à une ou plusieurs Puissances faisant partie de la Société des nations et ayant reçu mandat à cet effet.*" Under the supervision of the Council a permanent General Staff was to be created.

The European states represented at the Tenth Assembly met together on September 9, 1929, and entrusted M. Briand, French Foreign Minister, who had summoned the meeting, with the task of initiating a study of the possibility of organizing a "*lien fédéral*" among the European states. M. Briand, on behalf of the French Government now presided over by M. Tardieu, acquitted himself of this task in his *Memorandum sur l'Organisation d'un Régime D'Union Fédérale Européenne.* Official text issued by the French Foreign Office; also League Document, 1930. VII. 4. French and English texts, in *International Conciliation*, Special Bulletin, June, 1930.

The French delegation to the Disarmament Conference, under the leadership of André Tardieu, War Minister, submitted on February 5, 1932, three days after the opening of the Conference, proposals in which measures for disarmament were combined with the organization of an international police force. *Conference Documents*, I (1932. IX. 63), pp. 113-116. The recommendations were "for placing civil aviation and bombing aircraft, and also certain material of the land and home forces, at the disposal of the League of Nations; for the creation of a preventive and repressive international force; for the political conditions upon which such measures depend; and lastly, for new rules providing for the protection of civil populations."

Nine months later, the French Government, under Herriot, in an effort to devise a solution to the German demand for equality of rights and to bring Germany back to the Disarmament Conference from which she had withdrawn, sub-

National sovereignty was to be severely curtailed in favor of a council which would decide on matters as vital as national armaments. Of course, it was taken for granted that the League would always operate in favor of countries like France and her allies, the law-abiding and purely defensive group of powers in the League. They would naturally remain in control of the proposed super-state and of its police force, since its purpose was to protect the security of the peace-loving nations.

Notwithstanding her repeated failures to make the other members accept these proposals, membership in the League promised advantages to France which encouraged her to support the Geneva institution longer than any other Great Power.

In the first place, it was hoped that a large number of countries which would never have been willing to enter into an alliance with France would feel committed by the Covenant to assist her if she were attacked. While promises of assistance under the Covenant, in its existing form, might remain weak, they were not on

mitted on November 14, 1932, a new "plan" (1932. IX. 58). For the February proposals, limited to suggestions for an international police force, was substituted the security system of "concentric circles": the outer circle consisting of all the participants in the Disarmament Conference acting on the principles and consequences of the Kellogg Pact; the middle circle composed of states adhering to the League of Nations Covenant and supplementary general treaties; the inner circle consisting of a special European organization with a political arrangement for effective mutual assistance and military arrangements based on a unified short-service army for all continental countries and the maintenance of specialized units to be placed at the disposal of the League.

During the negotiations which followed Germany's remilitarization of the Rhineland in March, 1936, the French Government prepared a new "*Plan de Paix*," published April 8, 1936; *International Conciliation*, No. 320 (May, 1936), pp. 247-252. In view of the weakness of the League, it proposed a European regional organization within the framework of the League, which would fix the armament of its members by a two-thirds vote and have at its disposal permanent armed forces for the imposition of sanctions. The plan was, in fact, an adaptation of the "inner circle" of the Herriot–Paul-Boncour project of November, 1932.

this account to be regarded as negligible. In her struggle to make her system of defenses as comprehensive as possible, France was ready to incorporate into her organization of peace even weaker pledges than those contained in the Covenant if by so doing she could persuade still more countries to assure her of some kind of support. According to the Herriot plan of 1932, for instance, the "outer ring," composed of the non-European states including the United States, was not asked to pledge itself even to economic sanctions. Many efforts were made to bring these countries, and the United States in particular, into the organization of peace and of French security. The only one that met with any success was Briand's proposal for "outlawing war" between France and the United States. It resulted in the Kellogg Pact.[17] France claimed optimistically that the pact committed the United States to consultation in case of aggression and to a discriminatory policy against a violator of the pact. The American interpretation, however, destroyed practically all hope that France had succeeded in drawing the United States into her system of defenses. During the disarmament conferences it sometimes seemed as if a consultative pact with the United States was in the making. But no such agreement materialized.[18] The point to note is that in all of these attempts

[17] Shotwell refutes the suggestion that Briand "was intriguing for his country so as to secure an alliance that could be used against other Powers." Briand's proposal, he says, was intended "to provide for a world-wide structure of peace which would include nations like the United States." James T. Shotwell, *On the Rim of the Abyss* (1936), p. 134.

[18] The French delegation came to the London Naval Conference of 1930 determined to secure additional guarantees of security in exchange for its consent to further reduction of armaments. It made proposals for a Mediterranean pact, for a new interpretation of Article 16, and for a general consultative agreement supplementary to the Kellogg Pact. Although at first favorable to this last suggestion, the American delegation, it is rumored, turned away from it under pressure from home, and for fear that it might be interpreted as a *quid pro quo* for reductions in armaments. Royal Institute of International Affairs, *Survey of*

France was asking for commitments far less stringent than were contained in the Covenant. Any agreement was to be welcomed which would restrict the freedom of the United States to preserve "absolute neutrality," in the event of a new European war.

The French after all fully realized that even from their fellow members in the League they might receive no more than economic and financial assistance. All the discussions on collective action at Geneva centered around economic rather than military sanctions.

International Affairs, 1930, pp. 53-54; Giovanni Engely, *The Politics of Naval Disarmament* (1932), pp. 96-97, 150-154.

During the general Disarmament Conference the French renewed their efforts to give the United States a place in their security system. Encouraged by a statement of Secretary of State Stimson to the Council on Foreign Relations on August 8, 1932, the Herriot–Paul-Boncour plan of November 14, 1932, made the outer circle of its security proposals center around "the principles, which are generally recognized to be a necessary consequence of the Pact for the Renunciation of War." These were supposed to include agreement among the signatories to "concert together" in the event of a breach or threat of breach, "the prohibition of direct or indirect economic or financial relations with the aggressor country," and the agreement "not to recognize any *de facto* situation brought about in consequence of the violation of an international undertaking." The United States delegation did not commit itself regarding the proposals, but after President Roosevelt had taken office in the United States and the British Government had made the security proposals of their plan of March 16, 1933, center around a consultation procedure among the signatories of the Kellogg Pact, Norman Davis on May 22, 1933, declared to the General Commission of the Conference that the United States was ready to make its contribution to "the organization of peace":

"In particular, we are willing to consult the other States in case of a threat to peace, with a view to averting conflict. Further than that, in the event that the States, in conference, determine that a State has been guilty of a breach of the peace in violation of its international obligations and take measures against the violator, then, if we concur in the judgement rendered as to the responsible and guilty party, we will refrain from any action tending to defeat such collective effort which these States may thus make to restore peace." United States Department of State, *Press Releases*, No. 191 (May 27, 1933), p. 390.

It should also be mentioned that France's many suggestions for supervising the execution of the eventual disarmament convention and for measures to be taken in case of violation of the convention all had in view participation by the United States. With the failure of the Disarmament Conference no agreement was ever reached in regard to any of these proposals.

But while the French never shared the view, so widespread in Britain, that a country like Germany could be held in check by the mere threat or even actual use of no more than economic sanctions, they keenly appreciated the value of economic measures as a supplement to military action. The effectiveness of the British blockade during the World War had not been forgotten.

The universal character of the League offered a second advantage. The pledges of assistance under the Covenant were given not only to France, who might well have been able to find sufficient allies without the League, but also to weaker countries like her Central European allies, for whom it was difficult to acquire promises of assistance. Proof of this was Britain's reluctance to commit herself on the Danube. As long as the assistance to be given in case of aggression was available for some countries and not for others, the "potential aggressor" would be able to strike at the weak spots and hope that the conflict would be localized. France, wanting to link her western and eastern defenses together as closely as possible, was absolutely opposed to Hitler's suggestion for separate bilateral agreements and to the idea of localizing wars. Instead, the League was to give practical expression to "*l'indivisibilité de la paix.*"

But if the League, even in its existing form, offered France the two advantages we have just discussed—commitments by its members to participate at least in economic sanctions, and pledges, although hardly of a very reliable kind, to France's allies in Central Europe—what France hoped to make out of the League eventually was far more ambitious. It was to be a means of integrating all the pacts of mutual assistance which France and her friends might be able to conclude into a comprehensive and thoroughly organized whole. Endowed with an international police force, a general staff, and an administrative system for economic sanctions, it would develop into nothing less than a well-prepared potential war coalition, *"une coalition formée par la Société des nations,"* as Tardieu put it,[19] and erected on the model of the one-time victorious coalition of the World War.

It may sound cynical to interpret the French conception of the League and of *"l'organisation de la paix"* as in effect the establishment of a new "World War coalition." But from the French point of view, there was nothing objectionable in such an interpretation. The lessons of the last war had not been lost. They were constantly referred to. The coalition of the World War and the League were frequently compared: *"Dans la grande guerre, le concours de nombreux peuples, mus par la conscience universelle, nous a puissamment aidés, et pourtant la Société des nations n'existait pas. Aujourd'hui elle existe."* [20] It had taken months, if not years, to organize efficient common action by the Allied and Associated Powers. Bitter controversies had preceded the setting up of a unified high command. Long delays had ensued before the Supreme Council was properly established. It therefore behooved the peace-loving nations, warned by 1914, to provide in advance for a coalition which would at any moment be prepared, strong, and unified. It was firmly believed that so powerful a coalition would deter Germany from aggression. The old adage, *"Si vis pacem, para bellum,"* had been amended to read, "If you want peace, prepare sanctions against the country most likely to become the aggressor." The more nearly perfect the preparations, the more chance there would be of deterring the "potential aggressor," who would shape his course according to his appraisal of the "war coalition" which he would have to face. The more the League took on the character of such a super-alliance the less dangerous could Germany become

[19] André Tardieu, President of the Council of Ministers, radio interview, Geneva, April 9, 1932; *Le Temps,* April 10, 1932, p. 2.

[20] Yvon Delbos, Foreign Minister, June 23, 1936; Chambre, *Débats,* 1936, p. 1553.

for the peace of the world. This, even if it was not explicitly stated in so many words, was in the back of the minds of the French advocates of a rigorous and active League policy.

General Treaties and Special Accords

Whatever reliability the French might attribute to the League as an operating center for collective action of an economic or even military nature, there still remained advantages of a different and more important kind which could be gained only from alliances or from pacts of mutual assistance closely resembling alliances.[21] Under the existing "psychological circumstances," that is, in view of the dislike and distrust which Britain and other countries evinced for military alliances, it required a great deal of ingenuity and diplomatic skill to fit anything resembling alliances into an active League policy. Had not the League been set up primarily for the purpose of preventing a return to the pre-war European system, with its antagonistic military alliances? While Wilson had in mind

[21] Considering the importance of the French policy of alliances since the World War—"*eine der entscheidenden Tatsachen der europäischen Wirklichkeit,*" as Kraemer says (p. VII)—and the legal as well as political problems arising out of the co-existence of alliances and the League, it is surprising how little they have been discussed in any of the French, British, or American literature in this field. Most of the research has been carried on by Germans who are naturally critical of the French system of alliances and its compatibility with the League. See particularly: Fritz Berber, *Sicherheit und Gerechtigkeit* (1934), pp. 101-102; Graf Asche von Mandelsloh, *Politische Pakte und völkerrechtliche Ordnung* (1937); Heinrich Rogge, *Kollektivsicherheit, Bündnispolitik, Völkerbund* (1937), pp. 100 ff.; Fritz Kraemer, *Das Verhältnis der französischen Bündnisverträge zum Völkerbundpakt und zum Pakt von Locarno* (Frankfurter Abhandlungen zum modernen Völkerrecht, Heft 30, 1932); Baron Axel von Freytagh-Loringhoven, "Les Ententes Régionales," in Hague, Académie de Droit International, *Recueil des Cours,* Vol. 56 (1936, II), pp. 639 ff.; Paul Barandon, *Das System der politischen Staatsverträge seit 1918* (Handbuch des Völkerrechts, Vol. 4, Part 2), pp. 222 ff.; Walter Wache, *System der Pakte: die politischen Verträge der Nachkriegszeit* (1938), pp. 66 ff., 148 ff.

"that henceforth alliance must not be set up against alliance, understanding against understanding, but that there must be a common agreement for a common object,"[22] the French sought to have both alliances and the League. But was it not true that a "collective system and special alliances belong to different worlds?"[23]

As early as 1922, when France and her Central European friends held a dominant position in the League, the French succeeded in getting the League Assembly to vote a resolution which accepted the French thesis regarding the relationship between the League and pacts of mutual assistance among League members. During the ensuing years this resolution came to serve as an entering wedge by which pacts having all the features which made alliances valuable to France could be interpreted as being a part of the League system. The resolution stipulated that where "for historical, geographical, or other reasons, a country is in special danger of attack," it could enter into "detailed arrangements" with other countries, providing for "immediate and effective assistance in accordance with a pre-arranged plan."[24] In accepting this principle, the League drew a distinction between two different groups of countries. One group, being "in special danger of attack," "*ex-*

[22] Address before the League to Enforce Peace, Washington, May 27, 1916; in Ray S. Baker, and William E. Dodd, eds., *The Public Papers of Woodrow Wilson: The New Democracy* (1926), II, p. 186. In his note of December 18, 1916, to the belligerent powers, Wilson pointed out that the war aims of each were the same: "Each would be jealous of the formation of any more rival leagues to preserve an uncertain balance of power amidst multiplying suspicions; but each is ready to consider the formation of a league of nations to insure peace and justice throughout the world." *Ibid.*, II, p. 404.

[23] Alfred Zimmern, *The League of Nations and the Rule of Law, 1918-1935* (1936), p. 279.

[24] League of Nations, *Records of the Third Assembly, Plenary Meetings*, I, *Text of the Debates*, p. 291. Resolution XIV laid the bases for the Draft Treaty of Mutual Assistance framed the following year by the Temporary Mixed Commission and the Fourth Assembly; *Records of the Fourth Assembly, Minutes of the Third Committee, passim*, and Annexes, pp. 101 ff.

posées aux 'risques géographiques,' "[25] was not only to be permitted to have "partial treaties" or "special accords," as they were later called, but was declared to be actually in need of such accords. The significance of this becomes clear when one remembers the military alliances that France had already concluded with Poland and Belgium. If they could now be interpreted as the "detailed arrangements" described in this resolution, they would not only be tolerated by the League but even sanctified and transformed into a part of the organization of peace.

Once it was conceded that there was need for "special accords," the Covenant became merely a general treaty supplementing, as far as this particular group of countries was concerned, the far more solid foundation of security which these countries were laying down for themselves by stringent and reliable special agreements. Why the French were so eager to assure themselves of the right to enter upon special agreements is not hard to discover. General treaties, such as the Covenant, were expected to furnish security of no more than a "doubtful" and "indeterminate" nature. Even at best, the assistance in case of war which partners to a general treaty would be willing to offer would be "progressive" instead of "instantaneous," "conditional" instead of "automatic," and of "limited" instead of "total" efficiency. In these words the French described, in the abstract terminology common at Geneva, the two different types of assistance which they could expect from other countries in case of a new war with Germany.

The potential friends, allies, and supporters of France fell naturally into two categories. In the first group were countries like Belgium, Poland, and Czechoslovakia who, like France, were continental neighbors of Germany and therefore in fear not merely of a new war, but of German invasion of their soil. They needed

[25] Léon Bourgeois, Commission on the League of Nations, February 13, 1919; in David H. Miller, *The Drafting of the Covenant* (1928), II, p. 478.

promises of immediate assistance to be available in a few hours. At the same time, because of their geographical location and their common interests, they had no hesitation in giving promises of such immediate assistance to France. Whether other continental countries, like Italy or Soviet Russia, could be persuaded to join this inner circle was a matter of conjecture.

There was a second group of countries which was geographically distant from the area which the French unhesitatingly assumed to be the danger-center of the world. These countries were separated by the sea from the European continent and therefore from Germany, the potential aggressor. They were not in fear of invasion. It was unlikely that they would ever be ready to pledge the kind of immediate assistance which the other group needed; nor were they able, because of their remoteness from the probable scene of war, to give such assistance. As in the last war, they might eventually take up arms, but only after considering their interest in each specific case. Under an ideal system from the French point of view, France would have obtained from both groups of nations the maximum assistance compatible with their interests and abilities. It was logical to regard the "*accords spéciaux*" as suitable for the countries in danger of invasion, and the "general treaties" as best fitted for the more remote states. While this meant that primary interest would be focused on the special accords, it did not mean that attempts would not be made to make the general treaties as "alliance-like," as immediate, and as automatic as possible.

The inadequacy of the League to those who wanted immediate assistance becomes clear when it is compared with the typical bilateral military pact of mutual assistance. The outstanding difference between the League and the old-time alliances was that the former was not directed against any specific country. The "potential aggressor" was entirely anonymous. That left it quite uncertain in what direction coercive action might some day have to be taken.

But, said a report of the Permanent Advisory Commission, "immediate, pre-arranged and unlimited assistance . . . capable of providing guarantees which can be accurately measured," which was what France wanted, required an unequivocal definition of the *casus foederis*. This, it was said, would be easy to do in the "partial treaty," since the case of aggression against which the treaty was directed would be "expressly described in the treaty."[26] It is hard to see what this could have meant except the inclusion by name of the country regarded as the potential aggressor and against whose possible attack defensive measures were being prepared.

Such specific mention of the opponent was also necessary for another reason. Military assistance, as the French pointed out, was possible only if based on "pre-arranged military plans." But since nobody ever seriously suggested that military plans could be worked out by the general staffs except for a given military situation, and, therefore, against a specific opponent, the opponent would have to be known in advance. The plans would provide against what the French called *"certaines hypothèses de conflit déterminées."*[27]

Thus, because certain countries "in danger of invasion" were assumed to need promises of military assistance based on pre-arranged military plans which would be immediately effective, the special accords had, by their very nature, to be directed against specifically mentioned countries. The Little Entente was a case in point; it was explicitly directed against Hungary and Bulgaria.

[26] Opinion on Resolution XIV of the 1922 Assembly, submitted by the French, Belgian, and Brazilian members of the Permanent Advisory Commission; League of Nations, *Records of the Fourth Assembly, Minutes of the Third Committee*, pp. 120, 121.

[27] French memorandum of June 15, 1923, signed by Poincaré, on the Draft Treaty of Mutual Assistance; France, Ministère des Affaires Etrangères, *Documents Diplomatiques: Documents relatifs aux négociations concernant les garanties de sécurité contre une agression de l'Allemagne (10 janvier 1919–7 décembre 1923)*, p. 189.

Similarly, the French treaties of 1925 with Poland and Czechoslovakia were specifically directed against Germany.

It is therefore difficult to discover in what way these new particular accords differed from the pre-war defensive alliances. Certainly, they had neither of the two traits that distinguished the League. They were neither universal nor were they directed indiscriminately against any country that might resort to aggression. It was claimed, however, that special accords under the League system differed from the pre-war alliances in several other important respects.

In the first place, it was said, they would not form a part of a system of alliances and counter-alliances, splitting the Continent into hostile blocs. But this merely meant that France and the other partners of her special accords were to be granted a monopoly on alliances. Their prospective opponents would not be permitted to reciprocate by counter-accords. Herriot made this plain when he said that special accords were to be permitted only if they were "*conclus dans l'esprit général du pacte.*" [28] The Council, he declared, would have to assure itself of their purely defensive character. This was a diplomatic way of saying that revisionist

[28] Edouard Herriot, President of the Council of Ministers, January 28, 1925; Chambre, *Débats*, 1925, p. 359.

Article 18 of the Covenant provided that all treaties between League members, in order to be binding, "shall be forthwith registered with the Secretariat and shall as soon as possible be published by it." In Article 20 the Covenant abrogated "all obligations or understandings *inter se* [between League members] which are inconsistent with the terms thereof." These provisions were not interpreted as giving to the League any formal control over the negotiation and validity of treaties.

The Draft Treaty of Mutual Assistance, which was not accepted, stated in Article 7 that the Council would examine the "complementary agreements . . . with a view to deciding whether they are in accordance with the principles of the Treaty and of the Covenant."

On Articles 18 and 20 of the Covenant see Jean Ray, *Commentaire du pacte de la Société des Nations selon la politique et la jurisprudence des organes de la Société* (1930), pp. 545 ff., 568 ff.

countries, "*nations de mauvaise foi*," as they were often called, would not be allowed to join hands, since they could not be trusted to have purely defensive objectives. Herriot on one occasion went so far as to state that the Austro-German customs union project would violate the principle of the new order because it meant a return to the theory of "*forces antithétiques*."[29] Any attempt to set up "*combinaisons dirigées contre d'autres alliances*," Herriot insisted, would not be permissible, since the League was determined to "*mettre fin à cette vieille politique d'équilibre et de bascule qui, en effet, dans le passé a engendré plus de guerres qu'elle n'en a évité*."[30] Since France was determined to have her special accords, the correctness of the charge of monopoly should be sufficiently plain. Alliances were to be a privilege which only countries "in danger of invasion," not "potential invaders," were to enjoy. *Quod licet Jovi non licet bovi!*

The British placed more credence in a second difference which they believed would make the special accords inoffensive. They were to be open to any country that wished to join. The French put it more carefully in speaking of the pacts being "*perpétuellement accessible à tous les peuples de bonne foi, pourvu que ceux-ci fassent la preuve de leur bonne foi*."[31] Unfortunately, no country ever made an attempt to see what would happen if it asked to be included in an accord which it suspected of being directed against itself. If any country had made the experiment, we might know of what the "openness" consisted. It would seem to be in patent contradiction to the other features of the accords, particularly to the essential pre-arranged military plans. It was absurd to imagine that if the general staffs of two countries A and B had jointly

[29] Edouard Herriot, May 8, 1931; Chambre, *Débats*, 1931, p. 2663.

[30] Edouard Herriot, President of the Council of Ministers, January 28, 1925; Chambre, *Débats*, 1925, p. 359.

[31] Henry de Jouvenel, September 26, 1922; League of Nations, *Records of the Third Assembly, Plenary Meetings*, I, *Text of the Debates*, p. 252.

worked out plans against country C, similar plans could then be made by A and C against B, or by B and C against A. Military secrecy, quite apart from all political and psychological considerations, made such a procedure inconceivable. Whenever it was suggested in academic discussions it was discarded as impracticable. If, therefore, a given opponent against whom military plans had been worked out should have attempted to join such an accord, he could at best have become a secondary partner from whom the prearranged plans would have had to be kept secret. Even where no military agreements accompanied the treaty, as in the case of the Franco-Soviet Pact of 1935, it is hard to believe that politically it was "*ouvert à tous,*" and that therefore Germany had no reason to speak of "*encerclement, puisqu'il a été offert à l'Allemagne d'y participer.*" [32]

The differences, alleged or real, between the special accords and old-time alliances which we have discussed so far did not in any way affect the ability of France to negotiate any of the pacts of mutual assistance in which she was interested. But was there not perhaps another difference which would change the character of these pacts and justify the claim that the League had prevented a return to military alliances? It seemed logical to expect that special accords, since they were interpreted as being a part of the League system, would have been brought under the strict supervision of the League. Would not, therefore, some decision of the League Council or Assembly be required, for instance, before the partners to these special agreements would be permitted to go into military

[32] Henry Torrès, Rapporteur on the Franco-Soviet Pact, February 11, 1936; Chambre, *Débats*, 1936, p. 354.

Paul-Boncour put it more generally when he said, in referring to the Franco-Soviet Pact, that "*aucune nation n'a le droit de se dire menacée par lui ou victime d'un encerclement quelconque. On n'est pas encerclé quand il dépend de vous d'entrer dans le cercle de sécurité, . . .*" Joseph Paul-Boncour, Minister of State, March 12, 1936; Sénat, *Débats*, 1936, p. 264.

action? According to the official interpretation given to Article 16 of the Covenant this was not the case. Resolution 4 of the resolutions regarding sanctions, adopted by the League Assembly on October 4, 1921, declared, "It is the duty of each Member of the League to decide for itself whether a breach of the Covenant has been committed."[33] The special accords would have failed, in fact, to fulfill their primary objective if the League had insisted on controlling their execution. Their main aim was to assure countries of assistance within a period of hours in case of invasion. To submit the matter to Geneva first would have meant delay and would have defeated this purpose. The Locarno Treaty, which was often considered to be one of these particular accords, provided explicitly in Article 4 that the guarantors would, in case of flagrant violations of the treaty, be obliged to give immediate military assistance and not to await a decision by the League. The Council of the League would later, as the treaty said, "be seized of the question." But this did not give the League much chance to check the freedom of action of the signatories of the accords, since the most it could do, once they had gone into action, was to decide that there had not been any aggression in the first place and that the "allies" if they continued military action might themselves become guilty of aggression.[34]

[33] The League publication, *Reports and Resolutions on the Subject of Article 16 of the Covenant* (1927. V.14) is a complete documentary collection of materials relating to Article 16 before 1926. See also Georg von Gretschaninow, ed., *Materialien zur Entwicklung der Sicherheitsfrage im Rahmen des Völkerbundes*, Erster Teil, *1920-1927* (Vol. II, Part 1, of Viktor Bruns, ed., *Politische Verträge: eine Sammlung von Urkunden*), 1936, pp. 128 ff.

A proposal which would have specifically required the Council to note the breach of the Covenant before any sanctions could be applied was rejected by the 1921 Assembly. *Records of the Second Assembly, Plenary Meetings*, pp. 736 ff., 804 ff.

[34] In the protocol accompanying the Franco-Soviet Pact of mutual assistance of May 2, 1935, the League was given a greater measure of control because for once France herself preferred a special accord which was not subject to the

The League, it is no exaggeration to say, was never given any power over the special accords. Nations "in danger of invasion" were in practice left free to negotiate as many such accords as they saw fit, to direct them against any specific country by which they believed themselves to be menaced, to have their general staffs work out pre-arranged military plans, or even to set their military assistance in motion whenever they judged that they or one of their allies had become the victim of aggression. It is therefore hard to escape the conclusion that this freedom transformed the League into a shelter for a privileged system of French continental alliances. Paul-Boncour was not misleading his opponents at home when in answer to their demand for "alliances instead of the League" he exclaimed, "*Des alliances, des amitiés, nous en avons,*

"*automatisme brutal.*" (Henry Torrès, Rapporteur on the Franco-Soviet Pact, February 11, 1936; Chambre, *Débats*, 1936, p. 354.) She wished to assure herself that Britain, Italy, and Belgium agreed that France could go to Russia's assistance and would not interpret her attack or invasion of Germany as a violation of the Locarno Treaty. The treaty provided, therefore, that even in cases of flagrant aggression France and the Soviet Union should submit the matter to the League Council and give the Council reasonable time for decision before they went to each other's assistance.

In practice, action of the Council even in this case would not have been able to cause much embarrassment to France. In four out of six possible cases, France would have been free to assist the Soviet Union on the basis of her own decision regarding the *casus foederis:* first, if the Council had made no recommendation within the time the allies regarded as reasonable; second, if it had decided to make no recommendation at all; third, if it were unable to reach a unanimous decision, a result which France's friends on the Council could at any time have brought about; or, fourth, if the Council had unanimously concurred in France's opinion. Only in two cases could the Council have prohibited action which France might herself have taken: first, if the Council agreed unanimously that the Soviet Union had provoked the war; or, second, if by a similar decision it voted the Soviet Union the aggressor. Neither of these cases could easily have been established unless France herself regarded the Soviet Union as guilty and, therefore, desired a decision freeing her from her obligations.

The very fact that control by the League had to be explicitly provided for in the case of the Franco-Soviet Pact confirms our contention that special accords did not come *per se* under the supervision of the League.

et nous y sommes fidèles comme vous-mêmes. Là-deçu unanimité française." He then went on to accuse his opponents, who were demanding alliances of the pre-war type, of not realizing that France, as well as the countries with whom she wished to ally herself, had oriented themselves "*vers d'autres formules.*"[35] The change, as he rightly implied, was only to another "*formule.*"

Nothing has been said so far about the so-called "regional pacts" that came to play an increasingly important role as the earlier hopes of making the general treaties more stringent dwindled. They were said to be modeled on the Locarno Pact of Mutual Guarantee, the first agreement for mutual assistance among several countries in a specific region. The original Locarno Pact never really fitted into the French system of security. It was partly British, partly German in origin, as we shall see later.[36] The French had reason to hesitate before they agreed to it. It was not in harmony with either of the two seemingly contradictory principles, universality and particularity, on which they wished to base the general treaties and special accords. The special accord was to unite countries that had one and the same particular interest, namely, to protect themselves against some specific country. It was because of this particular common interest that their promises of mutual assistance were reliable. The general treaties, on the other hand, increased in value with their universality. Their purpose was to provide France and her allies with a maximum of commitments by as many countries as possible so as to insure ultimate victory.

With Locarno, the fact that Germany was one of the original signatories excluded the possibility of a common particular interest. The British welcomed the pact precisely because it helped to con-

[35] Joseph Paul-Boncour, Foreign Minister, March 9, 1933; Chambre, *Débats*, 1933, p. 1223.

[36] See below, p. 257.

ciliate countries with antagonistic interests. Locarno also differed most significantly from all other special accords in that, theoretically at least, it was not directed against any specific country. The guarantee by Britain and Italy was granted to France and Germany equally, much to the distress of French opponents of the pact, who bitterly resented having the term "potential aggressor" applied without discrimination to both France and Germany. "*Nous avons,*" complained Marin, "*l'humiliation d'être soupçonnés, au même titre que l'Allemagne, de pouvoir déclancher la guerre . . .*"[37] At the same time, Locarno was not universal either in the number of signatories or in its scope. The British committed themselves only for a certain specified geographical area in Western Europe, and the pact set up a bond only for the limited group of powers within that region. Had the League Covenant been supplemented merely by pacts of the Locarno type, it could with justice have been said that the pre-war type of alliances had not been revived.

The French Government was ready to agree to the Locarno Pact largely because in practice, though not in theory, the pact was expected to approximate very closely a special accord between Britain and France. Britain at the time desired to contribute to French security. Although she was also interested in giving Germany some support and satisfaction, it was virtually inconceivable that she would ever take sides with Germany in a war against France. Briand, when asked whether there was any danger that this might happen, exclaimed, "*Il suffit de lire les accords pour voir que c'est impossible. C'est évident!*"[38] The Locarno Treaty was

[37] Louis Marin, February 27, 1926; Chambre, *Débats,* 1926, p. 1050.

[38] Aristide Briand, President of the Council of Ministers, February 27, 1926; Chambre, *Débats,* 1926, p. 1045. Briand often argued that the Locarno Pact was the belated result of the negotiations for an Anglo-French alliance which he and Lloyd George had conducted at Cannes in January, 1922. Germany's

therefore in any case the best substitute—*"le maximum réalisable,"* said Briand—for a defensive alliance between the two countries that the French could hope to obtain at the time, and offered as binding and far-reaching a commitment as the British were then willing to consider.

In view of the fact that the Locarno Pact did not fully satisfy France's wishes, it is surprising that she should later have advocated new regional pacts, often spoken of as "new Locarnos," for other parts of the Continent. A Danubian pact was discussed in some detail during the Stresa Conference of 1935; an Eastern pact which we shall discuss in connection with Britain's policy in Central Europe was to become the subject of lengthy negotiations.[39] The Danubian pact was to protect Austria from absorption into the German Reich. Here no secret was made of the objective. In the case of the Eastern Pact, Poland, Czechoslovakia, and the Baltic states were also obviously seeking protection against Germany; there was no other common risk to which they considered themselves exposed at the time. In each of these cases, the purpose was to unite in a multilateral accord geographically adjacent countries which had the same particular interest in defending themselves against a specific country. Since these pacts were obviously intended to check Germany's expansionist ambitions in the East and Southeast, which so many of Germany's neighbors feared after 1933, they resembled the original Locarno Treaty only in their limitation to a particular geographical region. But the fundamental and unique concept of Locarno was lacking. The newly proposed regional pacts did not even pretend to reconcile former enemies or to set up a guarantee of the peace between them by disinterested

eastern border, he said, had finally been recognized as the *"frontière commune."* See his statements of February 26, 1926, Chambre, *Débats*, 1926, p. 1018; March 1, 1926, *ibid.*, p. 1090; December 20, 1929, Sénat, *Débats*, 1929, p. 1307.

[39] See below, pp. 273 ff.

third powers.[40] In other words, they did not actually differ from the rest of the "special accords" or alliances that characterized the French system of defenses.[41]

The League and the "German Menace"

It was all very well for France to interpret the League as an international guarantee and defense against Germany. But the other members of the League were in no way bound to reserve the League for that particular purpose. There was always a danger, therefore, either that they might take its general or universal purpose too literally and make the League operate indiscriminately against any country guilty of aggression, or that some powerful member might try to make the League serve its particular needs against a country other than Germany. This latent conflict of interests within the League was to have serious consequences for France, consequences with which she would never have been faced if the Allies of the World War, instead of setting up a League of Nations, had decided to continue their war coalition or had built up a new "Holy Alliance" for the avowed purpose of protecting the *status quo* of Versailles against any attempt of Germany to change it by the threat or use of force. As it was, Geneva became a battlefield for factions with opposing ideas about the purpose of the League.

What interested the French primarily was to make sure that

[40] Painlevé, in opening the Sixth Assembly of the League, spoke of two types of "*ententes régionales,*" one having "*pour objet d'assurer le maintien des frontières existantes; . . . elles laissent en dehors les Etats avec lesquels des conflits pourraient être vraisemblables,*" and others, like the proposed Locarno Pact then being negotiated, which "*englobent, au contraire, les Etats entre lesquels pourraient surgir des difficultés.*" *Actes de la Sixième Assemblée, Séances Plénières, Compte Rendu des Débats*, p. 24.

[41] See Vol. II, Part 1, of Viktor Bruns, ed., *Politische Verträge, op. cit.*, p. 462, n. 2.

they could count on the coercive powers of the League when, in their opinion, action against Germany was necessary. For this reason the definition of the *casus foederis* which would call for League sanctions was a matter of great political importance. While, as we have mentioned earlier, France did not succeed in broadening the *casus foederis* to include most of the steps which Germany might undertake to free herself from the restrictions of the Treaty of Versailles, it was nevertheless advantageous for her to have the League serve at least as a check on "aggression." Under any definition of aggression, the countries likely to become aggressors and against which punitive action would have to be undertaken were those who had grievances for which there was no remedy other than the use of force. "*Nul n'a droit de se faire justice lui-même*" had become the rule, said the French.[42] But if there was no other procedure by which to obtain justice some countries would be faced with a choice between continued injustice or breaking the law. Germany was in just such a situation, and was one of the few countries that was not only sufficiently hostile to the established order to take the risks of such unlawful action, but also powerful enough to do so. By trying to make the League first and foremost an instrument for the collective enforcement of the law against aggressors, France was adding to her defenses against revisionist Germany.

It has been contended that this was an unintentional and inevitable result of any attempt to strengthen the rule of law in international affairs. Legality, by its very nature, is a conservative force. Since judges and arbitrators are bound to apply, not to change, the existing law, enforcement of the law must discriminate against those who seek to alter it. It is "*inadmissible*," said a report of the Foreign Affairs Committee in 1929, "*qu'un tribunal*

[42] Chamber of Deputies Foreign Affairs Committee Report of April 3, 1925, on the Geneva Protocol; Rapporteur, Joseph Paul-Boncour; Chambre, *Documents*, 1925, Session ordinaire, Annexe No. 1515, p. 567.

arbitral quelconque puisse imposer au Gouvernement français la revision d'un traité quel qu'il soit. . . . La revision d'un traité est une opération politique."[43] The French deduced from this that the enforcement of the rule of law and the maintenance of the *status quo* of Versailles, which was "*le droit public européen*,"[44] were one and the same thing.

It should therefore be mentioned that a different interpretation of the provisions concerning aggression and League sanctions was conceivable. It would have considerably weakened the position of the *status quo* powers, and without infringing on the rule of law would have compelled them to react more favorably to suggestions for peaceful revision of the post-war settlements. If it had been made plain that a country accused of aggression might under certain circumstances be allowed to plead innocent on the ground that its attack had been provoked by the opponent, the Council could have proceeded to interpret undue insistence on certain treaty rights as an act of provocation.[45] It was feared that this might happen, since most treaties of assistance explicitly limited the *casus*

[43] Chamber of Deputies Foreign Affairs Committee Report of July 11, 1929, on the General Act of Arbitration; Rapporteur, Paul Bastid; Chambre, *Documents*, 1929, Session ordinaire, Annexe No. 2031, p. 1142.

[44] French memorandum of February 1, 1922, on the Genoa Conference; Ministère des Affaires Etrangères, *Documents Diplomatiques: Conférence économique internationale de Gênes (9 avril–19 mai 1922)*, p. 19.

[45] The mere fact that a treaty was unjust or unbearable, even in the opinion of a majority of the members of the League, might not have been sufficient, and a clear definition of the circumstances under which insistence on treaty rights would be considered provocative would have been imperative. The League, to give an example, might have regarded it as provocative for any member to insist on a certain solution of a problem when another was available which was regarded as fairer to both parties. The French warned of the danger of the "*agresseur*" being able "*de faire retomber sur sa victime le . . . soupçon d'avoir provoqué son agression.*" Chamber of Deputies Foreign Affairs Committee Report of April 3, 1925, on the Geneva Protocol; Rapporteur, Joseph Paul-Boncour; Chambre, *Documents*, 1925, Session ordinaire, Annexe No. 1515, p. 568.

foederis to "unprovoked aggression." The French, said Reynaud, therefore always insisted, "*Ce qui est capital, c'est l'automatisme des sanctions, car si un débat intervient sur les mobiles de l'agresseur, si on discrimine suivant les fautes ou les mérites de la victime, tout est perdu.*"[46] It is an indication of the preponderant position which the *status quo* powers had held earlier that the endless discussions on peace strategy and on the definition of aggression as well as on League sanctions were not accompanied by a single debate on provocation.[47]

There was another way the League might have become a help rather than an obstacle to Germany and the other revisionist powers without deviating from its purpose of protecting the rule of law. Article 19 of the Covenant had been incorporated in the Covenant for the very purpose of providing a kind of legislative procedure for peaceful change. But the policy of France and the Little Entente kept this article a dead letter. In theory the French disclaimed any intention to "*transformer l'histoire en un lac mort.*"

[46] He continued:

"*Nous précisions: le jour où l'Allemagne attaquerait l'Autriche, elle dirait: 'Mais la population de l'Autriche vient à moi, les bras ouverts.' Le jour où elle attaquerait la Tchécoslovaquie, elle dirait: 'Il y a en Tchécoslovaquie une majorité allemande et une minorité slovaque.' Le jour où elle attaquerait la Yougoslavie, elle dirait: 'Les Croates de Yougoslavie supportent difficilement le joug des Serbes.' Le jour où elle attaquerait la Roumanie, elle dirait: 'Il y a une puissante minorité hongroise.'*

"*Et nous ajoutions: 'C'est pourquoi il faut une formule sur laquelle aucun débat ne puisse s'ouvrir: Halte à l'agresseur quel qu'il soit et quelle que soit la victime.'*" Paul Reynaud, December 27, 1935; Chambre, *Débats*, 1935, p. 2813.

[47] The literature on international affairs which so fully expounded the doctrine of the League and the enforcement of law through League sanctions was equally silent on this question. German writers, as might be expected, paid more attention to the problem of provocation. See particularly: Heinrich Rogge, *Nationale Friedenspolitik* (1934), pp. 550 ff.; the same author's *Kollektivsicherheit, Bündnispolitik, Völkerbund* (1937), pp. 252-253; Wilhelm Steinlein, *Der Begriff des nicht herausgeforderten Angriffs in Bündnisverträgen seit 1870 und inbesondere im Locarno-Vertrag* (Frankfurter Abhandlungen zum Kriegsverhütungsrecht, Heft 5, 1927).

Modifications of frontiers, it was said in defense of the guarantee of the *status quo* contained in Article 10 of the Covenant, were to be the result of "*délibérations pacifiques sous l'égide salutaire de la Société des Nations.*" [48] Yet not only was nothing done to make the League capable of conducting such discussions with any chance of success, but when revision became a practical issue the mere suggestion of territorial changes was declared to endanger peace. "*Il est un principe,*" said Laval in 1934, "*dont chacun doit en fait reconnaître la nécessité: le maintien des frontières actuelles. Quiconque veut déplacer une borne-frontière trouble la paix de l'Europe.*" [49] Flandin went even so far as to say that "*toute revision territoriale des traités engendre toujours la guerre.*" [50] Some French statesmen of the Left, it should be added, criticized the attitude of their country. "*Nous pensons,*" said Léon Blum, "*que si les contrats ne doivent pas être déchirés par la violence, ils ne doivent pas davantage être maintenus par la contrainte quand ils s'opposent à la nécessité matérielle des choses ou quand ils contrarient l'intérêt suprême qui est celui de la paix.*" [51] To avoid "*la revision des traités par la guerre,*" said Bergery, "*c'est vous qui devez organiser une revision des traités par l'arbitrage.*" [52]

Whether, if France had been less adamant, a workable and practical procedure for "peaceful change" could have been developed is a controversial matter. On her side it must be admitted that there was dynamite in any policy that would encourage constant pressure for a change of the *status quo* and lead to a situation in which agreements between nations would be "*remis en cause à tout in-*

[48] Joseph Barthélemy, October 23, 1922; League of Nations, *Records of the Third Assembly, Plenary Meetings*, I, *Text of the Debates*, p. 214.

[49] Pierre Laval, Foreign Minister, November 30, 1934; Chambre, *Débats*, 1934, p. 2835.

[50] Pierre-Etienne Flandin, December 5, 1936; Chambre, *Débats*, 1936, p. 3359.

[51] Léon Blum, January 19, 1932; Chambre, *Débats*, 1932, p. 49.

[52] Gaston Bergery, February 23, 1932; Chambre, *Débats*, 1932, p. 753.

stant."[53] In the light of recent events, however, there would seem to have been at least as much dynamite, if not more, in a policy which branded as criminals nations seeking to change the established order by force and yet did not offer them any other means by which they could hope to redress their grievances.

Since Germany was the revisionist country *par excellence* and the League provided for action against aggression without recognizing provocation in the sense we have suggested and without making peaceful revision of treaties a real thing, the League was far more favorable to French than to German designs and worked to the advantage of powers interested in enforcing the *status quo*. But even so, a League that was directed indiscriminately against any potential aggressor was unfitted to meet French requirements either. The difficulty lay in making it a reliable instrument of security against one specific country. The French may not have been fully aware of this deficiency. It must, however, have been evident that Germany was not the only country which might some day be tempted to resort to force rather than submit to the maintenance of the established order. There was much dissatisfaction in Hungary, in the Balkans, and, as the Chaco War showed, in parts of Latin America. Intervention in conflicts between these smaller states was, however, not likely to cause France any embarrassment since it would not be necessary to apply the entire machinery of enforcement in such cases. The mere threat of sanctions, or even of moral pressure, would prove sufficient to forestall the outbreak of violence. The success which the League could hope to have in such instances might help to increase its prestige without diverting it unduly from its main purpose. The situation would be entirely different if ever a great power other than Germany should commit an act to which the general rules on aggression and sanctions

[53] Aristide Briand, Foreign Minister, June 12, 1930; Chambre, *Débats*, 1930, p. 2463.

would apply. If the League should then decide to go into action, France and her allies might be threatened in two different ways. First, the League and its members might become engaged in a campaign of such magnitude that the strength and freedom required to hold Germany in check might no longer be available; and, second, League action, if directed against a potential friend or ally of France, might destroy or weaken an essential part of her system of defenses.

The first time that such a danger arose was in 1931, when Japan invaded Manchuria. Fortunately for France, Britain was as reluctant as she herself to set the machinery of sanctions in motion against Japan. The "Manchurian incident," much to the despair of the "sanctionist" school of thought, was treated as a special case, to which the provisions for League sanctions did not apply. The Far East was said to be too remote for League action. It had also to be remembered that some of the great powers in the Pacific were not members of the League. The situation was exceptional, too, because of Japan's special rights in Manchuria. Whether these arguments were valid or not, the prestige of the League suffered greatly by its inaction. League-minded public opinion in the Anglo-Saxon and neutral countries was shocked and disheartened. While, therefore, the French could take satisfaction in the fact that the "coalition" had not been diverted from its primary purpose, they must also have realized that the effectiveness of the instrument which they were trying to forge was lessened by its loss of prestige.

Worse was yet to come. In 1935, Italy, another of the Great Powers, set out to revise the map of Africa and did not hesitate to give her conquest of Ethiopia the form of a war of undisguised aggression. Britain took the lead, followed by the vast majority of the members of the League, in demanding that Italy be voted an aggressor and be subjected to League sanctions. France had no choice as far as the vote on aggression was concerned. The case against Italy was too obvious. When, however, it came to the kind of sanctions to be employed and the vigor with which they were to be applied she faced a perplexing dilemma. There was apparently no way out of it that did not spell catastrophe for the entire French League policy.

France had a choice among three courses. The first and the one most in line with her obligations under the Covenant called for insistence on all the means of enforcement necessary to stop Mussolini and to save or restore the territorial integrity and independence of Ethiopia. Such a policy would have had the advantage of raising the League's prestige to great heights and would, as some suggested, have enabled France to rehearse the operation of the "great coalition." On the other hand, it would have had a disastrous effect on the "special accord" with Italy. After having just acquired promises of Italian assistance against Germany, the French had no desire to antagonize Mussolini or to take part in punitive actions which, if effective, might produce a major conflagration in the Mediterranean. This would provide Germany with a unique opportunity to regain her full freedom of action. It has been contended, it is true, that Germany might have been too profoundly impressed by such vigorous action of the League to risk any undertaking which would put her in the position of Italy and make her the next victim of League sanctions. This does not necessarily follow. If the League should prove itself capable of stopping or defeating Italy, it was not certain that it would be possible simultaneously or very shortly afterwards to undertake another vast sanctionist campaign. In any case, Germany would have had ample opportunity to render herself much less susceptible to outside pressure before the League was ready to act a second time. As it was, the diversion caused by League sanctions against Italy was sufficient to give Germany an excellent political opportunity for her *coup* in the Rhineland.

Incidentally, on this occasion an absurdity became apparent, which was inevitable if the League was to be expected to operate simultaneously against different "aggressors" carrying on independent campaigns. While the League powers were trying to defeat Italy in Africa, they needed her co-operation in defending the Locarno Pact on the Rhine. But as Grandi put it, the states which had taken sanctions against Italy "cannot expect my country to apply measures which would be incompatible with the position in which these same States have placed Italy." He pointed out the "contradiction which exists between the position of a country subjected to sanctions and the duties of a guarantor Power . . ."[54] However, no sanctions against Germany were considered, so that no acute problem arose in this particular case.

France did not choose the first course of action. Some French statesmen on the Left, to be sure, advocated rigid sanctions, even at the risk of war with Italy. Can France, exclaimed Herriot, "*répudier sa thèse constante,*"[55] by which he meant her insistence on the necessity of sanctions as a basis of the League and of security. Laval's government, however, did everything it could to preserve the newly acquired friendship with Italy. That accord seemed more important than the League. French action under Article 16 was at best half-hearted, and called forth none of the enthusiasm which might have been expected if the vigorous French support of sanctions at Geneva had come from a genuine desire to suppress all aggression, instead of German aggression exclusively. Pezet expressed French regret at having had to "*expérimenter le système des sanctions à l'égard d'un pays ami et allié.*"[56]

France might have chosen a second course, diametrically op-

[54] Dino Grandi, Italian Ambassador in London, League of Nations Council, March 18, 1936; *Official Journal*, XVII (April, 1936, Part 1), p. 328.

[55] Edouard Herriot, January 30, 1936; Chambre, *Débats*, 1936, p. 143.

[56] Ernest Pezet, June 23, 1936; Chambre, *Débats*, 1936, p. 1539.

posed to the first, by refusing to participate in sanctions altogether. Such a refusal on the part of France would have assured her the continued friendship of Italy. Indeed, this was the only way to preserve unbroken Italy's promises of military assistance against Germany. But, at the same time, such a course would have antagonized another French ally, Great Britain, and would have dealt a death-blow to the League. The Rightists would hardly have cared about the dissolution of the League; but nobody in France was willing to sacrifice the friendship and probable future assistance of Britain for the sake of cordial relations with Italy. Also it was not very sound policy to set out on a course which would destroy the League, when there was still some hope that some day it might help France in dealing with Germany. It was desirable to preserve, as far as possible, both the League and friendship with Italy. Therefore, no one in a responsible position proposed that France take the second course and refuse to participate in sanctions.

There remained a third and last course, and it was this that the Laval government undertook to follow. It was a compromise between the two extremes already discussed; but, instead of insuring the advantages which either of the two others would have offered, it combined the unfortunate consequences of both. France participated in sanctions but was largely, if not solely, responsible for their half-hearted application. She hoped by her compromise tactics to satisfy Britain, to keep the League intact, and yet to save her friendship with Italy. "*Je devais maintenir intacte notre collaboration amicale avec la Grande-Bretagne,*" Laval explained, "*marquer la fidélité de la France au pacte de la Société des nations, tout en sauvegardant les liens d'amitié avec l'Italie que j'avais moi-même scellés à Rome le 7 janvier dernier.*" [57] Actually, both the League

[57] Pierre Laval, President of the Council of Ministers, radio broadcast, November 27, 1935; *Le Temps*, November 28, 1935, p. 3.

as an instrument of sanctions and the friendship with Italy, two important links in the French system of defenses, were lost in consequence of this policy. Germany, at the same time, strengthened her power enormously by remilitarizing and fortifying the Rhineland, and reversed the military balance of power on the Continent.

Unsatisfactory as the conclusion may seem, there was no other outcome possible for France. The paradox which confronted her was of a fundamental nature. To set up a League against aggression in general proved to be incompatible with creating a "potential war coalition" against a particular country. To pursue the latter policy meant to let aggression by other countries go unpunished and thereby to discredit the universal purpose of the League. The resulting loss of prestige and loyalty was so great as to make the League incapable of effective action even in the particular case for which it was being reserved. If, on the other hand, League sanctions were applied indiscriminately against any great power guilty of aggression, the consequence would be to split the "coalition," perhaps at a crucial moment.

It has been argued that the French League policy was vindicated when Britain set out to organize the "Stop Hitler front" in 1939. This is not exact. What Britain did come to accept after years of resistance to French views was the plan of building up a "potential war coalition" with which to deter or if necessary to defeat Hitler, in case he should attack any one of Germany's neighbors. But the "peace front," since it was openly directed against Germany, suffered from none of the ambiguities which had beset the French attempts to make the League serve exclusively as an instrument of defense against the German menace.

The Reliability of Commitments under the Covenant

Even if the League could have been successfully reserved to stop only German aggression, France would still have had reason to be troubled. Would pledges which were expressed in so general and universal a treaty as the Covenant prove reliable when assistance was actually needed? Many of the members of the League, such as the small neutral countries, would obviously never have agreed to pledge any assistance specifically to France or to one of her allies in Central Europe. Great Britain, even after having become a member of the League, resisted every attempt which was made to draw her into anything approximating an automatic commitment in the East, and refused consistently to make any specific pledges to countries in the integrity of which she was not vitally interested. At Locarno she drew a line between her readiness to assist France in the West and her attitude toward countries in the East. It would seem, therefore, that France and her friends were counting on obtaining these pledges through the back door of the League, apparently expecting that nations which would not have been willing to promise assistance to France or her small allies directly would be willing to assist them under the Covenant if they became "victims of aggression." This expectation was justified only if we accept the premise that the establishment of the League introduced a new element into the international situation which would induce countries to go further in their willingness to assist others than they would have been ready to do had they not been members of the League. In terms of the doctrine of "collective security," which we shall discuss later, the question was whether France could count on a new solidarity between nations, and on a new devotion to the enforcement of the law which would prompt countries to participate in League action against any violator of the Covenant.[58]

The French were inclined to be skeptical about all pledges, whatever the nature of the instrument into which they were incorporated. This accounted for what has been called France's "pactomania." Her skepticism, curiously enough, led her to seek pact after pact, promise after promise, as if a multiplicity of repetitious pledges would assure her of the much-desired security. Léon Blum criticized *"cette recherche des moyens de sécurité nouveaux, qui paraîtront insuffisants à leur tour,"* and said:

"Depuis quelques années, une course à la sécurité s'est substituée à la course aux armements. On veut, sans cesse, entre les nations des instruments nouveaux. On ne les trouve jamais assez précis, assez formels, assez astreignants.

"Savez-vous à quoi on aboutit par cette recherche des instruments nouveaux? On vide petit à petit de leur contenu et de leur valeur les instruments qui existent." [59]

The Rightists reserved particular scorn for promises of assistance given in such general treaties as the League Covenant. This was a natural outgrowth of their entire philosophy of international affairs. They took the "realistic" view that the nations of the world had not changed their traditional course of policy after the World War, but were still conducting their affairs according to what they regarded as their national interests. If they still had the same national interests, as the Rightists believed they did, they would refuse to participate in any hostile action against other countries, whether it took the form of war or sanctions, unless their traditional "vital interests" were at stake. At the same time, they could

[58] For criticism of any such expectations see James M. Spaight, *Pseudo-Security* (1928). Speaking of assistance in the air, he says, "The certainty and promptness of mutual assistance . . . must always be conditioned first by vicinage, secondly, by solidarity of vital interests" (p. 161).

[59] Léon Blum, October 28, 1932; Chambre, *Débats*, 1932, p. 2909.

be counted upon to participate in any conflict which did affect their vital interests, whether or not they were obligated under the League Covenant.

The Rightists did not necessarily expect other countries openly to violate the obligations which they had incurred under the Covenant. The pledges given in a general treaty were vague enough to permit of a diversity of evasive legal interpretations. Experience with the League certainly justified this high opinion of the art of interpretation. France herself, being interested in reserving the League for a particular case in which she was vitally interested, resorted to this kind of legal strategy whenever there was any serious question of the application of League sanctions against a country other than Germany. This was evident in the Polish-Soviet War of 1920, the Corfu incident, the Manchurian invasion, and the Chaco dispute, no less than in the Italo-Ethiopian War.[60]

[60] Defending the League's failure to take an active part in stopping the war between Poland and Soviet Russia, Léon Bourgeois explained to the First Assembly, December 4, 1920, that "*le monde entier comprenait qu'il ne pourrait demander à la Société des Nations d'intervenir s'il était démontré que cette intervention serait non seulement inefficace, mais peut-être dangereuse.*" League of Nations, *Records of the First Assembly, Plenary Meetings*, p. 267.

Three years later, Henry de Jouvenel, who had been one of the French delegates to the Assembly during the Corfu crisis, explained in *Le Matin*, October 1, 1923, that there were delegations which had suggested the application of sanctions against Italy, "*et par là d'éterniser et d'étendre aux limites de l'univers un trouble local,*" but that, "*la France ne partageait pas cet enthousiasme guerrier. . . . Entre le prestige de la Société des Nations et l'intérêt de la paix,*" he added, "*pas d'hésitation possible: la paix d'abord!*" *Société des Nations*, V (1923), p. 855. M. de Jouvenel's fellow delegate, Gabriel Hanotaux, justified in the *Journal des Débats*, October 1, 1923, the attitude taken by the League: "*On ne saurait trop insister sur ce rôle de conciliation qui doit être bien compris si l'on veut arriver à la notion claire de ce que l'on peut faire à et par la Société des Nations.*" *Ibid.*, p. 853.

Addressing the Special Assembly on the Manchurian dispute, March 3, 1932, M. Paul-Boncour emphasized that "we have meticulously performed our duty, and have avoided allowing a precedent to be created which would have seriously hampered the League's future action." League of Nations, *Official Journal, Special*

Before considering the opposite view, taken by the supporters of the League in France, it might be pointed out that France herself was operating very definitely on the traditional principle of the vital national interest, since, as we have just pointed out, she was never desirous of having the League take action under Article 16 except against Germany. Her plan of incorporating the League as an international guarantee into her system of defenses was based on the assumption that the interests of the League were identical with French national interests. While, therefore, other countries might be faced with a conflict between their traditional

Supplement, No. 101, p. 22. On December 7 of the same year, he told the Special Assembly that it would be wrong to infer "that the League would display the same slowness and, to a certain extent, the same powerlessness if similar events were ever to occur in Europe." Unfortunately, in the Manchurian case there existed "a whole host of complexities such as could not be matched in any other part of the globe." *Ibid.*, No. 111, p. 48.

The same arguments regarding special circumstances and the desire to avoid creating precedents for future inaction were repeated in the Chaco case when M. Massigli told the Advisory Committee, March 12, 1935, that they "must not accumulate precedents to justify subsequent weakness," and that a "particular consideration" which might be sound in the Chaco case should "not lead to the enunciation of general principles which, if regarded as expressing the general universal truth of the Covenant, would so far undermine it as to destroy its efficacy." *Ibid.*, No. 134, p. 18.

During the application of sanctions against Italy, M. Franklin-Bouillon frankly asked of the Chamber of Deputies, January 30, 1936, "*Cet article 10, base de toute politique de sécurité collective, qui a songé à l'appliquer, qui a voulu l'appliquer dans les affaires allemandes?*" And, answering this question in the negative, he recommended "*moins d'enthousiasme pour les sanctions contre l'Italie, puisque vous n'avez pas le courage de les appliquer contre l'Allemagne.*" Chambre, *Débats*, 1936, p. 141. One of France's main reasons to regret having had to apply sanctions against Italy was well expressed by M. Flandin, who had been Foreign Minister during the later part of the Ethiopian crisis; addressing the Chamber of Deputies, February 26, 1938, he spoke of the development of forces "*pour obliger la France*" to apply Article 16 "*qui restait, pour elle, la garantie suprême, en cas de guerre européenne.*" And yet it was known in advance, said M. Flandin, "*qu'il serait inefficace, qu'il ne ramènerait pas la paix*" and that the only result would be "*de compromettre, pour l'avenir, le fonctionnement même du pacte de la Société des Nations.*" Chambre, *Débats*, 1938, p. 641.

policies and their new obligations under the Covenant, France never imagined that such a dilemma might arise for her.

Was there any foundation for the belief that loyalty to the League would provide France with additional support from other countries in case of a conflict in which Germany was violating the Covenant? Had other countries come to regard the defense of the Covenant as a new vital interest? For a time this did seem to be true as far as the small neutral countries in Europe were concerned. When Japan invaded Manchuria in 1931 they took a vigorous lead, quite unusual for countries of their size and power, in insisting that the League should take collective action. But after all, the small neutral countries had little or nothing to fear from League sanctions against Japan. Economic sanctions put little burden on them, since their economic relations with Japan were insignificant. It was moreover obvious that they would not have to fight if sanctions should lead to military action. At the same time, they had everything to gain by inducing the great powers to defend the integrity of a weak country and so to create a precedent which would tend to strengthen their own security. It was national interest which required them in this case to promote League sanctions.

The only other case in which a country vigorously urged the League to apply sanctions was during the Ethiopian War. Britain then insisted that they should be applied. This, however, was an exceptional interlude in the course of Britain's post-war policy, as will be shown later, and even in this case the British Government was lukewarm, to say the least.[61] But a majority of the British public was ready to have the country participate in any economic action by the League which might prove necessary to check Mussolini, although this same majority did not regard the integrity and independence of Ethiopia as a vital British interest in the tradi-

[61] See below, pp. 355 ff.

tional sense of the word. It was the enforcement of the League Covenant that was demanded. Under certain circumstances, therefore, the French could count on public opinion in Great Britain. It might force the government to assist countries to which no British pledge of assistance except that in the Covenant could have been given without violent opposition. It can easily be understood why the French Leftists hoped so fervently for the rise in power of the Leftist group in Britain which favored collective security and which in this particular case was demanding League sanctions against Italy.

However, from a remark by Lloyd George, as ardent a supporter of vigorous sanctions against Italy as could be found at the time, it may be seen that the French Leftists had little reason for their faith in British support, even from the exponents of collective security, much as that group seemed superficially to be in accord with French wishes. During a debate which took place in 1936, Lloyd George made the surprising statement that the British people would "never go to war again for an Austrian quarrel."[62] For once he was expressing more than a mere personal opinion and had revealed a fundamental difference between the views of France and the French supporters of the League on the one hand and those of the League-minded groups in Great Britain on the other. While both were in favor of sanctions and both regarded the League as an instrument for the enforcement of peace, they differed in defining the situations which required League action.

The British Leftists, whose views will be discussed in detail later,[63] had, after some hesitation, become willing to fight for the League. They adhered to the teachings of what one might call "Wilson-

[62] June 18, 1936; Great Britain, House of Commons, *Parliamentary Debates*, Vol. 313, col. 1226. See also the statement made by Hugh Dalton after the German reoccupation of the Rhineland, below, p. 340.

[63] See below, pp. 331 ff.

ian idealism"; their attitude had also been influenced by the French emphasis on the need for sanctions. The British public, it was often affirmed, had come to regard the enforcement of the "rule of law" as a primary interest for their country; but this is somewhat misleading. It has a formalistic and legalistic sound, and seems to imply that the British wanted to preserve all of the existing law and treaties, whether good or bad, just or unjust, negotiated or dictated. "Wilsonian idealism," however, was no legalistic matter. At the same time that it demanded international solidarity and a willingness to make sacrifices to the community wherever threatened by unlawful aggression, it promised justice to all nations and a new international order in which the right of self-determination and equality for all would be guaranteed. This strikes an ethical rather than a legalistic note. Sanctions were to be applied against an "evil-doer." Before supporting League action against any country, the exponents of collective security would therefore wish to make sure that the League was fighting a good cause and not, perhaps, defending treaties that were unjust or law that needed revision. This, of course, explains Lloyd George's statement. League-minded British public opinion had condemned the separation of Austria from Germany as unjust and contrary to the principle of self-determination. It is quite likely, therefore, that they would have refused to fight for the maintenance of Austrian independence. The fact that this independence was established by law and that Britain was legally bound to participate in League sanctions if Germany used force was of secondary importance. The same was true, at least for a large section of British public opinion, in the days of the dispute over the Sudetenland and did much to strengthen the hands of a government which did not desire to take action.

It follows then that France had little basis for her hopes that the League Covenant would provide her with additional support against Germany. She would either have to deal with Conservative governments in other countries, which would only too readily evade their pledges by means of clever legal interpretations whenever the conflict appeared to them not to fall within the vital interests of their country; or she would be dealing with Liberal or Socialist governments, on whose devotion to the League she could count, but which would question the justice of the law she might wish to enforce. She would discover to her dismay that in the very cases most important to her (the territorial integrity of her Central European allies, Austrian independence, and the maintenance of the demilitarized zone on the Rhine) they would deny that the treaties deserved to be enforced, and would refuse to commit their countries to what appeared to them to be the prolongation of a regrettable *status quo*. The "Wilsonian principles" called for international solidarity and League sanctions in defense of victims of aggression, but they did not help a country seeking to preserve settlements which in so many respects violated the very principles of justice which Wilson had proclaimed.

From France's dilemma may be drawn a general conclusion. Even if for some reason the feeling of solidarity among nations should grow to the point where the nations would be willing in principle to participate in collective action against any "aggressor," no nation even then could rely on the assistance of the League unless it could convince the other members of the justice of its cause. The effectiveness of the League as an instrument of coercion would, therefore, depend not only on the existence of an adequate sense of solidarity among its members, but also on the justice of the law which was to be enforced. Since every law has to undergo change if it is to remain just, "revision" would be the *conditio sine qua non* of collective enforcement. While a League providing effectively for the redress of grievances and changes of the law may be imaginable only in a Utopia, it nevertheless serves as a standard against which to measure the Geneva League.

PART TWO: BRITAIN

XI. Peace and Economic Recovery

IN recent years Britain and France have been able to bring their policies into such close accord that their co-operation has come to be looked upon as the most stable element in the political structure of Europe. However, this was far from true for most of the period after 1919. For nearly twenty years the outlook of France and Britain on European affairs, their aims, their interests, and their policies differed fundamentally. The conflict was not always visible, either because compromises were reached, often at the expense of a third power, or because one country, in order to gain some support which it needed, submitted to the will of the other. Britain's coolness or resistance to the desires of France helped to defeat French policy, while France at the same time blocked the path of Great Britain. Neither of the two countries was able to pursue unhampered the course it laid out for itself.

There must have been important reasons why the two great European victors and wartime allies left the Versailles Conference with such divergent views on the future. It is evident that geographic position played a very important role. This can be seen from the fact that once Germany was equipped with an air fleet large enough to rob Britain of the protection of the North Sea, her outlook began to merge with that of France. Differences of imperial and economic interests, as well as peculiarities of their respective national characters, national traditions, and doctrines, affected the views and policies of the two nations. Even when they were not the deciding factors in the difference of objective or of method, they were a source of mutual misunderstanding.

Both countries wished to retain the benefits which had accrued to them by the fact of victory. Both were "saturated countries." There was not likely to be any incentive in the near future for either of them to seek new territory or new rights and privileges beyond those with which the post-war settlements had provided them. They felt themselves to be "have countries," whose duty it was, according to Curzon, "to keep what we have obtained, sometimes almost against our will; . . ."[1] But this is about as far as the parallel goes. Although Britain fulfilled the requirements for a satisfied country better than France, who was continually demanding new assurances of security, it would be misleading to list her under the category of "*status quo* powers," of which France was the leader. If this classification applies to countries that intend to see as much as possible of the established order and existing treaty structure maintained without change, it does not describe the British position. One of the most firmly established elements in Britain's carefully guarded set of traditions was an inclination to regard every settlement as a temporary solution that would probably have to be changed in due time. This was the British attitude not merely in regard to the "dictated" settlements of 1919 but also toward other treaties and arrangements. It was, however, particularly true in respect to the Versailles Treaty and the other immediate post-war settlements in Europe. Fabre-Luce expressed the French reaction to this attitude of Britain when he said that she had been revisionist from the moment the Treaty of Versailles was signed.[2]

[1] ". . . not to seize anything else, to reconcile, not defy; to pacify, not to conquer." Earl Curzon, Foreign Secretary, statement to representatives of the United Kingdom, the Dominions, and India, June 22, 1921; Earl of Ronaldshay, *The Life of Lord Curzon* (1928), III, p. 225.

[2] Alfred Fabre-Luce, *La Crise des Alliances: essai sur les relations franco-britanniques depuis la signature de la paix (1919-1922)*, (1922), pp. 16 ff.

It is easy to see that conflicts would be inevitable between two countries when one regarded the permanent enforcement of the treaty as a minimum requirement for its security, while the other, for reasons of its own particular interest, which will be discussed later, looked at the same settlement as a temporary solution which would soon have to come up for reconsideration and readjustment.

The contrast between the British and French outlook goes further than that. The French were obsessed by the fear of a new war with Germany and therefore started out with a feeling of insecurity. They could not overlook the possibility of war in the future. Peace to them could be only the reward of an effective preparation for war. On this they desired the governments of the victorious countries to concentrate. Not so the British: security as far as Britain was concerned had been attained. A new war in Western Europe lay in too remote a future to be of any practical concern to her. The problem which worried her was how to "wipe out the past,"[3] that is, to "dissipate the surviving atmosphere of war,"[4] so as "to create a new temper in Europe"[5] and restore peace, normalcy, and economic stability. The British were pursuing a program of organizing peace in an even more literal sense than the French. While the French "*organisation de la paix*" was in reality a plan for organizing a potential war coalition, the British were seeking co-operation for the needs of a peacetime world and for the establishment on the Continent of a peaceful state of mind that would be conducive to normal economic activity.

[3] Earl Curzon, Foreign Secretary, statement to representatives of the United Kingdom, the Dominions, and India, June 22, 1921; Earl of Ronaldshay, *op. cit.*, III, p. 226.

[4] J. Ramsay MacDonald, Prime Minister, July 12, 1932; Great Britain, House of Commons, Official Report, *Parliamentary Debates*, Fifth Series, Vol. 268, col. 1146; hereinafter cited H. of C., *Parl. Deb.*

[5] H. A. L. Fisher, League of Nations Assembly, September 26, 1922; *Records of the Third Assembly, Plenary Meetings*, I, *Text of the Debates*, p. 260.

The lack of any feeling of insecurity on the part of the British may have been due to wishful thinking, to a tendency toward undue optimism, or to an inherent insularity, which made it difficult for them to grasp the depth of dissension existing in Europe. Certainly they did not awaken to the menace in the European situation until long after it had become quite obvious to observers on the Continent. The British Government at the start based its military plans "on the assumption that no great war was to be anticipated within the next ten years." [6] This it regarded as a broad margin of safety. Peculiarities of national character may have had something to do with the British belief that it was unnecessary to look ahead more than ten years, while the French were already wondering in 1919 what would happen after the evacuation of the Rhineland, scheduled for 1935. It is not without humor that the British in 1922 should have offered France a promise of military assistance for a period of only ten years when they were convinced that there would be no great war within that period.

In appreciating Britain's general attitude it is pertinent to remember that the post-war settlements actually left the British Isles as safe from attack and the communications connecting the parts of her Empire as secure as Britain could ever have hoped. None of the existing great powers or empires of the world is by nature more vulnerable than the British, with its long sea routes and the dependency of the homeland on uninterrupted imports. None, too, is in a sense more artificial, in that its security depends on its ability to curb the imperialistic designs of all of the other great powers. The British "life-line," stretching from the British Isles through the Mediterranean, the Indian Ocean to Singapore, and north to Hongkong, or even possibly to Shanghai, is safe only if Japan's ambitions are stopped north of the Yangtze, if Russia

[6] Great Britain, Committee on National Expenditure, *First Interim Report of Committee on National Expenditure* (1922), Cmd. 1581.

is barred from expansion into the Mediterranean, the Near East, and the Persian Gulf, and if Germany relinquishes all dreams of colonial or maritime empire and expansion into the Near East. It is necessary also that Italy be kept under control and that French aspirations in the Mediterranean and in the Near East be brought into close harmony with those of Britain. As a result of the World War the two most powerful rivals, the Soviet Union and Germany, were thrown back from the "life-line." Japan had, it is true, strengthened her position, but was as usual regarded with little apprehension by the British. Russia had eliminated herself by her internal upheaval. Germany was defeated, deprived of her colonies and of so much of her naval strength as to be powerless against Britain. She was completely stripped of military aircraft. Italy, of course, remained stationed on Britain's sea route to the East, but she was not at the time a world power and was counted upon to remain within the orbit of British influence. Thus with the exception of the United States, who was not located on the life-line, France was the only Great Power still in a position to oppose Britain and interfere with her vital interests if she so chose. This accounts for the critical nature of the Franco-British struggle in the Near East and in Europe in the early post-war years.[7] But Britain's security was not threatened. However much France might embarrass Britain and defeat her purposes, it would have been ridiculous to consider her a menace to British safety.

Although Britain for over a dozen years after 1919 therefore felt completely safe as far as any external attack on the British Isles or the Empire was concerned, she did not on that account retire into isolation and indifference toward the problems of Europe. All of her statesmen were emphatic in declaring that Britain needed to have peace established and perpetuated everywhere in

[7] See Henry H. Cumming, *Franco-British Rivalry in the Post-War Near East* (1938).

the world. "Our stake as a nation in peace," said Eden, "is probably greater than that of any other nation in the world." [8] According to the White Paper on Defence of 1935, "The first and strongest defence of the peoples, territories, cities, overseas trade and communications of the British Empire is provided by the maintenance of peace." [9] Certainly England's economic recovery was tied up with that of the whole world. The chances of becoming dangerously entangled in quarrels in any part of the globe were greater for the British Empire than for any other single country. The maintenance of the security which she was enjoying depended on continued general peace. The *pax Britannica* was not peace for Europe's sake or for the sake of the world, but a national British interest. Nevertheless, it did place Britain in the position of a peace-maker. Britain was, therefore, still "better placed than other nations," said Eden, "by the fact of that spirit of comparative detachment, which survived from the days of our isolation, to contribute to a pacification which was as much in our interest as in that of any nation upon the Continent of Europe." [10] Time after time the British repeated Lord Beaconsfield's parting words as Prime Minister in 1879: "So long as the power and advice of England are felt in the councils of Europe, peace, I believe, will be maintained, and maintained for a long period." [11]

There were two aspects of British peace strategy during the postwar era which might have been expected to find enthusiastic support in other countries, namely, her effort to foster world-wide

[8] Anthony Eden, Lord Privy Seal, March 14, 1934; H. of C., *Parl. Deb.*, Vol. 287, col. 390.

[9] *Cmd. 4827*, p. 2.

[10] Anthony Eden, Lord Privy Seal, speech in Swindon, March 7, 1935; *The Times* (London), March 8, 1935, p. 9.

[11] Quoted, for example, by Earl Stanhope, Foreign Under-Secretary, April 8, 1936; Great Britain, House of Lords, Official Report, *Parliamentary Debates*, Fifth Series, Vol. 100, col. 585; hereinafter cited H. of L., *Parl. Deb.*

economic recovery and prosperity, and her attempt to promote pacification, that is, to create a "peace psychology" among other nations. But while theoretically it was beneficial to all that a country with the power and influence of Great Britain should regard universal peace and recovery as her primary interests, the ways and the means by which she sought to attain this goal became in fact a source of much trouble between her and the Continental Powers.

We do not intend to deal in detail with the specific aspects of Britain's economic policy, which covered widely diversified matters and included efforts to scale down reparations and debts, to finance the defeated nations in need of working capital, to re-introduce the gold standard, to stabilize currencies, to re-open markets and to restore the confidence of the business man. In the days of the Dawes and Young Plans, when Britain's economic policy was strongly backed by the United States, it was frequently announced that the Anglo-Saxon countries were lifting the problem of reparation out of the political into the purely economic field. As a matter of fact, this demand for a purely economic approach was in itself a highly political measure, and one which was bound to lead to conflict with France. The "business-like deals" by their very nature favored the Germans. It was "business-like" to treat an opponent as an equal, unbusiness-like to use reparations as an instrument to protect one's security. It was to the interest of business men and private creditors to scale down reparations, to protect the stability of the German currency, to avoid political crises, and to prevent the execution of the treaty from retarding the return of good will and economic initiative. Every shift to economics, therefore, was accompanied by concessions to Germany and was essentially a victory for Anglo-Saxon over French peace strategy.

After the rise of German power on the Continent, a similar conflict developed between Great Britain and Germany. Then it was the Germans who accused the British of trying to evade political or territoral changes by suggesting merely economic settlements. Thus, for instance, agreements on raw materials or freer trade were advocated by Britain instead of a transfer of colonial mandates or colonies. Eden, in defining the policy of the British "in respect to the transference of territories at present held by them under Mandate," said that "they would, for their part, be entirely ready to discuss such problems as wider guarantees for access to Colonial raw materials and obstacles in the path of such access," but that, "the question of any transfer of Mandated Territories would inevitably raise grave difficulties, moral, political and legal, of which His Majesty's Government must frankly say that they have been unable to find any solution." [12]

It was unfair, however, to accuse the British of sacrificing everything to their base materialistic desire for economic profits and advantages.[13] A government that wanted to return to normalcy was quite naturally preoccupied with problems of economic policy and regarded it as a basic duty to promote reconstruction of the sadly shattered economic structure of Britain and of Europe. It was not because of any greater idealism that countries on the Continent, still harassed by the fear of war or driven by a desire to recover

[12] Anthony Eden, Foreign Secretary, July 27, 1936; H. of C., *Parl. Deb.*, Vol. 315, col. 1132.

Discussing the problems raised by Italy's colonial demands in Ethiopia, Sir Samuel Hoare, Foreign Secretary, told the League of Nations Assembly, September 11, 1935, that the problem of the distribution of the world's economic resources and raw materials "is economic rather than political and territorial" and that Britain would "be ready to take [her] share in an investigation of these matters." *Records of the Sixteenth Ordinary Session of the Assembly, Plenary Meetings, Text of the Debates*, p. 45.

[13] Declaring that the campaign for the revision of treaties resulted from a "*thèse d'origine anglo-saxonne, mâtinée d'infiltrations allemandes,*" Tardieu defined this hostile "*thèse*" as holding that "*les phénomènes économiques dominent le monde et le maîtrisent, et qu'ils doivent dominer et maîtriser les phénomènes politiques, les phénomènes de l'ordre moral, les phénomènes le l'ordre psychologique et de l'ordre national.*" May 23, 1922; Chambre, *Débats*, pp. 1540, 1541.

territory, power, honor, and prestige, continued to stress questions of a political or military nature. The British have themselves to blame, however, if their motives were misrepresented. Many of their statesmen did declare that Britain's main concern was trade and that she wanted peace for the sake of the economic advantages which it would offer her. "The interests of the British Empire in foreign countries," said Baldwin, "are first of all economic and commercial. When we speak of peace being the greatest British interest, we mean that British trade and commerce, which are essential to the life of our people, flourish best in conditions of peace"; [14] and MacDonald explained, "One of the reasons why we go to Geneva again and again for the purpose of getting agreements, getting tranquillity, getting international confidence upon which we can base a fabric of peace, is that we want security and stability for the working classes and for the economic interest of this country." [15] It would have been equally true and more acceptable to others if the British had said that they hoped that restoration of economic welfare would serve to appease war-minded nations and thus to benefit the cause of peace. It is certainly amazing that the British, even when dealing with Hitler, so frequently put faith in the ability of some purely economic arrangement or settlement to satisfy nations or to divert their attention from political or territorial aspirations unwelcome to Great Britain.

The second significant objective of British policy, pacification and appeasement, met with even greater obstacles. It may well be wondered whether the British ever realized what they were undertaking when they resolved to rid Europe, then under the yoke of the Versailles Treaty, of what seemed to them an outdated war

[14] Stanley Baldwin, Prime Minister, speech in London, November 9, 1923; *The Times* (London), November 10, 1923, p. 7.

[15] J. Ramsay MacDonald, Prime Minister, November 20, 1934; H. of C., *Parl. Deb.*, Vol. 295, col. 25.

psychosis. In the face of a situation in which age-old quarrels were still alive and new ones had been born, Britain had to cope with uncontrollable fear on one side, with the passions of resentment and dissatisfaction on the other. Every step she took to allay fear by giving more security to the *status quo* powers incensed the dissatisfied nations. And whenever she encouraged or made concessions to the revisionist countries with a view to making them more content, she increased the fear of the others, who were convinced that any surrender would result only in greater appetites and, at the same time, in more power with which to satisfy them.

The British probably found it hard to understand why they met with so much resistance and antagonism in both camps when, as Baldwin said, so many British statesmen believed "that by exhibiting a spirit of sweet reasonableness we could bend the whole of Europe to our will." [16] The French were skeptical, if not hostile, to the proposals for a psychological treatment of the Germans on British lines. They correctly foresaw that the result would be to strengthen Germany and to give her the power to carry her revolt to success if she were not appeased. Later it was the Germans who became impatient and, instead of becoming satisfied when the British believed them to have been granted enough concessions, they followed up every success by the presentation of new and greater demands. Certainly nobody should have expected passion-ridden Europe to be "reasonable." Distrust and fear, resentment and pride, nationalism and ambition for power, all were too deeply rooted. Any advantage for one country on the Rhine was bound to be gained at the expense of the other. However sincerely Britain may have tried to act as a disinterested mediator, it would have required superhuman skill to avoid eventually antagonizing both parties.

[16] Stanley Baldwin, Prime Minister, February 13, 1924; H. of C., *Parl. Deb.*, Vol. 169, cols. 848-849.

As a matter of fact Britain was not as disinterested politically as the terms "economic recovery" and "pacification" seem to suggest. She had made the quieting of unrest and economic upheaval in Europe the guiding principle of her continental policy, and therefore regarded it as her right and duty to bring about the political conditions which according to her view seemed best suited for that purpose. Happily for her, and not too surprisingly, this line of action was found to coincide with British traditions and certain well-defined national interests of a political nature. The details will be treated in the later discussion of British policy toward France and Germany. In general it can be stated that desire for pacification and economic restoration added new impetus to Britain's traditional desire for a balance of power in Western Europe. Would not the preponderance of any country on the Continent create fear and resentment and thus become an obstacle to pacification? How could prosperity return to the world if some nations were strong enough to strangle the political and economic life of the others? Every approach to a better balance of power between the warring factions on the Continent would serve to strengthen Britain's influence toward peace. While Britain therefore was interested in promoting a better balance of power, and France was trying on the contrary to maintain the superiority of the *status quo* powers, both regarded their objectives and the national interests of their respective countries as identical with those of Europe as a whole.

XII. Redress of Legitimate Grievances

FOR France, as we have seen, the post-war settlements represented the new and sacred law of Europe, on the complete and permanent enforcement of which she assumed that her security, as well as that of her continental allies, depended. Britain, on the other hand, as Lord Curzon stated as early as 1919, refused to regard the treaty as "sacrosanct." [1] Her statesmen repeatedly assured the public that they did not intend "to stamp the new territorial settlement as sacred and unalterable for all time." [2] Lord Curzon may have taken a more radical stand than many of his colleagues and successors. It remains significant, nevertheless, that, speaking in his capacity of British Foreign Minister only the month after the Versailles Treaty was signed, he should have declared that the "decisions arrived at in Paris will in many cases be hasty and provisional, but must in some cases be wrong," and should have concluded by saying that not only revision but "drastic alteration" might prove necessary in some cases.[3] Mr. Clynes went further when, in July, 1919, he welcomed the League of Nations in the name of the Labor party because it would be able to deal with "the blemishes of the Treaty" and help to remove some of its "defects." [4]

[1] Earl Curzon, Lord President of the Council, July 24, 1919, H. of L., *Parl. Deb.*, Vol. 35, col. 1034; and Foreign Secretary, February 10, 1920, H. of L., *Parl. Deb.*, Vol. 39, col. 24.

[2] Great Britain, Foreign Office, *The Covenant of the League of Nations with a Commentary thereon* (Miscellaneous No. 3, 1919), Cmd. 151, p. 15.

[3] Earl Curzon, Lord President of the Council, July 24, 1919; H. of L., *Parl. Deb.*, Vol. 35, col. 1025.

[4] John R. Clynes, July 21, 1919; H. of C., *Parl. Deb.*, Vol. 118, col. 960.

There has been much dispute, in and out of Great Britain, over the question whether the British Government, if it were indeed convinced of the need for changes in the treaties, ever put its views into practice with the proper energy. Certainly it was hindered by disagreement on a number of matters, such as the methods by which change could be accomplished, the choice of the appropriate time, or the concrete issues to be taken up. But even though many leading British statesmen were ready to acknowledge the great importance of obedience to law and respect for treaty obligations, none took exception to the opinion that in the long run peace in Europe depended on the ability of the leading powers to provide for "progressive regulation" (as the British commentary on the League Covenant expressed it in 1919).[5] "Redress of legitimate grievances" was the phrase used in a whole series of pronouncements, all through the post-war era. Although Lloyd George, for instance, in the early years, was a staunch defender of the treaty which he had negotiated, predicting that "unless Treaty faith is maintained" disorganization would result, and calling revision "an explosive word," in fact, "the most dangerous word" that could be used, he later advised Britain not to commit herself to the *status quo* under the guise of arbitration.[6] Even Sir Austen Chamberlain, who at times came very close to the French attitude in regard to the treaties, and warned people against raising "these frontier questions" which were keeping the minds of the nations "unsettled and disturbed," declared in 1936 that the guarantee of territorial integrity under Article 10 of the Covenant "ought to be subject to acceptance of any advice tendered under Article 19,"

[5] *Cmd. 151*, p. 15.

[6] David Lloyd George, Prime Minister, June 20, 1921, to the Imperial Conference, *Cmd. 1474*, p. 13; February 27, 1924, H. of C., *Parl. Deb.*, Vol. 170, cols. 616, 617; March 24, 1925, H. of C., *Parl. Deb.*, Vol. 182, cols. 328-329.

which provides for revision.[7] In the early period, the Labor party created considerable trouble for the government in its relations with France by coming out with drastic suggestions for a general revision of unpractical and unjust treaties; for without this revision "the future of Europe would be very dark," as Lord Parmoor put it.[8] It was the Conservatives, on the other hand, who later, in the days of Hitler's revisionist moves, argued for the need of a redress of Germany's grievances. Men as divergent in their philosophies as Chamberlain, Churchill, Londonderry, and Eden came out on one occasion or another in favor of "negotiated change." Whether they realized how radical it would have to be, if it were to achieve its end of satisfying and pacifying the "revisionist" powers, is another matter. There were also indications that the government often feared to raise the issue of change when it was likely to cause Britain trouble. Nevertheless, there existed quasi-unanimity on the desirability of revising the treaties and a deep conviction that an "explosion" would disrupt the peace of the world if such changes were not accomplished soon.

Why then did Britain, the second great beneficiary of the treaties, look upon them as provisional or even objectionable, in part at least, while the French at the same time clung to them with an almost desperate devotion? The explanation lies partly in Britain's traditions and the happy experiences which she has had in her relations with the Dominions and other parts of her Empire in applying a flexible policy. She has moved on from one temporary agreement to another, regarding each one only as a step in a continuous and inevitable historical evolution. It has also been suggested that a nation that has no written constitution and no codified law is more

[7] Sir Austen Chamberlain, Foreign Secretary, June 24, 1925, H. of C., *Parl. Deb.*, Vol. 185, col. 1563; July 27, 1936, H. of C., *Parl. Deb.*, Vol. 315, col. 1174.

[8] Lord Parmoor, July 22, 1920; H. of L., *Parl. Deb.*, Vol. 41, col. 431.

naturally skeptical about the permanency of any legal statutes and may at the same time have a more optimistic belief in the perfectibility of every settlement. But the point can be easily overstressed. It is dangerous to attribute to the French a stubborn inflexibility and a leaning toward the static and unchangeable, as if it were a national characteristic. It need only be remembered that throughout most of the nineteenth century France was the revisionist country. It is also not difficult to imagine that if certain matters had come up for serious discussion—the transfer of colonies, for instance—resistance would have come from the British rather than from the French. Leaving open, therefore, the fascinating but thorny problem of national character and national psychology, we shall try to discover other reasons for the difference that existed between the British and the French attitudes in regard to the treaty settlements of 1919.

To suggest that the British sense of justice may have been a contributing factor will be received with a condescending smile by the growing number of people who have become cynical about the conduct of world affairs and about European politics in particular. But some thought must be given to the peculiar role which the "Wilsonian principles of justice" have played in Britain since the World War. Before doing so, however, it is only fair to the French to warn the reader against inferring that, if a sense of justice prompted the British to urge peaceful change, France's opposition to "revision" proved that she was indifferent to matters of justice or morally to blame in any way. If nations could agree on what is just or unjust in international affairs, much conflict and difficulty could be avoided. But principles such as those invoked by President Wilson not only ran counter to egotistical demands and ambitions, but suffered quite as much from conflicting interpretations of international justice. To the French it appeared fitting and just, for instance, that in any European settlement primary consideration be given to the security of the victim of what they assumed to have been German aggression in 1914. It was also asserted that the new small states in Central Europe which had been emancipated from foreign yoke by the sacrifices of the Allies had a just and preeminent claim that they be given sufficient strength, both military and economic, to permit them to defend their new liberties. According to a further argument, any attempt to revise the law of Europe would only create new and greater injustice and would threaten to disrupt peace and order. It was better, therefore, to defend the established law and enforce the existing treaties, whatever their defects, than to run headlong into anarchy and new abuses of power. The French were, however, on the defensive. Their opponents had only to appeal to the Wilsonian principles of justice so dear to the Anglo-Saxon nations to put the French morally in the wrong, and thus very often to maneuver them into concessions of which they did not approve. French resistance was strengthened by fear lest "justice" be used as a cloak for interests hostile to France or for the mobilization of Anglo-Saxon opinion for the benefit of Germany and against France and her allies in Central Europe. Therefore, the price which she and her friends might be asked to pay for the sake of "justice" was a reason for caution.

These "principles of justice" might influence British governmental policy directly, or in an indirect way, by their effect on public opinion. To the continental observer of British affairs, naturally skeptical, nothing was more amazing than the hold which the Wilsonian principles were able to gain on public opinion throughout the British Isles and the Dominions, particularly on Leftist opinion. The result was that even in cases where the government did not approve of making these principles the basis of practical policies, it was constantly under great pressure to take them into consideration. How influential this factor must have been in Britain was apparent from the importance Germany attached to it in presenting her case. Hitler, whose realism even the cynics may be willing to admit, did not abandon the German practice of appealing to the sense of justice of British public opinion and of basing German claims on Wilsonian principles. The Germans insisted that they had a legal right to the application of these principles because they were promised to Germany in the pre-Armistice agreements as the basis of the peace settlement.[9] But the German Gov-

[9] The nature of the pre-Armistice negotiations, to which both Republican and National Socialist Germany referred in maintaining their protests against the Treaty of Versailles, may be briefly outlined. On October 4, 1918, a first note was sent to President Wilson by the German Government in which he was asked to take steps to bring about an armistice and restore peace. The note stated that the German Government "accepts the programme set forth by the President of the United States in his Message to Congress of January 8th [containing the Fourteen Points]." A second note of October 12 reaffirmed that Germany accepted the Fourteen Points and Wilson's "subsequent addresses on the foundation of a permanent peace of justice. Consequently its object in entering into discussions would be only to agree upon the practical details of the application of these terms. The German Government believes that the Governments of the Powers associated with the Government of the United States also adopt the position taken by President Wilson in his address." Further communications between the German Government and the President were exchanged, and in its fourth note of October 27 it was stated, "The German Government now awaits the proposals for an armistice which will introduce a peace of justice such as the President in his manifestations has described." The Allied Governments, after reviewing this correspondence, informed President Wilson that "subject to the qualifications which follow [regarding freedom of the seas and reparation], they declare their willingness to make peace with the Government of Germany on the terms of peace laid down in the President's Address to Congress of January 8, 1918, and the principles of settlement enunciated in his subsequent Addresses." This opinion was communicated to the German Government by the United States in a note of November 5 which declared that Marshal Foch had been authorized "to receive properly accredited representatives of the German Government, and to communicate to them the terms of an armistice." The German Government then communicated directly with the Allied military authorities and the Armistice was signed on November 11. Harold W. V. Temperley, ed., *A History of the Peace Conference of Paris* (1920), I, pp. 124 ff., and Appendix IV. Both the German Government and the Allied Governments referred to the pre-Armistice negotiations as constituting the basis for their subsequent policy. In its observations of May 29, 1919, on the draft peace treaty, the German Government referred to the pre-Armistice negotiations in detail, and contended that the

ernment could hardly have expected the legal argument to stir world opinion; it hoped that the favorable reaction of those wanting "justice" to be done to Germany would force the hand of the British Government. Post-war experience encouraged this hope. Hitler, it is true, managed so to antagonize the genuinely "Wilsonian" section of British public opinion that it became deaf to any German claims. But then the British Conservatives stepped in and began to argue the cases of the Rhineland, *Anschluss* with Austria, and the Sudetenland in terms of equality and self-determination.

It would be preposterous to suggest that the British Government was guided mainly by Wilsonian principles of justice. As a matter of fact it was very hesitant in its advocacy of drastic changes as long as the *status quo* powers were preponderant, and it became far more ready to listen to revisionist arguments when Germany rose to great power.

The role of the opposition was just the reverse. In the early period the Labor and Liberal opposition, assisted by Winston Churchill, clamored for more rapid and drastic redress of Germany's legitimate grievances. Later, when Germany's power had increased so much as to make her a threat to peace, ready to accomplish her objectives, if necessary by the use of force, the greater danger for Britain lay in opposing revision. Now the government began to argue in favor of rectifying past injustice, while the onetime revisionist opposition declared that it was too late for the adoption of such a policy, which was no longer justified in view of the attitude of the National Socialist Government. Britain, declared

agreements which had then been reached and which were binding were being violated by the Allies. The latter, in their reply of June 16, 1919, reaffirmed their pre-Armistice acceptance of the Wilsonian principles: "These are the principles upon which hostilities were abandoned in November, 1918, these are the principles upon which the Allied and Associated Powers agreed that peace might be based, these are the principles which have guided them in the deliberations which led to the formulation of the Conditions of Peace." *Ibid.*, II, p. 249.

Attlee, "will not countenance for a moment the yielding to Hitler and force what was denied to Stresemann and reason." [10] To some extent the government's policy must have been directly influenced by the Wilsonian principles, for, as has often been remarked, British policy when facing "legitimate grievances" gave every indication of operating under the shadow of an "uneasy consciousness" [11] that "Germany has not always had quite a fair deal." [12] Britain's resistance to demands for change weakened in proportion to the justifiability of the alleged grievances. Czechoslovakia, for instance, suffered from having a "poor case" in the light of the principle of self-determination. Britain's interest, it is true, generally corresponded to the impulses of her "bad conscience." The Wilsonian principles were useful when the government desired Anglo-German co-operation and sought a popular excuse for urging or demanding others to make concessions. In any case, these principles helped predispose Britain against rigid enforcement of the Versailles Treaty and in favor of the redress of grievances. Since a part of Wilson's program had been incorporated into the treaty, as, for instance, the promise of general disarmament, a feeling of moral, if not legal, obligation and a desire to fulfill Britain's pledges were added to the general wish to do justice. Woodrow Wilson had introduced the Trojan horse of revision into the fortress of Versailles and into the very heart of French defenses.

Britain's national interests, in contrast to those of France, permitted her to be more generous about the redress of grievances. There was much in the Versailles Treaty and the other post-war settlements that was unimportant if not distasteful to the British and which could be eliminated without affecting their interests.

[10] Clement Attlee, leader of the Labor opposition, April 13, 1933; H. of C., *Parl. Deb.*, Vol. 276, col. 2742.

[11] Sir Herbert Samuel, May 2, 1935; H. of C., *Parl. Deb.*, Vol. 301, col. 584.

[12] Lord Rennell, July 1, 1936; H. of L., *Parl. Deb.*, Vol. 101, col. 377.

This is true particularly for the territorial provisions in Central Europe, against which it was clear from the outset that the revisionist campaign would be mainly directed. The British may feel today that they underestimated the menace which changes in that region might harbor even for them. But they were convinced at the time that they could allow considerable leeway there. Here lay the main difference between the interests of Britain and France. "Redress of grievances" in the East threatened the vital interest of France in preserving the *status quo* in those regions; for Britain it implied merely the likelihood that the settlements on the Vistula and the Danube, of which she had never approved, would some day have to be replaced by new arrangements. If Germany should gain in strength by such a process, there was no reason to object; it would help restore a better and more stable balance on the Continent.

That does not imply that Britain was unwilling to consider any concessions which would involve sacrifices on her own part. The scaling down of reparations, for instance, affected her; German "equality" in armaments, to which she was willing to agree, meant a lessening of her security; the possibility of a transfer to Germany of colonial mandates or even of colonies was seriously advocated in some British quarters. While people objected that Britain was being too generous in giving away things that did not belong to her, the government, in the period of so-called appeasement of the dictators, was also criticized for sacrificing highly important strategic advantages of Great Britain in Spain, Ethiopia, and elsewhere. For instance, Attlee complained in 1937 that the government "are not even interested in the principle they used to profess of Imperial interests, because the strategic position in the eastern part of the Mediterranean and the Red Sea has been handed over to Italy."[13]

[13] Clement Attlee, February 18, 1937; H. of C., *Parl. Deb.*, Vol. 320, col. 1500.

It was true, however, that Germany's most urgent claims and Italy's most drastic demands hit France and her continental allies much more directly than they did Britain. The colonial issue, for instance, was to Hitler a matter of secondary importance as compared with the *Anschluss* or the union of Danzig with the Reich. It was even suspected that the British Conservatives expected Germany's ambitions in Eastern Europe to benefit Great Britain by distracting Germany away from naval and colonial ambitions and from other objectives in the West. "Realism; sacrifice liberty; sell Abyssinia, Spain and Czechoslovakia," taunted Sir Archibald Sinclair, "to curry favour with the dictators. Give them a free hand in the East to keep them busy for a few years." [14]

That redress of grievances or even outright revision was a necessary step in any peace policy which was directed toward the pacification of the dissatisfied nations was not difficult to see. But there was no certainty that any particular concession or series of concessions and changes would actually bring success to such a policy. Therefore, after every failure it became the "plain duty," as Eden put it, "to attempt to create out of the era of difficulty an era of opportunity." [15] It is rather pathetic to see with what optimism the British clung to the hope that each successive revision in favor of Germany—equality in arms, the remilitarization of the Rhineland, the incorporation of Austria and of the Sudetenland—would at last saturate the Germans and clear the way for that "new comprehensive settlement" that was to take the place of Versailles and, being satisfactory to everyone, was to lay a more stable and permanent foundation for peaceful and friendly co-operation. Neville Chamberlain spoke of the steps "towards . . . what has some-

[14] Sir Archibald Sinclair, Leader of the Liberal opposition, April 4, 1938; H. of C., *Parl. Deb.*, Vol. 334, col. 69.

[15] Anthony Eden, Foreign Secretary, July 27, 1936; H. of C., *Parl. Deb.*, Vol. 315, cols. 1116-1117.

times been called a general settlement, . . . when reasonable grievances may be removed, when suspicions may be laid aside, and when confidence may again be restored." [16] This, from the very beginning, was the goal toward which Britain was directing her efforts.

We do not know whether a policy based on the British theory of saturation ever had any chance of success. There is no way of proving now that, if Britain had been willing and able to break French resistance in the early thirties, and had given Germany the satisfaction for which the Brüning government was pleading, the German Republic would have been saved and subsequent German revisionism tempered with patience and moderation. There was a strong case in favor of the thesis that the elimination of justified causes of dissatisfaction and resentment would be a means of adjusting the balance of power. It would destroy much of that popular support which the revisionist countries could command at home as long as they were fighting for matters of vital importance; and it would at the same time strengthen the resistance of the "static" powers, since they would acquire a "good conscience" and find themselves in a better position to call a halt to further demands. Some believe, however, that the redress of grievances as a peace-preserving device becomes ineffective and dangerous once a country has become so thoroughly "dynamic" as to interpret any and every concession as a sign of weakness. If that was the case here, it is still possible that Europe might have been spared the rise of the "dynamic" régimes if radical changes had been effected earlier.

[16] Neville Chamberlain, Prime Minister, December 21, 1937; H. of C., *Parl. Deb.*, Vol. 330, cols. 1804-1805.

XIII. Schools of Thought in British Foreign Policy: Traditionalists and Collectivists

EVEN more than in the case of France, it is necessary to warn the reader against expecting an exposition of some consistent and unified policy which every British government and statesman accepted and pursued. A French minister, indeed, was once quoted in the House of Lords as having said, "It is better to have five Governments and one policy, like France, than to have one Government and five policies, like England." [1] While this is an exaggeration, we shall find two profoundly different schools of thought struggling for control over Britain's foreign policy, producing conflicts in outlook and principle, sometimes within the same cabinet. The one school we shall call the "traditionalist" school. The opposing group we shall refer to as the "collectivist" school. The use of new labels when so many already exist calls for justification. Why not simply use the terms Conservative, Liberal, and Laborite? The reason is that the two outstanding "ideological camps" in Britain did not coincide accurately with old party lines. The collectivists found adherents not only among the left-wing parties. While the members of the Labor party and most of the Liberals were to be found among them, they were forcefully represented by such groups as the non-partisan League of Nations Union and numbered several

[1] Quoted by Lord Lloyd, June 26, 1935; H. of L., *Parl. Deb.*, Vol. 97, col. 845.

outstanding Conservatives in their ranks. The name "collectivist" is chosen because this school came to lay emphasis mainly on collective security. Their opponents, who included only a few Leftists, were characterized by their desire to conduct foreign affairs on traditional lines, hence the name "traditionalist." While this latter school tended to consider any policy which follows established tradition to be good policy, the collectivists were prone to discard anything reminiscent of pre-war methods or objectives as outdated and reactionary.

Of course, any such sweeping division into two separate groups is a crude simplification. There were important differences of opinion within both groups. The views of Eden, in the days when he had turned collectivist, were certainly not identical with those of the leaders of the Labor party, such as Dalton or Attlee. The concepts of Lord Lloyd or Amery were not those of either Baldwin or Neville Chamberlain. A few statesmen, too, among whom Churchill stands out, did not fit into either of the categories.

The British, of course, were the last to expect that official policy would follow any doctrinaire program such as a political party might promise in times of elections. They have always been the masters and devotees of compromise. If we listen to some British statesmen, we might even conclude that the British never had any program or point of direction, but were groping their way through the dark, moving from decision to decision, "muddling through" without so much as a single principle or standard of judgment to guide them. "We have been content to deal at any one moment with the evil of the day and to provide the remedy which that evil required. It is not out of a logical system proceeding from general hypotheses that our freedom, our liberties, our safety have grown. It is from the wise spirit of compromise which has inspired all British parties in critical moments and from our careful concentration upon the immediate problems which required a solution at the moment."[2] This may be a typical attitude for men of action to take, but it is also a favorite diplomatic technique of the British. Not to commit oneself to any definite course means preserving one's freedom of choice. In fact there was more consistency and logic in British politics than the actors on the scene were aware of or wished to disclose, but there was also enough ambiguity and contradiction, enough confusion and lack of direction, to make British policy puzzling and hard for other countries to follow. There was no policy, from isolationism to the most extreme form of collective security that did not at times find a spokesman in high quarters; no orientation toward other countries, from a hard-and-fast military alignment with the Soviet Union to a clear-cut alliance with Germany, that failed to find its influential exponent. While the government steered clear of the extremes, it was unable to avoid the pitfalls of half-hearted compromises between the conflicting views. Sometimes, also, it reflected various pressures alternately, and pursued a zigzag path, confusing to other countries and damaging to British prestige.

To those statesmen in Britain who claimed that they conducted their foreign policy by sheer instinct and without principles, it must be distasteful to think of classifying the British into schools of thought or schools of political philosophy. But men who take this view are expressing traditionalist tenets. This school is characterized among other things by its skepticism in regard to general principles as a basis for conducting foreign affairs. The collectivists, on the contrary, took particular pride in having at last set out to make British policy conform with general rules and high moral principles. They criticized their opponents for having no other guide but opportunism. The issue, said Harold Nicolson, is "whether our foreign policy is to be conducted on a basis of ex-

[2] Austen Chamberlain, Foreign Secretary, League of Nations Assembly, September 10, 1925; *Records of the Sixth Assembly, Plenary Meetings, Text of the Debates,* pp. 38-39.

pediency or on a basis of principle."[3] Toynbee draws a distinction between "those of us who are mainly concerned with upholding British principles," and "those of us who are mainly concerned with preserving British property."[4] This is therefore part of the controversy and of the battle of political slogans which separated the two schools.

In trying to outline the course of Britain's policy since the World War, it must be remembered that during the period under consideration British foreign policy was conducted almost exclusively by Conservative or National governments. For only two short periods did Britain have a Labor government. The Prime Ministers of all these Conservative or National governments, as well as most of the members of their cabinets, belonged to the traditionalist school. While Conservative governments did yield occasionally, and on some very important occasions, to the pressure of a collectivist opposition outside and inside the Conservative ranks, most of their foreign policy was conducted on traditionalist lines. Since we are concerned with the actual policy of Britain, not with unfulfilled dreams of the opposition, we should be able to deal almost exclusively with the traditionalist school if it were not that the opposing doctrines influenced British foreign policy even when Labor was not in power. While the pressure of collectivist public opinion did not necessarily compel the traditionalists to take actions distasteful to them or to compromise, it very frequently led them to make their policies appear to be in line with the collectivist doctrines.[5]

When the collectivists are discussed, it will be necessary to outline their doctrines in detail; about the traditionalist ideas in general, much less explanation needs to be offered. They have few

[3] Harold Nicolson, February 21, 1938; H. of C., *Parl. Deb.*, Vol. 332, col. 99.

[4] Arnold J. Toynbee, "The Issues in British Foreign Policy," *International Affairs*, XVII (May-June, 1938), p. 318.

[5] Most of the discussion of this collectivist influence will be reserved for the chapters dealing with the League of Nations.

theories, and since in every country they are the predominant group and cling to traditional concepts, their main beliefs are familiar. The starting point of their approach to foreign policy is the "national interest." For the collectivists, as we shall see, it was the interest of an international community. The term "national interest" covers a long list of specific interests, some "vital," others of less importance. The protection and defense of the British Isles, the British Dominions, territories, and possessions, and of the lines of communication between them were regarded as the most vital interests. An extensive geographic zone on the globe was thereby defined as a region of vital British interest. This concept is essentially strategic. Britain is also recognized as having a vital interest in world trade in so far as it affects her own economic existence. The traditionalists recognize no other vital interests, and therefore no other issue for which the British people should or could be expected to fight. When a confirmed traditionalist raises general issues, moral or ideological (when for instance he proclaims that England's duty is to enforce world peace, democracy, or the rule of law), he either sincerely believes that Britain's vital interests run parallel to the need for defending these wider issues, or he may be pretending hypocritically that such general issues are involved, when some particular British interest is actually at stake. Some such hypocrisy occurred only too often, since the exponents of traditional vital interests often found it expedient to cloak their real objectives in terms which would appeal to that wide section of public opinion which was more devoted to certain general principles than to specific and traditional British interests. The traditionalists like to think of themselves as realists. "It is in our willingness to face realities which we cannot change, and to make the best of them," said Neville Chamberlain, "that the difference lies between this side and the other side of the House."[6]

[6] Neville Chamberlain, Prime Minister, May 2, 1938; H. of C., *Parl. Deb.*, Vol. 335, col. 535.

This "realism" is not necessarily indifference to a better world and to high moral principles, or an approval of aggression and the use of force. It rather confirms the conviction that no nation or group of nations can, without embroiling the world in greater and more disastrous troubles and unhappiness, afford "to take on the risks of other countries and become policemen of the world,"[7] or to enforce high moral standards and respect of the law upon nations involved in age-old and often insoluble conflicts and struggles. This is a pessimistic point of view, since it assumes that man is incapable in the present state of world society of enforcing his ideals or Utopias upon other nations, and must therefore accept the tragedy of international conflict as something beyond the power of nations to terminate.

It is not difficult to distinguish between traditionalists and collectivists. Only the former are concerned with geographic areas and geographic necessity, with regional interest and discrimination between vital and secondary interests. They discuss foreign affairs not in general and abstract terms, but with concrete allusions to this or that country, to German versus French power, to British military requirements to hold Germany in check, or to commitments in Western Europe as opposed to Eastern Europe. The collectivists, on the other hand, speak of security in general, or of disarmament and of arbitration. They avoid mention of specific countries and use the terms "victim of aggression" and "potential aggressor." We shall attempt to show that these differences were by no means academic or theoretical, but influenced directly the course of action British governments chose to take or were made to follow.

[7] Earl Stanhope, Foreign Under-Secretary, December 19, 1935; H. of L., *Parl. Deb.*, Vol. 99, col. 348.

XIV. France: Britain's Guardian on the Rhine

FROM the point of view of the "national interest," Britain's relations with her immediate neighbors across the Channel formed a natural starting point from which to map out a European policy. Relations with both Belgium and the Netherlands remained virtually unchanged by the World War, since these two small independent states continued to serve as guardians of the ports of the Lowlands. "It has been a cardinal principle of British policy in all times, and under all governments," wrote Sir Austen Chamberlain, "that we could not allow the Low Countries to be dominated by the greatest military Power of the day." [1] The real issue was France. The exigencies of modern warfare required the protection of the British Isles from the opposite coast to be on a larger scale than before. The French ports had to be in safe hands too, but it was no longer enough merely to keep the ports from falling into hostile hands. To make the ports and the British Isles safe from attack, a line of defense had to be drawn farther east. Stanley Baldwin stated it bluntly by saying, "When you think of the defence of England you no longer think of the chalk cliffs of Dover; you think of the Rhine. That is where our frontier lies." [2] Whether this was sound reasoning from a military point of view or not, the thesis was accepted as an article of faith. The "dogma of the Rhine" became as important in the shaping of Britain's European policy as the Monroe Doctrine in defining the role of

[1] *Down the Years* (1935), p. 166.

[2] Stanley Baldwin, Lord President of the Council, July 30, 1934; H. of C., *Parl. Deb.*, Vol. 292, col. 2339.

the United States in the Western Hemisphere. It was questioned only by those who would have preferred to place Britain's line of defense still farther east, or who wished the borders of any "victim of aggression" anywhere in the world to be treated as Britain's frontier.

The implications of the Rhine dogma are so significant and various that they will follow us throughout this study. Franco-British relations, of course, were most immediately affected. If the Rhine, or, to put it more exactly, if France's eastern frontier was equally Britain's frontier, then the territory west of this boundary had to be in the hands of a country from which Britain apprehended no threat to her safety. Belgium and the Netherlands, small neutral countries dependent on England, were, of course, ideally fitted to serve as guardians of the opposite coast. But to make a great power like France a guardian of British safety was no easy matter. She was, in 1919, the strongest military power on the Continent, held a prominent position as a naval power and as an empire, and had interests all over the world. In the Near East she was Great Britain's strongest rival for supremacy. Above all, France was engaged in a ceaseless struggle with Germany, which led her to take a vital interest in remote parts of Europe.

It is worth emphasizing at the outset that in accepting France as a guardian on the Rhine, Britain drew a distinction between her relations with France and those with Germany which was to have far-reaching consequences. France was looked upon as a "friendly Power" in whose possession the Channel ports should remain,[3] while it was said to be of vital interest to Britain that "no hostile force"—meaning German force—should cross the French or Belgian frontiers.[4] It is not being suggested that Britain, from the

[3] Austen Chamberlain, Lord Privy Seal, February 8, 1922; H. of C., *Parl. Deb.*, Vol. 150, col. 198.

[4] Anthony Eden, Foreign Secretary, March 26, 1936; H. of C., *Parl. Deb.*, Vol. 310, col. 1443.

point of view of her national interest, was wrong in drawing such a distinction. France was saturated; Germany was not. France was dependent on Great Britain as Germany was not. But since, rationally or irrationally, the British were convinced that a war with France was an impossibility, any idea of Britain's acting as a "disinterested mediator" between the two countries on the Rhine will have to be taken with a grain of salt. This does not mean, as might be prematurely concluded, that Britain would never act so as to weaken France or defeat her intentions. Indeed, not only were British sympathies at times definitely in favor of German arguments and claims, but the whole direction of Britain's policy was anything but agreeable to the French.

If politics obeyed the rules of simple logic, it would seem to follow from the "Rhine dogma" that France could at least count on British military protection against Germany without having to trouble about any specific British commitment. Britain would simply be protecting herself if she went to fight on the Rhine. But no French statesman, with the exception of Poincaré, dared to rely on such a conclusion. Several reasons can be given to explain this seemingly paradoxical situation. For one thing, it was some time before the British became convinced of the necessity for common defenses on the Rhine. In the years immediately following the World War, when France constantly demanded more security on the Rhine, the British saw little reason to worry about the safety of the British Isles, or to fear that Germany, weak and disarmed as she was, might some day become a threat to London. At that time, a guarantee of the eastern boundaries of France appeared to the British merely as a generous contribution to French security. The French, as we can readily understand, were not inclined to put unlimited trust in sheer generosity. Then, too, even after the British had acknowledged a common interest with France on the Rhine, they did very little for a long time to prepare the military assistance which would enable them to perform their part in defending this interest. Last, but not least, British and French ideas of how to prevent an emergency from arising on the Rhine differed so fundamentally that there was always a danger of acute conflict between the two countries which at a given moment might lead Britain to waive her "Rhine dogma" as long as it was not made binding by formal pledges.

Even when Britain had come to look upon France as her guardian on the Rhine she was still able, within the framework of traditionalist philosophy, to choose between at least two alternative policies in regard to France:

(1) It was possible for her to regard France as Britain's "sword" on the Continent, as the "policeman of Europe."

(2) France might take a far more modest and passive position, and serve as a "buffer state" between Britain and Germany.

The first alternative meant allowing or even helping to make France so strong that no "hostile force" would dare to move westward, thus making both France and Britain safe from future German attack. In this case France might never need British military assistance if she were left free to take whatever steps she saw fit in the way of armaments and alliances to strengthen her position. Britain might be able to enjoy "splendid isolation" once more, with France policing the European back yard of the Empire. However, should French power prove insufficient, it would then be logical and desirable for Britain to enter into a military alliance with her. In both cases it would be to Britain's interest to see that France was as strong as possible. Every advantage which France could gain would accrue to the benefit of the British. Churchill, who was convinced that any weakening of "that factor of stability, the unquestioned superiority of French military power, might open floodgates of measureless consequence in Europe at the present time," [5] also declared that he would "rather see another 10 or 20 years of one-sided armed peace than see a war between equally well-matched Powers or combinations of Powers—and that may be the choice." [6]

It was only after all other methods had failed to keep the Rhine and the British Isles safe from any German menace that Britain came to adopt an attitude which in many ways resembled this first alternative. But the fact that she did not do so in the earlier stages accounts for much of the conflict between herself and France. Why, if they had a common interest or even a common frontier on the Rhine, should there have been this lack of unity, when they agreed on the objective of keeping the Germans from invading French soil? The most obvious explanation is that they disagreed on the means by which to attain this goal.

The French, as we have tried to show, believed in the method of holding Germany firmly under control by the unquestioned superiority of the defenders of the established order and by giving Germany no chance to threaten the Rhine by any "indirect aggression" which would strengthen her at the expense of her eastern neighbors. The British objected even in principle to the idea of preserving peace by the preponderance of any country or group of countries on the Continent. Quite apart from any considerations of the balance of power or any fears of French hegemony, it was maintained that such a course would only increase Germany's resentment and lead her to renew the conflict on the Rhine. Clearly the British and the French both feared a possible future German revolt or "explosion." The French hoped to prevent this revolt by piling up insuperable odds against it. The British believed they

[5] Winston Churchill, June 29, 1931; H. of C., *Parl. Deb.*, Vol. 254, col. 963.

[6] Winston Churchill, November 23, 1932; H. of C., *Parl. Deb.*, Vol. 272, col. 88. Churchill's principal speeches during the critical period 1932-1938 are collected in *While England Slept: a survey of world affairs, 1932-1938* (1938).

could accomplish the same end by removing the incentives that might lead Germany to turn against the West. French nervousness, even at a time when Germany was "down and out," can only have strengthened the conviction in Britain that it was not good policy to rely on French superiority as a bulwark against Germany. "The holding down of Germany in a nervous grip," it was predicted, "was bound ultimately to lead to an explosion of which France herself would be the victim." [7] The insistence with which France sought a close military alignment between herself and Britain was not likely to increase British confidence in her. It meant that Britain would have to help her in preventing a dangerous outburst of German dissatisfaction, a function the British did not relish.

We must add to these considerations Britain's misgivings about France's Central European alliances. The policy of superiority over Germany apparently required that countries like Poland and Czechoslovakia be incorporated into the "preponderant group" that was called upon to defend the Rhine, directly or indirectly. But while these countries would add to the strength of Britain's "sword" on the Continent, they threatened at the same time to involve Britain in their quarrels, and thus to present an imminent danger in place of the remote possibility of a conflict on the Rhine. For all of these reasons, Britain's interest in strengthening her "guardian on the Rhine" came to be subordinated to her program of pacifying Germany, of drawing the latter's attention away from the West, and of keeping Britain free from any Central European entanglements.

When in 1939 Britain not only became a full-fledged ally of France but tried to check Germany by a coalition of superior power, it would seem as if she had, after the loss of much valu-

[7] Brigadier-General E. L. Spears, July 14, 1924; H. of C., *Parl. Deb.*, Vol. 176, col. 90.

able time, been converted to the idea of giving France as much strength as possible. It should not be forgotten, however, that by this time the reasons which had dictated her earlier course had lost their force. There was no longer any question of France's being made the *gendarme* of Europe, or of her gaining such strength as to make her the controlling factor in a Franco-British alliance. The Central European situation had completely changed. There was no longer any fear of specific French commitments which would unduly entangle Great Britain. The commitments entered upon in this period were of Britain's choosing. The entanglements which she was now willing to face were no longer the indirect effect of any French quest for preponderance but a consequence of the fight against German preponderance. The new policy, therefore, resembled only superficially the course which would have been called for if France in the earlier period had been treated as Britain's sword on the Continent.

In regard to the second alternative, namely, that France should be reduced to the status of a "buffer," there exists no proof that it was ever deliberately chosen or that the issue was ever put in such clear-cut terms as this discussion of alternatives might suggest. If, however, any concept of France's position and role in Europe can be discovered which would make the whole of the British traditionalist attitude toward France appear highly plausible and meaningful, this concept may be assumed consciously or subconsciously to have guided the British in their course of action. Certainly the relegation of France to the position of buffer state would fit into the picture of her treatment by the British traditionalists. France was to become one of the three guardians of Britain on the opposite shore of the Channel, together with Belgium and the Netherlands. The differences between France and the two others were, of course, too obvious and important for any British statesman to ignore. France was far too powerful to be neutralized and too determined on the course she meant to pursue to be forced to interest herself only in the defense of her own soil. Britain could hope only to limit, not to prevent, French commitments and actions beyond her borders. Later, when the possibility of an air attack on London came into the picture, the lack of reciprocity which usually distinguishes the relationship between a great power and a buffer state vanished. Britain became interested in assistance from France as well as in assisting her. But by this time the rise of German power had already driven Britain out of her initial course. That the original concept was not entirely abandoned can be seen, however, from the way in which, even after the British in 1935 became interested in French assistance, they still remained indifferent to the weakening of France which resulted from the German remilitarization of the Rhineland and later from the loss of Czechoslovakia's "Maginot Line." France was still believed to be strong enough to defend her own soil and thus to fulfill her functions as a buffer state. That was as far as Britain's interest went at the time.

A buffer state is characterized by two negative functions: that of not being provocative to its neighbors, and that of not becoming entangled in other people's conflicts.

Britain was constantly trying to keep France from provoking Germany. As Lloyd George put it, "A nation which is exasperated by incessant provocation will not reckon the cost . . ."[8] It was one of her basic assumptions that the pacification of Germany and of the Continent depended upon France's not taking any action or continuing any policy which would give Germany legitimate reasons for feeling provoked. The result was that practically any

[8] David Lloyd George, Prime Minister, August 16, 1921; H. of C., *Parl. Deb.*, Vol. 146, col. 1233. Already, during the Versailles Conference, he had written: "The maintenance of peace will . . . depend upon there being no causes of exasperation constantly stirring up the spirit of patriotism, of justice or of fair play." Memorandum of March 26, 1919; *Cmd. 2169*, p. 77.

move France undertook to enforce the treaty or to preserve her preponderance was open to the interpretation of provocativeness. Britain was taking it upon herself to be the judge of the psychological effects of French policy. The clash between Clemenceau and Lloyd George at Versailles on this very question gives some indication of how Frenchmen must have resented this attitude of Britain, though few of them dared to declare themselves as plainly as Clemenceau.[9] Germany's resentment and dissatisfaction, he said, did not depend upon what France and her continental allies did in the future. By destroying Germany's position as a world power, by taking her colonies, destroying her navy, and seizing her capital holdings abroad, the British themselves had provoked Germany and laid the foundation for German dissatisfaction. Germany would never allow herself to be compensated for her loss of world power and prestige by mere concessions on the Continent. According to this view, Germany was provoked to revolt by the war spoils that Britain had taken, and it was therefore unfair and highly hypocritical to demand that the French, the Poles, or any other continental country make concessions to Germany and risk their own security for the sake of mitigating the evil effects of a German state of dissatisfaction to which the British themselves had contributed so largely.

One of the thorniest problems of British "psychological policy" was how to make the French desist from further provocation. There were some who believed that the best solution would be for Britain to give France more security. She would then, they asserted, become less nervous and therefore less aggressive. "The provocative policy inspired by her present uncertainty will tend to diminish," said a Foreign Office memorandum, if, by a British guarantee "France will know that her ultimate security is regarded

[9] See above, p. 90 n. 20.

as of direct interest to the British Empire."[10] Lloyd George, in supporting a promise of assistance to France, declared, "You have to give to France the feeling that she is not isolated and that she is not left alone. . . . Give confidence and you give calmness, and calmness of judgment in the present disturbed state of the world is vital to wise decisions."[11] The collectivists, as we shall see, adopted this point of view. The government accepted it in a diluted form. They were willing to make some contributions to French security, but not to an extent which would commit Britain to military assistance in any automatic way. The pact of guarantee which had been offered at Versailles, and the similar pact which Lloyd George proposed later, typified the kind of contribution which the government and the traditionalists were willing to grant. Later this type of guarantee was incorporated into the Locarno Treaty. The collectivists, in advocating the Geneva Protocol, indicated their willingness to go further.[12] In every one of these cases, it was emphasized that the purpose of the British commitment was to make France feel more secure and therefore

[10] The text of this Foreign Office memorandum of February 20, 1925, to which further references will be made, was published in *The World* (New York) of May 10, 1925, several weeks after reports of its contents had already appeared in the press. The day after the publication of the text in *The World*, Austen Chamberlain refused, in accordance with traditional practice, either to deny or confirm its authenticity in replying to questions in the House of Commons. It has generally been accepted as authentic. An historical note accompanying Lord D'Abernon's diary, *An Ambassador of Peace*, III, p. 155, refers specifically to this memorandum as having been written by the Central European Department of the Foreign Office under Mr. Chamberlain's direction. The drafting period of the memorandum corresponded with Germany's overtures for a reciprocal pact of security in the West; the first German note to Great Britain was dated January 20, 1925, and it is probable that the memorandum was drafted in anticipation of the new security negotiations.

[11] David Lloyd George, Prime Minister, February 7, 1922; H. of C., *Parl. Deb.*, Vol. 150, col. 41.

[12] For the 1919 pact and the 1922 negotiations, see above, p. 14 n. 7, p. 79 n. 7. The Geneva Protocol is discussed below, pp. 343 ff.

to render her more amenable to reasonable British proposals, for example, for disarmament. Since unilateral German disarmament was regarded as provocative, it was here that one of the chief causes of German dissatisfaction might be overcome.

Others argued that the very opposite course was the one to be followed. The more secure France came to feel, they claimed, the less willing would she be to make concessions. Her attitude and that of her Central European allies would be stiffened; the redress of grievances would become even more difficult. Therefore, Britain should keep France sufficiently apprehensive and insecure so that she would be willing to yield to justified German demands for adjustment. Colonel Wedgwood argued that "by constantly supporting France they [the friends of France] are encouraging just that spirit in France which does not tend to European peace, and they are encouraging all these military adventures which in the interests of trade and peace had better be reduced rather than exaggerated."[13] And Lord Arnold, much later, contended that "France would have made a settlement with Germany long ago if it had not been that ever since the War she felt that she had got Great Britain behind her."[14]

Britain never made up her mind which of these two apparently contradictory psychological theories to adopt. It seemed wiser to apply them alternately according to the circumstances, that is, to resort to the old device of using sugar and whip at the same time, in this case the sugar of security and the whip of pressure.

The problem of how to keep France from entangling herself, and thus indirectly Great Britain, in the problems of Central Europe was even more difficult to solve. France had involved herself in an alliance with Poland and an agreement with Czechoslovakia soon after the World War. Britain lacked either the

[13] Colonel Wedgwood, May 5, 1921; H. of C., *Parl. Deb.*, Vol. 141, col. 1326.
[14] Lord Arnold, February 16, 1938; H. of L., *Parl. Deb.*, Vol. 107, col. 696.

desire or the foresight to object. As late as 1935 she gave her consent to a further pact of a similar nature, that with the Soviet Union. These alliances caused her much embarrassment. They interest us here as a further illustration of the difference between an ally and a buffer state. If Britain had been looking toward a new war in which she would need French assistance, every new ally of France would have been welcomed for the new strength it added to the original alliance. Britain, however, was not seeking assistance, at least not primarily; she was preoccupied with preventing a possible attack on France's eastern boundaries. If France, through her alliances, became involved in conflicts in Eastern Europe, just such an attack might result. The alliances would be like pipelines through which war would spread from East to West. Those who adhered to this argument were of course assuming either that the outbreak of war in the East would not involve France unless she were explicitly committed to give assistance in the East or that a French retreat from the East would avert a war over Germany's claims in those regions.

Both to prevent any provocative encirclement of Germany and to diminish the risks of entanglement, the British policy attempted to draw France back from Central and Eastern Europe, or, if that were impossible, at least to make it difficult for her to give military assistance there. Since the French regarded Germany's expansion over her eastern borders as constituting the chief menace to France's own security, it is easy to realize to what extent Britain's attitude was in conflict with theirs.

Not until after 1936, that is, not until France had suffered a grave setback in the Rhineland, could any Frenchman have conceived of his country's resigning itself to a position even remotely resembling that of a mere buffer state in Western Europe. To reduce France to such a position was not only incompatible with her status as a world power and empire, but seemed utterly fatal to her security in the broad sense of the term. The British, from the point of view of their own interests, so the French believed, were short-sighted in objecting to a French policy of strength and of comprehensive alliances. Some day Britain would need France as the sword on the Continent to protect her from Germany and would realize her mistake. It is therefore not without irony that some French statesmen began to advocate a policy of retrenchment for France, which was very much in line with the concept of a buffer state and with British suggestions ever since Versailles, just about at the moment when Britain in 1939 decided to change her course and to try to stop Germany in the East. The assistance which Britain now required from France was far beyond anything that a buffer state, capable of and interested only in defending its own soil, could be expected to provide.

XV. Germany and the Balance of Power

THE power and position of Germany have undergone tremendous changes since the days of Versailles. But while they affected the French attitude but little, since France was constantly bent on building up defenses against Germany, it is not easy to find a common denominator for Britain's policy toward Germany. Both before and after the advent of Hitler it was mainly characterized by attempts to assist Germany, but it ended in an effort to call a halt to her rise and expansion. Yet, although the British may often have been very much confused in regard to their own course of action and may have suffered from the lack of a clear-cut program, instinctively, at least, they were feeling their way along a line which, now that it can be viewed in perspective, appears not lacking in meaning and logic.

The French objective was easier to define. For security's sake, she was endeavoring to keep German power as close to the level set for her at Versailles as she possibly could. Even that level seemed none too low, if France and her allies were to enjoy full and satisfactory security. All other considerations, such as a desire to make Germany psychologically more peaceful, were subordinated to this primary interest.

Britain, too, was not indifferent to the extent of Germany's power. If there was ever any doubt as to this, it has since been dispelled. Britain has made it clear that her vital interests do not permit German power on the Continent to exceed a certain maximum, which will be more clearly defined when we discuss Britain's efforts to prevent National Socialist Germany from dominating the Continent. This, however, does not mean that the British were interested in holding Germany down to the level of power and influence set for her by the post-war treaties. On the contrary, we shall find that during most of the period under discussion she was helping to strengthen Germany. Her objective, therefore, whatever the motives behind it may have been, can be defined as an attempt to endow Germany with a "happy medium" of power lying somewhere between the Versailles level and a "maximum level" of Britain's determination. The policy, if it had been successful, would have held Germany permanently within these bounds.

The fundamental difference between the starting points taken by Britain and France, as has been mentioned, can be accounted for mainly by the fact that Britain, because of her insular position, had for a long period of years no reason for concern about a rise of German power. So remote was any German menace to the British Isles or the Empire that the fears of others were hardly understood, and the change when it came had to assume major proportions before it was fully realized. As Lord D'Abernon, Britain's first Ambassador in Germany after the World War, wrote from Berlin in 1923, Germany was disarmed "far beyond the point where any danger need be feared by England from the undue military or naval strength of Germany."[1] With the military menace so clearly negligible, the British could not conceive of the future in terms of a continued struggle with Germany.

There was also no cause for anxiety over German economic rivalry. On the contrary, since the British felt that "the economic

[1] "It is, indeed, probable," he added, "should the 'balance of power' theory again become a dominant English conception of policy, that future critics will consider that a mistake has been made . . . in disarming Germany so far without disarming other Powers of Europe." Diary, February 7, 1923; *An Ambassador of Peace,* II, pp. 167-168.

recovery of Germany was essential to Europe,"[2] what concerned them was the decomposition of Germany's internal market and the impending collapse of her financial structure. Herbert Asquith advised, regarding reparations, that "any steps that you take or propose must be of such a kind that whatever you ask or whatever you seek to enforce shall be such that it does not destroy, or even paralyse, the economic life of Germany, and thereby undermine the whole fabric of international trade."[3] The specter of social upheaval and growing Bolshevism in Germany increased Britain's desire to see the authority of the German Government strengthened and the Republic consolidated as quickly as possible. "As long as order was maintained in Germany," Lloyd George stated at Versailles, "a breakwater would exist between the countries of the Allies and the waters of revolution beyond."[4] Therefore, even if the British had not had reasons to wish for an actual rise in German power, they would have been inclined to tolerate it as long as it was of no immediate danger to them and tended to improve Europe's economic and social conditions.

The British policy of pacification worked even more directly than this to the advantage of Germany. In the case of France, Britain's general policy of eliminating the war psychosis of the Continental Powers called for allaying French fears. In the case of Germany, the question was how to make her less dissatisfied and therefore less rebellious. On the whole the British seem to have had more sympathy and understanding for the psychological reactions of the Germans than of the French. French fears they considered exaggerated, while German resentment appeared justified. The fact that the war spirit did not disappear was generally

[2] Marquess Curzon, Foreign Secretary, speech in London, November 8, 1922; *The Times* (London), November 9, 1922, p. 14.

[3] Herbert Asquith, February 13, 1923; H. of C., *Parl. Deb.*, Vol. 160, col. 31.

[4] David Lloyd George, Prime Minister, Supreme War Council, March 8, 1919; David H. Miller, *My Diary at the Conference of Paris* (1928), XV, p. 267.

attributed to the provocative policy of the French and to the injustice of some of the provisions of the Treaty of Versailles. The Germans were the ones who were being provoked. Thus, with no fear of German strength, with a desire to see that country economically and socially stabilized, and with a vital interest in pacifying her in order to avert any future explosion of resentment and new turmoil in Europe, the British developed a policy of promoting conciliatory moves, readjustments, and concessions, such as we have discussed in a previous chapter.

This, however, still leaves unanswered the question as to whether there was not another and perhaps basic motive which prompted Britain to act toward Germany as she did. Was it not perhaps the actual purpose of Britain's policy to create a more powerful Germany and to lift her from what in the British national interest was regarded as a state of dangerous and excessive weakness? It would be tempting in discussing this question simply to refer to the principle of the balance of power to which Britain has adhered with such unerring devotion over the centuries and to conclude from this British tradition that she was trying once again to equalize the power of France and Germany. The objection to this explanation lies partly in the difficulty in defining the balance of power, partly in the fact that up until the time when German preponderance became imminent, British statesmen of all parties explicitly disclaimed any intention to have Britain revert to this principle. Lord D'Abernon, a fervent adherent to the idea of the balance of power, who believed that it should have been employed to curb France's military superiority, regretted that it had become "unfashionable."[5] Lord Lothian thought it had "disappeared be-

[5] He regarded the unilateral disarmament of Germany as "a grave political mistake," and he believed that because of France's overwhelming superiority "no real pacification" was possible. Diary, April 4, 1923; D'Abernon, *op. cit.*, II, p. 186.

yond retrievement,"[6] while Ramsay MacDonald when Prime Minister went so far as to claim that Britain's policy of supporting the League was "exactly opposite" to the balance of power.[7] The list could be prolonged. What all of these men meant, however, particularly when they said that international co-operation or collective security had replaced the balance of power, was that Britain did not wish a return to a balance of two rival groups or hostile blocs in Europe, such as had existed at the beginning of the twentieth century. This they claimed had been one of the chief causes of the World War. But the tradition dated farther back than that, and did not originally mean a balance between two hostile groups of allies, as Professor Webster has explained, but "a Europe in which no Power was strong enough to attack the others."[8] In this definition there was no reference to any division of the Continent into two hostile camps. Therefore, even if Britain insisted that all nations become members of the League or of a concert of power, she might still refuse to allow any one power or group of powers to become too strong and capable of threatening the others. An active League policy was not incompatible with an attempt to build up whatever counterpoise was necessary to balance the weight and influence of some particularly strong continental power. The only countries which Britain might at the time have considered in need of being balanced were the Soviet Union and France.

It has often been suggested that Britain wanted to strengthen Germany so as to check the Soviets and protect Central Europe from the inroads of Bolshevism. While that may well have been

[6] Address at Chatham House, June 5, 1934, "The Place of Britain in the Collective System," *International Affairs,* XIII (September–October, 1934), p. 632.

[7] Interview in Berlin, July 28, 1931; *The Times* (London), July 29, 1931, p. 12.

[8] Remarks during discussion of address by the Marquess of Lothian, *International Affairs, op. cit.,* p. 649.

in the minds of some Conservatives after Hitler had come into power, such a policy could hardly have been applied with reason during the period of the German Republic. The danger from Russia in that period was that revolution might spread. It was important that Germany should not turn Bolshevist, but there was no need to set her up as a strong power against a Soviet Union which at the time had very little military strength. From the days of Rapallo, when Germany and the Soviet Union signed their first treaty of friendship and consultation, down to the beginning of the National Socialist régime, relations between Germany and the Soviet Union were so cordial that any increase in German power was quite obviously of benefit to Moscow, at least in the diplomatic field. All that Britain could do at that time was to try to wean the Germans away from too close an alignment with the Soviets.

If, therefore, Germany was to serve as a check on some power whose political influence and military superiority Britain might have feared, this country could apparently only have been France. It is easy to see why no documentary evidence should be available to prove that this was Britain's thought, and why no British government spokesman ever openly admitted to such a policy. During the Ruhr occupation, Ramsay MacDonald, then leader of the Labor opposition, asked, "Is it something essential to a demonstration of our amity to France that we are going to turn a blind eye to all the dangers that the development of an enormously powerful European Power is going to offer to us?" [9] The British had a paramount interest in remaining on friendly terms with their neighbor and "buffer" across the Channel quite apart from any sentimental ties or war memories, which were a strong influence. Yet everything seemed to point to an instinctive, if not intentional,

[9] J. Ramsay MacDonald, February 16, 1923; H. of C., *Parl. Deb.*, Vol. 160, col. 548.

desire to create a more even balance on the Rhine. At the Disarmament Conference Britain openly favored Germany's demand for "equality." While a feeling of justice and a desire to avoid further provocation may have led Britain to advocate equality, it is hard to believe that strong arguments on the other side would not have been discovered if British interests had not run parallel to those of Germany. The same holds true for the many other concessions which, under pressure from Britain, were made to Germany, and helped the latter to recover her strength. It may therefore have been merely a fortunate coincidence for the British that they were able to find plausible ideological and moral arguments for assisting Germany in her return to power, when basically they were following traditional precepts and seeking to re-establish a better balance between the two countries on the Rhine.

There were reasons enough why Britain might have wished to put a check on French preponderance on the Continent. Some we have already mentioned. The policy of pacification and economic recovery, for instance, made them fear that French policy on the Continent, if it were left free to follow its own course, would run counter to British wishes. The invasion of the Ruhr had come as a great shock and had proved that British persuasion was not in itself strong enough to prevent so disastrous an adventure. Also it was not the French alone, after all, with whom Britain had to reckon. France was the head of a powerful group of nations, her friends and allies in Central Europe, who for years had little effective opposition to fear on the Continent. Then, too, Britain's ability to act as a mediator and conciliator was in direct proportion to the degree of balance between the French group and any other powers with whom Britain was able to establish friendly relations. In the Near East, in the financial field, and in matters of naval armaments, France was at times capable even of interfering directly with British interests. It would seem, therefore, that national interests, reasonableness, and a sense of justice, all working together, combined to push Britain back into her traditional course. Whether her statesmen knew it or not, Britain's policy, in operating to restore a better balance of power on the Rhine, made her a firm opponent of the French policy of permanent superiority over Germany.

In any case and whatever her motives may have been, Britain was instrumental in helping Germany to get back on her feet after Versailles. Sir John Simon was able to say, "This country has led the way in restoring Germany to her position as an equal partner, and in removing the discriminations which pressed upon her." [10] But Britain was not willing at any time to see Germany replace France as the dominant power on the Continent. If there was ever any doubt in this respect, particularly after Neville Chamberlain's government came into office, the events of 1939 dispelled it.

The deep conflict which raged in Britain during the last few years did not bear upon the question whether Germany should be allowed to gain preponderance, but concerned the very thorny problem of how to decide when the critical moment had arrived to check her further rise lest she attain an undesirable degree of power. As long as Germany's strength was still well below the danger line, Britain's conciliatory policy toward her was backed almost unanimously by all political parties in Britain. Since the traditional policy of the balance of power and the policy of pacification ran parallel in that they both called for assistance to Germany,

[10] Sir John Simon, Foreign Secretary, November 7, 1933; H. of C., *Parl. Deb.*, Vol. 281, cols. 50-51.

The Germans since 1939 prefer to emphasize Britain's part in destroying Germany's world power at Versailles or to list the frequent cases where she failed to convert France to her viewpoint or to make concessions herself which would have alleviated Germany's position. In 1938 they went to the other extreme and persuaded themselves that Britain was ready to give Germany a completely free hand in Central and Eastern Europe.

conservatives and pacifists alike had reason to favor concessions and redress of German grievances.

This happy coincidence, as we hope to show in greater detail in subsequent chapters, disappeared from the moment Hitler came to power. The first to oppose any further continuation of a policy so advantageous to Germany were those who regarded any attempt to pacify National Socialist Germany as either futile or undesirable. It was impossible, they said, to satisfy Hitler. Every concession would be interpreted as a sign of weakness and encourage him to make greater demands toward the fulfillment of his ultimate objectives as laid down in *Mein Kampf*. Also, every success of Hitler in foreign affairs would only tend to strengthen the forces of National Socialism in the world. Later, opposition began to grow more and more among the Conservatives, too, who foresaw that German armaments, particularly in the air, would become a direct threat to Great Britain, and who believed that Germany was insatiable and aiming for hegemony on the Continent. Sir Austen Chamberlain, one of the first Conservatives to change from an attitude of conciliation to one of resistance, declared, "On the path of concessions to Germany we have already gone a very long way, and the time has come when we ought to indicate, on some points at any rate, quite clearly that there are limits, and that we make these concessions or come to these agreements in the hope that there will be a settlement and only in the hope that there will be a settlement; and that we are not ready to make all these concessions and then be faced next day with a new and more extreme set of demands, using what we have conceded merely as a jumping-off ground for these fresh claims."[11] There was increasing pressure

[11] Sir Austen Chamberlain, February 6, 1934; H. of C., *Parl. Deb.*, Vol. 285, cols. 1042-1043. Even those who were most favorable to the Third Reich were constantly endeavoring to secure an "exact statement of German aims," and "to see the Germans categorically pinned down to their programme," as the Marquess

on the government, therefore, to reverse its policy and not only to put an end to concessions, but to use every available means—armaments, alliances, collective security—to put a stop to any further rise of German power and expansion.

Not until the spring of 1939 did the government agree to discard its policy of pacification. It had justified the continuance of its earlier course first by the hope that Germany, even under Hitler's rule, might settle down as a satisfied country before reaching a point where she would threaten British vital interests and gain domination over Europe. When, later, this hope began to fade, it was pointed out that calling a halt to Germany too abruptly might mean war. It was then that the term "appeasement" came to mean not merely a willingness to make concessions and to favor pacification, but a readiness to bow to the *fait accompli* or even to the threat of force.[12] The same "psychological policy" was being followed, but its character and implications had changed under the new circumstances.

Although the government still pursued the old line of conduct after the rise of National Socialism, a new element entered into its relations with Germany. From a single-line policy it shifted to what the Germans called a double-line policy. The British Government did not drop the idea that Germany's advance might yet come to a halt of its own accord if justice were done to Germany's claims and if radical revision of the treaties in the East was achieved through negotiation; but it was not willing any

of Londonderry expresses it in *Ourselves and Germany* (1938), pp. 105, 154. The best known official attempt to secure a definition of the limits of German policy was the Eden "questionnaire" of May 6, 1936, drafted during the negotiations which followed the reoccupation of the Rhineland. *Cmd.* 5175, pp. 12 ff.

[12] The principal speeches made by Neville Chamberlain in defense of his policy of "appeasement" are collected in *In Search of Peace* (1939), which covers the period from May, 1937, when Mr. Chamberlain became Prime Minister, to May, 1939, after the "appeasement" policy had been discarded.

longer to run the risk of remaining unprepared in case its expectations were disappointed. If Britain waited too long (as many believe she did), she might be unable to check Germany's advance at the upper limit of power compatible with Britain's vital interests. The policy of appeasement was therefore now accompanied by feverish British rearmament and closer military understanding with France. While such a dual policy may not have been avoidable, its two aspects inevitably counteracted and weakened each other. Conciliatory moves were now interpreted by the Germans as only a device to gain time until rearmament should put Britain in a position from which she could dictate her own terms. At the same time, the policy of appeasement made it more difficult for Britain's rearmament to fulfill the task for which it was intended. Every success of Hitler added to the military strength and prestige against which the British were arming. However, the combination of the two policies also averted some of the undesirable consequences for Britain which either one applied alone would have had. As long as Britain was conciliatory it was more difficult for Germany to take offense at her rearmament and declare it to be intentionally provocative. Appeasement, on the other hand, could less easily be interpreted as a sign of British decadence and reluctance to fight, if it was accompanied by rearmament on a scale too tremendous to be lightly discounted as sheer bluff.

In the end, Britain's policy toward Germany went down to defeat. She was not able through conciliatory methods, coupled with the threat of her armaments, to halt a rise of Germany beyond the "maximum level." She had previously been in a position, even in the face of obstinate French resistance, to help Germany back onto her feet. There had been a time when the dream of a new general settlement among the Western Powers which would stabilize peace on the basis of a new balance of power on the Rhine seemed not

Utopian. But British diplomacy failed in the effort to make Germany a "satisfied" power or to convince her that there was an upper limit to the expansion of her power beyond which she would run up against British resistance. The outcome was a new war in Europe.[13]

[13] See below, pp. 292 ff., for a discussion of the policy of resistance to Germany over the Polish issue.

XVI. British Commitments in Western Europe and the Treaty of Locarno

IF Britain had been willing and able after the World War to retire into her one-time "splendid isolation," her influence on France and Germany and on the balance of their respective powers would have been slight. As it was, she became hardly less involved in Western Europe than France. "We are already, by the engagements we have undertaken, inextricably bound up with the fortunes of Europe whether for good or for evil," declared Austen Chamberlain in 1925, "and our safety lies, not in trying to ignore those obligations, not in seeking that isolation which is impossible, but in a wise and prudent use of our influence and power to maintain peace and prevent war from breaking out again."[1] Or, in Sir John Simon's words, ". . . the conditions for isolation have disappeared and cannot exist. We shall not increase our influence for peace by declaring that it does not matter to us what our neighbours in Europe do or do not do. We have an immense moral authority to assert, . . ."[2] No negotiations or conferences on European affairs took place, no diplomatic steps or actions were undertaken in which Britain did not play an active, if not a decisive, part. With the rise of Germany's power, her leadership in all negotiations with the Third Reich became increasingly marked.

[1] Austen Chamberlain, Foreign Secretary, June 24, 1925; H. of C., *Parl. Deb.*, Vol. 185, cols. 1560, 1561.

[2] Sir John Simon, Foreign Secretary, November 7, 1933; H. of C., *Parl. Deb.*, Vol. 281, col. 59.

The center of gravity in Western Europe moved from Paris and Geneva to London, and Anglo-German rivalry came to overshadow the old conflict on the Rhine. If there were any isolationists left in Britain their arguments were overruled by considerations of a strategic and economic character requiring close ties between Britain and the Continent, and not permitting any indifference or retrenchment behind the Channel.

To the Leftists, as we shall see later, it was not a question of whether Britain should commit herself on behalf of this or that country or should choose between the Continent and the Empire. They were eager to have Britain take an active part in the new community of nations which had been established at Geneva. The Conservatives favored a policy of caution in respect to continental commitments. The Empire and the command of the sea, according to them, remained Britain's primary interests. Any commitment likely to draw Britain too deeply into the affairs of a troubled and war-stricken continent would embarrass Britain in her relations with the Dominions and with the United States and would rob her of her freedom of action in the wide realm of her non-European interests. "The more our policy commits us to intervention in European affairs, to the probability or even the possibility of another European war, the more determinedly will the Dominions avoid sharing our responsibilities and stand aloof from any attempt at a closer and more effective organisation of the Empire for a common policy. I believe that the same is in large measure true of the United States."[3] As long as Germany had no air force capable of striking at the British Isles, it was hard to persuade the Conservative governments to undertake any continental commitment. They would have preferred to confine themselves to the League Covenant, which, even weakened as it was by

[3] Leopold Amery, November 7, 1933; H. of C., *Parl. Deb.*, Vol. 281, col. 108.

subsequent interpretations, was more of a pledge than Britain would traditionally have wished to countenance.

However, the Conservatives, as well as their opponents, realized that, whether they liked it or not, an additional pledge to France was a political necessity. It had been promised at Versailles, and France had made concessions to obtain it. The failure to ratify that pact of guarantee left Britain with a moral obligation and "in honour bound" [4] to substitute some other pledge. It was expected that the French would appreciate the "graciousness of the gift." [5] France, furthermore, was so obsessed by her desire for more security that Britain could not hope to gain any concessions from her unless in return she was willing to negotiate some new commitment. Arguments in favor of such a commitment were not lacking. The moral obligation was one; then there was the thesis that the World War would have been avoided if Germany had known in 1914 that Britain would stand by France. "Consider what might have been the altered condition of the world to-day had such a pact existed in 1914," exclaimed Austen Chamberlain.[6] France's state of nervousness, as explained before, was an obstacle to the pacification of the Continent, only to be removed by a promise of British assistance. Finally, it was said that Britain would have to fight on the side of France anyway, whether she was committed or not, since her strategic frontier was on the Rhine.

This left unsolved the problem as to what form an additional British promise of assistance to France should take. Was it to be an old-time military alliance setting Europe back on the road to the hostile blocs of pre-war days, or was it possible to satisfy

[4] David Lloyd George, Prime Minister, February 7, 1922; H. of C., *Parl. Deb.*, Vol. 150, col. 42.

[5] Marquess Curzon, Foreign Secretary, to British Ambassador in Paris, February 9, 1922; *Cmd. 2169*, p. 153.

[6] Austen Chamberlain, Lord Privy Seal, February 8, 1922; H. of C., *Parl. Deb.*, Vol. 150, col. 197.

France merely by rendering the obligations under the Covenant more stringent? The Leftists liked to believe the latter, since it would make Geneva the real center of European affairs. The British traditionalists rejected both of these alternatives. They defeated the French attempt to obtain a military alliance in 1922 and refused to ratify the Geneva Protocol, which the British Labor government had negotiated in 1924. If there was to be a new commitment, it would apparently have to take some novel form free of the unwelcome features of an alliance or of a "League with teeth."

The Locarno Pact or, as it was officially called, the Treaty of Mutual Guarantee, which was agreed to by Germany, Belgium, France, Great Britain, and Italy at Locarno in 1925, fulfilled the British traditionalist *desiderata* in an almost ideal fashion. Although today of purely historical interest, the pact assumes an important place in any study on British foreign policy because it contains so many of the concepts which guided British Conservative governments throughout the period under consideration and which may retain their influence in the future.

The original incentive which led to a new agreement was, as we have said, the French demand for more security. The initiative for this particular pact was taken by Germany.[7] However, once the

[7] Whatever part Britain, or the British Ambassador to Berlin, may have played in the early stages, German thought contributed to the original draft. An entry in Viscount D'Abernon's diary for April 9, 1923, refers to the possibility of reaching an agreement "guaranteeing both France and Germany from the danger of aggression," and speaks of the "necessity of bilateral protection." *An Ambassador of Peace*, II, p. 194. See also *ibid.*, III, pp. 125 ff., for Lord D'Abernon's day-by-day notes on the negotiations as viewed from Berlin.

The course of the negotiations is described in J. W. Wheeler-Bennett, and F. E. Langermann, *Information on the Problem of Security, 1917-1926* (1927), Part IV. The relevant documents are contained in *Cmd. 2435*, *Cmd. 2468*, *Cmd. 2525*, and in the publications of the French Foreign Office, *Pacte de Sécurité: Neuf pièces relatives à la proposition faite le 9 février 1925 par le Gouvernement allemand et à la réponse du Gouvernement français (9 février 1925–16 juin*

pact was signed, the most permanent and broad approval was that given by the British. Briand and Stresemann, the negotiators of the treaty for their respective countries, as well as their followers, of course praised the agreement. In both France and Germany, nevertheless, there was an outburst of violent nationalist criticism.

The French Rightists, as we have remarked earlier, regarded Locarno as a poor substitute for a straightforward Franco-British alliance. They resented the fact that France was being treated on no more than equal terms with Germany. Above all they feared the effect of the limitation of Britain's commitments to the Rhine which was a blow to the French policy of indivisible defenses on Germany's western and eastern borders.

The German Nationalists were in an uproar because, according to them, Germany had not been treated as an equal. It was she, they said, who had to make all the sacrifices. She was accepting voluntarily not only the reincorporation of Alsace and Lorraine into France, but the unilateral demilitarization of wide sections of German territory. What was she receiving in return? Would Britain ever protect Germany against a French attack?

No such complaint was raised by Britain's traditionalists. Locarno not only gave Britain's unavoidable new commitment a form against which there was no objection, but proposed a new order in Western Europe which was in complete accord both with Britain's interests and with ideas that were dear to the traditionalists. This accounts for the fact that many of the features of Locarno, as we shall see, turn up in every British traditionalist plan for a new settlement in Western Europe even down to the final period before the new war. The British Conservatives clung to the pact as a model with an unusual degree of consistency.

1925); and *Pacte de Sécurité, II: Documents signés ou paraphés à Locarno le 16 octobre 1925, précédés de six pièces relatives aux négociations préliminaires (20 juillet 1925–16 octobre 1925)*. See also Fritz Berber, *Locarno: a collection of documents* (1936).

The Locarno Treaty was not an alliance. It was not directed against any one country; it was fundamentally an agreement between one-time opponents who would normally have been expected to enter into alliances against one another. "It is the distinction between an alliance of certain Powers against another Power or group of Powers and a mutual guarantee of the peaceful settlement of disputes between a group of Powers interested in a particular area." [8] Therefore, it fulfilled Britain's often-expressed desire to avoid splitting the Continent into rival groups. They knew that "one defensive alliance is apt to call into existence a rival group, and this process might result ultimately in the division of Europe into hostile camps." [9] Military arrangements under these circumstances were out of the question, which had the advantage of making Britain's commitments less rigid and automatic. She retained her freedom to decide on how to fulfill her pledge.

At the same time, the pact differed no less fundamentally from the Geneva Protocol, since Britain's commitment was explicitly limited to a specified geographic region in which Britain had vital interests. This was a decisive victory of traditionalist policy over the collectivist idea of world-wide commitments and "indivisible peace." As Austen Chamberlain himself put it, Britain's obligations were "narrowly circumscribed to the conditions under which we have an actual vital national interest." [10] The *status quo* in Eastern Europe was not given the same guarantee as the *status quo* on the Rhine.

Thus the pitfalls of both forms of commitments that had been

[8] Austen Chamberlain, Foreign Secretary, June 24, 1925; H. of C., *Parl. Deb.*, Vol. 185, col. 1580.

[9] Second British memorandum to Committee on Arbitration and Security, February, 1928; League of Nations, *Documents of the Preparatory Commission for the Disarmament Conference*, Series VI (1928. IX. 6.), p. 184.

[10] Austen Chamberlain, Foreign Secretary, November 18, 1925; H. of C., *Parl. Deb.*, Vol. 188, col. 429.

suggested earlier were avoided. Britain was not to become a partner to either a bilateral or a general alliance. Like Italy, she was assigned the role of guarantor. Chamberlain stated that Locarno "enabled Britain once again to take her historic part as mediator and peacemaker in the new Europe created by the Great War," [11] and therefore theoretically, at least, she was able to act again as a disinterested party. The French nationalists who attacked Briand for accepting the pact fully understood the consequences if Britain, the one-time war ally, became the guarantor both of France, *"la grande victime,"* and of Germany, "the aggressor." [12] Britain had drawn "the real dividing point between the years of war and the years of peace" [13] by putting an end to any differentiation between victors and vanquished. "We were divided four years ago," said Baldwin in 1928, "into two camps, the victors and the vanquished; that distinction exists no longer. I hope those words will be forgotten." [14]

In fact Locarno did not entirely end British discrimination between France and Germany. Britain, with her frontier on the Rhine, was not really disinterested. France still represented the "friendly power" which protected the Channel ports from the potential "hostile force" which might some day cross the Rhine again. There was discrimination within the pact itself since some of its main provisions dealt with the demilitarization of German territory. More discrimination, the German Nationalists pointed out,

[11] Austen Chamberlain, Foreign Secretary, speech in Birmingham, November 2, 1925; in his *Peace in Our Time* (1928), pp.170-171.

[12] A full statement, from the French point of view, of Britain's gains from the Locarno Treaty, was made by Louis Marin during the debate on the treaty in the Chamber of Deputies, March 1, 1926; Chambre, *Débats*, 1926, pp. 1076-1078.

[13] Austen Chamberlain, Foreign Secretary, declaration to the press, October 23, 1925; *Société des Nations*, VII (1925), p. 499.

[14] Stanley Baldwin, Prime Minister, speech in London, November 9, 1928; *The Times* (London), November 10, 1928, p. 8.

would come to light if France should ever violate the pact, since nobody, either in Britain or France, could conceive of Britain's taking sides with Germany and fighting against the French.

This does not mean that British commitments to Germany were farcical and of no practical use to her. It was Germany, after all, who had proposed the treaty. Stresemann realized that it would be to the interest of Britain to prevent any situation from arising in which she would have to choose between helping Germany against France or violating her obligations to Germany. She would, therefore, use every means of diplomatic pressure to restrain France from attacking Germany and in particular from repeating her invasion of the Ruhr.[15] Germany's prestige was enhanced by being treated formally, at least, as an equal, and the wind was taken out of the sails of those who were still working for a bilateral Franco-British alliance.[16] British diplomacy had therefore succeeded in giving France additional security without provoking Germany and in lessening the vulnerability of Germany to new acts of French military pressure without thereby destroying the closer "entente" which linked Britain to France.

The satisfaction which the British traditionalists derived from

[15] In Harold Nicolson's opinion, Locarno served Germany as a "screen," and "because Locarno existed, because Germany had Great Britain's guarantee that she should never be invaded by France, Germany was able to build up, under that guarantee, a new system of armaments, . . ." Address given at Chatham House, March 18, 1936; in Royal Institute of International Affairs, "Germany and the Rhineland," special supplement to *International Affairs,* April, 1936, p. 9.

[16] The Foreign Office Memorandum of February 20, 1925, already referred to, which was drawn up under the direction of Austen Chamberlain, Foreign Secretary, recommended that it was "a necessity of British and, therefore, of imperial defense to reach some understanding with France and Belgium which may entail a guarantee on our part that these territories shall not fall into other hands." *The World* (New York), May 10, 1925, p. 2. This recommendation for a bilateral arrangement was, however, rejected by the cabinet, acting, it is said, on the advice of Balfour, Birkenhead, Churchill, and Curzon. Viscount D'Abernon, *An Ambassador of Peace,* III, p. 155.

the pact was not of a narrowly nationalistic nature. They saw in it the beginning, at least, of a new concert of the four great Western European powers. It was to become a close relationship based on a fair balance between France and Germany, which would be guaranteed by two powers, Britain and Italy, whose main interest was to preserve the balance and favor friendly relations between the two neighbors on the Rhine. At the same time this arrangement lessened the danger of German-Soviet intimacy and held the Bolshevist Government away from the councils of Europe.

Nothing, it would appear, could have offered more chance of real pacification than such a pact of reconciliation in Western Europe, provided that it really settled the main conflict between France and Germany. But this it did not do. It stabilized the *status quo* in the West, over which at the time there was no quarrel, but left the "powder box" in the East virtually unchanged. The fact that the pact emphasized British opposition to pledges in the East equal to those in the West and permitted Germany to give more binding promises in regard to her western than her eastern borders was anything but a solution to the problem which worried France and her allies.

The British Conservatives returned again and again to the idea of grouping the four Western Powers together in some form of close relationship. The Four-Power Pact of 1933 was based on the same configuration. It is likely that the Four-Power Conference at Munich in 1938 appealed to the Chamberlain government largely because it seemed to open the way for a new "general settlement" among these same four powers. As a matter of fact, the "appeasement" policy of the later period was for the most part an attempt at integrating the London-Paris entente and the Rome-Berlin axis. On each of these occasions the exclusion of the Soviet Union was an important feature. Furthermore, the agreement was in each case at the expense of the French policy on the Vistula and the Danube in that it gave Germany more freedom of action in the East. It is not to be wondered at, therefore, that the French had misgivings in regard to the British predilection for a purely Western European alignment and put obstacles in the way of its realization.

Nothing has been said so far about the attitude of the British Leftists toward the Locarno Pact. Since it suited the traditionalists so admirably, one might have expected that there would have been much opposition from the Left. This, however, was not the case. Criticisms of the pact developed only much later, when the consequences of Locarno came to be more clearly realized. At the time, all parties in Britain rejoiced over the apparent reconciliation between France and Germany which, it was believed, would inaugurate a new era of peace and friendship on the Continent. There was general satisfaction that Britain had avoided anything resembling the old-time military alliances. Her role as a friendly conciliator was lauded. The provisions for peaceful settlement of disputes and the promises of non-aggression which the Locarno Pact contained appealed to the pacifist sentiment on the Left. In many directions, therefore, all British parties shared the same outlook and preferences.

Where criticism was bound to arise was in regard to the effect of Locarno on the League and on British League policy. Austen Chamberlain confused the issue with much skill and made it appear that Locarno offered new support to the League. The League was not being forsaken; the purpose, he said, was "to underpin the general structure by agreements among nations in a particular region, whose fates are so knit one with another that they cannot be indifferent to what happens in that area and who on any aggression in that area will be found ready to help in the repression of the aggressor. That was the policy of Locarno."[17] How could the League be harmed by a treaty, the purpose of which was to stabilize peace in a region of acute conflict? But, as we have already said, the Locarno Pact was contrary to the whole concept of universal solidarity. Was not Britain, by explicitly limiting her guarantee to the Rhine frontier, saying in effect that "victims of aggression" in other parts of Europe or the world could not count on any British guarantee?[18] Attlee was right, from a collectivist point of view, when he stated in 1936 that "the Locarno Pact took a very big step in giving the League a twist out of its right course."[19]

Locarno did not turn out to be a permanent settlement. Hitler put an end to it in 1936 by remilitarizing the Rhineland and thus liberating Germany from restrictions which hampered her freedom of action in the East. Free access into Germany, as we have said earlier, was the *conditio sine qua non* for effective French influence on Germany's relations with Austria, Czechoslovakia, and Poland. Therefore, quite apart from the fact that the signing of a pact between France and the Soviet Union, the greatest power in the East, offered Germany an excuse for tearing up the Locarno Pact, the Western European agreement foundered on the rocks of the unsolved conflict over the power of Germany and France in the East and the future of Central rather than of Western Europe.

[17] Sir Austen Chamberlain, March 11, 1935; H. of C., *Parl. Deb.*, Vol. 299, col. 75.

[18] James M. Spaight, in *Pseudo-Security* (1928), approved the Rhine Pact precisely because it was a "break-away from the League" (p. 135) and "a return, within limits, to the older system, the principle of which was the recognition of the special interests of geographically circumscribed groups" (pp. 137-138).

[19] Clement Attlee, March 26, 1936; H. of C., *Parl. Deb.*, Vol. 310, col. 1535.

XVII. Germany's Eastern Neighbors

Britain's Interests on the Vistula and the Danube

AFTER Versailles the Continent of Europe divided itself for the British naturally into a number of geographic and strategic regions: first, Western Europe, including the Rhine, the Channel, and the North Sea; second, the Mediterranean area; and third, a section stretching eastward along the Vistula and the Danube. Further east lay the Soviet Union, but she was, as Neville Chamberlain put it, "partly European but partly Asiatic." [1] The third of these regions, which the Germans sometimes call "*Zwischeneuropa*," [2] was, according to British traditionalists, too far away to affect directly either the safety of the British Isles or British supremacy on the seas.

While France was deeply concerned and closely linked with the range of lesser countries that stretched from the Baltic to the Danube and down to the Balkans, Britain's attitude was one of marked indifference. France fully appreciated their strategic value and foresaw that they were predestined to be the first victims of any future efforts of Germany to expand her power on the Continent, but the British saw them primarily as potential trouble centers, filled with "national hatred, national greed, and the worst form of national pride." [3] Poland and Czechoslovakia had extended

[1] Neville Chamberlain, Prime Minister, February 21, 1938; H. of C., *Parl. Deb.*, Vol. 332, col. 154.

[2] See Giselher Wirsing, *Zwischeneuropa und die deutsche Zukunft* (1932).

[3] David Lloyd George, Prime Minister, speech in Portmadoc, June 15, 1921; *Société des Nations*, III (1921), p. 413.

their borders beyond the limits which the British had wished to concede to them, and contained "large masses of Germans clamouring for reunion with their native land."[4] They were, therefore, countries of mixed nationalities, minority problems, and disputed frontiers. The fact that France was bound to them by pacts and alliances hardly allayed British misgivings; indeed, this only increased the chances that Britain might become entangled in the struggles which were bound to arise. The fundamental credo of Britain's traditionalist policy was, therefore, to steer as free as possible of Central European affairs.

The British could not claim that they had no interests whatever in the course of political or economic events in Central Europe. After all, as a great power their security depended on the relative strength of their potential friends or enemies. If they had believed, for instance, that the Soviet Union might some day control all of these lesser powers, or if they had foreseen how little resistance German expansion might encounter if they did nothing to forestall such a development, their concern might have been far greater than it was. Furthermore, their interest in peace and economic prosperity was not regionally limited. It was, therefore, evident that the British could not be indifferent to an actual outbreak of violence or to serious economic troubles in those regions. The tendency was to minimize Britain's interest but not to deny it entirely. This was done by the use of negative terms. The British repeatedly stated, "We cannot, even if we would, disinterest ourselves in the course of events there, any more than we can disinterest ourselves in the course of events anywhere else on the earth's surface as conditions are to-day."[5] But, although Britain

[4] David Lloyd George, Prime Minister, Memorandum to Clemenceau, March 26, 1919; *Cmd. 2169*, p. 77.

[5] Anthony Eden, Foreign Secretary, June 25, 1937; H. of C., *Parl. Deb.*, Vol. 325, col. 1603.

was "not disinterested," it was emphasized at the same time that she was not "vitally interested" in Central and Eastern Europe. "Non-disinterestedness" was significant in several ways. Negatively, it implied that there was not enough of an interest for Britain to be willing to fight, or, in any event, to commit herself in advance to the use of military force on behalf of countries to the east of Germany. Positively, it meant that Britain was sufficiently interested, nevertheless, to refuse to give others a free hand in that region. She did not wish to be understood as "licensing or legitimising war" in that part of Europe.[6]

Although they minimized Britain's interests in Central and Southeastern Europe, the British Conservatives insisted that they had no intention of evading the commitments which Britain had assumed under the League Covenant. On the contrary, Article 16 (the sanctions article of the League) was, according to their interpretation, ideally fitted to serve a policy of "non-disinterestedness." The provisions were acceptable, inasmuch as they were "not capable of prior definition" and, therefore, did not conflict with what Viscount Halifax called Britain's inability to "define beforehand what might be our attitude to a hypothetical complication in Central or Eastern Europe."[7] At the same time the Covenant did give Great Britain not only the power but, what was more important, the right to interfere and to take forceful action in a case of unprovoked aggression if she should so desire. What Britain was trying to avoid, then, were rigid or automatic commitments. She wished to confine herself to the loose, general, and relatively noncommittal pledges contained in the Covenant.

Opposition to this attitude of relative aloofness on the part of

[6] Austen Chamberlain, Foreign Secretary, March 24, 1925; H. of C., *Parl. Deb.*, Vol. 182, col. 320.

[7] Viscount Halifax, Lord Privy Seal, March 3, 1937; H. of L., *Parl. Deb.*, Vol. 104, col. 498.

Great Britain was widespread and was voiced particularly by adherents to the collectivist philosophy. The opposition asserted that modern war could not be localized in any one region of Europe but would spread. Peace in the East and the West, according to this thesis, was "indivisible." "The point that I wish to emphasise," said Dalton, "is that in Europe there are no quarrels which are not our own. If the peace of Europe is disturbed anywhere then it is disturbed everywhere."[8]

The traditionalists did not deny the possibility that if a war should start in the East it might spread into Western Europe. Sir John Simon was of the opinion that "the beginning of a conflict is like the beginning of a fire in a high wind. It may be limited at the start, but who can say how far it would spread, or how much destruction it would do, or how many may be called upon to beat it out?"[9] The controversial question was how Britain could best avert such a war. Here was the old dilemma. Should Britain guarantee the territorial integrity of countries like Poland and Czechoslovakia, thereby stiffening their resistance and encouraging them to turn a deaf ear to any proposals for change or concession, even though she had little faith in the wisdom and permanency of the *status quo*? Or was it wiser to keep these countries in doubt as to whether British support would be forthcoming, at the risk, however, that this might encourage the revisionist powers to raise and perhaps realize unjustified claims against their weaker neighbors? Theoretically, the best plan of action for Great Britain would seem to have been for her to take a vigorous and courageous stand against the *status quo* powers in the days when they were strong and hostile to any suggestion for change, and later to have resisted the revisionist powers when they had become powerful and

[8] Hugh Dalton, March 26, 1936; H. of C., *Parl. Deb.*, Vol. 310, col. 1457.

[9] Sir John Simon, Chancellor of the Exchequer, speech in Lanark, August 27, 1938; *The Times* (London), August 29, 1938, p. 7.

had begun to dictate changes by the threat of force. We shall find that her policy in practice was exactly the opposite.

The French alliance system threatened to make any differentiation between the Rhine and *Zwischeneuropa* meaningless. On whatever grounds France might come to the assistance of her Eastern allies, Great Britain, with her strategic frontier on the Rhine, would have to throw her weight and active support on the French side. By virtue of her ties to France she was therefore indirectly committed to any power with which France chose to be allied. Eden spoke of the apprehension lest, "owing to obligations elsewhere, our neighbours may become involved in conflict and may call for help in a quarrel that is not ours."[10] The conclusion was inescapable that Great Britain had forfeited her freedom of action in Central Europe once she permitted France to enter upon treaties of alliance with powers in that region. All she could do was to use her influence either to prevent wars in which allies of France might become engaged, or to prevent France from living up to her obligations.

Because of the awkward consequences which French commitments to countries in the East were likely to entail for Great Britain if she wished to remain unentangled, one might have expected Britain to have consistently opposed such French alliances. She did not do so. The desire not to become entangled was frequently in conflict with other objectives in British foreign policy. Thus, at times, it seemed more expedient to allow France to satisfy her urgent demand for more security by further ties with other continental countries than for Great Britain to undertake new commitments to France. The opposition used this as an argument to accuse the government of actually having driven France into the

[10] Anthony Eden, Foreign Secretary, March 26, 1936; H. of C., *Parl. Deb.*, Vol. 310, col. 1443.

arms of the countries in the East by not being willing to give France the assurances which might have made her feel secure.

Status Quo VERSUS *Revision*

Since Britain had professed so little interest in Central Europe, it is amazing to see how in 1938 and 1939 she came to play not only a decisive role in the affairs of countries on the Danube and Vistula, but discovered that the fate of the Czechs and the Poles could under certain circumstances become as vital a matter to her as to France. Since Britain regarded her interest in these "far away" regions (as Neville Chamberlain called them)[11] as limited to the prevention of grave economic troubles and severe clashes of interest, she had no immediate concern either with the maintenance of the *status quo* or with its revision in any specific direction. From a short-term point of view, which was the one the British were inclined to take, anything was agreeable that helped preserve peace for the moment. This attitude eliminated any idea of actively suggesting and promoting some new and more satisfactory settlement which would offer a chance of more stable conditions, real pacification, and economic recovery in these troubled parts of Europe.

The French proposed such schemes as a Danubian confederation or the European Union; the Germans dreamed of a self-sufficient *Mitteleuropa*, or suggested a revision of the map of Central Europe on the basis of the principle of self-determination. No such plans were advanced by London. The British sought merely to avoid the acute outbreak of conflict. Whether at any given moment they would seek to preserve things as they were or support some specific demand for change depended on the answer to the ques-

[11] With reference to Czechoslovakia, in his radio broadcast, September 27, 1938; *The Times* (London), September 28, 1938, p. 10.

tion of how best to eliminate an acute threat of violence. This attitude had unfortunate consequences. It was bound in any given conflict to cause Britain to lean toward the stronger side, and to assist those countries which had the most power to back their intentions by force or were most likely to risk doing so. There was a time when the *status quo* powers were able to declare convincingly that the slightest suggestion of revision was provocative to them and would be met with force. If Britain wished to save peace under those circumstances, it was expedient to dissuade the weaker powers from attempting any change. This happened, for instance, in the case of the proposed customs union between Germany and Austria. Later, when the revisionist powers began to gain the upper hand, the situation was reversed, and Britain found herself persuading the *status quo* powers to make sufficient concessions to prevent the threat of force from becoming a reality. It was not difficult for other powers to take advantage of this British attitude and to threaten that peace would be endangered unless Britain helped them to secure the results they desired.

However, it would be unfair to say that Great Britain limited her activity to support of the stronger group. Her efforts were also directed toward moderating the course of the more powerful party so as to render its action less provocative. This accounts for the emphasis with which the British objected in every case less to the substance of the demands than to the form and methods which were being employed. Speaking of the Austrian *Anschluss*, Neville Chamberlain said, "I do not think that the people of this country would want to interfere in a case where two States desired to join together, but there were features about the methods which were employed in this particular case of union which were extremely distasteful to His Majesty's Government, and which profoundly shocked public opinion." [12] At the same time, it is true, persuasion

[12] Neville Chamberlain, Prime Minister, speech in Birmingham, April 8, 1938; *The Times* (London), April 9, 1938, p. 17.

and, when necessary, pressure were used to make the weaker powers acquiesce to the demands that the stronger party insisted on putting forward. Thus, in 1931, the plan for a customs union between Austria and Germany was dropped by "peaceful negotiation," and in 1938, under far more drastic pressure, the Sudetenland was annexed by "peaceful procedure." British "mediation" helped in both cases, but it might be more exact to call their policy "relative partisanship." The outcome depended on the relative strength (assumed or real) of the respective contestants rather than on any British plan for the fairest and most desirable settlement.

From 1918 until 1934, the distribution of power in Europe—in the West as well as on the Danube or the Vistula—was definitely favorable to the *status quo* powers. When disturbances occurred, the solution was bound to be to their advantage. Poland, for instance, was able to retain Vilna even though she had taken it by force. She also profited from a policy of the *fait accompli* in Upper Silesia, although Britain's moderating influence prevented Germany from losing as much of her territory as would otherwise have been the case. While Austria and Hungary were given financial assistance in meeting the disastrous economic consequences of the post-war political settlements, they had to pay the price by renewing their promises not to attempt to change the *status quo*. Our discussion of Britain's attitude toward French plans for an Eastern Pact will illustrate how the British, in 1934, still endeavored to assist those seeking to maintain the established order and yet to moderate their course. The discussion of the Czechoslovak crisis and the Munich agreement of 1938 will show the complete change in "relative partisanship" that came about as a consequence of Germany's rise in power. It was a passage from peace by stabilization of the existing order to peace by acquiescence to change.

A third stage followed only six months later, when the fear of

German predominance led Britain not merely to a relative shift of her partisanship, but radically to alter her whole attitude toward Central Europe. She suddenly judged her own vital interests to be at stake. Instead of seeking pacification, it became a matter of putting a stop to further successes of Germany's "revisionist" policy. That meant definitely taking sides with the weaker party. Even then, however, we shall find her more concerned with the methods employed by Germany than with the substance of her claims.

The Negotiations for an "Eastern Locarno"

Let us recall the historical setting. Germany withdrew from the Disarmament Conference and the League in October, 1933. Negotiations between the Great Powers continued throughout the winter in an effort to find a compromise for a disarmament convention, but were ended by the French in April, 1934. The greatly increased figures for armaments in Germany's newly published budget were, the French declared, an open confession that Germany intended to rearm in violation of the provisions of the Versailles Treaty. According to the political slogans of the day, the problem had been how to satisfy Germany's claims to equality and at the same time to meet French demands for more security. If Germany, having now regained her freedom of action, was going to attain "equality" by her own efforts, France was determined to set out and establish the kind of "security" which she desired. It was no longer from the lesser countries like Poland and Czechoslovakia that she wanted promises of military assistance, but from the great military powers on the Continent, namely, the Soviet Union and Italy. This was the aim of Barthou's and Laval's negotiations. There was to be no attempt to enforce the disarmament clauses of the Versailles Treaty, certainly not for the time being. But instead, Germany's rise in power was to be met by an increase in the French system of alliances which would permit her to retain her superiority. This was really possible only if she succeeded in linking together practically the whole of the Continent in a great defensive coalition against future German aggression. The French at that time spoke openly of wanting to forge an "iron ring" around Germany. It would be more exact to say that the small iron ring of the days of German disarmament was now to be supplemented by a greater ring of the big powers.

The French did not start by proposing a purely bilateral pact of mutual assistance with the Soviet Union. Partly because of their concern about Poland and Czechoslovakia and partly because of the need of British consent, they drew up a regional pact to include Poland, Russia, Germany, Czechoslovakia, Finland, Estonia, Latvia, and Lithuania, to be supplemented by a special Franco-Soviet agreement.[13]

What was to be Britain's role in this new scheme? The French refrained from asking Great Britain to link herself with the Continental Powers or to enter upon new commitments in Central and Eastern Europe. They knew that such commitments would not be forthcoming. In describing the initial stages of the Eastern Pact negotiations to the House of Commons on July 13, 1934, Sir John Simon declared, "We made it entirely plain from the beginning, whatever may be the interest or encouragement which this country may be prepared to offer in this new pact, we are not undertaking any new obligations at all. That is quite clearly and definitely

[13] On the negotiations, see above, p. 136 n. 7. The proposal consisted of an agreement for mutual assistance between the signatories, to be supplemented by a special Franco-Soviet arrangement whereby Russia would become a guarantor of the Locarno Treaty and France would accept obligations of assistance toward Russia. On British insistence this supplementary agreement was amended to ensure its operation for the benefit of Germany as well as of France and Russia. The relevant documents are contained in *Cmd. 5143*; the negotiations are described at length in Royal Institute of International Affairs, *Survey of International Affairs, 1935*, I, pp. 58-90.

understood, and there is no possible question or challenge about it. . . . this is not a case in which we are extending our own commitments in any way whatever."[14] But France knew that British consent to the plans was necessary if there was to be no estrangement from Britain and if France was to be assured that Britain would not regard her new pacts in Eastern and Central Europe as incompatible with previous agreements to which Britain was a partner, namely, the Pact of Locarno, or the Covenant of the League of Nations.

Britain was therefore given an opportunity to influence the course of events in those "far-away" regions of Europe which are being discussed here. Her attitude on that occasion illustrates the character of her policy at a time when Germany was not yet rearmed and France and her friends were still preponderant on the Continent. If the general considerations regarding Britain's Central European policy set forth earlier in this chapter are correct, Britain should be expected to lean to the French side, but to seek both to moderate the French course, particularly in regard to the forms and procedure, and to try through diplomatic pressure to get Germany to give her approval. This is exactly what happened.

Britain looked benevolently upon the proposal for a new pact of non-aggression and mutual assistance in the East, even though the Soviet Union was to be included. France thus won her main point and was free to obtain promises of military assistance from the Soviets, both in case Germany attacked her in the west or attacked her allies in the east, provided she gave to the agreements the form Britain required.

It might have seemed as if Britain were laying down more than formal conditions. She not only stressed the need of Germany's being invited to sign the Eastern Pact, but she was to be treated

[14] Sir John Simon, Foreign Secretary, July 13, 1934; H. of C., *Parl. Deb.*, Vol. 292, cols. 693, 694.

as an equal partner if she did. However, the pact, and with it the Franco-Soviet promises of mutual assistance, were not to be conditional on Germany's acceptance of the invitation. If she refused, the way was open, as was later to be proved, not only for a multilateral or regional pact, but for a bilateral alliance between France and the Soviet Union.

The British declared themselves to be as firmly opposed as ever to exclusive bilateral alliances directed against a specific country; it would be provocative to Germany to find herself encircled. Was it not natural, then, to seek a solution by the method that had worked so well in the West? Would not a new regional pact patterned after that of Locarno fulfill the French needs without antagonizing the Germans?

But was this really to be a new "Locarno"? Even the old Locarno Pact had, as far as Britain's pledge was concerned, been less favorable to Germany than to France, insofar as it was improbable that Britain would ever actually take up arms to defend Germany against French attacks. This partiality, however, was negligible compared to the one-sidedness of the treaty that was now being proposed for the East. This was to be a pact for the purpose of stabilizing the *status quo* in Northeastern Europe and of taking common military action against any country attempting to change it by force. No country except Germany was known to be dissatisfied with the *status quo* in this region. She was at that time the only country which all the other prospective signatories of the pact regarded as the "potential aggressor."[15] Legally, it is true,

[15] Discussing this aspect of the Eastern Pact, and explaining Germany's opposition to the plan, Seton-Watson writes that "it was fairly obvious that France and Russia were far more interested in the *status quo* than Germany could ever be, and not at all obvious whether Germany could rely on the active help of France against a Russian attack, . . ." On the other hand, discussing the Franco-Soviet Pact, he upholds its defensive and open character, and writes that "it was . . . at any moment within Germany's own power to put an end to her alleged

Germany was being offered the same protection as any other member of the group. It could be argued, therefore, that such a pact should have been as welcome to her as to any other country. Had not her statesmen constantly stressed the dangers of Bolshevism for Germany?

But even if these fears were genuine, the proposed pact tended rather to increase than to allay them. An agreement designed to assure France, the Soviet Union, and Germany's eastern neighbors of assistance against Germany could hardly be expected to provide Germany with French assistance against the Soviet Union; and as for Soviet assistance to Germany, this was the last thing the National Socialists wanted anyway in those days. The Germans maintained, therefore, that the proposed Eastern Pact only increased the Soviet danger. Russia's proposed status of guarantor of the Locarno Pact on the Rhine would open the way for her interference in Central and even in Western Europe. Why should France wish to ally herself with a Bolshevist government at the other end of Europe and to include Russia as a guarantor of the Rhine borders, if not for the purpose of heightening Russian pressure on Germany?

Sir John Simon, then Foreign Secretary, insisted that Great Britain would approve of the French suggestion for an Eastern Pact only if the pact were not a "selective alliance" and only if the engagements were really "mutual in expression and reciprocal in intention." [16] It is hard to believe that the British were so imbued with the formalistic type of thinking prevalent in some circles as not to realize that under the given political conditions in Europe there could be no question in the proposed pact of "reciprocity in intention."

'encirclement.'" *Britain and the Dictators: a survey of post-war British policy* (1938), pp. 124, 125.

[16] Sir John Simon, July 13, 1934; H. of C., *Parl. Deb.*, Vol. 292, cols. 693, 698.

The British were leaning toward the stronger side. They were willing to have France stabilize the *status quo* in the East with the assistance of the Soviet Union, and to add the Soviets to the other guarantors of the *status quo* in the West. Their efforts were limited to moderating the form by which this aim was to be achieved. A regional pact would be less provocative, they felt, than an alliance. A new "Locarno" would be more palatable to the German and the British peoples, both of whom were hostile to any Franco-Russian alliance of the pre-war type. If Britain could induce Germany to accept the pact, France would obtain her promises of assistance, without becoming as intimately and exclusively tied to the Soviet Union as she would have become by signing a clear-cut military alliance. The difference, even though it was only one of form, would still have its salutary effect on the political atmosphere. Britain was trying to prepare the ground for a "general settlement." If French fears could be allayed without stirring up new resentment in Germany, the British policy of pacification might at last have a chance of becoming effective.

Germany was very vulnerable at the time. She was beginning openly to challenge the Treaty of Versailles, but was not as yet sufficiently rearmed to defend even her own territory. She showed interest in promoting a Western air pact, which France was unwilling to consider unless the Eastern question were satisfactorily solved. The Germans might, therefore, be ready to make "a valuable contribution to the system of security," if they saw in it a means of gaining British sympathy, always a useful check on France. They were under strong pressure to do so, for if Germany refused to sign, she would be blamed for the failure of the Eastern Pact. She would become responsible, in the eyes of the British public, for driving France into a purely bilateral agreement with the Soviet Union and for plunging Europe back into the pre-war system of alliances. It may have been expected that she would not dare to run such a risk and would prefer to accept a pact that had Britain's approval. Some British statesmen who were unfriendly to Germany may, however, have favored the pact precisely because they expected that Germany would not put her signature to it, and thus justify a more openly pro-French course in the future.

To the extent that British policy was not hypocritical and was intended as friendly mediation, it failed to succeed. Germany and also Poland turned down the proposal. The Third Reich was already too strong to have to accept the purely formal status of equality offered her by the pact, and refused as in the past to tie herself down in any way to the territorial *status quo* in the East.

The Czechoslovak Crisis

No attempt will be made here to tell the "inside story" of Britain's role and actions during the greatest of Europe's crises between the two wars. The diplomatic documents which might throw new light on the actual succession of events or the real motives of the leading statesmen will not be available for some time to come. Writers on the subject have built up a whole series of theories, ranging from the proposition that Chamberlain's policy revealed him as the head of a pro-Fascist conspiracy to the argument that Britain's attitude bore witness to British pacifism and decadence.[17]

After 1934 drastic changes took place in Europe, and by 1937

[17] On the Czechoslovak crisis and the Munich Conference, see: Hamilton F. Armstrong, *When There is No Peace* (1939); Vera M. Dean, *Europe in Retreat* (1939); G. E. R. Gedye, *Betrayal in Central Europe* (1939); Graham Hutton, *Survey after Munich* (1939); R. W. Seton-Watson, *Munich and the Dictators* (1939); Alexander Werth, *France and Munich: before and after the surrender* (1939). The literature dealing with the Czechoslovak crisis is reviewed by René Maheu, "Quelques Ouvrages sur Munich," *Politique Etrangère*, IV (juin 1939), pp. 324-346. Relevant documents are contained in *Cmd. 5847* and *Cmd. 5848*.

the situation was vastly different from that of a year or two before. Germany had become one of the leading military powers on the Continent. Italy had been victorious in Ethiopia and had defeated League sanctions. The Rome-Berlin axis had been formed. The Spanish civil war was raising grave problems for the Western democracies. It was under these conditions that Hitler began making an issue of the "ten million Germans" living outside the German frontiers in Austria and Czechoslovakia. In March of 1938 Austria was united with the Reich. By the middle of May of the same year it became certain that Germany had decided to demand a change of conditions in Czechoslovakia. The question was whether Germany would go to war if her claims, the extent of which was unknown, were not satisfied.

Great Britain, while sharing the obligations of all the members of the League, was not an ally of Czechoslovakia; France and the Soviet Union were. It would seem, therefore, that the attitude of the latter, rather than that of Britain, should have decided the outcome of the impending struggle. France, however, had become entirely dependent upon Britain. The Soviet Union was bound to come to the assistance of Czechoslovakia only if France fulfilled her obligations. The final responsibility thus came to rest upon the British. This demonstrates how successfully Britain, by refusing to commit herself automatically and in advance, had gained control over the *status quo* powers and made it difficult for them to entangle her in Central Europe without having obtained her previous consent. But here it also becomes obvious that Great Britain had at the same time so involved herself in those "far-away" regions of Europe that the German-Czechoslovak crisis became a major Anglo-German diplomatic struggle. The Germans gained an advantage from the very outset by being able to deal almost exclusively with the one great power that had all along shown a lack of interest in the preservation of the *status quo* in Central

Europe, a country, moreover, in which all parties had expressed their disapproval of many important features of the post-war settlements, territorial and otherwise, in that region.

Britain's policy with regard to Central Europe during the earlier period after 1919 was, as we have tried to show, based, first, on the general conception held by the British traditionalists since the War, according to which the affairs of Central Europe were too remote to be of vital interest to the British, and, secondly, on the particular assumption that for the time being the *status quo* countries were the most powerful group in that region. It is essential to the interpretation of British policy during 1938 to discover whether the government still held to these two assumptions.

Some British statesmen, both on the Right and on the Left, gave voice to the opinion that any change in Czechoslovakia now, and certainly any that affected the territorial integrity or the independence of that country, would infringe upon vital interests of Great Britain. "The nazification of the whole of the Danube States is a danger of the first capital magnitude to the British Empire," exclaimed Winston Churchill.[18] Germany, it was said, would come to dominate Europe. Once she gained control of the strongly fortified strategic borders of Czechoslovakia, her drive to the East could no longer be checked and German influence would be extended down to the Black Sea and into the Near East. The government refused to be guided by these considerations. Never in an official statement was there any admission of governmental concern over the effects which the disappearance of Czechoslovakia's "Maginot Line" or the augmentation of German man-power would have on Britain's security, although one of the important factors in her security was the fate of France—a country which had relied heavily on the assistance and strength of Czechoslovakia.

[18] Winston Churchill, March 24, 1938; H. of C., *Parl. Deb.*, Vol. 333, cols. 1450-1451.

It was emphatically stated that Britain's sole interest in the matter was to avoid war. Only if Germany by her attitude toward British proposals were to give evidence that she sought domination rather than satisfaction of her demands for the Sudetenland, would the British Government have changed her policy and considered the issue as one of vital importance to the British. "However much we may sympathize with a small nation confronted by a big and powerful neighbour," said Neville Chamberlain, "we cannot in all circumstances undertake to involve the whole British Empire in war simply on her account. If we have to fight it must be on larger issues than that. . . . if I were convinced that any nation had made up its mind to dominate the world by fear of its force, I should feel that it must be resisted." [19]

There was less difference of opinion when it came to judging the relative strengths of the Continental *status quo* Powers and their opponents. This is shown by the fact that nobody, in or out of Great Britain, in or out of the government, seemed to have believed that Czechoslovakia had any choice but to make far-reaching concessions, unless Great Britain were willing to undertake the commitment to defend Czechoslovakia which she had so consistently refused to assume in the past. This is equivalent to saying that the Czechs and the French had themselves come to believe, rightly or wrongly, that they had lost control over the situation in Central Europe, and had become absolutely dependent on British assistance if the established order were to be maintained.

Could peace be more easily preserved by supporting the revisionist powers or the *status quo* countries? The answer depended on which group was more willing to risk a war. That group would be the one most dangerous to oppose. Was Hitler willing to risk a war even if Britain and France were certain to come in on the

[19] Neville Chamberlain, Prime Minister, radio broadcast, September 27, 1938; *The Times* (London), September 28, 1938, p. 10.

side of Czechoslovakia, or was he only bluffing? It is possible that we shall never know the answer. But this much is certain: the British Government based its policy on the assumption that Hitler was ready to risk war. To Chamberlain it was clear that "there was nothing that anybody could do that would prevent that invasion [of Czechoslovakia by German troops] unless the right of self-determination were granted to the Sudeten-Germans and that quickly. That was the sole hope of a peaceful solution." [20] The Germans undoubtedly used to advantage the reputation that Hitler had gained for being entirely unreasonable and capable, therefore, of the most unpredictable moves. The British Government, in any case, acted on the theory that resistance to Germany's revisionist demands by Czechoslovakia and her allies would threaten Great Britain with the most serious risk of becoming involved in a major war and set out to avoid such a war, no longer by helping to stabilize the *status quo* but instead by promoting its change (the term "peaceful change" is hardly applicable) in the hope of satisfying the revisionist powers.

It may be inexact to assert that Great Britain had simply decided once more that the safest course was to lean toward the preponderant group. Might she not have shifted her position because the change that was being demanded appealed to her sense of justice? Certainly the new policy was facilitated by the fact that British public opinion was far from enthusiastic about conditions in the Sudetenland or about the way in which Czechoslovakia's borders had originally been fixed. Had there been no question of self-determination and of oppressed minorities, the British Government would have found it even more difficult than it was to pursue the course adopted in 1938. "I saw that if we were obliged to go to war it would be hard to have it said against us that we were fight-

[20] In describing his visit to Berchtesgaden and the Anglo-French proposals that followed; September 28, 1938; H. of C., *Parl. Deb.*, Vol. 339, col. 15.

ing against the principle of self-determination," said Duff Cooper.[21] The little resistance Great Britain did offer to Germany's demands indicated a desire to limit concessions to what could be justified on the basis of principles of justice. On the other hand, the group that was in office in England in 1938 was suspiciously late in discovering its sympathies for the Sudeten Germans or for Wilsonian principles in general. How much pressure the British Government put on the Czechs to induce them to make concessions before Germany had reached the preponderant position which she now held cannot yet be judged.[22] The opposition which opposed concessions, just or unjust, to a country threatening the use of armed force if its demands were not satisfied, charged that "the Prime Minister's submission to Herr Hitler's demands was not due to a sudden conversion to the justice of his case, but was extorted by threats of force." [23]

It is possible now to analyze the character of Britain's actions in 1938. Britain's primary interest was to avoid an attack against Czechoslovakia by Germany, because "the immediate result must be that France will be bound to come to her assistance, and Great Britain and Russia will certainly stand by France." [24] By 1938, possibly even earlier, the British Government had also made up its mind as to the means by which this goal could be attained. Far-reaching changes of the *status quo* as it affected the Sudeten-Ger-

[21] Alfred Duff Cooper, October 3, 1938; H. of C., *Parl. Deb.*, Vol. 339, col. 35. (In explaining his approval of the Anglo-French proposals before he resigned from the cabinet because of his opposition to the Munich agreement.)

[22] Sir Samuel Hoare declared that as Foreign Secretary (from June to December, 1935) he had made "representations to the Czechoslovak Government that they must settle this Sudeten question," and that his successor, Anthony Eden, "pressed them even more strongly." October 3, 1938; H. of C., *Parl. Deb.*, Vol. 339, col. 154.

[23] Sir Archibald Sinclair, October 3, 1938; H. of C., *Parl. Deb.*, Vol. 339, col. 71.

[24] "Authoritative statement" issued in London, September 26, 1938; *The Times* (London), September 27, 1938, p. 12.

man minority in Czechoslovakia would have to take place. To the historian of this period it will have to be left to decide at what moment the British Government realized that the changes would have to include the territorial revision of the boundaries of Czechoslovakia, and from what date the French concurred with the British view.[25] For the purpose of clarifying the principles involved, these questions are of secondary importance.

Because of her interest in bringing about such changes as might prove necessary with as little delay and as little risk of a warlike explosion as possible, Britain gradually worked herself into the position of leader and active mediator in the negotiations, first by the customary diplomatic means, then by sending Viscount Runciman to Prague, and, finally, by the Prime Minister's visits to Hitler at Berchtesgaden and Godesberg. The British had not only to bring the two parties to agree on a solution of the conflict, but were also obliged to exert diplomatic persuasion and pressure, and use "their influence with both sides to urge the adoption of reasonableness in the efforts to reach a solution."[26] Pressure had to be employed against Germany if she were to be prevented from using force or from going so far in her demands that Czechoslovakia would choose to fight rather than to agree. Pressure had to be used against Czechoslovakia if she were to be induced to make concessions sufficient to restrain Germany from actually employing mili-

[25] Less than two weeks before the submission of the Anglo-French proposals which accepted the principle of cession of the Sudeten-German territory to Germany, an editorial published in *The Times* created a sensation because it suggested the possibility "of making Czechoslovakia a more homogeneous State by the secession of that fringe of alien populations who are contiguous to the nation with which they are united by race." This suggestion aroused violent opposition in many quarters and drew from the government a statement that it did not represent its views. *The Times* (London), September 7, 1938, p. 13; see also the editorials of September 8 and 9.

[26] Sir John Simon, Chancellor of the Exchequer, speech in Lanark, August 27, 1938; *The Times* (London), August 29, 1938, p. 7.

tary power to enforce her demands. The less successful the British were in moderating Germany's attitude, the more pressure they would have to bring to bear on Czechoslovakia.

It soon became evident that Germany would not be amenable to mere persuasion. Everything depended, therefore, as far as British influence was concerned, on the nature and extent of the pressure which she was willing to employ to moderate Germany's course. The most impressive threat that the British Government could have used and the one which the opposition urged as offering the only hope for success would have been a direct British commitment to go to war with Germany if she attacked Czechoslovakia. This the British Government refused to do. It was feared that "there would be a strong feeling within Czechoslovakia against making any concession to the minorities if that country felt that she had behind her an absolute guarantee from this country, France and Russia. There would have been practically no hope of a peaceful solution of that problem." [27] If Hitler was not bluffing and was not deterred by Britain's commitment, Britain would be "automatically" drawn into the war, and the guarantee would apply "irrespective of the circumstances by which it was brought into operation." [28] Britain therefore limited her intervention to stating that, since Czechoslovakia and her continental allies were prepared to fight in case of "unprovoked aggression," Britain, because of her ties to France, would inevitably be drawn into such a war.

Since no concessions were forthcoming from Germany, Britain's only chance of success lay in the pressure she could bring to bear on the weaker side, namely, on Czechoslovakia. It was evident that the Czechs, short of committing national suicide, could not put up any resistance to German demands, however far-reaching, unless

[27] Viscount Samuel, October 4, 1938; H. of L., *Parl. Deb.*, Vol. 110, col. 1385.

[28] Neville Chamberlain, Prime Minister, March 24, 1938; H. of C., *Parl. Deb.*, Vol. 333, col. 1405.

their allies were willing to share the consequences of such resistance. France, it would seem, was bound by treaty to stand by her if, after refusing further concessions, she became a victim of a German military invasion. This would make it appear as if British pressure could consist only in a threat, which of course presupposed Franco-British agreement, that France was prepared to break her word and violate a pledge which she had repeatedly and explicitly reaffirmed. In fact, the British have confessed that they told Czechoslovakia that they "would not stand by her" if she failed to accept the German terms which they had approved.[29]

It should be noted, however, that there was a loophole in the legal scaffolding, even in this case, which could have protected France from the accusation of a violation of her pledges. It was provided by the word "unprovoked" in the treaty by which France had promised Czechoslovakia assistance against "an unprovoked recourse to arms." [30] If Czechoslovakia had turned down a plan for the settlement of Germany's claims which France and Britain had found acceptable, she would have been blamed for her obstinacy in refusing a "redress of legitimate grievances." This would have been the same as saying that Germany's attack was "provoked" by the unreasonable attitude of her opponent. Of

[29] Earl Stanhope, President of the Board of Education, speaking in the House of Lords on October 5, 1938, said, "Is it not obvious that the only pressure that we could bring to bear on the Czech Government was to say that if they took certain action then we should not be prepared to stand behind them? That is the only pressure that we could bring, and that is what we did say, . . ." H. of L., *Parl. Deb.*, Vol. 110, cols. 1488-1489. The Czechoslovak Government was explicitly urged to accept the Anglo-French proposals so as to avoid "producing a situation for which we [the British] could take no responsibility." Telegram to Prague, September 21, 1938; H. of C., October 5, 1938, *Parl. Deb.*, Vol. 339, col. 450.

[30] Article 1 of the Treaty of October 16, 1925, between France and Czechoslovakia, referred to "an unprovoked recourse to arms" and to one of the parties being "attacked without provocation." Article 2 of the Soviet-Czechoslovak Treaty of May 16, 1935, spoke of assistance in case of "unprovoked aggression."

course, it is almost farcical to assume that France might have taken refuge in the idea of provocation when for twenty years her effort had been to make the definition of aggression automatic and free of any possible subterfuge. But the attitude which the British Government took when putting pressure on Czechoslovakia amounted to this in substance, if not in the terms that were actually used.[31]

By refusing to fight for the maintenance of the territorial integrity of Czechoslovakia, thus "persuading" that country to bow to Germany's ultimatum, Britain and France paved the way for a "peaceful solution." Again it was the weaker side that paid the price of pacification and suffered at the hand of Britain's "mediation." Britain, for the first time, took an active part in promoting territorial revision. But while the French had broken with a policy they had consistently pursued since Versailles, the British Government could still claim to have been acting along traditional lines. For the French the reduction of the Czechoslovak state to three undefended and indefensible provinces meant the end of her military bastion on Germany's southeastern borders, the end of her influence on the Danube, and the disappearance of a strong military ally. The British Conservatives, on the contrary, had never expressed any interest in the strategic aspects of the Czechoslovak problem. Britain was not pledged by any treaty with Czechoslovakia to defend the *status quo*. The success or failure of her policy at Munich could be measured by the traditionalists entirely by how much it had served the cause of peace, or, more precisely, whether the "redress of Germany's legitimate grievances" in regard to the Sudetenland had made her a satisfied power and at last paved the way for that "general settlement" which was to end the period of

[31] We are not suggesting that an accusation of provocation would have been justified in this case. But since the "law" of political treaties depends on the interpretation given by those who are in power, the "revisionist" interpretation had as good a chance of being accepted in 1938 as the no less partisan "*status quo*" interpretation had had during the twenty preceding years.

dangerous transition from the Versailles *status quo* to a more satisfactory order. It is one of the most perplexing aspects of the fight between the parties or schools of thought in Britain that the Leftists showed concern about the strategic disadvantages which Britain and France would suffer with the elimination of Czechoslovakia's military power, while the Conservatives, hopeful of an agreement with Hitler and trusting his promises, refused to be impressed by these consequences of the change, or to be disturbed over Britain's loss of prestige.

There is one other aspect which needs to be emphasized. Britain's traditional policy in Central Europe was based on the premise that although Germany might be strengthened by events in that region, she was not to be allowed to dominate Europe. For several reasons the British Government chose not to regard Germany's demands for the Sudetenland as an indication of a will to acquire such domination. In the first place, Germany's claim appeared justified. In the second, Hitler gave the most explicit assurance that after this Germany would have no further territorial claims to raise. Thirdly, he was willing in the end to meet the other Western Powers in conference. The last point gave to the outcome the semblance of peaceful and negotiated change. "The real triumph," declared Chamberlain, was that the Munich Conference had shown "that representatives of four great Powers can find it possible to agree on a way of carrying out a difficult and delicate operation by discussion instead of by force of arms." [32]

Whatever may have been thought about Germany's intentions and about the direct effects on her new position on the Continent, it is surprising that there should have been so few expressions of skepticism as to Hitler's trustworthiness, and that so few precautions were considered necessary to make sure that Germany's ex-

[32] Neville Chamberlain, Prime Minister, October 3, 1938; H. of C., *Parl. Deb.*, Vol. 339, col. 45.

pansion would remain within the limits which with British consent had been reached at Munich. Except for continuing and accelerating Britain's program of rearmament, neither the British nor the French Government did anything to counteract the dangers which so sudden a change in the balance of power in Central Europe was certain to create. Germany's success was so sweeping that it acted as an almost irresistible stimulus to further demands and further action. The precedent which one case of territorial revision had established was in itself a new incentive to push the change of other boundaries which from the point of view of self-determination had equally good justification. Instead of balancing these unsettling factors by immediate and unmistakable diplomatic countermoves, the British Government rejoiced over the establishment of "peace for our time" [33] with such satisfaction and optimism as to create the impression that further "Munichs" would be acceptable if they were presented as the necessary price for continued peace. The Munich settlement was acclaimed much in the same way that the British had sought to make the best of every previous crisis, as "only a prelude to a larger settlement in which all Europe may find peace." [34] Just before Munich all parties in Britain helped to confirm this impression of satisfaction, when the House of Commons, with the exception of its lone Communist member, enthusiastically applauded Hitler's invitation to the conference, as if the struggle were already over, even before actual negotiations had started. How could subsequent criticism by the opposition, however sharp and persistent, offset the fact that the invitation to a conference on the procedure to be followed in transferring the Sudetenland to Germany had been accepted without reservations or dissent?

[33] Declaration by Chamberlain to the crowd in Downing Street, after his return from Munich. *The Times* (London), October 1, 1938, p. 14.

[34] Declaration by Chamberlain at the airport, on returning from the Munich Conference, September 30, 1938; *The Times* (London), October 1, 1938, p. 12.

In view of the violent British controversy over the Munich settlement, it would seem worth while to review the stands taken by the government and the opposition. In the eyes of the latter, as we shall see when we discuss the collectivist theory, the Czechoslovak crisis was but another case in a series of acts of aggression by the dictators. Britain, according to this view, should have taken the lead years earlier to stop such aggression. Hitler should have been deterred by a show of overwhelming force on the part of the members of the League and particularly by the combined forces of Britain, France, and the Soviet Union. By refusing to commit Britain to the defense of Czechoslovakia and of all other victims of aggression and by allowing "class prejudice" to stand in the way of an agreement with the Soviet Union, the British Government, according to the opposition, had encouraged Germany's threatened invasion and made the Conference of Munich necessary. The government had thereby sacrificed vital strategic advantages of Britain and one of the strongest bulwarks of democracy against Fascist aggression. "Munich" therefore became the symbol of humiliation and moral abdication. It caused deep resentment and was branded as the final step in a dishonorable and cowardly retreat before the dictators, which had already called for the betrayal of China, Ethiopia, Spain, and Austria.

The point of view of the government and of most of the traditionalists, it need hardly be said, was diametrically opposed. What they sought was not collective security against aggression but a new settlement between the four Western Powers. They believed that they had previously eliminated the danger of war or grave conflict in the Mediterranean by agreement with Mussolini and by localizing the Spanish civil war. They had made effort after effort to come to terms with Germany. Now the problem of the Sudetenland was pictured as the last serious hindrance to such an understanding. If Hitler's assurances were to be trusted, the goal of pacification had come within reach. Germany would have become a satisfied power without having grown to dimensions that endangered British vital interests or the security of Western Europe. But was the price of appeasement not too high? The government decided that it was not. It should be paid, because Britain could not be expected to fight for the sake of keeping a minority within a country to which it did not wish to belong. Besides, Britain was not in a position, from a military point of view, to fight effectively for Czechoslovakia even if she had wanted to, and could, therefore, not save that country if, as the government expected, Hitler could not be deterred from attacking. But what if Hitler's assurances were broken afterwards? Since the government did not reply to this question, there is no way of telling whether it had made up its mind about what it would do in that case or whether it was satisfied, in the true spirit of "muddling through," with merely having settled one problem and with waiting until the next one emerged. From the government's attitude toward rearmament, it is possible, however, to conjecture that it believed time would work for Britain and would enhance her chances of calling a halt to Hitler later, if it should become necessary after all. If this expectation was justified, although Czechoslovak assistance was being forfeited and the Soviet Union antagonized, then Britain was running little risk by her great experiment in "appeasement through revision."

The Pledge to Poland

On March 14, 1939, German troops began to occupy Bohemia and Moravia. Within a few days the two provinces were formally given the status of a German protectorate, and Slovakia was put under Hitler's "protection." It was this invasion of non-German territory more than anything else that marked the end of Britain's policy of appeasement and opened a new chapter in British and European history.[35] The change in policy became evident in connection with the German-Polish negotiations which followed almost immediately upon the occupation of Czechoslovakia. Hitler demanded the union of Danzig with the Reich and a strip of land across the Polish Corridor. After Poland had rejected these demands, so the British say, the British Government pledged its country to come to the assistance of Poland with all the power at its command "in the event of any action which clearly threatened Polish independence, and which the Polish Government accordingly considered it vital to resist with their national forces."[36]

[35] Whether Prime Minister Neville Chamberlain personally decided on an immediate change in policy has been questioned. Although the answer is not essential to the present discussion it is nevertheless interesting to compare his speech to the House of Commons on March 15, 1939, the day German troops entered Prague, to that delivered two days later to the Birmingham Unionist Association. On the first occasion he attributed Czechoslovakia's collapse largely to internal disintegration, and while expressing his bitterness as to the methods employed by Germany, he said, "But do not let us on that account be deflected from our course. . . . The aim of the Government is now, as it has always been, to promote that desire [for peace and good will] and to substitute the method of discussion for the method of force in the settlement of differences." In spite of "checks and disappointments" this objective was too important "for us lightly to give it up or set it on one side." H. of C., *Parl. Deb.*, Vol. 345, col. 440. Two days later he explained in Birmingham that this initial statement to the House had necessarily been "cool and objective." He proceeded to voice his grievance against Hitler for having betrayed his promises and "shattered the confidence which was just beginning to show its head." He repeated a previous statement "that any demand to dominate the world by force was one which the democracies must resist," and spoke with confidence of "resisting such a challenge if it ever were made." *In Search of Peace* (1939), pp. 269-275.

[36] Announced in a statement by Chamberlain to the House of Commons, March 31, 1939; H. of C., *Parl. Deb.*, Vol. 345, col. 2415.

The unilateral pledge announced at this time was supplemented on April 6 by a reciprocal assurance from Poland of assistance to Britain; on August 25 a formal treaty of mutual assistance was signed. *Cmd. 6106*, pp. 36-39. On April 13, one week after Italy's occupation of Albania, Britain gave promises to Rumania and Greece that "in the event of any action being taken which clearly threatened the independence" of those countries and which they "considered it

We propose to look for an explanation of Britain's pledge to Poland and to define its connection with the preceding events and the policies which have been discussed in the foregoing chapters. Was it, as it might seem, a clear-cut break with all tradition? Was it a victory of the opposition over the traditionalist government, or did the two opposing schools for once find themselves united in outlook and intentions?

Whatever the arguments or reasons may have been that influenced the course of the British Government, it is necessary to emphasize at the outset that the events that took place in Britain during the spring and summer of 1939 were due to more than a mere change of mind. There was every indication of a wide popular revolt against permitting any new acts of "wanton aggression" by Hitler and against further "shameful retreat" before the dictators. This popular feeling was no less strong and effective because it found its outlet in the orderly processes of British parliamentary debate and public discussion. Moral indignation was coupled with national resentment at Britain's being "pushed from pillar to post."[37] Emotion swept the country and carried with it even the bulk of the Conservatives, who had hitherto remained immune to the earlier waves of "collectivism." Whatever may have been left after Munich of the hopes for appeasement had disappeared with the German march on Prague. All political decisions now had to obey the relentless popular demand for "no more Munichs."

For the opposition there was nothing in the new events that called for a revision of its previous stand. Aggression was again on the march, and Britain's duty, as always, was to take the lead in stopping the aggressor. The demand for an alliance with the

vital to resist" Britain would come to their assistance. France gave similar assurances to both countries. H. of C., *Parl. Deb.*, Vol. 346, col. 13.

[37] Winston Churchill, April 3, 1939; H. of C., *Parl. Deb.*, Vol. 345, col. 2499.

Soviet Union, on which the opposition had always insisted, had become only more urgent and was now regarded as essential for the success of what Eden called the "peace front," [38] and Churchill described as the "Grand Alliance against aggression." [39] There was no doubt in the minds of the critics of the government that Britain could obtain this alliance if she put all her energies to the task. Hitler's "bluff" might still be successfully called and his future aggressions deterred if overwhelming force were arrayed against him. But the emphasis was no longer, as in the earlier years, on the League and collective security. There was an open demand for a military coalition of the "peace-loving nations" directed against German aggression. There was also no hesitation in insisting that Hitler should be stopped by force if he could not be deterred by persuasion. The slightest semblance of compromise was looked upon with the utmost distrust. Any hint of a peaceful settlement was suspected as foreshadowing a "new Munich" and was rejected with bitterness. The logic and consistency of this attitude of the opposition will become clearer when we discuss the "collectivist doctrine" and the earlier outbreak of collectivist passions in the days of the Ethiopian War.

The position of the government was far less simple and obviously less consistent, if not diametrically opposed to its previous course. We do not yet have sufficient data to know with any degree of certainty whether, when the British Government decided to make the pledge to Poland and later to turn down the kind of "settlement" which Hitler proposed, it acted under the pressure of public sentiment or whether it had come of its own accord to the conclusion that this was the proper course for Britain to take.

For the sake of clarifying the various possible explanations which history may give to the momentous decision on the part of Britain,

[38] Anthony Eden, April 13, 1939; H. of C., *Parl. Deb.*, Vol. 346, col. 46.
[39] Winston Churchill, April 3, 1939; H. of C., *Parl. Deb.*, Vol. 345, col. 2501.

we shall consider whether a cabinet reasoning on traditionalist lines could without inconsistency justify the new course. As a matter of fact, the members of the government argued on traditionalist lines when they emphasized the threat of German domination. They also used arguments which the opposition would have wanted them to listen to earlier. For example, Chamberlain wrote to Hitler: "It has been alleged that, if His Majesty's Government had made their position more clear in 1914, the great catastrophe would have been avoided. Whether or not there is any force in that allegation, His Majesty's Government are resolved that on this occasion there shall be no such tragic misunderstanding." [40] For this argument to be in line with traditionalist thinking, it was not enough that there be a chance of deterring an "aggressor." "Realistic" proof had to be given that Britain's vital interests, either in the particular geographic zone or in relation to the balance of power, made it necessary for Britain to stop the expansion of Germany at this point.

Chamberlain himself spoke of having "departed from our traditional ideas" and of the beginning of a "new epoch" in Britain's foreign policy.[41] But Sir John Simon qualified this statement when he declared that Britain had not "forgotten its traditions" but was adapting them to the "change that has taken place in Europe." [42] Both statements contained a kernel of the truth. While it had been Britain's traditional policy ever since the World War to refuse to give in advance any automatic commitments on behalf of countries in Central Europe, this policy had rested all along on the assumption that events in that region would not lead to German domination on the Continent. "As a matter of history, successive Brit-

[40] Letter of August 22, 1939; *Cmd. 6106*, p. 97.

[41] Neville Chamberlain, Prime Minister, April 3, 1939; H. of C., *Parl. Deb.*, Vol. 345, col. 2482.

[42] Sir John Simon, Chancellor of the Exchequer, April 13, 1939; H. of C., *Parl. Deb.*, Vol. 346, col. 139.

ish Governments have felt obliged to resist attempts by a single Power to dominate Europe at the expense of others, . . ."[43] It had been one of Britain's unshakable traditions to consider that her vital interests were threatened by such domination and to take steps to prevent or defeat it. The whole policy of non-commitment in Central Europe and of appeasing Germany by means of changes in that region was based, therefore, on the hope that it would be possible to satisfy Germany and to bring her into a new "general settlement" before she attained hegemony. As each succeeding attempt at appeasement gave more and more power to Germany without producing this final settlement, the critical point in the process was brought nearer and nearer.

Why should this point have been reached as a consequence of the events of March, 1939? There was no way of predicting when it would come, since it depended entirely on the views of the British Government regarding Germany's power and intentions. The Germans may not have expected the crisis to come when they marched on Prague or when they made their demands on Poland. Some people inside and outside of the British cabinet may have doubted whether it was wise to reverse Britain's policy at that moment. The statements made by members of the government, however, would make it appear that it was this question of domination that decided the issue.

This, it is important to note, does not mean that it was the substance of Germany's demands on Poland for the reunion of Danzig with the Reich and for the creation of a "corridor through the Corridor" which in the eyes of the government justified Britain's commitment to Poland. The increase of German territory as such was not what would give her domination. No doubt was left by the British that any settlement reached between Germany and

[43] Viscount Halifax, Foreign Secretary, House of Lords, August 24, 1939; *Cmd. 6106*, p. 112.

Poland on the basis of "equal negotiations with the threat of force removed" would be welcomed by Great Britain, and the wording of the pledge itself, already quoted, makes it plain that Britain left to Poland the responsibility for deciding whether at any given time she should resist German claims. This implied that, as far as the balance of power or any other British interest was concerned, there was no objection to a reunion of Danzig with the Reich or even to more far-reaching concessions, provided they were agreed to freely and not under threats of force. It would, in fact, have been awkward, to say the least, if Britain, after having stood up for the "redress of legitimate grievances" in the Czechoslovak case, had had to reverse her stand on Germany's claim to Danzig and to a solution of the Corridor issue. There is no question that it would have been incomparably easier for Britain to have gained general support for her policy of appeasement if, in 1938, the Germans had made their claims against Poland instead of demanding the annexation of the Sudetenland. The British public, rightly or wrongly, had always regarded the Versailles solution in regard to Danzig and Poland's access to the sea as particularly unfortunate and unjust. Also, the threat to Poland's independence embodied in the union of Danzig with the Reich was slight compared to the loss which Czechoslovakia had been made to suffer by the separation of the Sudetenland. The reversal of British traditionalist policy cannot, therefore, be explained by any particular "illegitimacy" of Hitler's specific demands on Poland, as judged by British standards, nor by any fear that the fulfillment of these claims in itself would increase Germany's political or strategic position to such an extent as to give her predominance.

Instead, all the arguments of the government concerned not the claims themselves, but the circumstances which preceded and accompanied them and the methods which Hitler was employing. This is easily comprehended. As Chamberlain had stated during the Czechoslovak crisis of 1938, Britain was determined to stop the rise of German power as soon as it should become evident that Germany intended "to dominate the world by fear of its force."[44] He stated later that in September, 1938, he had not felt that such a will to dominate was "necessarily involved."[45] Subsequent events, however, might and did destroy this conviction. That a country has the will to dominate is, of course, impossible to prove. But obviously the circumstances under which a claim is raised may give as much evidence of this will as the nature of the claim itself. The British Government in 1938 justified its stand by pointing to the assurances given Britain that, as Chamberlain put it, "the foreign policy of the German Government was limited, that they had no wish to dominate other races, and that all they wanted was to assimilate Germans living in territory adjacent to their country. . . . when that was done that was to be the end, and there were to be no more territorial ambitions to be satisfied."[46] The limitations thus set to Germany's objectives, assuming that Hitler's word could be trusted, disproved the contention that Germany's goal was predominance. With the military occupation of the non-German-speaking part of Czechoslovakia these assurances were "thrown to the winds." The disappearance of the limitations which seemed to have been established at Munich and the complete destruction of confidence raised the question, said Chamberlain, whether "further reasons may not presently be found for further expansion."[47]

That Hitler had ambitions, as expressed in *Mein Kampf*, which went far beyond anything Britain would have been willing to

[44] See above, p. 282.

[45] Neville Chamberlain, Prime Minister, April 3, 1939; H. of C., *Parl. Deb.*, Vol. 345, col. 2483.

[46] *Ibid.*, col. 2484.

[47] *Ibid.*, col. 2484.

concede was nothing new. But what seems to have determined the British at this point to resist what appeared to be "a will to dominate" was the fact that, for the first time, Hitler appeared to have a real chance of obtaining his ultimate objectives, if he was not immediately stopped. The government gave special reasons for believing this to be the case. Once Germany had invaded territory to which on ethnical grounds she had no claims, no country in her neighborhood, it was argued, could feel safe any longer. Assurances could no longer be trusted. Contradiction between acts and assurances had "completely undermined the sense of security in Europe, and it created a widespread feeling that the independence of no small State was safe if it stood in the way of German ambitions." [48] If, therefore, a capitulation of Poland or another "Munich" were to allow a new expansion of Germany, the impression would be created that there was nothing for a weaker country to do but to yield to Germany. None of the lesser states from the Baltic down to the Black Sea and the Near East would dare to resist German demands. "Unless some new stabilising factor could be introduced into Europe," said Chamberlain, "the dissolution of a large part of Europe might be imminent." The pledges to Poland, Rumania, and Turkey were the means to supply this new "stabilising factor." [49] Their purpose was to reinforce the resistance of Poland as well as of the other non-German countries in Eastern Europe, a resistance which the occupation of Czechoslovakia had already undermined and which a capitulation of Poland, in particular, might have swept away completely.[50]

[48] Neville Chamberlain, Prime Minister, May 19, 1939; H. of C., *Parl. Deb.*, Vol. 347, col. 1832.

[49] *Ibid.*, cols. 1832, 1833.

[50] Chamberlain insisted that "nothing that we have done or that we propose to do menaces the legitimate interests of Germany. It is not an act of menace to prepare to help friends to defend themselves against force." House of Commons,

It would seem, then, that the government may have reached its decisions in conformity with traditionalist philosophy, and could justify as consistent therewith its break with the Central European policy it had pursued up to that time. Under this hypothesis, however, the earlier course opens itself to new criticism. If there was any chance that the expansion of Germany within Central Europe could make that country predominant and dangerous to Britain's vital interests, Britain was taking extraordinary risks when, only six months earlier, she helped to destroy the main bulwark against such German predominance and antagonized or alienated countries which might now have helped Britain.

All along, from Versailles to Munich, the French had insisted that Germany would seek to gain predominance by striking in the East, where she would find no adequate resistance unless France and Britain were willing to oppose her, while the view of the British Conservatives had been that Germany's moves in the East were not vitally important to Britain. It would now seem that they must have erred either in regard to the extent to which Germany's revisionist ambitions would go or in not foreseeing what would happen if Germany, after not having received satisfaction earlier, would come to take matters into her own hands.

Since it cannot positively be known whether the British Government acted in 1939 on the grounds which we have outlined and by which it declared itself to have been motivated, it is to the point to consider a possible second line of traditionalist reasoning which, while more in line with Britain's earlier policy in Central Europe, would not explain the pledge to Poland. If any members of the cabinet took this second view, they must either have been outvoted or have remained silent in the conviction that public

August 29, 1939; *Cmd. 6106*, p. 109. For the same reason it was "fantastic to suggest that a policy which is a policy of self-defence can be described as encirclement. . . ." April 3, 1939; H. of C., *Parl. Deb.*, Vol. 345, col. 2485.

opinion would not accept their reasoning. But they might personally have felt that Britain had not only been right in disinteresting herself in Central and Eastern Europe earlier, but also should continue to do so. Their argument would have been that any lasting pacification of Europe required that Germany be granted extensive political and economic opportunities in those regions, the exact nature and extent of which were not of primary importance to Britain. She had no vital interests in the region nor was there any reason to expect that Germany's domination of *Mitteleuropa* would give her complete hegemony in Europe. She would still remain wedged in between Britain and France on the one side and the Soviet Union on the other. The likelihood of a clash between Germany and the Soviet Union, or even between Germany and Italy, would increase with every additional increase of Germany's power toward the East or toward the Balkans. Even if the submission of Poland to her demands should give her control over that country and should lead to the "dissolution" of the Danubian countries, Britain could still remain undisturbed and wait until Germany's expansion was stopped by others or until the difficulties which she was bound to encounter with the Poles, Czechs, Rumanians, Hungarians, and other peoples, drove her to seek a settlement with the Western Powers. Furthermore, if Britain and France remained on friendly terms with her and held out the possibility of a general settlement in Western Europe, she might be induced to concentrate her efforts toward the East and might be distracted from the West as well as from any colonial or naval aspirations. This seemed to be the attitude that the British Conservatives were taking in 1938. If they had wanted to continue it in 1939, they would never have considered such a pledge to Poland as was actually made. It was certain to stiffen Poland's resistance so much that "negotiated change" sufficient to satisfy Hitler was practically precluded. It is conceivable that Hitler forced those members of the cabinet who might have reasoned along these lines into the other camp, both by the aggressiveness of his methods and by the contempt which he showed for Britain. Also, his actions in response to Britain's conciliatory attitude at Munich created such a revolt even of British Conservative opinion that a continuation of the former policy could easily have proved suicidal for the government.

By which line of reasoning the British Government actually reached its decision we have no way of telling. Some members of the government may have acted out of conviction, others, out of an opportunistic respect for the pressure of public opinion. There may have been a great deal of vacillation between the two lines of traditionalist reasoning. And finally, no man is immune to strong emotional influences. The statesmen who had been responsible for the Munich accord may well have been afraid of being accused of cowardice and weakness, or may have been stirred by resentment and anger at Hitler's abuse of their confidence. The sudden emphasis which the government came to lay on the fact that "Hitlerism" was the real enemy which Britain must fight would seem to show how strongly the clash with Hitler and his methods impressed Britain's responsible statesmen in the crucial weeks and days that preceded the new war.

XVIII. Britain and the Soviet Union

A LONG history of rivalry and antagonism rather than of friendship forms the background of Anglo-Soviet relations. Only a common fear of German expansion drew Britain and Russia together at times. It was for this reason that they became co-members of the Triple Entente before the World War and fought together during the first three years of that conflict. The only time since then that Britain made any serious bid for close political and even military ties with the Soviet Union was in 1939, when she set out to stop the rise of Germany. It might be noted that any *rapprochement* between Britain and Germany, as for instance at the time of Locarno, or in the days of Munich, was regarded unfavorably by the Soviet Government as presaging the formation of an anti-Bolshevist coalition. Similarly, such signs of German-Soviet co-operation as the Treaty of Rapallo of 1922, the Treaty of Berlin of 1926, not to speak of the non-aggression pact of 1939, were viewed apprehensively by the British.

British relations with Soviet Russia after the World War were dominated by the fact of the Bolshevist Revolution. The Bolshevists had signed a separate peace treaty with Germany in 1918. Great Britain had intervened with armed force on the side of the White Russian armies. World revolution was written on the flag of the Bolshevists. Whereas, before the World War imperial rivalries and conflicts had caused friction between the two countries, fear of Bolshevism on the part of Britain, and the fear of an anti-Soviet "capitalist plot" on the part of the Moscow government now created suspicion and ill-feeling. In no sphere of Britain's foreign affairs did party sentiment come to play so significant a role as in her policy toward the Soviet Union.

The Conservatives, it is true, always disclaimed any intention of allowing the nature of the internal régime of Russia to affect British relations with her. Speaking of the Soviet Union, Sir Samuel Hoare declared, "Any State sincerely desirous of maintaining the peace of Europe, whatever may be its government, will have our collaboration in that aim."[1] In practice, however, relations with the Soviet Government could not be clearly isolated from the widespread hostility of the Conservatives to Bolshevism. The opposition accused them, therefore, of allowing "class prejudice" to interfere with the interests of Britain, although the Leftists, as a matter of fact, were to experience similar difficulties in the case of Italy. But whatever the reasons for the antipathy may have been, it certainly existed, and had the effect that arguments against co-operation with the Soviet Union were heard with much readiness.

The Labor party and the Liberals, on the other hand, were outspoken in their friendliness toward the Soviet Government from the very outset, and never wavered in their support of *rapprochement*. The government headed by Lloyd George was the first to sign a trade agreement with the Bolshevists and also invited the Soviets to the Genoa Conference. MacDonald, as head of both British Labor governments, twice interrupted the British course of aloofness, if not open hostility, by recognizing the Soviet Government in 1924 and by renewing diplomatic relations in 1929, after they had been broken off by the Conservatives in the meantime.

Conservative aversion to Bolshevism did not keep the British Government, even under traditionalist guidance, from realizing

[1] Sir Samuel Hoare, Foreign Secretary, July 11, 1935; H. of C., *Parl. Deb.*, Vol. 304, col. 522.

the possible disadvantages of a policy of complete disregard of the Soviet Government. There was first an economic interest in opening the Soviet market to British goods. Then there was the danger that Germany and Russia might draw together. Lloyd George had hoped that the Genoa Conference would serve both to reopen the Russian market and to eliminate the danger of what he called a "community of debasement" between the two "Pariahs," Germany and Soviet Russia.[2] Ironically enough, it was during this very conference that they lined up together and signed the Treaty of Rapallo. The Conservative governments concentrated their efforts on Germany, seeking to attract her away from Russia. They were accused of having favored and signed the Locarno Pact for the purpose of establishing a hostile coalition against the Bolshevists. Austen Chamberlain denied suggestions by Ramsay MacDonald that Locarno had been "engineered for the purpose of uniting Western civilisation against Russia."[3] But he did not deny Britain's desire to see Germany turn toward the West and loosen her ties with the Soviet Government. As Ormsby-Gore put it, "The significance of Locarno was tremendous. It meant that as far as the present Government of Germany was concerned, it was detached from Russia and was throwing in its lot with the Western Powers."[4] Once the National Socialists, with their violently anti-Bolshevist program had come into power, the British were satisfied that the danger of an alignment between the two countries was past. There was even less need now to try to wean the Soviets away from Germany. This, at least, would seem to be the only

[2] David Lloyd George, Prime Minister, May 25, 1922; H. of C., *Parl. Deb.*, Vol. 154, col. 1456.

[3] Austen Chamberlain, Foreign Secretary, November 18, 1925; H. of C., *Parl. Deb.*, Vol. 188, col. 441.

[4] William Ormsby-Gore, Colonial Under-Secretary, speech in Manchester, quoted by J. Ramsay MacDonald, November 18, 1925; H. of C., *Parl. Deb.*, Vol. 188, col. 438.

explanation for their continued bold expressions of antipathy to the Bolshevist Government and for their permitting relations between the two countries to remain as cool as they were, even after the fear of German domination of the Continent had been officially expressed in 1938.

But how does British concern over the distribution or balance of power in Europe fit into this picture? It is hard to believe that even the most rabid anti-Bolshevists among the British Conservatives could have forgotten this principle completely. The difficulty is that the concept of a balance of power, while it indicated with relative clarity a line of action for dealings on the Rhine, supplied no such simple answer to Britain's problems in Eastern Europe. As long as Germany was disarmed and the Central European countries between Germany and Russia were weak and internally unsettled, Bolshevist power in the East hung over France and Britain like a "storm cloud upon the Eastern horizon of Europe" and was "the most menacing of our uncertainties." [5] The French hoped to keep this danger in check with the help of their Eastern allies, Poland and Rumania. The British, on the other hand, favored German recovery, arguing that it would give more solidity to Central Europe and thus decrease susceptibility to infection by the Bolshevist germ. Here as elsewhere the situation was completely changed when Germany became a military power once again.

After 1934 the danger that she might become overwhelmingly strong could no longer be overlooked. Now the role of the Soviet Union, whose rearmament had also gained momentum in the meantime, took on a different character. The British, as well as the French, became aware of the possibility that Germany's rising power might be offset or balanced by that of the Soviet Union. Growing tension between National Socialist Germany and the Bol-

[5] Foreign Office memorandum, February 20, 1925; *The World* (New York), May 10, 1925, p. 2.

shevist Government was paving the way for a realignment. The French method was to bind the Soviet Union to Western Europe by pacts of mutual assistance and the Covenant of the League of Nations. The British traditionalists did not like this procedure, since it was far more likely that the Germans would move against the Soviet Union, and therefore much more probable that France and consequently Britain would be drawn into conflict to aid the Soviet Union than that she would have to call upon Soviet assistance against German aggression in the West. In British Conservative opinion there was an alternative course to the French plan. Britain and France should seek to arrive at a new general settlement with Germany and thereby completely remove the danger of a German threat to the West. "I was at a loss to understand," wrote the Marquess of Londonderry, "why we could not make common ground in some form or other with Germany in opposition to Communism." [6] If such a settlement could be reached, Germany would turn all her attention to the East, where the Soviet Union, it was assumed, out of sheer self-interest, would have to bar her way. It is impossible, of course, to guess whether it was expected that Germany and the Soviet Union would be so well-balanced that neither would dare to strike at the other, or whether, as some believe, the Conservatives cherished the Machiavellian idea that the two countries would eventually go to war and weaken each other mutually.

The concept we have just described could be called that of an "isolated balance of power" between Germany and the Soviet Union in Eastern Europe. There were, however, two serious flaws in this view. In the first place, it was too obviously an attempt to throw all the burden of Germany's rise in power onto Russia. Therefore, it served as an invitation to the Soviet Union to try to reverse Britain's plan and promote conflict between Germany and

[6] *Ourselves and Germany* (1938), p. 129.

the Western Powers. In the second place, since Germany and the Soviet Union were not neighbors, a German drive toward the East did not immediately affect Russia, but did involve Britain and France, who were committed, morally at least, not to permit German acts of unprovoked aggression against the lesser states in Central Europe. Therefore, even if Britain undertook no pledges toward the Soviet Union, she was not in a position to offer Germany a free hand in the East as she might have liked to do. This accounts for the paradoxical situation of 1939 when Britain and France went to war to bar a German thrust eastward, while the Soviet Union, supposedly the most threatened by such a German move, sat back and played Germany's game.

Many reasons have been suggested for Britain's inability to come to terms with the Soviet Union in 1939, when at last she made an effort to do so, and even started staff conversations: mutual suspicion or bad faith, unwillingness to make the kind of concessions Stalin demanded or inability to do so because of conflicting obligations to other countries, doubts with regard to the value of Soviet assistance, or inadequate realization of Stalin's freedom to change over into the German camp. In reality, the determining factor may have been that when Britain finally turned to the Soviets for a pact, her bargaining power, compared with that of the Soviets, was at a low ebb. The rift with Germany was already so wide that in the triangular struggle between Germany, Britain, and the Soviet Union, only the last-named of these three was in a position to choose her course. She could therefore set a price for her friendship which no government in Britain could have paid without disgrace.

It cannot yet be predicted whether the failure of the British and French to draw the Soviet Union into the "anti-Hitler" front will prove harmful to them. But that Britain's approach to the Soviets should have come so much later than the French alignment with Moscow offers a further illustration of the difference between the policies and attitudes of the two countries: France, seeking to incorporate into her system of defenses as many of the Slavic powers to the east of Germany as she believed at a given time necessary for her security; Britain, trying to dissociate herself as long as possible and to draw France back from the "danger zone" of Eastern Europe.

XIX. Britain and Italy

THE Mediterranean, after the World War, retained its traditional position in Britain's foreign policy primarily as an essential link in the "life-line" connecting the British Isles with important parts of the Empire. It was therefore regarded as a zone of vital interest in much the same way as the Lowlands and later the Rhine. When Mussolini stated that, after all, it was only a "short cut" for the British system of communications,[1] he was consciously contradicting the British. True, his assertion was correct, if commercial shipping alone was taken into consideration. From the point of view of the strategic defense of the Empire, however, the Mediterranean was a "main arterial road."[2] British rights and possessions in the Mediterranean, although originally established to protect the sea route to India and the Far East, had an importance of their own, particularly after the World War, which made them of direct and primary interest. We need only remind ourselves of the economic importance of the Sudan, of Britain's responsibilities in Palestine, or of the pipe-lines connecting the Mosul oilfields with eastern Mediterranean ports. Then, too—a point rarely mentioned explicitly in Britain—her freedom of naval action in the Mediterranean was essential to her power on the Continent. How otherwise, for instance, could she have drawn countries like Turkey, Greece, and Rumania into her orbit in 1939? How could she ever

[1] Speech in Milan, November 1, 1936; *International Conciliation,* No. 326 (January, 1937), p. 125.

[2] Anthony Eden, Foreign Secretary, November 5, 1936; H. of C., *Parl. Deb.,* Vol. 317, col. 283.

have hoped to influence the course of Italian foreign policy, if it were not for her ability to make her naval superiority felt in those waters? The Mediterranean was thus not only a scene for wartime operations but also for diplomatic moves, backed by force, in times of peace. It entered into Britain's relations with all other European powers.

British interests in the freedom of her communications and the safety of her rights and possessions required that Italy should not be able to interrupt these communications or successfully attack any of Britain's Mediterranean holdings. Italy, on the other hand, was vitally concerned about the freedom of entry to and exit from the Mediterranean, in which she would otherwise, as Mussolini often said, be held as a prisoner of Great Britain. Besides, she had an even greater interest in assuring the security of her own territory and possessions. Any war between the two countries, whatever the outcome, was certain to destroy the freedom of traffic through the Mediterranean as well as the freedom of entry and exit. If Britain and Italy ever went to war with each other, both of them would, therefore, be sacrificing interests which they claimed to be vital, at least for the duration of the war. With interests so interlocked, conflict between the two countries was bound to react disadvantageously on both.[3]

Italy was the more vulnerable of the two. While the "main arterial road" was not a matter of life and death to Britain, it was doubtful whether Italy could survive the economic effects of a complete closing of the Mediterranean to outside traffic. Even if her military preparations were as effective as she claimed, the consequences of a military clash with Great Britain must necessarily involve more serious risks for the country located within the

[3] On Anglo-Italian relations, see Maxwell H. Macartney and Paul Cremona, *Italy's Foreign and Colonial Policy, 1914-1937* (1938), Chapter VIII; R. W. Seton-Watson, *Britain and the Dictators* (1938), Chapter VII.

Mediterranean than for a state defending only a part of its imperial possessions and interests.

It did not, however, follow that Italy would under all circumstances avoid such a conflict. Realizing her vulnerability under the existing conditions, she might prefer to stake her whole future on the outcome of an attempt to break the hold that Britain had over her. Perhaps she hoped that Britain would prefer to recede step by step, rather than to become involved in a fight for Mediterranean interests and thereby endanger her Empire. Finally, if Italy's colonial aspirations and ambitions for power were such that nothing less than the defeat of the British Empire could render their satisfaction possible, she might prefer even to risk her existence rather than sacrifice these wider aims. In planning her policy toward Italy, Britain had always to keep in mind, therefore, the possibility that Fascist Italy might gamble with her future and challenge the British Empire.

The British Conservatives never gave up hope that Mussolini, realizing the interdependence of the two countries, would try to maintain their mutually advantageous friendship and prevent Italy from entering a war on the opposite side from Great Britain. They were willing, as they proved on more than one occasion, to go far to disperse any clouds of discord and to further friendly co-operation. Thus, when Italy, in the years following the World War, accused Britain and France of having violated the pledges made to Italy in the Treaty of London of 1915 and the St. Jean de Maurienne agreement of 1917, on the basis of which she had fought the War on the side of the Allies, Britain ceded the territory of Jubaland to the Italians and re-established friendly relations. This was in 1924, eleven years before France was ready to make similar concessions.[4] Britain was also willing the following year to give

[4] On the cession of Jubaland, see Royal Institute of International Affairs, *Survey of International Affairs, 1924*, pp. 463-470. On France's negotiations with Italy, see above, p. 145 n. 14, p. 148 n. 19.

Italy a free hand in parts of Ethiopia as far as economic penetration was concerned. The agreement was dropped, however, when Ethiopia, supported by France, protested before the League.[5] In June, 1935, Britain took a step which was unusual for a third and disinterested party and offered to cede the port of Zeila to Ethiopia so that she would more readily make concessions satisfactory to Italy.[6]

The abrupt interruption of friendly relations which followed when Britain took the lead in applying sanctions against Italy did not fit into either Britain's traditional policy or the convictions of the Conservatives.[7] Their desire to maintain friendship with Italy expressed itself in the continued efforts at conciliation which culminated in the Hoare-Laval plan. It became even more marked after the conquest of Ethiopia had been successfully accomplished. Britain was the first Great Power to suggest that sanctions be terminated, and followed this up later with the recognition of the conquest. Even after the strain which Italian intervention in the Spanish civil war put upon the relations between the two countries, an agreement confirming their common vital interests in the Mediterranean and their intention not to change the *status quo* there, was reached in 1937.[8] The British Government persisted in

[5] See *ibid., 1929*, pp. 208-232.

When, in 1935, Mussolini inquired about Britain's attitude toward his plans in Ethiopia, an inter-departmental committee, set up under the chairmanship of Sir John Maffey, came to the conclusion that with the exception of Lake Tsana, the waters of the Blue Nile, and certain tribal grazing rights, Britain had no important interest in Ethiopia. This was the same as saying that from an imperial point of view, which was the chief traditionalist concern, Britain had no reason to oppose the absorption of Ethiopia by Italy. Statement by Anthony Eden, Foreign Secretary, February 24, 1936; H. of C., *Parl. Deb.*, Vol. 309, cols. 6-9.

[6] This proposal was made by Anthony Eden, Minister for League of Nations Affairs, during his visit to Rome, June 24-26, 1935.

[7] On the application of sanctions against Italy, see below, pp. 355 ff.

[8] This "Gentleman's Agreement" of January 2, 1937, was accompanied by an exchange of notes dated December 31, 1936, confirming Italy's intention not to modify the integrity of Spanish territories. *Cmd. 5348*.

maintaining and redoubling efforts to restore the traditional friendship with "the country which has been our friend since the Risorgimento." [9] Another agreement was signed with Italy in 1938, intended, by the British at least, to "remove the danger spots one by one," and to clear away the "clouds of mistrust and suspicion." [10]

The Leftist groups in Great Britain had been skeptical about Italian friendship ever since Mussolini had come into power, although the ideological issue became serious only after National Socialism had been established in Germany. Open hostility toward Italy did not develop until she had attacked Ethiopia in violation of the League Covenant. It increased as Italy and Germany drew closer together, and reached its peak when Italy went to the support of General Franco in the Spanish civil war. Both the Leftists and the group of Conservatives supporting Anthony Eden, who was Foreign Secretary at the time, then took the view that any further attempts to restore the traditional harmony between British

[9] Sir Samuel Hoare, Foreign Secretary, July 11, 1935; H. of C., *Parl. Deb.*, Vol. 304, col. 519.

[10] Neville Chamberlain, Prime Minister, May 2, 1938; H. of C., *Parl. Deb.*, Vol. 335, cols. 535, 541. To the Labor party, however, the accord was essentially "an imperialist agreement of the pre-war variety." Herbert Morrison, *loc. cit.*, col. 549.

The Anglo-Italian agreement signed at Rome on April 16, 1938, consisted of a Protocol, eight Annexes, and six Exchanges of Notes. The two countries agreed: to reaffirm the exchange of notes of December 31, 1936, regarding the integrity of Spain, and the "Gentleman's Agreement" of January 2, 1937, regarding the *status quo* in the Mediterranean; to exchange periodic information regarding troop movements in Africa and naval and air forces in the Mediterranean; to seek no privileged position or political control in the Arabian States and neighboring territories; and not to employ propaganda against each other. Special provisions covered mutual interests in the Suez Canal and Lake Tsana. Italy agreed to reduce her forces in Libya, withdraw her volunteers from Spain, and accede to the London Naval Treaty of 1936. Britain agreed to take steps toward the recognition of Italy's sovereignty over Ethiopia. A special Bon Voisinage agreement, to which Egypt was a party, provided for co-operation in preserving good relations between Egypt, the Sudan, and adjoining British and Italian possessions. Texts in *Cmd. 5726.*

and Italian interests were now not only hopeless, since Mussolini would violate every agreement and would never give up his anti-British aspirations, but were dishonorable as well. They would amount to putting a premium on the violation of treaties and covenants. Eden resigned over this issue.[11]

We have mentioned the fact that the traditionalists counted on the reluctance of the Fascist Government to risk a war with so superior a naval power as Britain. Even if this speculation were right, they had no reason to believe that Mussolini would in peacetime spare them any inconvenience and shrink from using intimidating threats or from entering into hostile combinations. The less Britain was willing to antagonize Italy or to go to war with her, the greater were the chances for Mussolini to gain concessions without having to use force. His policy in Spain and the Arabian world, his collaboration within the Rome-Berlin axis, and the anti-Comintern pact would indicate that such was his intention.

Aside from Mediterranean issues, the interests of the two countries in the rest of Europe contained elements both of harmony and of discord. Before the Ethiopian crisis, their common aims were predominant and formed a broad, strong foundation for their traditional friendship. The geographic positions of Italy and Britain in regard to the Continent show striking similarities. Although Italy is not an island but a peninsula, she is separated from the rest of Europe by the Alps in much the same way that the British Isles are separated from the mainland by the Channel. The role of Holland and Belgium as buffer states on the opposite

[11] In explaining his resignation to the House of Commons on February 21, 1938, Eden declared that the "immediate difference" leading to his resignation was his insistence that Italy give adequate guarantees regarding her policy in Spain before Britain should open official conversations looking to an Anglo-Italian agreement; but he emphasized that this was not an isolated issue between him and Prime Minister Chamberlain, and that recently "upon one most important decision of foreign policy which did not concern Italy at all, the difference was fundamental." H. of C., *Parl. Deb.*, Vol. 332, col. 49.

shore is practically identical with the role which Switzerland and, for a time, Austria played for Italy in post-war Europe. The influence of both Britain and Italy on the Continent was in direct proportion to the degree of balance that existed between France and Germany. Both of them were more interested after the World War in overseas regions than in the area between the Alps and the North Sea, and were hence eager to establish a balance on the Rhine which would give them more freedom of action elsewhere. It is not surprising, therefore, to find Britain and Italy serving together as guarantors in the Locarno Treaty and collaborating harmoniously in all of the negotiations on reparations and German armaments.

But there were also differences of interest and outlook between them which contained the seeds of possible conflict. In the first place, there was a sharp contrast between their respective attitudes toward treaty revision. Britain was not averse in principle to changes in treaties, even in their territorial provisions, when they offered an alternative to the greater evils of conflict or war. She was as willing to discuss such changes with Italy as she was with Germany, although in the Italian case she might have to pay a larger part of the price herself. But while, for a satiated country like Britain, revision was at best a lesser evil which offered no direct benefit, Italy meant to profit by it. When she backed the revisionist claims of Hungary or Germany, she did so for the advantages which she hoped to gain herself by loosening the *status quo* and thereby preparing the way for a redistribution of colonies and for the satisfaction of her imperial aspirations. A comparison between the Locarno Treaty of 1925, which incorporated British traditionalist ideals, and the Four-Power Pact in the form originally drawn up by Mussolini in 1933—two agreements which both Britain and Italy accepted—gives an idea of this difference of viewpoint. The Locarno Treaty was primarily intended to guarantee the *status quo* on the Rhine. By implication only did it allow for "peaceful change" on the eastern borders of Germany. Mussolini's draft of the Four-Power Pact, on the contrary, put revision of treaties first. The sensation which the original text created was due to its second clause, which stated that "the four Powers confirm the principle of the revision of treaties . . . in cases in which there is a possibility that they will lead to conflict among the States." [12] This was interpreted as an invitation to the Great Powers to seek a new territorial settlement for Central Europe and to negotiate a new distribution of colonies or colonial mandates.

The contrast was no less marked in the attitudes of the two countries toward the League of Nations, and was to lead to their severest clash when in 1935 Italy violated the provisions of the Covenant, while Britain set out to defend them by applying sanctions. The British traditionalists had never been happy about the rigidity of the Covenant, and had done everything in their power, mainly by means of interpretation, to weaken the guarantee of the territorial *status quo* contained in the Covenant. Yet they admitted

[12] Article 2 of the original Italian draft of March 18, 1933, read as follows: "The four Powers confirm the principle of the revision of treaties in accordance with the clauses of the Covenant of the League of Nations in cases in which there is a possibility that they will lead to conflict among the States. They declare at the same time that the principle of revision cannot be applied except within the framework of the League and in a spirit of mutual understanding and solidarity of reciprocal interests."

Article 2 of the final text initialed in Rome on June 7, 1933, read as follows: "In respect of the Covenant of the League of Nations, and particularly Articles 10, 16, and 19, the High Contracting Parties decide to examine between themselves, and without prejudice to decisions which can only be taken by the regular organs of the League of Nations, all proposals relating to methods and procedure calculated to give due effect to these articles."

On the negotiations for the Four-Power Pact see John W. Wheeler-Bennett, *The Pipe Dream of Peace: the story of the collapse of disarmament* (1935), Chapter VII; a comparative table of British, French and Italian drafts, German amendments, and the final text is contained in Royal Institute of International Affai s, *Documents on International Affairs, 1933*, pp. 240-249.

that Britain was legally bound by her pledges to the League to participate in "steady and collective resistance to all acts of unprovoked aggression."[13] Fascist Italy regarded the League at best as an expedient instrument of diplomacy, and was unwilling to accept any limitations which the Covenant might place on her freedom of action.

Although differences of ideology, as well as Italy's dissatisfaction and aspirations as a new empire-builder, put a strain on the friendship between the two countries, the British traditionalists, if they had had a free hand to follow their policy of "imperialist bargaining," as their opponents called it, might have succeeded in holding the two countries together. The real obstacle to success was Italy's rivalry with France. As long as France was preponderant on the Continent, Italo-French friction was not disturbing to Britain, since it led Italy to align herself more firmly with Britain. It was only after Germany had begun to regain her power that a new alternative presented itself to Italy, who could now seek assistance from Germany. She gained thereby greater independence from Britain and immediately launched a program of aggressive action. It might have been expected that Britain would do everything in her power to strengthen the ties between France and Italy. She did favor their *rapprochement* in the days of the Stresa Conference of 1935, but soon after helped to alienate them by drawing France into League sanctions against Italy. If, after the Ethiopian episode, she did attempt to restore harmony between the two countries, she was unsuccessful. Italy started pressing claims for colonial concessions from France and joined Germany in a military alliance, while Britain and France were drawing ever more closely together and had in fact become steadfast military

[13] Sir Samuel Hoare, Foreign Secretary, League of Nations Assembly, September 11, 1935; *Records of the Sixteenth Ordinary Session of the Assembly, Plenary Meetings, Text of the Debates*, p. 46.

allies. Anglo-Italian relations came to rest, therefore, on an ambiguous foundation: Italian hostility to Britain's closest ally and what, in diplomatic language, would be called "cordiality" toward Great Britain. Which of the two would have more influence on Italy's course in case of an emergency was a matter of guesswork, leaving future alignment in a state of great uncertainty.

There exists a striking parallelism between the French and British relations with the Soviet Union and with Italy, respectively. Co-operation between the Soviet Union and France was rendered difficult, if not actually defeated, by British aversion and hesitation. In the case of the attempt at co-operation between Britain and Italy, the stumbling-block was France. We do not intend to decide whether Britain in the one case or France in the other was wrong in not paying the price which might have removed the obstacles in the way of the desired alignments. It would also be premature to claim that the "appeasement" of Italy had borne no fruit for Britain. In any event, Britain and France, when they came to fight Germany again, found themselves without the assistance of either the Soviet Union or of Italy.

XX. The League of Nations: Instrument of National Policy

AN extreme Conservative might say that all that was of real importance in Britain's post-war policy toward Europe has now been discussed and that the rest—the League, collective security, disarmament—can be dismissed as mere verbiage or Utopianism. It might perhaps be of practical value, but only as a smoke screen or as a means of providing the government with convenient slogans with which to satisfy the masses. But most British Conservatives would not subscribe to this opinion. The League played a significant role in Britain's policy even when the traditionalists were firmly established in power and had no reason, therefore, to make concessions to an opposition which adhered to the "collectivist school of thought." Even though the "League aspects" of British policy were much more in evidence when the Leftists were in office, the remarkable amount of time that was given to debates on the theory and practice of collective security, both in the House of Commons and in the House of Lords, gives an indication of how much political importance was generally attached to the issue. In no country was the government under such severe and relentless pressure to bring the foreign policy of the nation into line with the new League concepts. The traditionalists fought back, not by discrediting the League, but by interpreting it in their own way. While the struggle often seemed to bear mainly on terms and definitions, the passions aroused were enough to show that the basic issue was more than a theoretical controversy on doctrine.

The collectivists wished to make the League the heart and center of world affairs; in the traditionalist scheme it was considered only as one instrument of national policy among others, which, if not necessary, could nevertheless be very useful to supplement the traditional methods of diplomacy. An eclipse of the League, such as occurred after the failure of sanctions against Italy, was obviously of much less consequence from this point of view than from that of the collectivists, who had pinned all their hopes on Geneva.

It is hard to distinguish between what was mere lip service to the League, intended to satisfy a League-minded populace, and what was a realistic appreciation of the usefulness of the Geneva institution in terms of British national interests. The collectivist doctrine had a very broad following among the British electorate. If any proof of this were needed, it was supplied by the so-called Peace Ballot in 1935.[1] No British government could, therefore, fail to realize the expediency of making its foreign policy appear, at least, to be based on the League, if it wished to gain popular support. It became customary for the Speech from the Throne to include a reference to the importance of the League in British policy, so that its omission after the failure of sanctions was interpreted as indicating a serious change of attitude on the part of the government and was severely criticized. Many a time, when a Conservative government made a move which could have been regarded as hostile to the League, it hastened to interpret its action in terms of League principles. Rejection of the Geneva Protocol, for instance, was defended on the ground that there was no need for any reform of the Covenant, since it contained all that the true friends of the League desired. The Locarno Pact, as has been shown, was declared to be not a break with the League, but, on the contrary, a device to "underpin" the Covenant and thus to make it more effective. Even Britain's great rearmament program

[1] See Dame Adelaide Livingstone, *The Peace Ballot: the official history* (1936).

was justified by the contention that if Britain wished to participate effectively in collective security, she would have to equip herself with the armaments necessary for that purpose. There is reason to believe that in these instances, if in no others, the government and its supporters were more interested in securing popular support than in promoting the cause of the League. Professions of faith in the League became so much a matter of routine that in most cases it is difficult to discover whether there was any serious intention behind them that was real enough to affect Britain's policy in actual practice.

It is to be assumed that support of the League resulted from a mixture of motives, some nationalistic and realistic, others genuinely idealistic. That the majority of the British people, whether they adhered to the Left or the Right, hoped for progress toward a world of lawfulness and peace and welcomed the League as the most promising means to this end need not be doubted. Although some thorough-going "die-hards" openly derided the whole idea, calling the League a "mutual admiration society manned by well-meaning busybodies,"[2] most of the traditionalists merely expressed skepticism as to how much progress could be realistically expected. They emphasized the fact that the League "will serve you well if you do not overload it,"[3] that it was in its infancy and should, therefore, be kept "within the limits of what is possible at the present moment."[4] Development, they said, should be slow and steady, as with the British Commonwealth. Hence there was little hesitation in pushing the League into the background whenever it threatened to interfere with urgent needs. When at last it

[2] Lord Newton, February 24, 1937; H. of L., *Parl. Deb.*, Vol. 104, col. 315.

[3] Arthur Balfour, Lord President of the Council, June 17, 1920; H. of C., *Parl. Deb.*, Vol. 130, col. 1507.

[4] Stanley Baldwin, Prime Minister, speech in Edinburgh, November 3, 1927; *The Times* (London), November 4, 1927, p. 9.

came to be a real obstacle to policies which the traditionalists believed necessary—for instance, negotiation with the Fascist powers—opposition to further support of the League became strong. Of what loyalty there had been, nothing remained but a pious wish for a dim and remote future, in which "those great and splendid ideals" might become a reality.[5] But the attitude of the British Conservative governments toward the League was not as negative as would appear from the debates in which the "splendid ideals" of the collectivist opposition were being rejected. From the point of view of British national interest and traditional principles there was much to recommend an institution like the League, provided it did not involve Britain, by an unwarranted emphasis on positive commitments, in conflicts that were outside of the realm of her own interests. British peace strategy, attempts to achieve pacification and economic recovery, as well as to negotiate "new settlements" could profit immensely by the proper use of the Geneva institution. There were also a number of particular British national interests which it could serve.

For one thing, the League provided a means to strengthen the ties with the Dominions. It was frequently called "the main bridge between the United Kingdom and the Continent,"[6] but it would have been more exact to speak of it as the only bridge to the Continent over which the Dominions were legally bound to follow Great Britain. It was very much in doubt, up to the outbreak of the new European war, whether the Dominions would fight at Britain's side if she should become entangled in military action on the Continent except if she were participating in League sanctions.

Another way in which the League served British purposes has

[5] Neville Chamberlain, Prime Minister, speech in Birmingham, April 8, 1938; *The Times* (London), April 9, 1938, p. 17.

[6] Sir Samuel Hoare, Foreign Secretary, League of Nations Assembly, September 11, 1935; *Records of the Sixteenth Ordinary Session of the Assembly, Plenary Meetings, Text of the Debates*, p. 46.

been mentioned earlier in connection with Central Europe. The Covenant, it is true, committed Britain to help defend any country that should become a victim of aggression. But by the interpretation given to Articles 10 and 16, Britain believed she had preserved her freedom of action in such a way that she was entitled rather than committed to interfere in regions where she had no vital interests. The Covenant also contained the important provision of Article 11 which declared "any war or threat of war" in any part of the world to be "a matter of concern to the whole League." This gave Britain, as a member of the League, a valuable legal basis for using her mediatory and conciliatory influence whenever she wished to do so. Geneva was an ideal medium for the kind of mediatory services on which by long tradition British diplomacy had come to rely.

This brings us to the chief advantage of the League as an instrument of British national policy and, at the same time, to the main difference between the traditionalist attitude toward the League and that of the collectivists. Everybody in Britain agreed that the preservation of peace was the essential purpose of the League. But peace could be sought in two different ways, the one generally spoken of as "conciliation," the other as "coercion." In the early days of the League, British opinion was unanimous in laying the emphasis on conciliation. The provisions for sanctions and for the organization of collective force were minimized or passed over in silence. If there had to be any use of sanctions, it would be the moral sanction of world opinion. With the negotiation of the Geneva Protocol in 1924, the collectivists, as we shall see, went their separate way and became staunch supporters of a "League with teeth." The traditionalists persisted in the earlier attitude. The League, they affirmed, was to be "a great co-operative commonwealth," not an "armed guarantee of peace," nor an instrument of "international sabre-rattling." [7] Although they could not, of course, deny that the Covenant contained provisions both for coercion and for conciliation, it made all the difference in practice which of the provisions were to be stressed and what interpretation they were to receive. Much to the distress of the exponents of the coercive method—the French, and later the British collectivists—the Conservative governments in Britain consistently relegated the coercive, or "sanctionist," aspects of the League to a secondary position. "The less we hear of the Sanctions of the League," said Sir Austen Chamberlain, "the stronger its moral authority will be, and unless its moral authority be strong, whatever the Sanctions are they will not prevent war, . . ." [8] And he also insisted that "the League must work in the main not by force but by persuasion. Its policy must be one of conciliation, not coercion." [9] What the British traditionalists were aiming at therefore resembled very closely the old Concert of Europe. That Concert had disappeared with the World War. To restore it in its old form would not be advantageous because there was need for a broader one embracing the new great non-European powers. Without some such institution the world would break up into separate groups and perhaps hostile camps. There was nothing the British feared more than that. It was in the true spirit of British tradition to wish that nations might join in conference and consultation with one another. Many Englishmen believed that if Lord Grey's conference proposal of July, 1914, had been successful, the World War might have been avoided. The League should serve as a "permanent

[7] Lord Eustace Percy, December 13, 1933; H. of C., *Parl. Deb.*, Vol. 284, cols. 479, 482.

[8] Sir Austen Chamberlain, March 22, 1932; H. of C., *Parl. Deb.*, Vol. 263, col. 916.

[9] Sir Austen Chamberlain, speech at the University of Glasgow, November 2, 1926; in his *Peace in Our Time* (1928), p. 161.

Round Table of the nations in conference,"[10] "a clearing house for international disputes."[11] It would offer opportunity for discussion and would bring all nations within the influence of the community of nations. The collectivists, for their part, had nothing but scorn for this conception of the League as a "mere debating chamber."[12]

It seems paradoxical that Conservatives and even "die-hard" Imperialists should be found in the camp of conciliation, while Liberals and Laborites, among whose ranks were so many pacifists, should have come to back coercion. The reason most frequently given by the traditionalists for their hostility to League sanctions was that the League was not universal, as had been originally expected, and was, therefore, incapable of fulfilling its coercive duties. What they meant when they spoke of the disappointed hope for universality was that the United States had remained outside the League. This was supposed to have fundamentally changed the conditions under which the Geneva institution was originally designed to operate and, therefore, to justify British reluctance toward a policy of sanctions. While it has often been said that it is a convenient habit of the British to provide an alibi for themselves by laying the blame for their own failings on the United States, it was not merely an excuse in this case. The absence of the United States made it more difficult for the British to participate in collective action by the League. In the first place, without the help of the United States, economic sanctions had little chance of being effective, and secondly, naval action on the part of the British might lead to conflict with the United States over the freedom of the seas. "Never so long as I have any responsibility in gov-

[10] Leopold Amery, October 23, 1935; H. of C., *Parl. Deb.*, Vol. 305, col. 182.

[11] Foreign Office memorandum, February 20, 1925; *The World* (New York), May 10, 1925, p. 2.

[12] Brigadier-General Spears, December 13, 1933; H. of C., *Parl. Deb.*, Vol. 284, col. 461.

erning this country," exclaimed Baldwin, "will I sanction the British Navy being used for an armed blockade of any country in the world until I know what the United States of America is going to do." [13] If both great Anglo-Saxon naval powers had become members of the League, the idea of "policing the world" together with the other members might have appealed to the traditionalists. As it was, they were unwilling to have "collective security mean that all the work is to be done by the British Navy." [14] The task of "policing the world" was a colossal one to undertake under any circumstances, but it was considerably more dangerous if it contained any risk of conflict with the United States.

When, however, in 1931 and 1932, sanctions became a real issue because of Japan's invasion of Manchuria in violation of the Covenant, it became evident that American aloofness had not been the sole cause of the traditionalist dislike for collective coercion. The government of the United States was ready at that time to go further than the British and was disappointed at the coolness with which suggestions for pressure on Japan were received.[15]

The British traditionalists were opposed to a sanctionist League for a number of reasons that were firmly rooted in their philosophy of international affairs. They were opposed to the obligations it involved for Britain, who would be called upon to police the

[13] Stanley Baldwin, Lord President of the Council, speech in Glasgow, November 23, 1934; *The Times* (London), November 24, 1934, p. 7.

[14] Stanley Baldwin, Prime Minister, speech in London, May 14, 1936; *The Times* (London), May 15, 1936, p. 11.

Zimmern writes that "of the two leading sea-powers, who together could have provided a Police-power for civilisation, one was out of action and the other determined at all costs to deny or ignore the responsibility." *The League of Nations and the Rule of Law, 1918-1935* (1936), p. 302.

[15] Henry L. Stimson, who was Secretary of State at the time, writes that the British Government failed to accept a proposal made by him in February, 1932, that Great Britain and the United States, as a prelude to the imposition of economic measures against Japan, make a joint *démarche* reaffirming their intention not to relinquish their rights under the Nine-Power Treaty. *The Far Eastern Crisis: recollections and observations* (1936), pp. 161-164.

world for the benefit of others and would incur grave risks for quarrels that were not hers. They also refused to believe that Britain could count upon the support of others even if she decided to act on behalf of the League. Finally, "collective security," as it came to be called, meant committing Britain to the enforcement of the *status quo* even where she had no vital interest in its preservation and no faith in its wisdom. In the discussion on Locarno, it was shown how much the traditionalists rejoiced at having limited Britain's commitments to the *status quo* on the Rhine. For all of these reasons, therefore, the British traditionalists clung to the so-called conciliatory functions of the League.

The policy of conciliation stressed the skeptical or realistic point of view in international relations. It meant that the idea of guaranteeing permanent peace was discarded as Utopian. For nobody, of course, could be so naïve as to believe that all conflicts which might lead to the use of force could be solved peacefully by mere persuasion, friendly discussion, or compromise. Conciliation was not a panacea for peace. It could not be expected to do more than reduce occasions for war, or at best to shorten or localize the use of force. But that was all the traditionalists expected from it or from any peace strategy. If it did that, and did it successfully, it would render a great service, although it would not fulfill the prophecies of a new millennium of peace which the establishment of the new peace machinery, the League of Nations, was to have inaugurated.

It may seem as if Britain's sanctionist policy during the Ethiopian War contradicted these assertions regarding traditionalist doctrine. In fact, as we shall see, it rather proves the rule by standing out as an exception. From the traditionalist point of view, it was an aberration. When, therefore, the "Ethiopian interlude" ended in failure, which to no small extent resulted from the lack of conviction with which the British Government acted, the reaction against League sanctions became all the more violent. It was now stated that "it would be madness to delude ourselves with the notion that we could depend upon collective security, . . ."[16] Moreover, because of its coercive provisions, the Covenant now appeared as an obstacle to a policy of conciliation and appeasement. With Germany and Italy outside the League, there was danger, it was said, of "the division of Europe into *blocs*."[17] What British statesmen meant was that "collective security" under League auspices implied lining up a group of countries against the Fascist powers. Therefore, as long as the traditionalists hoped to reach an agreement with Germany and Italy, a League that branded these countries as "aggressors" stood in the way of "conciliation" and "appeasement."

We can see how far the two schools had diverged in thought. The traditionalists ridiculed their opponents for "being able to bamboozle themselves into thinking that if they take a pre-war alliance, and mumble these words, 'Collective Security,' over it, they can change its character and the consequences which are bound to flow from it."[18] The collectivists, on the other hand, were scornful of a policy of conciliation as pursued by the traditionalists, which they defined as a series of "imperialist deals" with aggressor nations, intended to "buy off" the violators of the law at the expense of the weaker states. It is hardly to be wondered that the attempt to combine the ideas of two so strongly conflicting attitudes in one and the same British foreign policy, which was undertaken during the Ethiopian War, should have failed and have harmed not only the League, but also Britain's prestige and leadership.

[16] Neville Chamberlain, Chancellor of the Exchequer, speech in Edinburgh, March 5, 1937; *The Times* (London), March 6, 1937, p. 16.

[17] Viscount Halifax, Foreign Secretary, speech in Bristol, April 8, 1938; *The Times* (London), April 9, 1938, p. 17.

[18] Neville Chamberlain, Prime Minister, April 4, 1938; H. of C., *Parl. Deb.*, Vol. 334, col. 60.

XXI. The League of Nations: Instrument of Collective Security

The Collectivist Doctrine

NOTHING illustrates more clearly the difference between the two schools of political thought in Britain than the divergence already referred to of their views regarding the importance of general principles in the conduct of international affairs. While the traditionalists preferred to describe themselves as acting by political instinct in the light of the particular circumstances existing at the moment, the collectivists, or at least their intellectual spokesmen, elaborated a logical system from which the proper objectives and the right courses of action could be deduced. On closer analysis, it is true, the statesmen of the first school are found not to be completely devoid of basic conceptions to which they cling with some consistency. The statesmen belonging to the latter group also appear to be more influenced by realistic considerations than they are likely to confess. However, it will be impossible to understand the collectivist aims properly without first outlining the underlying doctrine.[1] Much of it is well known, especially in the United States, where it may be said to have originated. It will be sufficient, therefore, to review briefly the main principles and to point out some of the differences between this and British traditionalist thought.

[1] See the report, "British Opinion on Collective Security," in Maurice Bourquin, ed., *Collective Security: A Record of the Seventh and Eighth International Studies Conferences, Paris, 1934, London, 1935* (1936), pp. 79-90.

It was the basic assumption of all collectivist thinking that with the establishment of the League of Nations a universal "community" of nations had come into existence, to be the acting center of world affairs. The individual sovereign nations were merely the parts of an embracing whole, to which they and their inhabitants owed loyalty. National interests in the traditional sense of the word, therefore, should be subordinated to the interests of the community. "To my mind," said Attlee, "the essential thing about the League is . . . that any one Member of the League should feel that the other States have an obligation towards it whether it is a near neighbour or not, or whether this or that State has any particular interest of its own." [2]

This did not mean that the concerns of Britain were to be neglected. The exponents of the collectivist doctrine claimed that, on the contrary, they had a truer conception of the "national interest" than their opponents, who were clinging to antiquated theories. While people had spoken in the nineteenth century of geographically limited regions of national interest and had insisted that wars in remote regions were none of their business, the development of modern methods of warfare and closer economic relationships between all parts of the globe, so it was said, had now made impossible the localization of war. This meant that aggression in any part of the world constituted a threat to all nations. To defend a victim of aggression anywhere in the world had become an act of self-preservation. "Peace, justice and the rule of law for all" were declared to be "the real British interest." [3] If it is put in these terms the controversy can be said to bear merely on the definition of what constitutes Britain's national interests. But it can also be looked at as a conflict over the views and loyalties of the British people. "The common people," Baldwin

[2] Clement Attlee, October 22, 1935; H. of C., *Parl. Deb.*, Vol. 305, col. 37.
[3] Clement Attlee, December 21, 1937; H. of C., *Parl. Deb.*, Vol. 330, col. 1797.

claimed, have "such a loathing of war . . . that I sometimes wonder if they would march on any other occasion than if they believed their own frontiers were in danger." Speaking of "men's hearts" as they are today, he doubted whether the peoples of Europe would "be ready to fight to restrain the aggressor." [4] The collectivists took the exactly opposite view. Their opponents did not understand "the immense feeling there is behind the principles of the League and the immense difference it makes to people whether they are to be called upon to make sacrifices for an ideal or for a little bit of British property." [5] According to this reasoning, it would be dangerous for a government to lead its country into war except to defend some great and general principle such as the rule of law. This controversy can be represented as being between "realism" and "idealism," "patriotism" and "internationalism." It reveals a deep conflict of values and philosophies.

The British collectivists identified the community of nations with the League of Nations. They wanted, therefore, British foreign policy to be based on the League and to center at Geneva. But the logic of their reasoning drove them to demand a particular kind of a League, or rather, a development of the existing League in a specific direction which coincided less with that advocated by the British Conservatives than with that desired by the French. The following would seem to have been the underlying argument.

The community of nations requires the establishment of the rule of law if it is to function like a national community and enjoy peace and order. Its enemy is therefore the aggressor, that is any nation that resorts to force in violation of the law. What the community needs primarily if aggression shall be wiped out or punished is the

[4] Stanley Baldwin, Prime Minister, June 18, 1936; H. of C., *Parl. Deb.*, Vol. 313, cols. 1236-1237.

[5] Clement Attlee, March 24, 1938; H. of C., *Parl. Deb.*, Vol. 333, col. 1417.

readiness for common coercive action by its law-abiding members. If the threat of such coercion is strong enough it will deter the aggressor in most cases. If it does not do so it will be able to defeat any criminal violator of the law. The function of the League, its most essential function at least, is therefore to organize and to set in motion the "police forces" of the community. In doing so it protects every potential victim of aggression. This, then, is collective security. It means putting "irresistible force behind the rule of law." [6] It means making the League a center of international "police action." There was obviously no place in this scheme for a merely consultative and conciliatory League such as the traditionalists favored. Mediation, conciliation, and the redress of grievances were not to be excluded from the international peace machinery, but they were thought of as coming after the enforcement of the law. They are not the means by which a law-abiding community deals with its criminals.[7]

Several perplexing aspects of the theory call for closer analysis. One is its hypothetical character. When an adherent of collectivism speaks of a community of nations or of a spirit of solidarity between the peoples of the world, it is difficult to discover whether he is speaking of a world as he imagines it actually to exist, or whether he is referring to a world which he believes should be established in the future. If it had been the latter only, the hopes of these men for a better world and their appeal to men of all countries to bring it to pass would not have met with great po-

[6] Sir Archibald Sinclair, October 29, 1936; H. of C., *Parl. Deb.*, Vol. 316, col. 68.

[7] One of the purposes of the discussion below of the Geneva Protocol will be to show how the British Labor party, despite its strong pacifist leanings, came to support a theory and policy which laid so much emphasis on the preparation and application of collective force and which came so near in practice to the policy of security against Germany which France and the Little Entente powers were pursuing on the basis of their national interest, in the traditional sense of the word.

litical opposition in Britain. But when, for instance, Henderson, speaking for the Labor party, said that "the security of each nation shall be the concern of every other nation," [8] or when Attlee proclaimed that "you have to put loyalty to the League of Nations above loyalty to your country," [9] they were demanding from the British Government that it proceed *as if* the "concern" and the "loyalty" were already in existence and could be counted upon. The assumption apparently was that if a government, particularly the British Government, would only take the lead in an act of international solidarity, and call for collective action against an aggressor, the rest of the world would follow. According to the Leftists the responsibility was chiefly Britain's: "We know that when this country does take a lead other States of the League follow." [10] The peoples of the world, assumed to be in sympathy with collectivist ideas, would compel their governments to cooperate. The world would thus be made over into what it should be, if it were not already so.

Through all the discussions of collective security there was evident an almost religious faith that the mass of the common people was intensely international-minded and was only waiting for courageous leadership to throw off the restraining influence of reactionary nationalistic governments and vested interests. The sincerity of the adherents of this school of thought cannot be questioned. It could be seen in their missionary zeal, as well as in their willingness to have their governments take risks which might involve the country in heavy sacrifices. Nowhere did this sentiment gain more momentum and political significance than in England. The "Wilsonian" trend in British post-war politics may well appear to the future historian as one of the great emotional mass

[8] Arthur Henderson, March 2, 1937; H. of C., *Parl. Deb.*, Vol. 321, col. 234.
[9] Clement Attlee, November 7, 1933; H. of C., *Parl. Deb.*, Vol. 281, col. 148.
[10] Clement Attlee, February 24, 1936; H. of C., *Parl. Deb.*, Vol. 309, col. 152.

movements of our times. We have encountered it in discussing Britain's pledge to Poland in 1939, and shall find it reaching an earlier climax in the days of sanctions against Italy.

It is obvious that whenever practical political consequences were involved, as for instance in the case of the Ethiopian War, these views, or articles of faith, were bound to clash violently with the opinions of the traditionalists. There was a sharp line of demarcation between those who were willing to commit Britain only within the limits of her traditional national interest and believed that other nations would act in a similar manner, and the collectivist school. The latter regarded the willingness of the peace-loving nations of the world to defend the law and fight the aggressor as an overwhelmingly powerful though dormant force which could be awakened and brought into action if only the League were not left "in the hands of people who do not want to work it." [11] What the collectivists regarded as reactionary and nationalistic relics of pre-war days that could be swept aside, the traditionalists regarded as still the most real, stable, and potent factors in the world, which should, therefore, be given first consideration. These included, for instance, the desire of the United States to keep out of foreign entanglements, the conviction of the French that collective action should be reserved to deal with Germany, the hesitation of many small countries to give up their neutrality, the aversion of the bourgeois classes to co-operate with the Soviet Union, or the refusal of the average citizen to fight except in defense of his country's vital interests. In view of such a cleavage of opinion and sentiment, it is not surprising that the political pendulum, after having swung to collective security under British leadership in the days of sanctions against Italy, should have reverted in 1937 to an extreme type of traditionalist "realism," characterized by a willingness not only to "face the facts" of the world as it was, but

[11] Clement Attlee, March 24, 1938; H. of C., *Parl. Deb.*, Vol. 333, col. 1416.

to condone practically every *fait accompli* as if Britain had no part to play in shaping the course of events.

The abstract type of reasoning which characterized every collectivist debate at Geneva and elsewhere is also worth considering more closely. In theoretical discussions on matters of peace machinery or peace strategy, it is obviously necessary to speak in abstract terms, and to describe and analyze problems of a general nature, such as "collective security," "peaceful change," or "disarmament," without reference to any particular political situation or to any specific countries. But it is quite another matter when statesmen are debating questions of practical application and actual policy. When they use the abstract approach, the chances are that it serves some political purpose. Thus when, during the period of sanctions against Italy, Eden declared that "these old phrases 'pro' this country or 'anti' that country belong to a past epoch,"[12] he was merely telling the Italians that British participation in League sanctions represented no British hostility toward Italy or no clash of national interests. The collectivists would have wished this phrase to mean that such conflicts between nations had ceased to exist altogether and had given way to conflicts between the law-abiding community and the law breaker. Abstract phraseology in the mouth of the collectivists was, therefore, an attempt to deny or minimize the particular national interests of individual countries and to speak as if they had been merged into the interests of the community.

Abstractness also served another purpose. Although it was hardly a secret which countries were regarded as being on the side of the "police force," and which were the "potential aggressors," it was considered to be politically wise not to mention them by name and thus to avoid provocation and the splitting of the community.

[12] Anthony Eden, Foreign Secretary, speech in Warwick, January 17, 1936; *The Times* (London), January 18, 1936, p. 8.

Therefore, instead of saying that Britain should not limit her commitments to Western Europe but should promise aid to Czechoslovakia and Poland, in case Germany should attack them, it was better to say, "The real League position does not differentiate between frontiers." [13] It is not being suggested that it was a conscious act of political expediency to use this abstract phraseology. Certainly this was not true for sincere collectivists. They quite obviously believed that in not mentioning names they were actually preventing the League from being pointed against any specific country or from serving any particular national interests.

Abstractness, it should be noted, faded away as soon as sanctions against aggressors became a serious political issue, that is, after the Japanese attack on Manchuria and the development of Fascist power. Instead of speaking of a universal community of nations, the collectivists now came to use the term "community of the peace-loving nations." Its security was to be defended by common action against the "aggressor nations." Soon the differentiation became even more concrete; the Fascist nations were considered by their actions and principles to have defined themselves as the "actual or potential aggressors." From that time on, Japan, Germany, and Italy were very regularly mentioned by name as the "aggressor countries."

There was now no further objection to preparing police action clearly directed against this specific group of countries. Was not every country free to decide whether it wished to be on the peace-loving or on the aggressive side? "If Germany nourished no aggressive designs," Churchill declared, "let her join the club and share freely and equally in all its privileges and safeguards." [14] Certain countries, it was assumed, had made their choice long ago

[13] Clement Attlee, March 26, 1936; H. of C., *Parl. Deb.*, Vol. 310, col. 1534.
[14] Winston Churchill, speech in Chingford, May 23, 1938; *The Times* (London), May 24, 1938, p. 18.

and could be counted on the peace-loving side of the eventual "police force." It had always been taken for granted, for instance, that Great Britain, and also France and the United States, would never be found in the camp of the aggressors; the citizens of a democracy would not accept a policy of aggression on the part of their government. This had made it possible from the beginning to be quite concrete about the kind of police action the League might undertake. Discussions centered upon economic sanctions, which could never be successful unless assured of the support of the Anglo-Saxon naval powers and which, on the other hand, could never be effective against self-sufficient nations like the United States or against so dominant a naval power as the British Empire.

Even after the early "abstractness" had been discarded, the attitude of the British collectivists was not in harmony with French views. While the French were pleased with the emphasis on "collective enforcement," there was still too much abstract generalization in the differentiation between "peace-loving nations" and "Fascist aggressors." This was clearly revealed during the Manchurian and Ethiopian crises. On both occasions the British collectivists fought hard to have the League take effective action against the aggressors and regarded the failure to do so as a major catastrophe for the collective system. The French, on the other hand, were making every effort to distinguish between an aggressor with war-like intentions in Europe (*i.e.*, Germany) and other aggressors who were merely taking action of a colonial character in remote regions. Therefore, when, in 1935, the British public, after much hesitation, at last came out overwhelmingly in favor of League sanctions and in support of strong collective measures against Italy, adopting what for years had been the favorite French thesis, they took the abstract terms used at Geneva far too literally for the French, who for good reasons disliked taking action in this case.

Another contrast between the British collectivist and the French conceptions has been mentioned earlier. While the French sought to extend the *casus foederis* so that sanctions would be put in motion in cases of treaty violations, particularly of demilitarized zones and other acts not involving a resort to war, the Labor party drew a clear distinction between "aggressive war" beyond the frontiers of a country and other violations of the law, however reprehensible, such as Hitler had taken in 1935 or 1936. When the Germans marched into the Rhineland, it was declared that "the Labour party would not support the taking of military sanctions or even economic sanctions."[15] This was said at the very moment when the sanctionist campaign against Italy was being pushed so vigorously by the British Leftists. "Collective security" in the British sense, therefore, meant a collective fight against wars of aggression in any part of the world; French "sanctionism" was a means of combating any German threats or acts which were aimed at the treaty structure of 1919.

The British traditionalists objected even more than the French to the attitude of the British collectivists. Abstract discussions about security, disarmament, or arbitration seemed to them irrelevant to the problem with which British national policy was faced. It might be opportune to participate in the "new diplomacy" of Geneva, but it must be understood that what was really being discussed were British commitments to this or that country, ratios of armaments between certain powers, and other concrete issues. The fight against the "Fascist aggressors" was more explicitly and more strenuously opposed. It antagonized such traditional friends of Great Britain as Italy and Japan; it tended to unite the three great revisionist powers; and it made extremely difficult, if not impossible, the "general settlement" with Germany which for years was one of the main objectives of the British Government.

[15] Hugh Dalton, March 26, 1936; H. of C., *Parl. Deb.*, Vol. 310, col. 1454.

Winston Churchill, with a group of Conservative friends, took an attitude which differed from that of either of the two schools. He advocated a policy of the national interest, in the traditionalist sense of the term, but based wholeheartedly on a sanctionist League. When he first advanced his ideas, they seemed to indicate a complete break with traditionalist philosophy. Had he deserted to the collectivist camp and become just another passionate exponent of the idea of collective security? He did advocate "collective security"; but as he interpreted it, it was a very different thing from the ideal for which the collectivists were striving. He was not concerned with any abstract community of nations, with the rule of law, or with the punishment of aggressors, although he did use these terms. His one and only concern, now as always, was Britain. He was seeking to defend the safety of the British Isles and the British Empire against the threat of a German attack, which he believed was to be feared. Between him and the collectivists there was an identity of views, however, with regard to the means which Britain should employ. Both wanted a "League with teeth" and wholehearted British support for League sanctions. This identity between collectivist internationalism and British nationalism existed, as he explained, because Britain's national interest coincided with the interests of humanity and civilization. "The fortunes of the British Empire and its glory are inseparably interwoven with the fortunes of the world. We rise or we fall together," he exclaimed.[16] The British had every reason to profit by this happy coincidence. They would gain the support of all peace-loving nations and of all classes of British society if, instead of taking a stand on the ground of British safety, they set out to

[16] Winston Churchill, October 24, 1935; H. of C., *Parl. Deb.*, Vol. 305, col. 361.

Churchill's principal speeches on international affairs since 1932 are collected in *While England Slept: a survey of world affairs, 1932-1936* (1938), and *Step by Step, 1936-1939* (1939).

fight for the great moral cause of collective security. Thus the one-time isolationist turned collectivist, not because he was converted from nationalism to internationalism, but because he had become convinced that Britain's safety could no longer be protected by the British navy alone, or even by Britain and France together, but needed the support of a "grand alliance." The League as a kind of super-alliance presented itself as an ideal solution. A strong British navy and a strong League, Churchill said, were "allied insurances for our peace and safety," serving both the security of Great Britain and the moral cause of humanity.[17] His was the same stand that France had taken all along, not merely because both regarded the function of the League to be that of a great coalition, but because both thought of it exclusively in terms of the "German menace."

Churchill and collectivist Laborites were curious bedfellows. Their alignment for the cause of collective security was not without irony. Both had gone a long way before they united; and it was National Socialist Germany who had brought about this union. The one-time pacifists had first come to espouse the cause of collective coercion in an idealistic hope of saving the community of nations from aggressive violators of the law. Then the policy of collective security had gained new impetus from a desire to call a halt to "Fascist aggression." Churchill had started by opposing the League, lest it should entangle Britain in other people's quarrels, and had turned to collective coercion later because he thought Britain needed allies against a rearmed and aggressive Germany. Thus "collective security" came to mean three different things: an international organization of peace against potential aggressors; a common defense of the democracies against Fascist

[17] Winston Churchill, October 24, 1935; H. of C., *Parl. Deb.*, Vol. 305, col. 361.

aggression; and a grand alliance of Britain and her friends to protect British security from a German attack.

The clash of opinion within Britain was more than a conflict of philosophies. Beneath the debates over the true nature of Britain's national interest, the proper extent of international solidarity, police action, and lawfulness, there operated all the stimuli—personal, social, and economic interests, prejudices, and emotions—that lead the British to align themselves with one party rather than with another, or to prefer one group of powers or one type of régime to another. However, the enunciation of two sets of opposing philosophies on foreign policy and international affairs did become a powerful factor itself, with considerable influence on the course of British foreign policy in world events.

"Putting Teeth" into the Covenant: The Geneva Protocol

The collectivist doctrine which we have described, with its emphasis on deterring or punishing the aggressor, and, therefore, on "police force" and coercion, was not by any means the program with which the Leftist parties and particularly the Labor party in Britain started out after the close of the World War. At a time when the French were already demanding that the League be equipped with an international police force and were endeavoring to make the coercive provisions of the Covenant more rigid, the British Leftists were committed to what one may call a pacifist philosophy, that is, to disarmament, to the "moral pressure" of public opinion as the sole sanction, to reconciliation of the one-time enemies, and to the revision of unjust treaties.

It is, therefore, interesting to inquire why collectivist views came to gain the upper hand, so that at the time the League applied sanctions against Italy "collective security" had come to be regarded as a panacea by the British Leftists even more than by the French.

What might be called the basic peace programs of both major parties in Britain, Conservative and Labor, took shape in the years 1924, when Labor approved the Geneva Protocol, and 1925, when the Conservatives accepted the Locarno Treaty. Both instruments were primarily intended to give France an additional guarantee of security, the Locarno Pact serving as a substitute for the Protocol, which the British Conservative government had refused to ratify.[18]

The Geneva Protocol is of interest because the British Labor

[18] The Geneva Protocol had its origins in the labors of the Temporary Mixed Commission which was set up on the initiative of the First Assembly with the task of preparing a plan for the execution of the disarmament obligations contained in Article 8 of the Covenant. The Commission made little progress until the principles which were to guide it were laid down by the 1922 Assembly in Resolution XIV (see above, p. 168). The Commission was instructed to prepare a draft treaty, accepting as its starting point the interdependence of the reduction of armaments and further guarantees of security. On the basis of drafts submitted by Lord Robert Cecil and by Lieutenant-Colonel Réquin of the French delegation, the Commission prepared the Draft Treaty of Mutual Assistance which was amended by the Fourth Assembly in 1923 and submitted for approval. See the *Records of the Fourth Assembly, Minutes of the Third Committee.* The reaction was not generally favorable, and from the British Labor government, in particular, came an answer rejecting the draft.

In the meantime, a movement was in progress for the addition of a third element, "arbitration," to the twin bases of the Draft Treaty, "disarmament" and "security." In this way, it was hoped to remove the objections that the Draft Treaty had been too concerned with sanctions and not enough with the settlement of disputes, and, at the same time provide a means for "defining the aggressor" which would remove this task from the political hands of the Council. A draft treaty submitted in the summer of 1924 by a private American group under the chairmanship of Professor James T. Shotwell, supplied the key to the problem in its suggestion that the acceptance or rejection of arbitration be made the "automatic" test of aggression, a proposal that had been advanced by Lord Grey in the House of Lords a year before.

The Fifth Assembly, acting under the initial stimulus provided by the presence of Herriot and MacDonald, set out to draft a new plan based on the famous trilogy, arbitration, disarmament, and security. The Assembly's First and Third Committees (concerned with legal matters and armaments, respectively) devoted themselves to this task under the guidance of MM. Politis and Beneš, the two

party, by accepting its principles, became the backbone of the collectivist school in Britain and, at the same time, took a big step in the direction of the French thesis of the League and European peace strategy. After 1924, spokesmen of the Labor party in Britain and of all parties in France constantly referred with regret to the rejection of the Protocol, which they believed would have gone far toward stabilizing peace and making the League effective.

It would be both inexact and unfair to say that the Protocol was limited only to strengthening the coercive provisions of the Covenant or that, as the French might have wished, it added materially to the execution of League sanctions.[19] According to the

rapporteurs. The Protocol for the Pacific Settlement of International Disputes was the result of these labors. On October 2, 1924, the Assembly recommended its acceptance, and within a short time seventeen signatures, including that of France, had been affixed to the Protocol. But after its rejection by the British Conservative government in March, 1925, it was dropped, and attention was turned to the negotiations for a Western security pact which were already in progress. See League of Nations, *Arbitration, Security and Reduction of Armaments*, C. 708. 1924. IX, which contains all of the debates, resolutions, and reports relating to the Geneva Protocol. See also Philip J. Noel Baker, *The Geneva Protocol for the Pacific Settlement of International Disputes* (1925), and David H. Miller, *The Geneva Protocol* (1925). The relevant documents are also to be found in Georg von Gretschaninow, ed., *Materialien zur Entwicklung der Sicherheitsfrage im Rahmen des Völkerbundes*, Erster Teil, *1920-1927* (Vol. II, Part 1 of Viktor Bruns, ed., *Politische Verträge: Eine Sammlung von Urkunden*), 1936, pp. 389 ff.

[19] The main provisions of the Protocol were the following. The preamble declared a "war of aggression" to be an "international crime," and declared that the purpose of the Protocol was to facilitate the application of the system provided in the Covenant for the pacific settlement of disputes, to ensure the repression of international crimes, and to realize the reduction of armaments contemplated in Article 8 of the Covenant. The signatory states agreed not "to resort to war" except in resistance to acts of aggression or in agreement with the League and accepted compulsory procedures for the settlement of disputes (Articles 2-6). They undertook not to mobilize or increase their armaments, either before or during the procedure for pacific settlement, nor to take any action which might constitute a threat of aggression, and agreed to entrust the Council, voting by a two-thirds majority, with the enforcement of these provisions (Articles 7 and 8). A state resorting to war in violation of its undertakings, or violating rules laid

British interpretation, only the occasions on which sanctions were to be applied were extended. Disarmament and arbitration played an important role in the new agreement. But, as we shall see, an agreement on armaments was left to the future; it was merely made a condition for bringing the Protocol into force, and arbitration, as well as other forms of peaceful settlement of dispute, was incorporated not primarily for its own sake, but as a means of making the definition of aggression automatic.

There was general agreement, then, that the value of the Protocol was to be sought in the fact that "it will restrain aggressors by making greater the deterrent power of the obligations already enshrined in the Covenant."[20] Philip Noel Baker, one of the Protocol's fervent exponents, calls it "the outlawry of war with a vengeance."[21] Henceforth, then, the British Leftists were going to base their peace policy primarily on the "determination to resist

down for a demilitarized zone, was declared to be an aggressor. Presumptions of aggression were established which were to be applied unless a unanimous vote of the Council should decide otherwise (Article 10). Sanctions were to be applied by all states "loyally and effectively" and in application of special agreements where they existed (Articles 11-15). The signatories agreed to participate in a conference for the reduction of armaments (Article 17) and it was provided that the Protocol would not go into effect until a disarmament plan had been accepted, and that it would become null and void if such a plan were not carried out (Article 21).

[20] Arthur Henderson, Home Secretary, League of Nations Assembly, Third Committee, September 22, 1924; *Arbitration, Security and Reduction of Armaments, op. cit.*, p. 174.

[21] Baker, *op. cit.*, p. 30.

Austen Chamberlain, Foreign Secretary in the Conservative government which rejected the Protocol, explained the Conservative attitude toward the Protocol when he declared, "The fresh emphasis laid upon sanctions, the new occasions discovered for their employment, the elaboration of military procedure, insensibly suggest the idea that the vital business of the League is not so much to promote friendly co-operation and reasoned harmony in the management of international affairs as to preserve peace by organising war, . . ." Declaration to the League of Nations Council, March 12, 1925; *Official Journal*, VI (April, 1925), p. 448.

all unscrupulous attempts to plunge the world again into the disaster of war." [22]

Neither the statements of the spokesmen of the Labor party nor what was known of its pacifist philosophy foreshadowed a sudden swing to a collectivist program such as the Protocol represented. Up until the very month during which it was negotiated at Geneva, the party had been strongly opposed to "the theory that you must have force before you can have friendliness or security"; the introduction of force was said, moreover, to be "the introduction of a new era of fear such as led to the war of 1914." [23] "Our interests for peace are far greater than our interests in creating a machinery of defence," said MacDonald at a meeting of the same Assembly which voted the Protocol.[24] What, then, converted him and his colleagues to a "League against the aggressor"? [25]

Before seeking an explanation, it should be said that the majority of the British people, even on the Left, were far from becoming sanctions-minded overnight.[26] Even those who welcomed the

[22] Report of the British delegation, November 1, 1924; *Cmd. 2289*, p. 9.

[23] Lord Parmoor, Lord President of the Council, July 24, 1924; H. of L., *Parl. Deb.*, Vol. 58, col. 982, explaining the Labor government's rejection of the Draft Treaty of Mutual Assistance.

[24] J. Ramsay MacDonald, Prime Minister, League of Nations Assembly, September 4, 1924; *Arbitration, Security and Reduction of Armaments, op. cit.*, p. 13.

[25] Before 1924, collectivist ideas had received their warmest support from British Liberal circles and from Lord Robert Cecil, a Conservative. The Draft Treaty of Mutual Assistance was partly based on a draft presented by Cecil, and was then turned down by the British Labor government. Since the British governments which Cecil represented at Geneva were conducting a traditionalist policy in London, they apparently regarded Cecil's work at Geneva merely as an academic exercise.

[26] See Maurice Bourquin, ed., *Collective Security: A Record of the Seventh and Eighth International Studies Conferences* (1936), p. 83, where the report of a British group says that the impression that Great Britain was asked in the Protocol "to pledge her armed forces in advance to co-operative action with other

more explicit threat of sanctions did not expect that this would ever lead to the actual use of military force. Deterring, not punishing, the aggressor was, in the optimistic views of the British Leftists, the real purpose of any "array of forces against the aggressor." The sanctions of the Protocol would so impress the potential aggressor as to be "an almost insuperable barrier to future warfare."[27] If coercive action should, however, become necessary, "economic sanctions alone," according to Henderson, were expected to be sufficient because of the "supreme value of supplies of raw materials and foodstuffs, and, conversely, the enormous effect of a blockade."[28] Not until the days of the Ethiopian War was there any inclination to apply or even any willingness to consider military measures.[29]

This, then, is the reason why the shift from a pacifist faith in the "moral sanction of world opinion" to League sanctions was not felt to be so great. Were not economic sanctions a new and bloodless device with which to bring "aggressors" to reason? In addition, it should be remembered that the whole problem of aggression was a highly academic matter in 1924 and for many years thereafter, as far as the British were concerned. It was a period of hope and relative peacefulness. Conciliation and disarmament could always remain in the foreground, whatever the agreements on sanctions might contain. These were, therefore, regarded mainly as a means of appeasing nations that were still hypnotized by fears

States came as something of a shock—and this not merely to the Conservative part of the nation."

[27] Lord Parmoor, March 24, 1925; H. of L., *Parl. Deb.*, Vol. 60, col. 663.

[28] Arthur Henderson, Home Secretary, League of Nations Assembly, Third Committee, September 22, 1924; *Arbitration, Security and Reduction of Armaments*, *op. cit.*, p. 173.

[29] Anthony Eden, Foreign Secretary, once said, "The truth is that while hon. Gentlemen opposite profess to support the League with horse, foot, and artillery, they really only mean to support it with threats, insults and perorations." May 6, 1936; H. of C., *Parl. Deb.*, Vol. 311, col. 1736.

of actual aggression. By the time the scene changed and "aggression" became real, in the years when Japan and Italy resorted to war, pacifist sentiment had receded and given way to an increasingly more militant and anti-Fascist feeling, to which both the array and the use of collective force against the violators of the "law" could appeal.

Turning now to the question of how the "conversion" can be explained, we shall find that in 1924 a number of elements concurred in pushing the Laborites into a new path. There was a strong desire on the part of the Labor government in Britain to improve Franco-British relations, so that progress could be made in matters of reparations and particularly disarmament. In 1922, attempts to negotiate a satisfactory bilateral Anglo-French pact of guarantee had failed. The following year, which saw the French occupation of the Ruhr and Anglo-French clashes over the treaty with Turkey, had made tension between the two countries very serious. The Labor party, before coming into office, had itself contributed greatly to this situation by demanding the revision of the Versailles Treaty in its electoral program.[30] The fact that a

[30] The Labor party's election manifesto of November 17, 1923, declared that the party stood for "the immediate calling by the British Government of an International Conference (including Germany on terms of equality) to deal with the revision of the Versailles Treaty, especially reparations and debts." *The Times* (London), November 19, 1923, p. 21.

After the Labor government had come into office, Arthur Henderson, the Home Secretary, in a speech in Burnley on February 23, 1924, declared that "the revision of the Treaty of Versailles with all expedition possible" was "an absolute essential" for the restoration of peace and co-operation. *The Times* (London), February 25, 1924, p. 7. But when Ramsay MacDonald, the Prime Minister, was questioned in the House of Commons as to whether the Labor government accepted this declaration as its own, he declined all responsibility for it, and spoke, in moderate terms that satisfied even his critics, of a future "complete survey of all the problems, debts and everything else, with the intention of attacking them in detail and clearing them out of the way." The responsibilities of office had left their mark. February 27, 1924; H. of C., *Parl. Deb.*, Vol. 170, col. 610.

Leftist government under Herriot now took the place of Poincaré's ministry, aroused hopes for a close co-operation between the liberal forces in the two countries. This was the general political constellation which predisposed the British at this time to make concessions to France.

But there was also a more specific and pressing reason. Labor's panacea during the early years, before the collectivist doctrine came to predominate, was disarmament. If all nations would disarm, it was argued, the most dangerous cause of war would disappear, and nations could at last feel secure. The Labor government was committed to promote a general agreement on disarmament, which it had called "the only security for the nations." [31] But the French were blocking every such move toward disarmament. They insisted that their country could not afford to reduce its armed forces unless it received other equally reliable safeguards, by which, as we have said earlier, they meant promises of military assistance. A deadlock was reached, with Britain advocating disarmament as a means of giving security, and France demanding security as a prerequisite for disarmament. The debates on this subject at Geneva, carried on in the abstract, sounded like theoretical discussions regarding the respective merits of two types of peace strategy. But, in reality, the conflict concerned the most fundamental political issues facing the countries of Europe. "Disarmament" meant for France a demand on her that she sacrifice a part of her military superiority over Germany; for Britain, "security" was equivalent to saying that she should give France and her allies new or more binding promises of assistance. Would the British, for the sake of achieving some progress toward a general reduction of armaments, make some "contribution . . . to

[31] Labor party's election manifesto, November 17, 1923; *The Times* (London), November 19, 1923, p. 21.

give a greater sense of security"? [32] This was the phraseology usually employed.

If the British felt that they had won a victory because the signatories of the Protocol promised to take part in a Disarmament Conference (Article 17), and because the Protocol was to come into force only if a plan for the reduction of armaments was adopted (Article 21), the French in turn could rejoice at having obtained a concession of even greater importance. The British had accepted the idea that it is impossible to persuade "continental countries which had been the victims of aggression," meaning of course France, "to abandon their armaments, reduce them, or limit them, unless you gave to them some kind of alternative security." [33] This meant, "If you ask people to reduce armaments you must guarantee them assistance in case of unprovoked assault." [34] Since Germany had disarmed, the implication was that France was justified in maintaining the advantage over Germany obtained at Versailles, either by superior national armaments or by additional promises of assistance equivalent to the reduction of her armaments which she would be expected to make. That was her thesis all along. It was in clear contradiction to the views generally held in Britain, according to which France and the other allies were morally, if not legally, committed to follow up Germany's unilateral disarmament by reductions of their own armaments.[35]

If faith in disarmament made the price in terms of commitments seem worth paying, there was still another reason which helped induce the British. The Protocol, so it seemed, supplied at last a real and complete substitute for war, by providing "an

[32] Viscount Grey, July 24, 1924; H. of L., *Parl. Deb.*, Vol. 58, col. 964.

[33] Viscount Cecil, July 24, 1924, H. of L., *Parl. Deb.*, Vol. 58, col. 985.

[34] Lieutenant-Commander Kenworthy, July 14, 1924; H. of C., *Parl. Deb.*, Vol. 176, col. 147.

[35] See above, p. 41.

alternative form of settling international disputes applicable to disputes of every kind." [36] It made peaceful settlement and arbitration compulsory. But to believe that actually all disputes were in this way provided with a procedure other than war was an illusion which the commentators on the Protocol, even in the Labor party, did not share.[37] Conflicts over claims for a change of the law and for a revision of treaties, the only type of conflict which France and her allies seriously feared, and the only conflicts over which countries in Europe were likely to go to war, were not included within the "alternative solution." For the Protocol was silent on what is now called "peaceful change." Arbitration, as we have said earlier, means the application, not the change, of treaties.[38] Instead of facilitating revision, the effect of the Protocol was "unquestionably to consecrate the international *status quo* with a definite position of legality, not to be disturbed by force." [39]

If it was surprising to find the British Leftists swing from pacifist tenets to a sanctionist League, it is even more astonishing that the party which had been most vociferous in attacking the

[36] Lord Parmoor, Lord President of the Council, December 10, 1924; H. of L., *Parl. Deb.*, Vol. 60, cols. 68-69.

[37] See Baker, *op. cit.*, pp. 169 ff.

[38] The original draft discussed by the First and Third Committees of the 1924 Assembly contained a provision specifically excluding "disputes concerning the revision of a treaty or convention" from the arbitral procedures being devised. M. Titulesco, the Rumanian delegate, not satisfied with this proposal, wished also to have specifically excluded from arbitration "the modification of the existing territorial situation of the various States signatory to the present Protocol." These suggested provisions were, however, regarded as superfluous because they were self-evident and were not included in the final text. The final report to the Assembly did, however, specifically declare that the new system of pacific settlement of disputes included in the Protocol could not be applied to "disputes which aim at revising treaties and international acts in force, or which seek to jeopardise the existing territorial integrity of signatory States." Although a number of voices expressed the fear lest the Protocol "petrify" the *status quo*, suggestions for facilitating the procedure of Article 19 had no results. *Arbitration, Security and Reduction of Armaments*, *op. cit.*, pp. 202-204, 353.

[39] Miller, *op. cit.*, p. 44.

injustices of Versailles should, implicitly at least, have become a defender of the *status quo*. Arguments were offered in 1924, and from then on, to justify this stand. One was that the Protocol would not lead to any stereotyping of conditions because it would encourage "the spirit of assent and agreement."[40] This was hardly more realistic than to say that "when change becomes again a pressing need," there is no "cause to doubt that article 19 will suffice to meet the situation."[41] According to another argument, the continuance of the *status quo*, whether just or unjust, was in any case a lesser evil than the use of force. Those who accepted this thesis went on to console themselves by saying that the consent to change would more likely be given, once insecurity and the threat of force were removed. If you create stability and enforce the law, justice will follow. The collectivists were not impressed by the opposing argument, that if the *status quo* powers, the *beati possidentes* in international affairs, were made to feel safe the little incentive which they might have to redress the grievances of countries whose resentment they feared would be removed.

Since the collectivists reasoned in abstract terms, they were probably little aware of the fact that to agree to the Protocol, heralded as a means of strengthening the *status quo*, meant committing themselves to a British guarantee of the settlements in the East, of which they were the sharpest critics. The contrast between the Protocol and the Locarno Treaty, which came to the forefront a year later, brought this out clearly. Because Britain dropped the "general guarantee" in favor of a guarantee limited to the Rhine, the Eastern allies of France felt that they had lost Britain's backing for the defense of their existing frontiers.

It was one of the curious paradoxes of the European situation

[40] Lord Parmoor, March 24, 1925; H. of L., *Parl. Deb.*, Vol. 60, col. 669.
[41] Baker, *op. cit.*, p. 176.

after Versailles that the British Labor party, which for years showed so much hostility to France because of her efforts to force Germany into compliance with the treaty, should have swung nearer to the French point of view than the Conservatives. The latter, under their most pro-French Foreign Secretary, Austen Chamberlain, negotiated the Locarno Pact which represented Britain's opposition to "indivisible peace" and universal commitments. The reason may be found in the fact that Britain's vital interests, in the traditional sense, were in conflict with those of France, whereas the ideals of collective security coincided to a considerable extent with the French interest in "*paix indivisible*" and equal protection for the *status quo* in East and West.

Apparently the idea of collective resistance against criminal nations, which came to be so strongly emphasized in the days of the Protocol and thereafter, cannot in practice be dissociated from the defense, pure and simple, of the established order and the existing treaties, at least not as long as procedures for a peaceful change of the law are non-existent. It is significant that the collectivists, while expressing much sympathy for such procedures, neither insisted that the guarantee of the *status quo* be made conditional on their establishment, nor made much effort to discover whether such procedures were possible. Adherence to the principles of the Protocol and of collective security obviously rested on the assumption, not only that the maintenance of the existing order was the lesser evil to war, but that its enforcement would prevent war. However, by taking this attitude, the collectivists committed themselves to fighting any nation disagreeing with this philosophy and preferring to risk war rather than to put up with a *status quo* which it regarded as unjust or unbearable.

An Experiment in League Sanctions

The latent conflict between a policy of the national interest and a policy of collective security was bound to break into the open sooner or later. As long as no great power challenged the League, the issue of collective security could lie dormant. Backed by Britain and France, the League had sufficient authority, without resorting to coercive measures, to settle disputes between minor powers or to deal with a great but disarmed power like Germany. Until the early thirties, therefore, the British traditionalists had little reason to quarrel with the League Covenant; the consultative concert of powers at Geneva was working to their satisfaction. Even when Japan invaded Manchuria, the question of Britain's attitude toward the League was not definitely raised. The real test came with the Italo-Ethiopian War.

During the thirties, one after another of the great dissatisfied powers—first, Japan and Italy, and later, Germany—set out to alter the map of the world by the use or threat of armed force. According to British traditionalist conceptions, Britain had no reason to oppose this process of change and expansion as long as her vital interests were not affected. Her policy should be not to allow her long-standing friendly relations with such countries as Japan and Italy to be disturbed. But Britain would have found herself at variance with the whole peace machinery which she had helped to set up after the World War if such an attitude had been unreservedly maintained. The Versailles Treaty, the League Covenant, the Nine-Power Treaty of 1922, the Locarno Treaty, the Kellogg Pact, to mention only the most important agreements, all contained various prohibitions of the use of force or of acts of war such as the revisionist powers were employing. Such actions were not only contrary to the law, as some of them would have been even before the World War, but were now declared to be a matter of concern to all members of the League and to call for some kind of collective action, either preventive or repressive. The British traditionalists had compromised with these new concepts, without apparently foreseeing the dilemma into which this course would lead them.

Traditionalist policy in its "pure form" would, in the cases of Japan and Italy, have advocated "friendly deals," with China and Ethiopia paying the price—a price which might have been lower than the one they actually came to pay. Britain would have acted as a mediator and sought to safeguard whatever immediate interests she might have; China and Ethiopia would certainly not have received any encouragement to resist. The disputes might have ended in settlements similar to the one proposed during the Ethiopian War in the abortive Hoare-Laval plan. But in both instances the League Covenant and the League-mindedness of the British people prevented the adoption of such policies.

In the case of Manchuria, it is true, the British course came very close to this traditionalist type of program. The coercive provisions of the Covenant were not set in motion. Britain's role in the League and outside was openly proclaimed to be that of a friendly and impartial mediator and conciliator. Britain did not believe that the League should "seek to start a larger fire in order to put out a smaller one." [42] But a policy of conciliation could not work successfully under League auspices, once a country had used force in violation of its covenants. Concessions to Japan would have been regarded as a "premium on aggression." Furthermore, the Covenant excluded any radical concessions anyway, since they were certain to infringe on the territorial integrity and independence of China, which were guaranteed by Article 10. The role of impartial conciliator was incompatible with the condemnation of

[42] Sir John Simon, Foreign Secretary, November 24, 1933; H. of C., *Parl. Deb.*, Vol. 283, col. 439.

Japan by the League and with the threat of coercive action implied in the Covenant. "Constant references to the stick that the League is supposed to have in the cupboard, is not the very best way to secure compliance with advice," said Sir John Simon.[43] The conciliatory policy was doomed to failure, while at the same time coercion was not applied. The British Government has been blamed by its opponents ever since for having allowed a dangerous precedent to be set in permitting Japan to "get away with aggression."[44] But whether collective action could have stopped her, in view of the fact that economic sanctions were as much as even the most fervent collectivists were willing to apply, must remain an open question.

The crucial test came with the Italian invasion of Ethiopia.[45] It disclosed all the dangers inherent in a policy which was self-contradictory, and involved Britain in a course of unfortunate compromise resulting from the vain search for a line of action acceptable to both schools of thought in the country.

With the exception of Anthony Eden, the men in control of British foreign policy at the time of the Ethiopian crisis were staunch believers in traditionalist principles. Stanley Baldwin, Sir Samuel Hoare, Neville Chamberlain, Sir John Simon, all were

[43] Sir John Simon, Foreign Secretary, March 22, 1932; H. of C., *Parl. Deb.*, Vol. 263, col. 923.

[44] For authoritative Leftist criticism of the National government's policy during the Manchurian crisis, see "Vigilantes," *Inquest on Peace: an analysis of the National Government's foreign policy* (1935), Chapter I.

[45] For a survey of the British standpoint during the Italo-Ethiopian War, see the Royal Institute of International Affairs, *Survey of International Affairs, 1935*, II, pp. 39-70; this volume is devoted entirely to the Ethiopian War. All relevant documents are contained in the companion volume, *Documents on International Affairs, 1935*, II; see also George Martelli, *Italy Against the World* (1937).

For a Leftist condemnation of the National government's policy during this crisis, see "Vigilantes," *op. cit.*, Chapter V, and the companion volume, *The Road to War: being an analysis of the National Government's foreign policy* (1937), Chapter IV.

known for their skepticism with regard to League sanctions. Only a few months before the Ethiopian War, Baldwin spoke of a system of collective security as something that "we hope may come" but which it "is difficult to look for . . . in the present state of the League."[46] Throughout the period during which sanctions were being applied, he, Neville Chamberlain, and others continued to express their doubt as to the possibility of solving what they had called the "extraordinarily difficult question"[47] of making sanctions effective. Even Anthony Eden had never expressed himself as firmly in favor of collective coercion as had either the leaders of the Labor party or Winston Churchill, who by their favorite and unvarying theme of "how to combine formidable forces with which to confront an aggressor" gave expression to their collectivist fervor. It was an overwhelmingly traditionalist British cabinet that decided to apply League sanctions against Italy.

It must be left to the future historian to uncover and to weigh all the reasons and influences which prompted this decision. The pressure of collectivist sentiment which had just been disclosed by the Peace Ballot, and which threatened to express itself again in the imminent General Election, must have been one of these factors, if not the decisive one. The influence of Eden, who was now the official exponent of strong League action, with his hold on a broad and important part of the electorate, probably had considerable weight. Imperialist interests, on the other hand, of which Britain was suspected, seem to have played no role. Nobody was more hostile to League sanctions against Italy than the imperialists, who regarded the whole affair as an unfortunate fuss

[46] Stanley Baldwin, Lord President of the Council, March 11, 1935; H. of C., *Parl. Deb.*, Vol. 299, col. 48.

[47] Stanley Baldwin, Lord President of the Council, February 7, 1934; H. of C., *Parl. Deb.*, Vol. 285, col. 1203.

caused by one of Britain's "periodic fits of morality." [48] But there was still another reason, the official one, which may well have played a significant role. The decision to support sanctions was claimed to have been motivated by the fact that Britain, being pledged by the "precise and explicit obligations" of the Covenant, could not refuse to act without breaking her word.[49] In the case of Manchuria it had not been clear beyond doubt that Japan had gone to war in violation of the Covenant. Mussolini, on the other hand, went out of his way to give his attack on Ethiopia the character of a war of conquest and of unprovoked aggression in its most classical form. The League would have been doomed if the members had refused to act when they were so clearly obliged to do so. It is hard to believe that any British government could have remained in office if it had allowed the League to collapse at this stage and had so clearly violated its own pledges. Some members of the government may have hoped that the attempt would prove how futile the sanctions of the Covenant really were. Others may have believed that such a test case would show how badly Great Britain was in need of larger armaments if sanctions were to be successful in the future. Finally, not all of the men who were responsible may have realized how extremely serious the consequences of sanctions against a great power would be, regardless of whether they ended in success or failure.

The League, under British leadership, embarked upon a dual policy, that is, one that attempted to combine conciliation with coercion. But even more than in the Manchurian case, the League members were immediately hampered by the contradictions of such a course.

[48] Lord Mottistone, December 19, 1935; H. of L., *Parl. Deb.*, Vol. 99, col. 307.

[49] Sir Samuel Hoare, Foreign Secretary, League of Nations Assembly, September 11, 1935; *Records of the Sixteenth Ordinary Session of the Assembly, Plenary Meetings, Text of the Debates*, p. 46.

During the preliminary stages, that is, until September 11, 1935, the day on which Sir Samuel Hoare startled the world by announcing at Geneva that "the League stands, and my country stands with it, for the collective maintenance of the Covenant in its entirety, and particularly for steady and collective resistance to all acts of unprovoked aggression,"[50] the efforts of Great Britain and France were directed exclusively toward bringing about a peaceful settlement, acceptable to Italy, Ethiopia, and the League. Yet even during this period, the conciliatory policy, as in the case of Manchuria, was narrowly hedged in by the provisions of the Covenant, which guaranteed the territorial integrity and independence of Ethiopia and promised her the support of the League in case she refused to comply with the far-reaching demands of Italy. At the same time, the British Government and the other League members, desirous of reaching a friendly compromise, postponed threatening Italy with the application of sanctions until it was too late to deter Mussolini from going to war. Thus the collectivist theory that the threat of sanctions would be enough to deter an aggressor was not tested. It was inexpedient for the purposes of conciliation to wield the "big stick" and thereby to provoke Mussolini. But conciliation failed and Italy started her war of conquest.

The next stage found the League in no less of a quandary. Sanctions were applied, but, at the same time, Britain, together with France, insisted on continuing her mediatory efforts directed toward a friendly arrangement. It is hard to see how collective force could be applied with enough effect to defeat Mussolini as long as the two leading powers in the League were making "great professions of friendship for the country which [they were] attempting to coerce."[51] But so skillful were they in handling this

[50] Sir Samuel Hoare, League of Nations Assembly, September 11, 1935; *ibid.*, p. 46.

[51] Viscount Cecil, July 29, 1936; H. of L., *Parl. Deb.*, Vol. 102, col. 364.

ambiguous task that, as far as Italy was concerned, their policy of conciliation, culminating in the Hoare-Laval proposals, was almost crowned with success.[52] The trouble was that the Hoare-Laval plan was incompatible with the coercive policy, since it was more favorable to Italy than anything proposed before the war started. In terms of collectivist doctrine, it meant "buying off the aggressor" and thus defeating the purpose of collective security. The second stage ended, therefore, with this last abortive effort to negotiate a settlement and to end the war.

Conciliation having been ruled out, the British traditionalists were faced with the unwelcome task of pursuing a policy of collective security pure and simple. Coercion even then was not extended beyond economic and financial sanctions. It had always been very optimistically maintained that these would suffice to defeat an aggressor. Since Italy was particularly vulnerable to economic pressure, the stage was set for an ideal test of the new peace machinery. It failed because, contrary to the elaborate sanctionist theories, it proved impossible in practice for the League powers to apply effective economic sanctions without running the risk of

[52] The Hoare-Laval plan was agreed to by Sir Samuel Hoare and M. Laval during the Foreign Secretary's visit to Paris, December 7 and 8, 1935. The two statesmen, claiming that they were carrying out a mission entrusted to them by the League, drafted a plan which proposed an "exchange of territory" whereby Italy would annex practically all of those parts of Ethiopia which she had already occupied, in return for which Ethiopia would receive a strip of Eritrea giving her access to the sea. In the second place, in southern Ethiopia, which had not yet been conquered, there was to be formed "a zone of economic expansion and settlement reserved to Italy." Administration of this zone, although under Ethiopian sovereignty, was to be placed under the control of the League, but put chiefly in Italian hands. The nature of the plan was prematurely divulged in the French press on December 9, after it had been sent to the Ethiopian and Italian Governments. The concessions which it offered to Italy created such a sensation and aroused such opposition, particularly in Britain, that the plan was dropped by its authors and officially buried by the League Council. As a result of the affair, Sir Samuel Hoare resigned from the British cabinet and was replaced by Anthony Eden.

being forced to take military action as well. They were not willing to take this risk. The British Government, under collectivist pressure, had submitted to the necessity of applying sanctions, but "never even proposed . . . the consideration of any military measures." [53] In fact, they had been ruled out from the beginning by agreement with France. In the course of later events, and under growing collectivist pressure, this stand was somewhat modified. The British Government then took the view that it would be ready to go to any length, provided it were "satisfied that all members of the League at any rate who matter are not only ready to give us assurances but are prepared to take their part in meeting an attack." [54] Since no other country pressed for additional sanctions or took any steps to prepare for military action, Britain was able to adhere to her original intention of avoiding any risk of war. After the failure of sanctions she could justify her policy by saying that the British had gone "to the furthest length to which the League was prepared collectively to go." [55]

Under these conditions the question was not what economic measures were necessary to defeat Italy, but which economic sanctions could be applied without involving the League powers in a possible war. This, ironically enough, left the decision up to Mussolini. He could declare his intention to go to war over any economic measure of the League; if this threat was taken to be more than sheer bluff, it would create a risk of war. Opposition to oil sanctions, for instance, could therefore be justified on the ground that Mussolini might respond to them with an act of war. The more likely it was that sanctions would prove effective, the

[53] Sir Samuel Hoare, Foreign Secretary, October 22, 1935; H. of C., *Parl. Deb.*, Vol. 305, col. 30.

[54] Neville Chamberlain, Chancellor of the Exchequer, December 19, 1935; H. of C., *Parl. Deb.*, Vol. 307, col. 2117.

[55] Anthony Eden, Foreign Secretary, May 6, 1936; H. of C., *Parl. Deb.*, Vol. 311, col. 1740.

more reason there was for taking him at his word. As a result, sanctions which Mussolini deemed effective were automatically excluded. The only chance for success that remained was that the sanctions to which Mussolini had not objected might nevertheless prove to be effective in the long run. The outcome showed, however, that Mussolini was a good judge in deciding which economic measures his country could stand. Thus the third and last stage, characterized by the use of a limited set of economic sanctions, also ended in failure.

The British traditionalists had many reasons for not wanting their country to incur the risks of war, especially with Italy. They had never agreed to have Great Britain fight another country merely because it had committed an act of aggression. They had always maintained that the British people should and would fight only for British vital interests. Cries of "Not one battleship," "Not one British soldier" for Ethiopia were heard from Conservative benches. In addition to these general considerations, arguments of no less strength could be drawn from the particular circumstances. Italy and Britain were friends. If Britain's leadership in the League should make an enemy of this traditional friend, Britain's life-line in the Mediterranean might be at the mercy of hostile forces.

Even more serious, though not so freely discussed, was the reaction which stronger British moves against Italy were likely to have on relations between Britain and France, and on the French position on the Continent. The reluctance of France to impose sanctions was known. The opposition wanted the British Government to overlook this and to see whether France would publicly dare to oppose measures which the League Covenant demanded. The government was unwilling to pursue a course so provocative to France, especially at a moment when the dangers threatening France on the Rhine were so obvious.

As it was, Ethiopia suffered a cruel defeat and lost her independence. The League received a setback from which it was unable to recover. British prestige suffered greatly and Italy, after a victory not merely over Ethiopia, but over the League and fifty-two of its members, moved from the side of France and Britain into the arms of Germany.

Those who believe that if Britain had taken a firmer stand, both during the Manchurian crisis and again in this case, France and the other powers would have followed her lead and would, thereby, have enabled the League to stop aggression, will continue to blame the British traditionalists for the defeat of collective security. Those sympathetic with the traditionalist viewpoint must place the responsibility on the sanctionist provisions of the League Covenant and on the collectivist doctrine, which made it impossible for Britain and France to save the League for conciliatory purposes and to satisfy Italy by a compromise over Ethiopia.

XXII. From Disarmament to Rearmament

THE course a country takes in the matter of national defense is a good barometer of its outlook on world affairs. Britain's armament policy after the close of the World War was that of a country which did not expect another great war on the Continent for years to come and did not, therefore, feel the need for extensive land armaments. Her policy confirms the thesis that large armaments are an effect of the fear of war rather than a cause of war; not fearing war, Britain had little use for armaments. Of course, the facts do not suggest that Britain denuded herself of all military protection, least of all on the seas. But it does appear as if she sought to keep her armaments at the lowest level compatible with her safety and that, inclined as she was to optimism, she was modest in estimating her military requirements.

What Britain called her "unilateral disarmament" consisted, in the first place, in a rapid and drastic demobilization of the large land and air forces which she had built up during the World War. They were almost immediately reduced to approximately the pre-war level. After that, Britain continued to effect further reductions every year, with only a few exceptions, and in every branch of her military establishment. By 1932, armaments on land, to give an example of the general trend, had not been raised even to the limit set for them by the government in 1923. The expansion of the air force which the government initiated in 1923 was slowed down after Locarno. Even British naval building was affected by this policy in that it lagged behind the maximum standards set in the naval treaties. The result was a relative decline of British military power, particularly in the air, as compared to that of other countries. From being the strongest air power in the world at the close of the World War, she had dropped to fifth or sixth place by 1932.[1]

These few facts give an indication of the policy to which the British became accustomed, and allow us to appreciate the distance they had to go after German rearmament awakened them to what Churchill called "the iron realities."[2] They then set out, with much hesitation and against obstinate opposition, to make Britain by 1939 one of the strongest powers in the air, and finally to equip her with a conscript army.

In the present state of affairs in Europe, Britain's earlier policy of "unilateral disarmament" seems more puzzling than her later rearmament. British "pacifism," in the broadest sense of the term, is usually blamed for the lag in military preparedness which became evident in the thirties. Yet, while this was perhaps the most effective single factor, it could never have decided Britain's course if the party which was in control of the government most of the time and which was least affected by pacifist ideas had not, for very different reasons, favored the same policy with almost equal fervor. Conservative opposition to large armaments was prompted by a desire to keep public expenditures low; it was prompted by a deep concern for the taxpayer, already overburdened as a consequence of the World War, and with the economy of the country which had great difficulty in recovering from the war. This is not the place to go into the decidedly orthodox financial views of the Conservatives and their faith in a balanced budget, a stable currency, and a reduction of the public debt. Whether they

[1] See Rolland A. Chaput, *Disarmament in British Foreign Policy* (1935).

[2] Winston Churchill, November 23, 1932; H. of C., *Parl. Deb.*, Vol. 272, col. 80.

were sound or not, they account for the hostility of the Conservatives to large military expenditures. Leading members of the party have confessed their share of responsibility for the policy pursued prior to 1934. Lord Londonderry, for instance, certainly not to be suspected of pacifist leanings, spoke of it as "a deliberate policy" on the part of Conservative governments that wished to restore the financial position of the country before raising the budget for armaments.[3] Winston Churchill, the first to realize that the scene had changed, admitted that he had been personally responsible for five budgets before 1929 and that he shared the responsibility "for what was done, or not done" in the field of armaments.[4]

The Liberals and Laborites, being the chief exponents of the pacifist sentiment in the country, were decidedly in favor of reducing British armaments. Although "collective security" became the main Leftist slogan after the collapse of the Disarmament Conference, "disarmament" had been "the supreme objective" of the policy of the Labor party in the earlier period.[5] The British public was told, in never-ending variations, that peace depended on disarmament. The armament race, the conscript armies of the Continent, and the military spirit were all in turn declared to be the real cause of war. The new peace machinery was regarded as dispensing with the need for armaments. "National security under a 'balance of power' policy required armaments; national security under the British policy of international co-operation was best attained by disarmament."[6] These arguments strengthened the

[3] The Marquess of Londonderry, speech in Newcastle-upon-Tyne, June 26, 1936; *The Times* (London), June 27, 1936, p. 8.

[4] Winston Churchill, March 8, 1934; H. of C., *Parl. Deb.*, Vol. 286, col. 2073.

[5] Hugh Dalton, Foreign Under-Secretary, March 26, 1931; H. of C., *Parl. Deb.*, Vol. 250, col. 589.

[6] J. Ramsay MacDonald, Prime Minister, interview in Berlin, July 28, 1931; *The Times* (London), July 29, 1931, p. 12.

opposition to military expenditures among all who were emotionally hostile to anything military or otherwise associated with war.

It would seem, therefore, that the love of peace and the desire for economy had worked together to minimize any conflict between government and opposition. The main reason for this harmony and for the low level of British armaments during the twenties was, of course, the degree of actual safety enjoyed by Britain. The history of the naval conferences shows clearly enough that she was not willing to neglect her necessary defenses, even when her only serious rival was a friendly nation like the United States. In the air, where France, another friend of Britain, was at the time the only country with an air force strong enough to menace the British Isles, the government decided on a "one-power standard" for the purpose of protecting Britain, as Baldwin put it, "against Air attack by the strongest Air Force within striking distance." [7]

Since Britain, although bent on limiting her armaments, did not overlook the dangers that might some day threaten her from what were then her most trusted friends, it was to be expected that she would be even more on the alert with regard to Germany when that country began to rearm, and that she would certainly not permit preparedness in the air to lag behind that of Germany. But when the hope of preventing German rearmament by means of a disarmament convention was thwarted, the British either failed to estimate the consequences at their full value, or hesitated, for reasons which we shall discuss, to act on the advice of those who warned them.

England's Laborites, Liberals, and collectivists of every shading pinned their hopes on the Disarmament Conference which finally

[7] Stanley Baldwin, Prime Minister, June 26, 1923; H. of C., *Parl. Deb.*, Vol. 165, col. 2142.

opened in February, 1932. How sincerely the government and its Conservative supporters shared their hopes of a general arms convention and believed that the cause of disarmament would be materially furthered is impossible to judge. Tory opinion, on the whole, was skeptical of the League and of its conferences. Churchill scorned disarmament conferences, in general, as "a positive cause of friction and ill-will,"[8] and Londonderry, one of Britain's delegates to the Disarmament Conference, referred to its "pacifist and sentimentalist atmosphere," where he felt "most out of place discussing these fatuous doctrines."[9] Some Conservatives may, therefore, have welcomed the Disarmament Conference not so much for its possible benefits if successful, as with a hope that by failing it would convince the British people of the necessity of strengthening Britain's armaments. Others may have regarded it merely as a means of postponing the inevitable financial sacrifices which an increase of British armaments would involve.

According to the statements of its official spokesmen, the government expected a convention on the reduction of armaments to result from the negotiations. The opposition criticized it for lack of leadership and fervor for the cause of disarmament.[10] But while the traditionalists were not willing, as we shall see, to pay the price for disarmament which their opponents would have approved, they had good reasons for desiring the success of the Conference. Britain, it was claimed, had "gone pretty nearly to the limit of example."[11] If others did not follow her example she would not

[8] Winston Churchill, June 29, 1931; H. of C., *Parl. Deb.*, Vol. 254, col. 955.

[9] The Marquess of Londonderry, Air Secretary, letter from Geneva, July 17, 1932; in his *Ourselves and Germany* (1938), p. 49.

[10] The British Government's alleged lack of leadership and policy of obstruction at the conference are described in "Vigilantes," *Inquest on Peace: an analysis of the National Government's foreign policy* (1935), Chapter II. The course and failure of the Disarmament Conference are described in John W. Wheeler-Bennett, *The Pipe Dream of Peace: the story of the collapse of disarmament* (1935).

[11] J. Ramsay MacDonald, Prime Minister, June 29, 1931; H. of C., *Parl. Deb.*, Vol. 254, col. 916.

be able to remain at the low level that had been reached. As long, therefore, as none of the weapons, airplanes, or ships which Britain possessed or needed were prohibited, she could only profit from having others reduce their armaments.[12] This last consideration was true only because the government did not regard Britain to be in need of military assistance from any of the other countries, France included, and was, therefore, not concerned about whether or not their military power might be relatively weakened by a convention. Churchill, disagreeing with this attitude, exclaimed, "The awful danger, nothing less, of our present foreign policy, is that we go on perpetually asking the French to weaken themselves. . . . there is nothing to be said for weakening the Power on the Continent with whom you would be in alliance." [13]

If the British Government, as well as the opposition, wished the Conference to succeed, the question arises why Britain was unable to prevent its failure. If anybody really did believe that negotiations on disarmament would again be successful because, both at Washington in 1922 and at London in 1930, naval armaments had actually been reduced or limited by agreement between the leading naval powers, they must have failed to realize the fundamental difference between naval disarmament of the kind which had succeeded and the nature of the European disarmament

[12] "We are proud to think that we have done a great deal for disarmament, but I think that our attitude has sometimes been, or at any rate appears to the outside world to be like the Pharisee who said:

'Lord, I thank thee, that I am not as other men'—

French, German, or even Russians. I have reduced my armaments more than anyone else. I am ready to give up submarines, which I do not want, and tanks over 20 tons which I have not got. But when it comes to action, when we pass from general declarations and come down to business, we are like the other Powers, we always

'Compound for sins we are inclined to
By damning those who have no mind to.'"

Clement Attlee, November 10, 1932; H. of C., *Parl. Deb.*, Vol. 270, col. 530.

[13] Winston Churchill, March 14, 1934; H. of C., *Parl. Deb.*, Vol. 287, col. 397.

which was being proposed. While the former had meant proportionate limitation or reduction of the armed forces of all of the countries involved, leaving the ratios of strength between them virtually untouched, the latter was directed toward the reduction of the military strength of one group of powers only. Germany had already been disarmed. There was, therefore, no question of any further reduction of her armaments. She attended the Conference, so to speak, as a creditor, demanding that her continental neighbors pay the debt of disarmament which they had incurred at Versailles. France and her continental allies, in other words, were to be induced to give up some part of their military superiority.

The Conference was the scene of a triangular struggle between Britain, France, and Germany, in which France was supported by her continental allies, Germany by the other defeated and disarmed countries, Britain by the United States, the neutrals and Italy.

Britain's position, as compared with that of either France or Germany, was a peculiar one. She was not directly involved in the Franco-German dispute over the duty of the Allies to disarm. She had not only voluntarily reached a very low level of air and land armaments, which were the particular concern of the Conference, but nobody, not even Germany, was interested in reducing British armaments any further. The French even felt that Britain had neglected the armaments which in case of conflict with Germany both countries might need. But if Britain believed, therefore, that her only role in making the Conference a success could be that of an impartial and friendly mediator, she was greatly mistaken.

The collectivists had tried for many years to persuade the French that disarmament was beneficial and meant greater security to everyone. In view of the fact, however, that its most obvious effect was to reduce French superiority over Germany, it is not surprising that this theory did not appeal to the French. Having discovered this, the British collectivists were realistic enough, as was pointed out in the previous chapter, to understand that France could be brought to reduce her armaments only if she were granted new guarantees of security to compensate her for the surrender of any part of her national means of defense. They were willing to have Britain give her such guarantees. What they had in mind when they urged their government to make "constructive proposals" was for Britain, together with other countries, to give France and her continental allies new pledges of assistance in the form of more rigid commitments, both under the League and for the execution of the future arms convention. This suggestion, whatever its other merits, at least showed a way by which France might have agreed to reduce her armaments and thus have enabled the Conference to reach an agreement.

If the British Government was not willing to offer France adequate compensation and make this kind of "contribution," it is difficult to understand on what its hopes for an arms convention may have rested. Friendly mediation alone could certainly not be sufficient, since there was no room for any give-and-take between France and Germany that might have offered the chance of a compromise. Nothing Germany could do would add to the security of France, unless one believed that the French would put much faith in new German promises of non-aggression and good behavior. If there was to be any give-and-take, Germany would "take" French disarmament and Britain would have to be the one to "give" France more security. Britain showed no inclination to do this. But what the British traditionalists may have hoped was that France could be brought under sufficient pressure so that she would yield, whatever her views on military superiority and on new pledges of assistance might be. Would she not fear isolation if she antagonized all the countries like Britain, Italy, and the United States, which were urging her to make concessions and accept the principle of equality on which Germany was basing her claims? If France refused, she risked being blamed for destroying a great and idealistic effort toward world disarmament. If that did not impress her, she might be moved by the fear that Germany would not wait much longer and would in complete freedom arm far beyond the limits which a convention would set to her armaments. But France was not impressed, preferring the risks which her resistance involved to making the concessions both to Germany and to Britain which were being demanded from her.

The Conference soon degenerated into a struggle between France and Germany to throw the blame for failure on each other. In April, 1934, France finally broke off the negotiations, which had been carried on through diplomatic channels after Germany had left the League and the Disarmament Conference in the fall of 1933. Britain's mediatory efforts and hopes of limiting or reducing European armaments by international agreement had been conclusively defeated.

The stage was now set for a reversal of Britain's policy on armaments. From a traditionalist point of view, there could be no doubt as to the necessity for such a change. Germany had already started to rearm. An Anglo-German conflict might be a very remote contingency, but a cautious policy of national defense on traditional lines demanded that every potential menace be taken into consideration. If there was any reason which might have been accepted by the military experts for moving without great haste, it was the fact that Germany had to start virtually "from scratch," particularly with regard to armaments in the air. In spite of Germany's reputation for thoroughness and military efficiency, only those few who shared Winston Churchill's special gift for accurate and pessimistic predictions foresaw the speed with which the Germans would move and the dimensions their future air force might reach.

Lack of foresight alone does not explain the extreme caution with which the government proceeded to increase its estimates for arms expenditures.[14] Nor can it be said that the government and the parties supporting it were ready to go to any length in rearmament and that the parties not participating in the National government were solely responsible for slowing down Britain's efforts at rearmament. If the government had been sure of its own aims and of the support of its followers, Baldwin would hardly have given his word "that there will be no great armaments."[15] Since the government had an overwhelming parliamentary majority, it should have had little difficulty in overruling any opposition. As a matter of fact, the Liberals voted for increased military estimates on every occasion, and the Labor party moved for token reductions only. The most obstinate resistance which the government had still to fear came from the deeply ingrained popular aversion to anything connected with war and "militarism." Faith in collective security (with all its emphasis on the array of overwhelming force), which had replaced the earlier pacifism, paradoxical as it may seem, did little to reduce the opposition to the British rearmament program. The fear of financial expenditures, which prompted the Conservatives to oppose larger military estimates in

[14] A start was made in June, 1934, with the air force (*Cmd. 4521*). The increases, however, as Baldwin explained, were not even enough to bring Britain up to the standard of parity accepted eleven years earlier. The White Paper of March, 1935 (*Cmd. 4827*), allowed for further increases, but again only in the air force. A radical break with the past came only in March, 1936, when Britain proclaimed her vast all-round program of rearmament on the sea, on land, and in the air (*Cmd. 5107*). Even so, it was another three years before conscription was introduced. During the long and possibly decisive interval between what the British had called "unilateral disarmament" and the beginning of an ambitious rearmament scheme, Germany was pushing ahead from her status of forced "unilateral disarmament" to the rank of the world's leading and most dreaded air power.

[15] Stanley Baldwin, Prime Minister, speech in London, October 31, 1935; in his *This Torch of Freedom* (1935), p. 339.

the early period, had faded before the greater fear of external dangers. But there were still enough of the long-ingrained prejudices in Conservative and financial circles against anything that would lead toward militarization of the economic life of the country to embarrass any government that sought to compete with the rearmament measures of totalitarian states. There was also, even at this time, enough optimism left from the long period of faith in Britain's conciliatory and mediatory role to make many traditionalists hesitate before taking steps which might irrevocably destroy the chances of an agreement with Germany. British rearmament was thus retarded and limited until 1936, when the European situation finally became so menacing that further postponement was impossible. The British were then forced suddenly to spring upon the world a rearmament program of amazing proportions, which, since it was obviously directed against Germany, became a new source of profound political tension on the Continent. It may well have been a prime factor in encouraging the speed and urgency with which the Fascist powers pushed on to accomplish their objectives.

Never before had the British collectivists been in so grave a quandary. In the face of "Fascist aggression," none but the most radical pacifists persisted in demanding that the "peace-loving nations" should disarm. Unilateral disarmament by Great Britain was now obviously helpful to the "aggressors," since Britain was unquestionably to be counted on the side of the "police forces" of the world. "If the peace-loving democratic Powers like Britain, France and the United States were to disarm and if the militarist Powers were to increase their armaments, the affairs of mankind would be handed over to them," said Sir Herbert Samuel.[16] The British navy had, of course, always been regarded as the predes-

[16] Sir Herbert Samuel, October 22, 1935; H. of C., *Parl. Deb.*, Vol. 305, col. 56.

tined and ideal deterrent to aggressors. To this, the British air force had now to be added. The "promised land" had not yet been reached in which the use of force in international relations could be discarded. Progress toward the "new order" would, therefore, have to be made, not by abolishing the old-time national armed forces, but by dedicating them to collective service for the enforcement of the law. Therefore, while objections could no longer be raised in principle against increases of the armaments of peace-loving nations, a rearmament program of a traditionalist government, based "on the old lines of balancing and comparison with other countries" [17] and on "reliance on the old, anarchic principle of self-defence," [18] still met with intense opposition.

The two schools spoke such different languages that the Parliamentary debates from 1934 to 1938 often sounded like sheer sophistry in which people could hide their real thoughts under a pyramid of generalities. Whether armaments are good or bad, said the opposition, depends on the policy which they are intended to serve. Calling for a policy in support of collective security, Attlee said, "Give us that policy and we will agree to the arms." [19] To this the traditionalists, the spokesmen of the government, replied, "It is futile and dangerous to attempt to distinguish between the armament necessary for our own defence and what is required for the fulfilment of our international obligations," [20] and, "You must have your armaments and your defence, whether you are pursuing a policy of alliances, or a policy of isolation, or a League policy." [21] Collective security, they said, presupposes national de-

[17] Clement Attlee, October 22, 1935; H. of C., *Parl. Deb.*, Vol. 305, col. 45.

[18] Clement Attlee, July 30, 1934; H. of C., *Parl. Deb.*, Vol. 292, col. 2340.

[19] Clement Attlee, October 29, 1936; H. of C., *Parl. Deb.*, Vol. 316, col. 141.

[20] Neville Chamberlain, Chancellor of the Exchequer, speech in Margate, October 2, 1936; *The Times* (London), October 3, 1936, p. 7.

[21] Sir Austen Chamberlain, July 27, 1936; H. of C., *Parl. Deb.*, Vol. 315, col. 1171.

fense by each country. No, answered the collectivists: armament needs can be estimated only if it is known whether "we are fighting our own battles, or [whether] we form part of a system of collective security."[22] There was no need to worry about "national defense," if you have "collective defense," the common defense of all by all. But, answered the traditionalists, in any case collective security adds to the commitments of Great Britain and, therefore, demands armaments even larger than those needed for national defense. On the contrary, their opponents replied, pooled security means pooled military resources and, therefore, diminishes the burden for each participating country.

In the abstract these arguments are an interesting subject of debate. The trouble is that they appear to give no answer to the practical problems with which Britain was faced. Tactical reasons, however, explain the use of this theoretical pageantry. The government spokesmen were trying to avoid basing their case on traditionalist arguments so as to gain support from the collectivist-minded section of the British people. The collectivists, on the other hand, were seeking to cover up the dilemma which they faced in wanting to be anti-militarist and anti-government, while at the same time urging the government into a stronger and more militant stand against the "Fascist aggressors." It was no enviable task to reconcile two such diametrically opposed objectives.

What the government was trying to obtain is easy to see; it was rearmament, both for the purpose of meeting the threat which the rise of the military power of the totalitarian states held for British vital interests, and for the purpose of giving Britain enough diplomatic weight to enable her to reach an agreement with Germany and Italy.[23]

[22] Arthur Henderson, February 17, 1937; H. of C., *Parl. Deb.*, Vol. 320, col. 1211.

[23] The official statement of the purpose of British armaments and of the relation of these armaments to British commitments was made by Anthony Eden,

The opposition was no less realistic and concrete in what it wished to achieve or to prevent. The "magic incantation" of collective security [24] was no longer a matter of general ideas or abstract theory. Apart from having to hide the above-mentioned contradiction from the eyes of the electorate, the unwillingness of the collectivists to consent to the program of rearmament which the government advocated expressed suspicion of the intentions which lay behind the policy of the government. Strong armaments, it was feared, would be made to serve the policy of "appeasement" by making Britain more capable of striking "imperialist deals" with the dictators. They would also make Britain feel strong enough to require no assistance from others and, therefore, less willing than ever to stand behind "collective security" and to help build up a "grand alliance" of peace-loving nations. In practice, this meant even more specifically that British rearmament would enable the

Foreign Secretary, in a speech to his constituents in Leamington, November 20, 1936:

"These arms will never be used in a war of aggression. They will never be used for a purpose inconsistent with the Covenant of the League or the Pact of Paris. They may, and if the occasion arose they would, be used in our own defence and in defence of the territories of the British Commonwealth of Nations. They may, and if the occasion arose they would, be used in the defence of France and Belgium against unprovoked aggression in accordance with our existing obligations. They may, and, if a new Western European settlement can be reached, they would, be used in defence of Germany were she the victim of unprovoked aggression by any of the other signatories of such a settlement.

"Those, together with our Treaty of Alliance with Iraq and our projected treaty with Egypt, are our definite obligations. In addition our armaments may be used in bringing help to a victim of aggression in any case where, in our judgement, it would be proper under the provisions of the Covenant to do so. I use the word 'may' deliberately, since in such an instance there is no automatic obligation to take military action. It is, moreover, right that this should be so, for nations cannot be expected to incur automatic military obligations save for areas where their vital interests are concerned." *The Times* (London), November 21, 1936, p. 14.

[24] Viscount Cranborne, Foreign Under-Secretary, May 6, 1936; H. of C., *Parl. Deb.*, Vol. 311, col. 1841.

government to claim that there was no need for an alignment with the Soviet Union for which the opposition was clamoring.

Thus a conflict over the proper course to take in regard to British armaments led to a curious paradox. Those who called for resistance to the "Fascist aggressors" opposed vigorous rearmament, while those who were accused of condoning these aggressors were eager to have Britain make a maximum effort at rearmament, directed unmistakably against the powers with which they were assumed to be sympathizing. It is not surprising that both the participants in the debate and the outside observers were confused. Clarification was not made any easier by the fact that there were still other points of view which found expression in the debates. Winston Churchill, to mention only the most conspicuous example, was in favor both of the "grand alliance" and of an even more ambitious program of rearmament than that proposed by the government. By combining elements from both theories, he foreshadowed the policy to which Britain ultimately had recourse and that on which, in the face of growing external danger, the opposing factions finally came to agree. By 1939, Britain was not only arming feverishly with practically no more opposition at home, but was, at the same time, trying to establish as broad a coalition against Hitler as she could obtain. That she should, however, have introduced conscription only a few months before again going to war with Germany is a last and significant illustration of the British dislike of large land armaments and militarism. The necessity of stopping Germany overcame this resistance, just as it had swept aside the general Leftist abhorrence of national rearmament and the traditionalist opposition to advance commitments in Central and Eastern Europe.

Conclusion: Britain, France, and the Peace of Europe

BY discussing the foreign policies of Britain and France separately, we have emphasized the characteristics distinguishing their respective concepts and courses of action. But both the incidental comparisons which have been introduced and the significant cases of conflict between the two which have been described have shown how much the success or failure of the policies of each was contingent upon the views and actions of the other. It has also become evident that during most of the period under consideration Britain and France were working at cross-purposes and defeating rather than assisting each other.

It would be tempting, in drawing conclusions, to explain the discord between Britain and France by attaching labels to their respective attitudes and thereby deriving some simple formula. The discussions, it may be recalled, have indicated that France was possessed by a desire to organize preponderant force and prepare coercive measures, while Britain was engaged in establishing a better balance of power and in applying methods of conciliation and appeasement. Or it might be affirmed that, while both countries feared a German revolt against the new order of 1919, France hoped to prevent it by making the defenders of the *status quo* strong and invincible, whereas Britain wished to avert the danger by removing what she believed to be its main causes.

Such statements, however, are misleading and unfair to France, since they do not explain why the two countries came to take such divergent views. They give the false impression that France was motivated by some irrational predilection for coercive methods and the strict enforcement of the *status quo,* while Britain, moved by greater generosity or wisdom, preferred gradual adjustments and the redress of grievances. Even if the real conflict had concerned general principles, which it did not, a value-judgment such as this would be open to question. Skeptics could point to the fact that the British collectivists, who were the champions of high moral principles in the conduct of foreign affairs, came much nearer in their views to the French attitude than to the traditional British stand. They, too, were in favor of organizing overwhelming force, only in their abstract terminology it was to be that of the peace-loving nations arrayed against the potential aggressors. They sought just as persistently as the French to reinforce the *status quo* by the threat of coercive means, only they meant not a threat directed specifically against Germany by a group of allies, but the threat of League sanctions against any country using force to attack the established order.

The basic issue underlying the controversy between Britain and France was not a matter of general attitudes, but the concrete political problem of Germany's power and position. How strong could Germany be permitted to become without menacing the vital interests of the two countries? The British and the French disagreed on the answer to this question; this disagreement accounts for most of the discord between them.

France worked on the assumption that for the sake of her security she could not allow any rise of German strength above the limits prescribed for Germany at Versailles. Britain, who was obviously more remote, was not opposed to the restoration to Germany of much of her previous power, but even wished for it. Such a change would be to Britain's advantage, since it would improve the balance of power on the Continent and since, by satisfying the

Germans to a reasonable extent, it might prevent a great explosion which would carry Germany beyond permissible limits.

It should, however, be added immediately that Britain made two important reservations, which account for what harmony there was between her and France. While she wanted Germany to strengthen herself, it was not to be at the expense of Britain's vital interests and was not to give Germany domination over Europe. All along, therefore, the British and the French concurred in a desire to protect and stabilize the settlements in Western Europe, in which Britain had a vital interest. Also in 1939, in the face of what Britain regarded as a drive for domination, she and the French joined their efforts to stop the rise and expansion of Germany, and unity was established.

Harmony of opinion in regard to Western Europe meant little, since Germany did not challenge the territorial *status quo* in the West. At least, she was not likely for a long time to seek to increase her power by an attack on France. Rather would she try to accomplish such an increase through changes of the territorial settlements in the East. Even the remilitarization of the Rhineland, which barred French access to Central Europe, was essentially part of a program aimed toward revision in the East. For this reason the Locarno Pact, so highly regarded in Britain, was no more than a temporary solution to the Franco-German and Franco-British conflicts. Because it did not determine what Germany's total strength and position was to be, it was nothing more than a truce.

This explains why the difficulties on the Vistula and the Danube should have come to play so decisive a role. To keep Germany at the level set at Versailles required putting the same obstacles in the way of her rise in the East as in the West. To France, Austrian independence and the territorial integrity of Poland and Czechoslovakia were therefore almost as important as the safety of her own soil. This made her a party to the age-old conflict between Teuton and Slav in Eastern Europe and committed her to the pro-Slav solution that had been formulated in 1919. Since Britain had no objection to a rise of German power, her attitude in regard to those regions ran at cross-purposes to that of France. As far as she was concerned, the East was an ideal place for making concessions to Germany. Not only would they divert German attention from the regions of vital interest in the West, but they might also improve the existing settlement of the Slav-Teuton conflict, a solution in the wisdom, justice, and durability of which Britain had little faith. While France, therefore, opposed concessions to Germany, regardless of what region they affected, and stood for "indivisible peace," Britain made every effort to discriminate between East and West. She tried to limit her own commitments to the Rhine and, if possible, to draw France away from the regions east of Germany.

It is interesting to note that the British collectivists, unwittingly perhaps, sided with France on the Eastern issue. The program of collective security and universal solidarity militated against any discrimination between different regions. Security to them also was indivisible. Therefore, had collective security under the League become effective, Poland and Czechoslovakia, even if they refused to countenance "redress of legitimate German grievances," would have been assured of League assistance (which meant British, as well as French, aid), if their territorial integrity and rights were menaced by any German threat or use of force.

This makes it clear why the conflict over Germany's power and position also gave rise to a Franco-British controversy over the primary functions of the League. A sanctionist League meant British commitments in the East and strengthened the *status quo* in that part of Europe. An emphasis on conciliation, on the other hand, meant that the League, instead of protecting the Eastern settlements of 1919, would serve as a means to bring about in a peaceful and orderly fashion the change which was inevitable sooner or later. Since both Britain and France used the League as an instrument of their traditional policies of the national interest, their attitude toward the German problem, which held a key position in their European policies, necessarily determined the course they took in regard to the League.

The question might be raised whether any one of the policies advocated respectively by France, Britain, and the British collectivists would have met with success if it had been pursued without opposition, and whether it would then have prevented the catastrophe of another war. If the French had had the wholehearted support of Britain, they might claim, Germany could never have acquired the power with which to break loose. Instead, Britain had not only encouraged Germany to strike but, by forcing others to make concessions to her, had provided her with the power to do so with impunity. To this the British could reply that the need for stopping Germany by force would never have arisen if France and her allies had been willing to halt their provocation of Germany before it was too late and had given her the satisfaction to which she was entitled. Germany would then have found her place among the great Western powers and become an element of stability and order in Central Europe. Finally, the collectivists for their part might insist that if Britain and France had abandoned their antiquated policies of the national interest, as traditionally interpreted, and had given wholehearted support to the League, there never would have been any reason for conflict between them or with Germany. In a true international community such as they proposed, Germany would not only have been forced to obey the law, but would have had her just claims satisfied and therefore no cause for revolt.

However, to discuss these hypothetical possibilities is of purely academic interest. That any nation would risk sacrificing for the sake of the League what it believed to be necessary in its national interest was hardly probable. Nor could a policy that suited either France or Britain and was not acceptable to the other be expected to deal successfully with the problems of Europe. Peace on that continent requires, in the first place, that the two Western Powers agree on a mutually satisfactory solution.

It may now be asked whether there is anything in the history of the period between the two wars indicative of what the nature of such an agreement might be. Such a query, incidentally, has point only if Europe continues to remain under the rule of a number of Great Powers. Such a rule would not be excluded by the mere establishment of a European concert of powers, or of a European League, for the League of Nations since 1919 has given ample evidence of the fact that the strength of such an organization does not supersede the control which the Great Powers have over their own foreign policies. Rather does the success of such an institution depend on the degree of harmony existing among its members.

But there are two cases in which the old problems would become entirely irrelevant. The first is the emergence of a United States of Europe. This would put an end to the existence of the Great Powers as separate entities and would therefore eliminate the entire problem of their inter-relationships. But this we can dismiss as a Utopia for the present. The second case is more probable. One of the Great Powers may gain hegemony over the Continent, with the result that none but its foreign policy will have any further importance for Europe. Theoretically, either Germany, the Soviet Union, or France might become master of Europe. If the war should end with German or Russian domination of the Continent, there would be no opportunity for analogies with the period after Versailles and nothing in the past would offer any suggestions regarding the course Britain and France would or should take. For France, experience since Versailles seems, however, to exclude the practical possibility of another "Napoleonic" era. Even by her own admission, she is not strong enough to maintain preponderance, to say nothing of actual hegemony, except as the head of a vast anti-German coalition. This requires British co-operation and raises the same problems that followed Versailles.

It may seem very rash to discard the idea of a solution based on the unquestioned preponderance of France. Did the last peace fail, perhaps, because Germany was not weakened enough in 1919? Let us assume, for the purpose of argument, that French superiority is given a better start by a more drastic reduction of German power. France once again would have to fear a possible German revolt. Again she would be seeking not only British assistance, but the support of a grand coalition to control a neighbor whose potential superiority is undeniable. But unless there is an unpredictable change in British attitude, such assistance will not be forthcoming. Fatigued and ridden by the passions of war, the British may accept many things at the close of a war, but treaties that are at variance with Anglo-Saxon ideals of political wisdom and justice and with Britain's own interests will in the long run find no support in Britain. It should be remembered that Britain has always opposed any French scheme of this kind. The conflict between the British and the French would break out again, and France would again be defeated.

But, might French predominance not be established without antagonizing British and world opinion, and without giving the Germans any justified cause for resentment? The renewal of the idea of "internationalizing" such superiority must be tempting to the French. If a settlement basically inimical to Germany could be presented as a new *"organisation de la paix,"* predominance would appear to rest with the community of peace-loving nations rather than with France. The collectivists in Britain and elsewhere may again be ready to back the enforcement of a new *status quo*, whatever it be, if it is presented to them as a step toward a "League with teeth" or a "European federation," equipped with the power to apply collective sanctions. They will delude themselves with the theory that enforcement of the law must have precedence over all other considerations, and will again argue that if there is collective security, justice will follow. They will also claim that national boundaries, armaments, colonies, and any of the other elements of national power will, as the time goes on, lose their present significance. Why should Germany, therefore, be disturbed by the preponderance of France? But the Germans, whether National Socialist or not, far from sharing such hopes or illusions, will resent them as sheer hypocrisy even more than they resent undisguised domination by others. If they are told that superiority of one nation in the "international community" means nothing, they will ask why France insists so vehemently on having it, just as when it was argued that colonies were after all of no use to their holders, their answer was that what was worthless to others might well be handed over to them. It is obvious that a collectivist policy, if it accepts a "French solution" as a starting point, does not prevent the German revolt against which France seeks in vain for British assistance.

If we assume, for the sake of drawing comparisons, that after the present war none of the Great Powers will hold a position of hegemony, it then remains to be seen once more whether Britain, France, and the others can find a way to live together in peace. The central theme of Franco-British relations and of British, as well as French, policy toward Europe will again be Germany. Two great wars fought with that country over the extent of its power and position give ample and tragic evidence of this. The outstanding condition for peace in Europe is that the "German problem" be solved. This is not, to be sure, the only condition. Relations of Europe proper with the Soviet Union will increase in importance. And if Italy is not brought to an agreement, her rebellion, though less powerful than Germany's, may disrupt any settlement and cannot therefore be dismissed as a secondary matter. However, if Britain, France, and Germany can come to terms on a basis satisfactory to all three of them, their influence is so great that there should be no insuperable obstacles in the way of settling these other problems.

Experience since Versailles does not suggest the existence of any objective standard of justice with which to measure the rightful position of Germany, any more than that of any other power. Fortunately, such standards are neither necessary nor relevant. All that matters is whether Britain and France and Germany can agree on a particular solution and whether, once they have done so, they can make it permanent. Some indications of what the settlement should not be, if there is to be real peace, seem to follow from the events which carried Europe from the World War to another armed conflict.

If Germany's power, in terms of territory, armaments, and economic influence, is either forced below a certain minimum level or is allowed to exceed a certain maximum, it will become a threat to the vital interests of the other European countries. Below a certain point German resentment and revolt will become so violent and "dynamic" that France, with what assistance she can command in such a case, will be incapable of coping with the situation. The minimum level is therefore the point below which the readiness of Germany to rebel under provocation, as after Versailles, cannot be deterred by the available powers of the defenders of the *status quo*. The maximum level is that level beyond which the chances of keeping Germany from aspiring to domination are equally slim. The aftermath of Munich illustrates this. The temptation would become irresistible to take advantage of the weakness of others and to seek an end to European strife by a one-power domination of the Continent. Only if France, Britain, and Germany can agree on a level for German power somewhere between these two limits is there any chance of a lasting settlement.

This has been Britain's traditional thesis. Before it can become a basis for future peace in Europe, however, a drastic change of attitude must take place in both Germany and France. As long as Germany remains under the sway of National Socialism, the British are almost certain to share the French conviction that German aspirations will never stop short of domination or permit of any fair solution for the Slav-Teuton struggle, that besetting nightmare of Europe. But for France the dilemma is even more complex. At a time when she is once again hoping to establish durable peace by victory over Germany, she is asked to surrender her claims to superiority for the sake of that peace. She cannot fail to realize that Germany under any régime will accept no settlement as permanent that does not take into account the size of her population, nearly twice that of France, and recognize the advantages or glories of empire which Britain and France enjoy.

But surely, if all that France wants is security from attack, statesmanship should be capable of giving it to her. The question is how to hold a Germany that is stronger than France within limits which she herself is willing to accept. Experience suggests one and only one way to do this. It bears the name of "balance of power." The difference between the old balance, which was mainly a tool of British diplomacy, and that of the future lies only in the fact that instead of balancing the others all of Britain's weight must now be put into the scales.

Some people may be disappointed to think that Europe may have to go on with the dangerous game of balancing power. But such critics, if they are free of illusions, should find every other solution even more distasteful. As long as there are many great sovereign powers in Europe, a balance of power is the only available alternative to the domination of one nation or of one group of nations over the others.

To create a new balance of power does not solve the question of European peace; it is not a "peace plan," but merely one necessary element of an agreement on Europe's crucial problem, Germany's place and power. Such a balance is also no substitute for close union and co-operation between Britain, France, Germany, and Italy, the *conditio sine qua non* for any real pacification of the Continent. On the basis of an agreement on the extent of their respective power and positions in the East and West, which would eliminate causes of unrest not only on the Rhine but on the Vistula, the Danube, and in the Mediterranean as well, the four powers could start off where they stopped at Locarno. There would at last be a chance for the development of institutions which in time might limit and control their arbitrary will and lead them toward the ultimate goal of "federation." However great the difficulties may be that stand in the way of such a program, the sad history of the twenty-year "truce" that ended in the cataclysm of a second war does not suggest to us any other way by which Europe can be saved from self-destruction and defeat.

Chronology 1919-1939

Britain	*France*	*General*
1919		
Lloyd George * *Balfour* ‡	*Clemenceau* * *Pichon* ‡	
		JANUARY 19 Peace Conference opens
MARCH 26-31 Correspondence between Lloyd George and Clemenceau on the nature of the peace settlement		
JUNE 28 Signature of Anglo-French pact of guarantee (fails to go into effect due to refusal of United States to ratify similar pact)		JUNE 28 Signature of Treaty of Versailles with Germany; in force, January 10, 1920
		SEPTEMBER 10 Signature of Treaty of St. Germain with Austria
OCTOBER 23 *Curzon* ‡		
		NOVEMBER 27 Signature of Treaty of Neuilly with Bulgaria
1920		
	JANUARY 18 *Millerand* §	

NOTE—The following symbols are used:

* Prime Minister—Président du Conseil des Ministres

‡ Secretary of State for Foreign Affairs—Ministre des Affaires Etrangères

§ Both above offices held simultaneously

Britain	*France*	*General*
	1920	
APRIL 6 French occupation of five Rhineland towns, followed by British protests; withdrawal, May 17.	APRIL 6 French occupation of five Rhineland towns, followed by British protests; withdrawal, May 17.	
		JUNE 4 Signature of Treaty of Trianon with Hungary
	SEPTEMBER 7 Military agreement with Belgium	
	SEPTEMBER 24 *Leygues* §	
		OCTOBER 12 Preliminary agreement ending Polish-Soviet war
	1921	
	JANUARY 16 *Briand* §	
	FEBRUARY 19 Military alliance with Poland	
		MARCH 8 Allied occupation of Ruhrort, Duisburg, Düsseldorf; withdrawal, August 25, 1925
MARCH 16 Trade agreement with Soviet Russia		
		MAY 5 London ultimatum on reparations; accepted by Germany, May 11
		NOVEMBER 12–FEBRUARY 6, 1922 Washington Conference

Britain	*France*	*General*

1921

DECEMBER 5

French overtures for Anglo-French pact; active negotiations continue during Cannes Conference, but end shortly afterward

1922

General — JANUARY 6-13
Cannes Conference

France — JANUARY 13
Poincaré §

General — APRIL 10-MAY 19
Genoa Conference

General — APRIL 16
Treaty of Rapallo between Germany and Soviet Russia

Britain — OCTOBER 23
Bonar Law *
Curzon ‡

General — OCTOBER 30
Mussolini, Italian Prime Minister; beginning of Fascist régime

Britain — NOVEMBER 15
General elections

General — NOVEMBER 20-JULY 17, 1923
Lausanne Conference on peace with Turkey

General — DECEMBER 13
Cuno offer of a Rhine pact

General — DECEMBER 26
Reparation Commission votes German default by a vote of three to one

Britain	*France*	*General*
	1923	
	JANUARY 11 Occupation of Ruhr by French and Belgian troops; withdrawal, July 31, 1925	
MAY 22 *Baldwin* * *Curzon* ‡		
AUGUST 11 Curzon note protesting French occupation of Ruhr		
		AUGUST 12 Stresemann, German Chancellor and Foreign Minister
		SEPTEMBER 2 Stresemann suggests conclusion of a Rhine pact
		SEPTEMBER 27 End of German passive resistance in the Ruhr
		SEPTEMBER 29 Draft Treaty of Mutual Assistance adopted by League of Nations Assembly (not ratified)
		NOVEMBER 30 Reparation Commission creates Committee of Experts
DECEMBER 6 General elections		
	1924	
JANUARY 22 *MacDonald* §		

Britain	*France*	*General*
	1924	
	JANUARY 25 Treaty with Czechoslovakia	
FEBRUARY 1 Recognition of Soviet Union		
		APRIL 9 Dawes Plan submitted by Committee of Experts
	MAY 11 General elections	
	JUNE 14 *Herriot* §	
JUNE 20–22 Herriot and MacDonald meet at Chequers		
		AUGUST 16 London agreement on reparations (Dawes Plan)
		OCTOBER 2 Adoption of Geneva Protocol for the Pacific Settlement of International Disputes by League of Nations Assembly (not ratified)
	OCTOBER 28 Recognition of Soviet Union	
OCTOBER 29 General elections		
NOVEMBER 4 *Baldwin* * *Austen Chamberlain* ‡		

Britain	*France*	*General*
	1925	
		FEBRUARY 9 German note initiating Western pact negotiations
MARCH 12 Chamberlain in speech to League of Nations Council rejects Geneva Protocol		
	APRIL 16 *Painlevé* * *Briand* ‡	
MAY–JUNE Franco-British negotiations regarding German proposal for Western pact		
		OCTOBER 16 Locarno agreements initialed
	NOVEMBER 27 *Briand* §	
	1926	
		JANUARY 31 Evacuation of first Rhineland zone (Cologne)
		MARCH 8–17 Failure of special Assembly to admit Germany to the League of Nations
		APRIL 24 Treaty of Berlin between Germany and Soviet Union

Britain	*France*	*General*
	1926	
		MAY 18 First meeting of Preparatory Disarmament Commission
	JUNE 10 Treaty with Rumania	
	JULY 23 *Poincaré* * *Briand* ‡	
		SEPTEMBER 8 Germany elected to membership in the League of Nations
		SEPTEMBER 17 Thoiry meeting between Briand and Stresemann
	1927	
		JANUARY 31 Allied Military Commission of Control over German disarmament dissolved
	APRIL 6 Briand message to United States proposing bilateral treaty of non-aggression	
MAY 27 Severance of diplomatic relations with Soviet Union		
		JUNE 20–AUGUST 4 Geneva Naval Conference
	NOVEMBER 11 Treaty with Yugoslavia	

Britain	France	General
	1928	
	APRIL 22, 29 General elections; *Poincaré** and *Briand*‡ remain in office	
JUNE-OCTOBER Anglo-French naval compromise negotiations		
		AUGUST 27 Signing of Kellogg Pact for renunciation of war
		SEPTEMBER 16 Geneva agreement opening the negotiations regarding reparations and evacuation of Rhineland which led to the Young Plan
		SEPTEMBER 26 Adoption of General Act for the Pacific Settlement of International Disputes by League of Nations Assembly
	1929	
MAY 30 General elections		
JUNE 5 *MacDonald** *Henderson*‡		
		JUNE 7 Young Plan submitted by Experts Committee
	JULY 29 *Briand* §	
		AUGUST 6-31 First Hague Conference on reparations

Britain	*France*	*General*
	1929	
SEPTEMBER 19 Signature of optional clause of Permanent Court of International Justice	SEPTEMBER 19 Signature of optional clause of Permanent Court of International Justice	
OCTOBER 3 Resumption of diplomatic relations with Soviet Union		OCTOBER 3 Death of Stresemann
	NOVEMBER 2 *Tardieu* * *Briand* ‡	
		NOVEMBER 30 Evacuation of second Rhineland zone (Coblenz)
	1930	
		JANUARY 3-20 Second Hague Conference on reparations; adoption of Young Plan
		JANUARY 21-APRIL 22 London naval conference
		MARCH 31 Brüning, German Chancellor; Curtius, Foreign Minister
	MAY 17 Briand memorandum on European Union	
		JUNE 30 Evacuation of third zone (Mainz); end of Rhineland occupation

Britain	*France*	*General*
	1930	
		SEPTEMBER 14 Reichstag elections; National Socialists win 107 seats
		DECEMBER 5 Adoption of draft convention by Preparatory Disarmament Commission
	DECEMBER 12 *Steeg* * *Briand* ‡	
	1931	
	JANUARY 26 *Laval* * *Briand* ‡	
		MARCH 19 Austro-German customs union protocol signed
		MAY 11 Failure of the Austrian *Kreditanstalt*
		JUNE 20 President Hoover proposes moratorium on inter-governmental debts
		JUNE 24 Renewal of 1926 Treaty of Berlin between Germany and Soviet Union
AUGUST 25 National Government formed; *MacDonald* * *Reading* ‡		

Britain	*France*	*General*
	1931	
		SEPTEMBER 3 Austro-German customs union protocol abandoned
		SEPTEMBER 18 Japanese seizure of Mukden; beginning of Sino-Japanese hostilities
SEPTEMBER 21 Abandonment of the gold standard		
	OCTOBER 22-25 Laval visits President Hoover to discuss financial questions	
OCTOBER 27 General elections		
NOVEMBER 5 *MacDonald* * *Simon* ‡		
	1932	
		JANUARY 9 Brüning announces German inability to continue reparation payments
	JANUARY 13 *Laval* §	
		FEBRUARY 2 Disarmament Conference opens
	FEBRUARY 5 First French (Tardieu) plan submitted to Disarmament Conference	
	FEBRUARY 20 *Tardieu* §	

Britain	*France*	*General*
	1932	
	MARCH 7 Death of Briand	
		APRIL 26 Brüning-Stimson-MacDonald conversations on disarmament in Geneva
	MAY 1, 8 General elections	
		JUNE 1 von Papen, German Chancellor
	JUNE 3 *Herriot* §	
		JUNE 16-JULY 9 Lausanne Conference on reparations
JULY 13 Anglo-French declaration regarding future European co-operation		
		SEPTEMBER 14 Germany withdraws from Disarmament Conference for first time
	NOVEMBER 4 New French (Herriot–Paul-Boncour) plan presented to Disarmament Conference	
	NOVEMBER 29 Signature of Franco-Soviet non-aggression pact	
		DECEMBER 2 von Schleicher, German Chancellor

Britain	*France*	*General*
	1932	
		DECEMBER 11 Five-Power declaration regarding Germany's equality of status; Germany returns to Disarmament Conference
	DECEMBER 18 *Paul-Boncour* §	
	1933	
		JANUARY 30 Hitler, German Chancellor; beginning of National Socialist régime
	JANUARY 31 *Daladier* * *Paul-Boncour* ‡	
MARCH 16 British (MacDonald) plan submitted to Disarmament Conference		
		MARCH 18 Rome negotiations between Simon, MacDonald, and Mussolini leading to Four-Power Pact
APRIL 21-26 MacDonald visits President Roosevelt to discuss economic matters and war debts		
	APRIL 23-28 Herriot visits President Roosevelt to discuss economic matters and war debts	

Britain	*France*	*General*
	1933	
		MAY 5 Renewal of 1926 Treaty of Berlin between Germany and Soviet Union
		JUNE 7 Four-Power Pact initialed in Rome
		JUNE 7–JULY 27 World Economic Conference
		OCTOBER 14 German withdrawal from Disarmament Conference and League of Nations
	OCTOBER 26 *Sarraut* * *Paul-Boncour* ‡	
	NOVEMBER 27 *Chautemps* * *Paul-Boncour* ‡	
	1934	
		JANUARY 26 German-Polish non-aggression pact
	JANUARY 30 *Daladier* * *Paul-Boncour* ‡	
	FEBRUARY 9 *Doumergue* * *Barthou* ‡	

Britain	*France*	*General*
	1934	
FEBRUARY 16–MARCH 1 Eden (Lord Privy Seal) visits Paris, Rome, Berlin		
		FEBRUARY 17 Three-Power declaration by Britain, France, and Italy regarding Austrian independence
		MARCH 17 Italo-Austro-Hungarian Rome Protocols
APRIL 17 Barthou note to Britain closing disarmament negotiations		
	MAY 18 Barthou and Litvinov meet in Geneva; discuss Eastern Pact	
		JUNE 14–15 Hitler visits Mussolini in Venice
	JUNE 27 Memorandum on Eastern Pact	
JULY 8–10 Barthou visits London to discuss Eastern Pact		
		JULY 25 Unsuccessful Nazi *Putsch* in Vienna; murder of Dollfuss. Italian troops reported sent to the Brenner
		SEPTEMBER 27 Reaffirmation of declaration of February 17 regarding Austria

Britain	*France*	*General*
	1934	
	OCTOBER 13 *Laval* ‡	
	NOVEMBER 8 *Flandin* * *Laval* ‡	
NOVEMBER 12 Vote on Peace Ballot begins (results announced June 27, 1935)		
	DECEMBER 5 Franco-Soviet preliminary agreement on treaty of mutual assistance	DECEMBER 5 Walwal incident between Italy and Ethiopia
	1935	
	JANUARY 4-7 Laval visits Rome; negotiates Franco-Italian agreements, signed January 7	
		JANUARY 13 Saar plebiscite favors return to Germany
FEBRUARY 1-3 Flandin and Laval visit London; Franco-British communiqué on general European settlement		
MARCH 4 Publication of White Paper on Defence		
		MARCH 16 Re-introduction of conscription in Germany; abrogation of Part V of Treaty of Versailles

Britain	*France*	*General*
	1935	
MARCH 25-26 Simon and Eden visit Berlin (Eden goes to Moscow, Warsaw, Prague)		
		APRIL 11-14 Stresa Conference on German rearmament and Central Europe
		APRIL 16-17 League of Nations Council meets to condemn German rearmament
	MAY 2 Signature of Franco-Soviet pact of mutual assistance	
		MAY 16 Signature of Czechoslovak-Soviet pact of mutual assistance
JUNE 7 *Baldwin* * *Hoare* ‡ Eden, Minister for League of Nations Affairs	JUNE 7 *Laval* §	
		JUNE 18 Anglo-German naval accord
JUNE 24-26 Eden visits Rome in attempt to settle Ethiopian dispute		

SEPTEMBER 10-OCTOBER 18

Franco-British correspondence regarding sanctions and mutual support in the Mediterranean

Britain	*France*	*General*
	1935	
SEPTEMBER 11 Hoare addresses League of Nations Assembly on British policy and collective security		
		OCTOBER 3 Italy invades Ethiopia
		OCTOBER 10 Members of League of Nations Assembly note Italian aggression and create Co-ordination Committee on sanctions
NOVEMBER 14 General elections		
		DECEMBER 9 Hoare-Laval plan for settlement of Ethiopian conflict
DECEMBER 22 *Eden* ‡ replaces Hoare, resigned		
	1936	
	JANUARY 24 *Sarraut* * *Flandin* ‡	
	FEBRUARY 27 Chamber of Deputies approves Franco-Soviet Pact	
		MARCH 7 German military re-occupation of Rhineland; abrogation of Locarno Pact

Britain	*France*	*General*

1936

General — MARCH 12-13
London meeting of four Locarno Powers (followed by meeting of League of Nations Council)

General — MARCH 19
Locarno Powers submit proposals

General — MARCH 31
German peace plan in reply to March 19 proposals

Britain/France — APRIL 1
Britain reaffirms Locarno obligations to France (and Belgium)

France — APRIL 8
Peace plan

Britain/France — APRIL 15-16
Anglo-French (Belgian) staff conversations

France — APRIL 26, MAY 3
General elections

General — MAY 9
Annexation of Ethiopia by Italy

France — JUNE 4
Blum *
Delbos ‡

General — JUNE 22-JULY 20
Montreux Conference on the Straits

General — JUNE 30-JULY 4
League of Nations Assembly approves the end of sanctions

Britain	*France*	*General*
	1936	
		JULY 18 Beginning of Spanish civil war
	AUGUST 2 Appeal for non-intervention in Spain	
		SEPTEMBER 9 First meeting of non-intervention committee on Spain
		OCTOBER 14 King Leopold announces Belgium's new policy of neutrality
		OCTOBER 20-25 Ciano, Italian Foreign Minister, visits Berlin; formation of Rome-Berlin axis
		NOVEMBER 25 German-Japanese anti-Comintern pact
DECEMBER 4 Delbos promises French assistance to Britain in case of attack		
	1937	
		JANUARY 2 Anglo-Italian Mediterranean agreement
MAY 28 *Neville Chamberlain* * *Eden* ‡		
	JUNE 22 *Chautemps* * *Delbos* ‡	

Britain	*France*	*General*
1937		
		JULY 7 Renewal of Sino-Japanese hostilities
		SEPTEMBER 14 Nyon accord on Mediterranean piracy
		SEPTEMBER 25-29 Mussolini visits Hitler in Germany
		NOVEMBER 3-24 Brussels Conference on Far East
		NOVEMBER 6 Italy adheres to anti-Comintern pact
NOVEMBER 17-21 Halifax (Lord President of the Council) visits Berlin		
		DECEMBER 11 Italy withdraws from League of Nations
1938		
		FEBRUARY 4 Changes in German army high command; Ribbentrop, Foreign Minister
		FEBRUARY 12 Schuschnigg visits Hitler in Berchtesgaden
FEBRUARY 25 *Halifax* ‡ replaces Eden, resigned		

Britain	*France*	*General*
	1938	
	MARCH 13 *Blum* * *Paul-Boncour* ‡	MARCH 13 Official proclamation of *Anschluss*, following entry of German troops into Austria
	APRIL 10 *Daladier* * *Bonnet* ‡	
		APRIL 16 Signature of Anglo-Italian agreements regarding Spain and the Mediterranean
APRIL 27-29 Daladier and Bonnet in London; strengthening of Anglo-French alliance		
		MAY 3-9 Hitler visits Mussolini in Rome
		MAY 21 Czechoslovak mobilization during Sudeten crisis
JULY 19-22 King and Queen pay state visit in Paris		
JULY 25 Runciman sent to Prague		
		SEPTEMBER 15 Chamberlain meets Hitler in Berchtesgaden
SEPTEMBER 18-19 Daladier and Bonnet visit London; drafting of Anglo-French proposals regarding Sudetenland		
		SEPTEMBER 22 Chamberlain meets Hitler in Godesberg

Britain	*France*	*General*
	1938	
SEPTEMBER 25-26 Daladier and Bonnet visit London		
		SEPTEMBER 29-30 Munich Four-Power Conference on the cession of the Sudetenland to Germany
SEPTEMBER 30 Hitler-Chamberlain declaration on Anglo-German relations		
		NOVEMBER 30 Italian agitation on colonial claims against France
	DECEMBER 6 Franco-German declaration of friendship	
		DECEMBER 17 Italian denunciation of Rome accords of January 7, 1935
	1939	
JANUARY 11-14 Chamberlain and Halifax visit Rome		
		MARCH 14 German occupation of Bohemia and Moravia begins; Slovakia proclaims independence
		MARCH 15 German protectorate over Bohemia and Moravia proclaimed

Britain *France* *General*

1939

MARCH 21-24
President Lebrun pays state visit in London

MARCH 21
Germany proposes to Poland a settlement regarding Danzig and the Corridor

MARCH 22
German occupation of Memel

MARCH 23
Signature of German-Slovak treaty placing Slovakia under German protection

MARCH 26
Poland rejects German proposals regarding Danzig and the Corridor

MARCH 28
General Franco's troops enter Madrid; virtual end of Spanish civil war

MARCH 31
Chamberlain declaration on behalf of Britain and France guaranteeing Poland

APRIL 6
Anglo-Polish declaration exchanging reciprocal promises of assistance

APRIL 7
Italian occupation of Albania

APRIL 13
British and French declarations guaranteeing Greece and Rumania

Britain	*France*	*General*
	1939	
APRIL 26 Chamberlain proposes compulsory military service		
		APRIL 28 German denunciation of Anglo-German naval agreement and German-Polish non-aggression pact
MAY 12 Agreement on mutual assistance with Turkey		
		MAY 22 Signature of German-Italian alliance
	JUNE 23 Agreement on mutual assistance with Turkey	
AUGUST 11 Franco-British military mission arrives in Moscow to pursue negotiations begun in March		
		AUGUST 23 Signature of German-Soviet non-aggression pact
AUGUST 25 Signature of Anglo-Polish alliance		
		SEPTEMBER 1 Germany invades Poland; Danzig's return to Germany is proclaimed
SEPTEMBER 3 A state of war with Germany is declared to exist	SEPTEMBER 3 A state of war with Germany is declared to exist	

Bibliography

I. OFFICIAL DOCUMENTS: DOCUMENTARY COLLECTIONS

A. France

Ministère des Affaires Etrangères

Documents Diplomatiques: Conférence économique internationale de Gênes, 9 avril–19 mai 1922. Paris: Imprimerie nationale, 1922.

Documents relatifs aux Réparations. Tome premier. Paris: Imprimerie nationale, 1922.

Documents Diplomatiques: Conférence de Washington, juillet 1921–février 1922. Paris: Imprimerie nationale, 1923.

Documents Diplomatiques: Demande de Moratorium du Gouvernement allemand à la Commission des Réparations (14 novembre 1922), Conférence de Londres (9–11 décembre 1922), Conférence de Paris (2–4 janvier 1923). Paris: Imprimerie nationale, 1923.

Documents Diplomatiques: Documents relatifs aux Notes allemandes des 2 mai et 5 juin sur les Réparations (2 mai–3 août 1923). Paris: Imprimerie nationale, 1923.

Documents Diplomatiques: Réponse du Gouvernement français à la lettre du Gouvernement britannique du 11 août 1923, sur les Réparations (20 août 1923). Paris: Imprimerie nationale, 1923.

Documents Diplomatiques: Documents relatifs aux Négociations concernant les Garanties de Sécurité contre une Agression de l'Allemagne (10 janvier 1919–7 décembre 1923). Paris: Imprimerie nationale, 1924.

Documents relatifs aux Réparations. Tome deuxième. Paris: Imprimerie nationale, 1924.

Documents Diplomatiques: Conférence de Londres, 16 juillet–16 août 1924. Paris: Imprimerie nationale, 1925.

Pacte de Securité. Neuf pièces relatives à la proposition faite le 9 février 1925 par le Gouvernement allemand et à la réponse du Gouvernement français (9 février 1925–16 juin 1925). Paris: Imprimerie des Journaux Officiels, 1925.

Pacte de Sécurité, II. Documents signés ou paraphés à Locarno le 16 octobre 1925, précédés de six pièces relatives aux négociations préliminaires (20 juillet 1925–16 octobre 1925). Paris: Imprimerie des Journaux Officiels, 1925.

Limitation des Armements navals. Trente cinq pièces relatives aux travaux préparatoires du désarmement et à la limitation des armements navals (21 mars 1927–6 octobre 1928). Paris: Imprimerie des Journaux Officiels, 1928.

Pacte général de Renonciation à la Guerre comme instrument de politique nationale. Trente pièces relatives à la préparation, à l'élaboration et à la conclusion du traité signé à Paris le 27 août 1928 (6 avril 1927–27 août 1928). Paris: Imprimerie des Journaux Officiels, 1928.

Documents relatifs à l'Organisation d'un Régime d'Union Fédérale Européenne. Paris: Imprimerie des Journaux Officiels, 1930.

Pacte d'Entente et de Collaboration paraphé à Rome le 7 juin 1933. Paris: Imprimerie des Journaux Officiels, 1933.

Les Négociations relatives à la Réduction et la Limitation des Armements. Vingt-quatre pièces (14 octobre 1933–17 avril 1934). Paris: Imprimerie nationale, 1934.

Documents Diplomatiques, 1938-1939: Pièces relatives aux Evènements et aux Négociations qui ont précédé l'Ouverture des Hostilités entre l'Allemagne d'une part, la Pologne, la Grande-Bretagne et la France d'autre part. Paris: Imprimerie nationale, 1939.

Chambre des Députés

Journal Officiel de la République Française, Chambre des Députés, *Débats Parlementaires*, 1919-1939.

Journal Officiel de la République Française, Chambre des Députés, *Documents Parlementaires*, 1919-1939.

1919, Session ordinaire, pp. 305-322, Annexe No. 6657; Committee on the Peace report of August 5, 1919, on the Treaty of Versailles, Louis Barthou, general rapporteur.

1919, Session ordinaire, pp. 385-466, Annexe Nos. 6663-6673; Committee on the Peace reports of August 6, 1919, on the individual parts of the Treaty of Versailles.

1920, Session ordinaire, pp. 571-580, Annexe No. 660; Foreign Affairs Committee report of March 31, 1920, on the Treaty of Saint Germain, M. Margaine, rapporteur.

1920, Session extraordinaire, pp. 274-285, Annexe No. 1649; Foreign Affairs Committee report of November 23, 1920, on the Treaty of Trianon, Charles Daniélou, rapporteur.

1921, Session ordinaire, pp. 1474-1475, Annexe No. 2603; Foreign Affairs Committee supplementary report of April 29, 1921, on the Treaty of Trianon, M. Guernier, rapporteur.

1921, Session ordinaire, pp. 2118-2120, Annexe No. 3025; Foreign Affairs Committee report of July 6, 1921, on the Permanent Court of International Justice, Joseph Barthélemy, rapporteur.

1922, Session ordinaire, p. 100, Annexe No. 3818; government bill of February 2, 1922, on loan to Austria.

1922, Session ordinaire, pp. 427-432, Annexe No. 4104; Finance Committee report of March 18, 1922, on loan to Austria, M. Noblemaire, rapporteur.

1922, Session ordinaire, p. 566, Annexe No. 4245; Foreign Affairs Committee opinion of April 4, 1922, on loan to Austria, M. le comte de Lastours, rapporteur.

1923, Session ordinaire, p. 172, Annexe No. 4833; government bill of July 8, 1922, on loan to Rumania.

1923, Session ordinaire, pp. 210-213, Annexe No. 5467; Foreign Affairs Committee report of January 22, 1923, on the Washington Treaty regarding the Pacific, M. Raynaldy, rapporteur.

1923, Session ordinaire, p. 330, Annexe No. 5561; Foreign Affairs Committee opinion of February 9, 1923, on loan to Poland, M. Raynaldy, rapporteur.

1923, Session ordinaire, p. 760, Annexe No. 5865; government bill of March 23, 1923, on loan to Kingdom of Serbs, Croats, and Slovenes.

1923, Session ordinaire, pp. 712-713, Annexe No. 5870; Finance Committee report of March 23, 1923, on loan to Rumania, Louis Marin, rapporteur.

1923, Session ordinaire, pp. 718-719, Annexe No. 5888; Foreign Affairs Committee opinion of March 27, 1923, on loan to Rumania, Henry Roulleaux Dugage, rapporteur.

1923, Session ordinaire, pp. 1517-1527, Annexe No. 6293; Finance Committee report of June 30, 1923, on loan to Kingdom of Serbs, Croats, and Slovenes, Louis Marin, rapporteur.

1923, Session extraordinaire, pp. 697 ff., Annexe No. 5229; Finance Committee report of December 9, 1922, on loan to Poland, Louis Marin, rapporteur.

1924, Session extraordinaire, pp. 196-199, Annexe No. 773; government bill of November 28, 1924, on the Geneva Protocol.

1925, Session ordinaire, pp. 564-572, Annexe No. 1515; Foreign Affairs Committee report of April 3, 1925, on the Geneva Protocol, J. Paul-Boncour, rapporteur.

1925, Session extraordinaire, pp. 358-359, Annexe No. 2238; government bill of December 15, 1925, on the Locarno accords.

1926, Session ordinaire, pp. 194-200, Annexe No. 2615; Foreign Affairs Committee report of February 23, 1926, on the Locarno accords, J. Paul-Boncour, rapporteur.

1929, Session ordinaire, pp. 64-65, Annexe No. 1078; government bill of January 17, 1929, on the Kellogg Pact.

1929, Session ordinaire, pp. 305-314, Annexe No. 1288; Foreign Affairs Committee report of February 15, 1929, on the Kellogg Pact, Pierre Cot, rapporteur.

1929, Session ordinaire, pp. 406-408, Annexe No. 1368; government bill of March 1, 1929, on the General Act of Arbitration.

1929, Session ordinaire, pp. 1130-1143, Annexe No. 2031; Foreign Affairs Committee report of July 11, 1929, on the General Act of Arbitration, Paul Bastid, rapporteur.

1930, Session ordinaire, pp. 322-326, Annexe No. 3071; Foreign Affairs Committee opinion of March 24, 1930, on the Hague accords, Edouard Soulier, rapporteur.

1930, Session extraordinaire, p. 296, Annexe No. 4198; government bill of December 4, 1930, on the Convention for Financial Assistance.

1935, Session ordinaire, pp. 374-375, Annexe No. 4817; government bill of February 26, 1935, on the Franco-Italian Rome accords.

1935, Session ordinaire, pp. 642-643, Annexe No. 5023; Foreign Affairs Committee report of March 19, 1935, on the Franco-Italian Rome accords, Edouard Soulier, rapporteur.

1935, Session ordinaire, pp. 1211-1212, Annexe No. 5524; government bill of June 27, 1935, on the Franco-Soviet Pact.

1935, Session extraordinaire, pp. 161-169, Annexe No. 5792; Foreign Affairs Committee report of December 10, 1935, on the Franco-Soviet Pact, Henry Torrès, rapporteur.

Sénat

Journal Officiel de la République Française, Sénat, *Débats Parlementaires*, 1919-1939.

Journal Officiel de la République Française, Sénat, *Documents Parlementaires,* 1919-1939.

1919, Session ordinaire, pp. 569-600, Annexe No. 562; Foreign Affairs Committee report of October 3, 1919, on the Treaty of Versailles, Léon Bourgeois, rapporteur.

1920, Session ordinaire, pp. 256-263, Annexe No. 266; Foreign Affairs Committee report of June 23, 1920, on the Treaty of Saint Germain, Imbart de La Tour, rapporteur.

1921, Session ordinaire, pp. 584-586, Annexe No. 205; Foreign Affairs Committee report of March 29, 1921, on the Permanent Court of International Justice, M. de Las Cases, rapporteur.

1921, Session ordinaire, pp. 817-819, Annexe No. 507; Foreign Affairs Committee report of June 30, 1921, on the Treaty of Trianon, Georges Reynald, rapporteur.

1922, Session ordinaire, pp. 364-368, Annexe No. 325; Foreign Affairs Committee report of April 8, 1922, on loan to Austria, Louis Dausset, rapporteur.

1922, Session ordinaire, pp. 404-405, Annexe No. 362; Finance Committee opinion of June 9, 1922, on loan to Austria, Henry Bérenger, rapporteur.

1923, Session ordinaire, pp. 794-797, Annexe No. 422; Finance Committee report of June 7, 1923, on credits for Ruhr occupation, Henry Bérenger, rapporteur.

1923, Session ordinaire, Annexe No. 680; Foreign Affairs Committee report of July 10, 1923, on Washington naval treaty, Georges Reynald, rapporteur.

1923, Session extraordinaire, pp. 143-146, Annexe No. 798; Finance Committee report of December 7, 1923, on loan to Kingdom of Serbs, Croats, and Slovenes, Henry Bérenger, rapporteur.

1923, Session extraordinaire, pp. 146-149, Annexe No. 799; Finance Committee report of December 7, 1923, on loan to Poland, Henry Bérenger, rapporteur.

1923, Session extraordinaire, pp. 156-157, Annexe No. 805; Foreign Affairs Committee opinion of December 10, 1923, on loan to Poland, Georges Reynald, rapporteur.

1923, Session extraordinaire, p. 212, Annexe No. 814; Foreign Affairs Committee opinion of December 12, 1923, on loan to Kingdom of Serbs, Croats, and Slovenes, Georges Reynald, rapporteur.

1926, Session ordinaire, pp. 890-898, Annexe No. 194; Foreign Affairs Committee report of March 31, 1926, on the Locarno accords, M. Labrousse, rapporteur.

1930, Session ordinaire, pp. 739-744, Annexe No. 194; Foreign Affairs Committee opinion of April 1, 1930, on the Hague accords, Henry Bérenger, rapporteur.

1935, Session ordinaire, pp. 226-228, Annexe No. 301; Foreign Affairs Committee report of March 22, 1935, on the Franco-Italian Rome accords, Henry de Jouvenel, rapporteur.

1936, Session ordinaire, pp. 89-94, Annexe No. 152; Foreign Affairs Committee report of March 5, 1936, on the Franco-Soviet Pact, Yves Le Trocquer, rapporteur.

1936, Session extraordinaire, p. 631, Annexe No. 953; Foreign Affairs Committee opinion of December 31, 1936, on loan to Poland, Aimé Berthod, rapporteur.

B. Great Britain

Foreign Office

British and Foreign State Papers, Vol. 112 (1919) —. London: H.M. Stationery Office.

London Naval Conference, 1930, Documents. London: H.M. Stationery Office, 1930.

Treaty Series, 1919—. London: H.M. Stationery Office.

Foreign Office memorandum, February 20, 1925; *The World* (New York), May 10, 1925, pp. 1, 2.

Parliament

Parliamentary Debates, Fifth Series, House of Commons, *Official Report,* Vol. 110 (November, 1918) to Vol. 351 (September, 1939).

Parliamentary Debates, Fifth Series, House of Lords, *Official Report,* Vol. 32 (November, 1918) to Vol. 114 (September, 1939).

Parliamentary (Command) Papers:

Cmd. 151, *The Covenant of the League of Nations with a Commentary thereon,* Miscellaneous No. 3 (1919).

Cmd. 153, *The Treaty of Peace Between the Allied and Associated Powers and Germany* (1919).

Cmd. 221, *Treaty respecting assistance to France in the event of unprovoked aggression by Germany* (*with an Appendix of the similar treaty between the United States of America and France*) (1919).

Cmd. 1325, *Protocols and correspondence between the Supreme Council and the Conference of Ambassadors and the German Government and the German Peace Delegation, between 10th January, 1920, and 7th July, 1920, respecting the execution of the Treaty of Versailles of 28th June, 1919*, Miscellaneous No. 15 (1921).

Cmd. 1474, *Conference of Prime Ministers and Representatives of the United Kingdom, the Dominions, and India, held in June, July, and August, 1921: Summary of Proceedings and Documents* (1921).

Cmd. 1614, *Memorandum circulated by the Prime Minister on 25th March, 1919* (1922).

Cmd. 1621, *Resolutions adopted by the Supreme Council at Cannes, January 22, as the basis of the Genoa Conference* (1922).

Cmd. 1667, *Papers relating to the International Economic Conference, Genoa, April, May, 1922* (1922).

Cmd. 1742, *Correspondence between His Majesty's Government and the French Government respecting the Genoa Conference*, Miscellaneous No. 6 (1922).

Cmd. 1812, *Inter-Allied Conferences on Reparations and Inter-Allied Debts, held in London and Paris, December, 1922, and January, 1923*, Miscellaneous No. 3 (1923).

Cmd. 1943, *Correspondence with the Allied Governments respecting Reparation Payments by Germany*, Miscellaneous No. 5 (1923).

Cmd. 1987, *Imperial Conference, 1923: Summary of Proceedings* (1923).

Cmd. 1988, *Imperial Conference, 1923: Appendices to the Summary of Proceedings* (1923).

Cmd. 2169, *Papers respecting negotiations for an Anglo-French Pact*, France No. 1 (1924).

Cmd. 2184, *Correspondence concerning the Conference which it is proposed to hold in London on July 16, 1924, to consider the measures necessary to bring the Dawes Plan into operation*, Miscellaneous No. 10 (1924).

Cmd. 2200, *Correspondence between His Majesty's Government and the League of Nations respecting the proposed Treaty of Mutual Assistance (with a draft of the Treaty)*, Miscellaneous No. 13 (1924).

Cmd. 2258, *Minutes of the London Conference on Reparations, August, 1922*, Miscellaneous No. 16 (1924).

Cmd. 2270, *Proceedings of the London Reparation Conference, July and August, 1924*, Miscellaneous No. 17 (1924).

Cmd. 2289, *League of Nations, Fifth Assembly. Report of the British Delegates relating to the Protocol for the Peaceful Settlement of International Disputes*, Miscellaneous No. 21 (1924).

Cmd. 2368, *Statement on behalf of His Majesty's Government by the Rt. Hon. Austen Chamberlain, M. P., to the Council of the League of Nations, Geneva, March 12, 1935*, Miscellaneous No. 5 (1925).

Cmd. 2429, *Collective Note of the Allied Powers presented to the German Government on June 4, 1925, in regard to the fulfillment of the obligations of the Treaty of Versailles with regard to Disarmament*, Germany No. 2 (1925).

Cmd. 2435, *Papers respecting the Proposals for a Pact of Security made by the German Government on February 9, 1925*, Miscellaneous No. 7 (1925).

Cmd. 2458, *Protocol for the Pacific Settlement of International Disputes. Correspondence relating to the position of the Dominions* (1925).

Cmd. 2468, *Reply of the German Government to the Note handed to Herr Stresemann by the French Ambassador at Berlin on June 16, 1925, respecting the proposals for a Pact of Security*, Miscellaneous No. 9 (1925).

Cmd. 2525, *Final Protocol of the Locarno Conference 1925 (and Annexes), together with Treaties between France and Poland, and France and Czechoslovakia, Locarno, October 16, 1925*, Miscellaneous No. 11 (1925).

Cmd. 2527, *Correspondence between the Ambassadors' Conference and the German Ambassador in Paris respecting German Disarmament, Evacuation of the Cologne Zone and Modification of the Rhineland Régime*, Miscellaneous No. 12 (1925).

Cmd. 2768, *Imperial Conference, 1926: Summary of Proceedings* (1926).

Cmd. 2769, *Imperial Conference, 1926: Appendices to the Summary of Proceedings* (1926).

Cmd. 2964, *Speeches (in Plenary Session of the Geneva Conference for the Limitation of Naval Armaments, June to August, 1927) by the Rt. Hon. W. C. Bridgeman, First Lord of the Admiralty* (1927).

Cmd. 3109, *Correspondence with the United States Ambassador respecting the United States' proposal for the renunciation of war*, United States No. 1 (1928).

Cmd. 3211, *Papers Regarding the Limitation of Naval Armaments*, Miscellaneous No. 6 (1928).

Cmd. 3421, *Declaration made on behalf of His Majesty's Government in the United Kingdom at the time of the Signature of the Optional Clause, Geneva, September 17, 1929*, Miscellaneous No. 8 (1929).

Cmd. 3417, *International Agreement on the Evacuation of the Rhineland Territory, The Hague, August 30, 1929*, Miscellaneous No. 7 (1929).

Cmd. 3452, *Memorandum on the Signature by His Majesty's Government in the United Kingdom of the Optional Clause of the Statute of the Permanent Court of International Justice*, Miscellaneous No. 12 (1929).

Cmd. 3717, *Imperial Conference, 1930: Summary of Proceedings* (1930).

Cmd. 3718, *Imperial Conference, 1930: Appendices to the Summary of Proceedings* (1930).

Cmd. 3803, *Memorandum on the Proposed Accession of His Majesty's Government in the United Kingdom to the General Act of 1928 for the Pacific Settlement of International Disputes*, Miscellaneous No. 8 (1931).

Cmd. 3906, *Memorandum respecting the International Convention on Financial Assistance signed at Geneva, October 2, 1930*, Miscellaneous No. 13 (1931).

Cmd. 4131, *Declaration by the United Kingdom and France regarding future European co-operation, July, 1932*, Miscellaneous No. 9 (1932).

Cmd. 4189, *Declaration of the Policy of His Majesty's Government in the United Kingdom on Disarmament, in connexion with Germany's Claim to Equality of Rights*, Miscellaneous No. 11 (1932).

Cmd. 4342, *Despatch to His Majesty's Ambassador at Rome in Regard to the Agreement of Understanding and Co-operation between France, Germany, Italy, and the United Kingdom. London, June 7, 1933*, Miscellaneous No. 3 (1933).

Cmd. 4498, *Memorandum on Disarmament communicated by His Majesty's Government in the United Kingdom to the Governments represented at the Disarmament Conference*, Miscellaneous No. 2 (1934).

Cmd. 4512, *Memoranda on Disarmament issued by the Governments of the United Kingdom, France, Germany, and Italy in January, 1934*, Miscellaneous No. 3 (1934).

Cmd. 4521, *Memorandum by the Secretary of State for Air to Accompany Air Estimates, 1934* (1934).

Cmd. 4559, *Further Memoranda on Disarmament, 14th February to 17th April, 1934*, Miscellaneous No. 5 (1934).

Cmd. 4798, *Joint communiqué issued on behalf of His Majesty's Government in the United Kingdom and the Government of the French Republic as the result of the Conversations between the French and British Ministers in London, February 1 to 3, 1935*, Miscellaneous No. 1 (1935).

Cmd. 4827, *Statement relating to Defence issued in connexion with the House of Commons Debate on 11th March, 1935* (1935).

Cmd. 4880, *Joint Resolution of the Stresa Conference including the Anglo-Italian Declaration and the Final Declaration. Stresa, April 14, 1935*, Miscellaneous No. 2 (1935).

Cmd. 4953, *Exchange of Notes between His Majesty's Government in the United Kingdom and the German Government regarding the Limitation of Naval Armaments. London, June 18, 1935*, Treaty Series No. 22 (1935).

Cmd. 5044, *Documents relating to the Dispute between Ethiopia and Italy*, Ethiopia No. 1 (1935).

Cmd. 5072, *Dispute between Ethiopia and Italy. Correspondence in connexion with the application of Article 16 of the Covenant of the League of Nations, January, 1936*, Ethiopia No. 2 (1936).

Cmd. 5107, *Statement relating to Defence* (1936).

Cmd. 5118, *Memorandum by the German Government respecting the Franco-Soviet Treaty, the Treaty of Locarno and the Demilitarised Zone in the Rhineland, communicated to the Secretary of State for Foreign Affairs by the German Ambassador on March 7, 1936*, Germany No. 1 (1936).

Cmd. 5134, *Text of Proposals drawn up by the Representatives of Belgium, France, United Kingdom of Great Britain and Northern Ireland, and Italy. London, March 19, 1936*, Germany No. 2 (1936).

Cmd. 5143, *Correspondence showing the course of certain Diplomatic Discussions directed towards securing an European Settlement*, Miscellaneous No. 3 (1936).

Cmd. 5149, *Correspondence with the Belgian and French Ambassadors relating to "Text of Proposals drawn up by the Representatives of Belgium, France, the United Kingdom of Great Britain and North-*

ern Ireland, and Italy. London, March 19, 1936. Cmd. 5134." *London, April 1, 1936,* Miscellaneous No. 4 (1936).

Cmd. 5175, *Correspondence with the German Government regarding the German proposals for an European Settlement, March 24–May 6, 1936,* Miscellaneous No. 6 (1936).

Cmd. 5348, *Declaration by His Majesty's Government in the United Kingdom and the Italian Government (with an Exchange of Notes regarding the "status quo" in the Western Mediterranean, dated December 31, 1936). Rome, January 2, 1937,* Italy No. 1 (1937).

Cmd. 5374, *Statement relating to Defence* (1937).

Cmd. 5437, *International position of Belgium. Documents exchanged between His Majesty's Government in the United Kingdom and the French Government and the Belgian Government. Brussels, April 24, 1937,* Belgium No. 1 (1937).

Cmd. 5482, *Imperial Conference, 1937: Summary of Proceedings* (1937).

Cmd. 5682, *Statement relating to Defence, March 2, 1938* (1938).

Cmd. 5726, I—*Agreement between the United Kingdom and Italy, consisting of a Protocol with Annexes and Exchanges of Notes;* II—*Bon Voisinage Agreement and Exchanges of Notes between the United Kingdom, Egypt, and Italy. Rome, April 16, 1938,* Treaty Series No. 31 (1938).

Cmd. 5847, *Correspondence respecting Czechoslovakia, September, 1938,* Miscellaneous No. 7 (1938).

Cmd. 5848, *Further documents respecting Czechoslovakia, including the agreement concluded at Munich on September 29, 1938,* Miscellaneous No. 8 (1938).

Cmd. 6101, *Agreement between the Government of the United Kingdom and the Polish Government, London, August 25, 1939,* Poland No. 1 (1939).

Cmd. 6102, *Correspondence between His Majesty's Government in the United Kingdom and the German Government, August, 1939,* Miscellaneous No. 8 (1939).

Cmd. 6106, *Documents concerning German-Polish relations and the outbreak of hostilities between Great Britain and Germany on September 3, 1939,* Miscellaneous No. 9 (1939).

Cmd. 6115, *Final report by the Right Hon. Sir Nevile Henderson, G.C.M.G., on the circumstances leading to the termination of his mission to Berlin, September 20, 1939,* Germany No. 1 (1939).

C. League of Nations

Assembly

Records of the Assembly, First Assembly, 1920—. (Published in *Official Journal Special Supplement*, beginning *Records of the Fourth Assembly*, 1923.)

Plenary Meetings; Text of the Debates.

Meetings of the Committees; Minutes.

Council

Minutes of the Sessions of the Council, First session, January 16, 1920—. (Published in *Official Journal* beginning *Minutes of the Sixteenth Session.*)

Preparatory Commission for the Disarmament Conference

Documents

Series I. C.9.M.5.1926.IX.

Series V. *Minutes of the Fourth Session of the Preparatory Commission for the Disarmament Conference and of the First Session of the Committee on Arbitration and Security.* C.667.M.225.1927.IX (1928.IX.2)

Series VI. *Minutes of the Second Session of the Committee on Arbitration and Security and of the Fifth Session of the Preparatory Commission for the Disarmament Conference.* C.165.M.50.1928.IX. (1928.IX.6)

Series VII. *Minutes of the Third Session of the Committee on Arbitration and Security.* C.358.M.112.1928.IX. (1928.IX.8)

Series IX. *Minutes of the Fourth Session of the Committee on Arbitration and Security.* C.357.M.149.1930.IX. (1930.IX.3)

Conference for the Reduction and Limitation of Armaments

Records

Series A. *Verbatim Records of Plenary Meetings*, Vol. I, *February 2nd–July 23rd, 1932.* (1932.IX.60)

Series B. *Minutes of the General Commission*, Vol. I, *February 9th–July 23rd, 1932.* (1932.IX.64)

Minutes of the General Commission, Vol. II, *December 14th, 1932–June 29th, 1933.* (1933.IX.10)

Minutes of the General Commission, Vol. III, *October 16th, 1933–June 11th, 1934.* (1936.IX.1)

Series C. *Minutes of the Bureau*, Vol. I, *September 21st, 1932–June 27th, 1933*. (1935.IX.2)

Minutes of the Bureau, Vol. II, *October 9th, 1933–November 20th, 1934*. (1936.IX.2)

Series D. *Minutes of the Political Commission, February 27th, 1932–March 10th, 1933*. (1936.IX.8)

Conference Documents

Vol. I (1932.IX. 63)

Vol. II (1935.IX. 4)

Vol. III. (1936.IX. 4)

Miscellaneous

Application of the Principles of the Covenant of the League of Nations. Communications from Governments. A.31.1936.VII. (1936.VII.9)

Arbitration, Security and Reduction of Armaments. Extracts from the Debates of the Fifth Assembly including those of the First and Third Committees. Reports and Resolutions adopted by the Assembly and the Council. C.708.1924.IX.

Committee for the Amendment of the Covenant of the League of Nations in order to bring it into harmony with the Pact of Paris. Geneva, February 25th to March 5th, 1930. Minutes. C.160.M.69.1930.V. (1930.V.10)

Documents relating to the Organisation of a System of European Federal Union. A.46.1930.VII. (1930.VII.4)

Monthly Summary. Vol. I, No. 1, January, 1921—.

Official Journal. Vol. I, No. 1, February, 1920— (including minutes of sessions of the Council).

Official Journal, Special Supplement (including minutes of the sessions of the Assembly and of the special meetings called to deal with the Chaco, Manchurian, and Ethiopian conflicts).

Particulars with regard to the Position of Armaments in the Various Countries. Communication from the French Government. Memorandum of July 15th, 1931, and Annexes. 1931.IX.9.

Report of the Special Committee set up to Study the Application of the Principles of the Covenant. Adopted by the Committee on February 2nd, 1938. A.7.1938.VII. (1938.VII.1)

Report of the Temporary Mixed Commission for the Reduction of Armaments. A.35.1923.IX. Part I.

Reports and Resolutions on the Subject of Article 16 of the Covenant, Memorandum and Collection of Reports, Resolutions and References pre-

pared in Execution of the Council's Resolution of December 8th, 1926. A.14.1927.V. (1927.V.14)

Systematic Survey of the Arbitration Conventions and Treaties of Mutual Security deposited with the League of Nations. (Prepared by the Legal Section of the Secretariat of the League of Nations in pursuance of the Council's resolution of December 12, 1935.) Second edition, revised and augmented, containing all Treaties registered before December 15th, 1927. C.653.M.216.1927.V. (1927.V.29)

Treaty of Mutual Assistance, Replies from Governments. A.35.1924.IX.

Treaty Series, Vol. I, 1920—.

D. United States

Department of State

Conference on the Limitation of Naval Armament, Washington, November 12, 1921–February 6, 1922. Washington: U.S. Government Printing Office, 1922.

The London Naval Treaty, 1930. Conference Series No. 2. Washington: U.S. Government Printing Office, 1930.

The London Naval Conference, 1935. Report of the Delegates of the United States of America. Text of the London Naval Treaty of 1936 and other Documents. Conference Series No. 24. Washington: U.S. Government Printing Office, 1936.

The Conference of Brussels, November 3-24, 1937, convened in virtue of Article 7 of the Nine-Power Treaty of Washington of 1922. Conference Series No. 37. Washington: U.S. Government Printing Office, 1938.

Senate

Records of the Conference for the Limitation of Naval Armaments Held at Geneva, Switzerland, from June 20th to August 4, 1927. Senate Document No. 55, 70th Congress, 1st Session. Washington: U.S. Government Printing Office, 1928.

E. Documentary Collections

Berber, Fritz, ed.: *Das Diktat von Versailles: Entstehung, Inhalt, Zerfall, eine Darstellung in Dokumenten,* 2 vols. Veröffentlichungen des Deutschen Instituts für aussenpolitische Forschung, Band 3. Essen: Essener Verlagsanstalt, 1939.

Locarno: a collection of documents. London: W. Hodge and Company, Ltd., 1939.

Bruns, Viktor, ed.: *Politische Verträge: eine Sammlung von Urkunden.* Band I, *Garantiepakte, Bündnisse, Abkommen über politische Zusammenarbeit, Nichtangriffs—und Neutralitätsverträge der Nachkriegszeit.* Band II, *Materialien zur Entwicklung der Sicherheitsfrage im Rahmen des Völkerbundes.* Erster Teil, *1920-1927.* Zweiter Teil, *1928-1935* (bearbeitet von Georg von Gretschaninow). Berlin: Carl Heymanns Verlag, 1936.

La Documentation Internationale, politique, juridique et économique, monthly, Vol. 1, No. 1, 15 avril 1934—.

L'Europe Nouvelle, weekly, Vol. I, No. 1, janvier 1918—.

Harley, John E., ed.: *Documentary Textbook on International Relations: a text and reference study emphasizing official documents and materials relating to world peace and international co-operation.* Los Angeles: Suttonhouse, 1934.

Hoetzsch, Otto, ed.: *Abrüstung und Sicherheit.* Dokumente zur Weltpolitik der Nachkriegszeit, Heft 2. Leipzig und Berlin: B. G. Teubner, 1932.

Honnorat, André: *Un des Problèmes de la Paix: le désarmement de l'Allemagne; textes et documents.* Paris: Costes, 1924.

Un des Problèmes de la Paix: la sécurité de la France; textes et documents. Paris: Costes, 1924.

Hudson, Manley O., ed.: *International Legislation: a collection of the texts of multipartite international instruments of general interest, beginning with the Covenant of the League of Nations,* 5 vols. Washington: Carnegie Endowment for International Peace, 1931, 1936.

Langsam, Walter C., ed.: *Documents and Readings in the History of Europe since 1918.* Chicago, Philadelphia, New York: J. B. Lippincott Co., 1939.

Lapradelle, Albert G. de, ed.: *La Paix de Versailles,* 12 vols. La Documentation Internationale. Paris: Les Editions Internationales, 1929-1939.

Le Fur, Louis, and Chklaver, Georges, eds.: *Recueil de Droit International Public,* 2nd ed. Paris: Dalloz, 1934.

Niemeyer, Theodor, ed.: *Friedensverträge, Völkerbunddokumente, Vergleichs-, Schieds- und Sicherheitsverträge, Allianzverträge, 1919-1926.* Jahrbuch des Völkerrechts, IX Band. Kiel: Institut für internationales Recht an der Universität Kiel, 1926.

Handbuch des Abrüstungsproblems, 3 vols. Berlin: W. Rothschild, 1928.

Royal Institute of International Affairs (Wheeler-Bennett, John W., ed.), *Documents on International Affairs, 1928—.* London: Oxford University Press, 1929—.

Société des Nations, monthly and quarterly, Bern, Vol. I, 1919— (reprints of speeches, resolutions, debates).

Weltgeschichte der Gegenwart in Dokumenten. Essen: Essener Verlagsanstalt, 1936—.

1934-1935, Teil I, *Internationale Politik* (bearbeitet von Michael Freund).

1935-1936, Internationale Politik (herausgegeben von Werner Frauendienst).

1936-1937, Internationale Politik (herausgegeben von Werner Frauendienst).

II. MEMOIRS, ADDRESSES, BOOKS BY FRENCH AND BRITISH STATESMEN

A. France

Barthou, Louis: *Le Traité de Paix.* Commission chargée d'examiner le projet de loi portant approbation du traité de paix conclu à Versailles le 28 juin 1919. Louis Barthou, rapporteur. Paris: E. Fasquelle, 1919.

Blum, Léon: *Les Problèmes de la Paix.* Paris: Librairie Stock, 1931. (English ed., *Peace and Disarmament.* London: J. Cape, Ltd., 1932.)

L'Exercice du Pouvoir: discours prononcés de mai 1936 à janvier 1937. Paris: Nouvelle Revue Française, 1937.

Bourgeois, Léon: *L'Oeuvre de la Société des Nations (1920-1923).* Paris: Payot, 1923.

Le Pacte de 1919 et la Société des Nations. Paris: Bibliothèque Charpentier, E. Fasquelle, 1919.

Le Traité de Paix de Versailles, 2nd ed. Paris: F. Alcan, 1919.

Briand, Aristide: *Paroles de Paix.* Paris: E. Figuière, 1927.

Caillaux, Joseph: *Où va la France? Où va l'Europe?* Paris: Editions de la Sirène, 1922.

Cambon, Jules: "France," in *The Foreign Policy of the Powers,* pp. 3-24. New York: Harper and Brothers for the Council on Foreign Relations, 1935. Reprinted from "The Permanent Bases of French Foreign Policy," *Foreign Affairs,* VIII (January, 1930), pp. 173-185.

Clemenceau, Georges: *Discours de Paix.* Paris: Librairie Plon, 1938.

Grandeur and Misery of Victory. New York: Harcourt, Brace and Company, 1930.

Daladier, Edouard: *In Defense of France.* New York: Doubleday, Doran and Company, 1939. (French ed., *Défense du Pays.* Paris: Flammarion, 1939.)

Flandin, Pierre-Etienne: *Discours, le Ministère Flandin, novembre 1934–mai 1935.* Paris: Nouvelle Revue Française, 1937.

Paix et Liberté. Paris: Flammarion, 1938.

Foch, Ferdinand: "Du Malaise Mondial," *Revue de France*, VIII (janvier 1928), pp. 5-13.

François-Poncet, André: "Ce que la France attend de l'Allemagne," *Revue de Genève*, décembre 1923, pp. 762-777.

Herriot, Edouard: *La France dans le Monde*. Paris: Hachette, 1933.

"The Program of Liberal France," *Foreign Affairs*, II (June 15, 1924), pp. 558-570.

La Russie nouvelle. Paris: J. Ferenczi et fils, 1922.

The United States of Europe. New York: The Viking Press, 1930.

Jouhaux, Léon: *Le Désarmement*. Paris: F. Alcan, 1927.

Jouvenel, Henry de: "France and Italy," *Foreign Affairs*, V (July, 1927), pp. 538-552.

La Paix Française: témoignage d'une génération. Paris: Les Editions des Portiques, 1932.

Klotz, Louis L.: *De la Guerre à la Paix: souvenirs et documents*. Paris: Payot, 1924.

Larnaude, Ferdinand: *La Société des Nations*. Conférences faites à MM. les officiers du Centre des hautes études militaires, de l'Ecole supérieure de guerre et de l'Ecole supérieure de marine les 20, 28 février et 12 mars, 1920. Paris: Imprimerie nationale, L. Tenin, 1920.

Marin, Louis: *Le Traité de Paix*. Paris: Floury, 1920.

Painlevé, Paul: *Paroles et Ecrits*, publiés par la Société des Amis de Paul Painlevé. Paris: Les éditions Rieder, 1936.

Poincaré, Raymond: *Histoire Politique: chroniques de quinzaine*, 4 vols. Paris: Plon-Nourrit, 1920-1922.

Messages, Discours, Allocutions, Lettres et Télégrammes, 3 vols. Paris: Bloud et Gay, 1919-1921.

Au Service de la France: neuf années de souvenirs, 10 vols. Paris: Plon-Nourrit, 1926-1933.

"Since Versailles," *Foreign Affairs*, VII (July, 1929), pp. 519-531.

Reynaud, Paul: *Courage de la France*. Paris: Flammarion, 1939.

Tardieu, André: *L'Epreuve du Pouvoir*. Paris: Flammarion, 1931.

France in Danger! London: D. Archer, 1935.

Notes de Semaine, 1939: l'année de Munich. Paris: Flammarion, 1939.

La Paix. Paris: Payot, 1921. (U. S. ed., *The Truth about the Treaty*. Indianapolis: The Bobbs-Merrill Company, 1921.)

"The Policy of France," *Foreign Affairs*, I (September, 1922), pp. 11-28.

Sur la pente. Paris: Flammarion, 1935.

Le Temps, daily, 1919-1939 (texts of speeches, resolutions, etc.).

B. Great Britain

Amery, Leopold S.: "The British Empire and the Pan European Idea," *Journal of the Royal Institute of International Affairs*, IX (January, 1930), pp.1-22.

Empire and Prosperity. London: Faber & Faber, Ltd., 1930.

The Forward View. London: G. Bles, 1935.

The German Colonial Claim. London and Edinburgh: W. & R. Chambers, Ltd., 1939.

Attlee, Clement R.: "The Socialist View of Peace," in *Problems of Peace*, ninth series, *Pacifism is not Enough*, pp. 96-127. London: Allen & Unwin, Ltd., 1935.

Baker, Philip J. Noel: "Disarmament," *International Affairs*, XIII (January-February, 1934), pp. 3-25.

"The Future of the Collective System," in *Problems of Peace*, tenth series, *Anarchy or World Order*, pp. 178-198. London: Allen & Unwin, 1936.

Baldwin, Stanley: *Service of Our Lives: last speeches as Prime Minister*. London: Hodder and Stoughton, Ltd., 1937.

This Torch of Freedom. London: Hodder and Stoughton, Ltd., 1935.

Balfour, Arthur J., Earl of: *Opinions and Arguments from Speeches and Addresses of the Earl of Balfour, 1910-1927*. London: Hodder and Stoughton, Ltd., 1927.

Birkenhead, Earl of; Bliss, General Tasker H.; Kerr, Philip H.: *Approaches to World Problems*. New Haven: published for the Institute of Politics by the Yale University Press, 1924.

Cecil, Robert, Viscount: *The Way of Peace*. London, P. Allan & Co., Ltd., 1928.

Cecil, Lord Robert; Amery, Leopold S., and others: "The Draft Treaty of Mutual Assistance," *Journal of the British Institute of International Affairs*, III (March, 1924), pp. 45-82.

Chamberlain, Sir Austen: *Down the Years*. London: Cassell and Company, Ltd., 1935.

"Great Britain," in *The Foreign Policy of the Powers*, pp. 54-77. New York: Harper and Brothers for the Council on Foreign Relations, 1935.

Reprinted from "The Permanent Bases of British Foreign Policy," *Foreign Affairs*, IX (July, 1931), pp. 535-546.

"Great Britain as a European Power," *Journal of the Royal Institute of International Affairs*, IX (March, 1930), pp. 180-188.

The League of Nations. Address delivered to the students of the University of Glasgow. Glasgow: Jackson, Wylie & Co., 1926.

Peace in our Time: addresses on Europe and the Empire. London: P. Allan & Co., Ltd., 1928.

Chamberlain, Neville: *In Search of Peace.* New York: G. P. Putnam's Sons, 1939. (English ed., *The Struggle for Peace.* London: Hutchinson & Co., Ltd., 1939.)

Churchill, Winston S.: *Step by Step, 1936-1939.* New York: G. P. Putnam's Sons, 1939.

While England Slept: a survey of world affairs, 1932-1938. New York: G. P. Putnam's Sons, 1938. (English ed., *Arms and the Covenant.* London: G. G. Harrap & Co., Ltd., 1938.)

The World Crisis, 1918-1928, The Aftermath. New York: C. Scribner's Sons, 1939.

Clynes, John R.: *Memoirs*, 2 vols. London: Hutchinson & Co., Ltd., 1937.

Cooper, Duff: *The Second World War: first phase.* New York: C. Scribner's Sons, 1939.

Cripps, Sir Richard Stafford: *The Struggle for Peace.* London: V. Gollancz, Ltd., 1936.

Cushendun, Roland McNeill, Lord: "Disarmament," *Journal of the Royal Institute of International Affairs*, VII (March, 1928), pp. 77-93.

D'Abernon, Edgar Vincent, Viscount: *An Ambassador of Peace: pages from the diary of Viscount D'Abernon*, 3 vols. London: Hodder and Stoughton, Ltd., 1929-1930. (U. S. ed., *The Diary of an Ambassador, Viscount D'Abernon*, 3 vols. Garden City, New York: Doubleday, Doran and Company, 1929-1930.)

Foreign Policy. Sidney Ball lecture, October 31, 1930. London: Oxford University Press, 1930.

Dalton, Hugh: *Towards the Peace of Nations.* London: G. Routledge & Sons, Ltd., 1928.

Eden, Anthony: *Foreign Affairs.* New York: Harcourt, Brace and Company, 1939.

Greenwood, Arthur: *The Labour Outlook.* London: Chapman, 1929.

Henderson, Arthur: *Consolidating World Peace.* Burge memorial lecture, 1931. Oxford: The Clarendon Press, 1931.

Labour's Way to Peace. London: Methuen & Company, Ltd., 1935.

Lloyd, George, Lord: "The Need for the Re-armament of Great Britain: its justification and scope," *International Affairs,* XV (January–February, 1936), pp. 57-79.

Lloyd George, David: *Is It Peace?* London: Hodder and Stoughton, Ltd., 1923.

Memoirs of the Peace Conference, 2 vols. New Haven: Yale University Press, 1939. (English ed., *The Truth about the Peace Treaties,* 2 vols. London: V. Gollancz, Ltd., 1938.)

Slings and Arrows. Sayings chosen from the speeches of the Rt. Hon. David Lloyd George; edited with introduction by Philip Guedalla. London: Cassell and Company, Ltd., 1929.

The Truth about Reparations and War-Debts. Garden City, New York: Doubleday, Doran and Company, 1932.

Londonderry, Charles Vane, Marquess of: *Ourselves and Germany.* London: R. Hale, Ltd., 1938.

Lothian, Philip Kerr, Marquess of: "Europe and the United States: the problem of sanctions," *Journal of the Royal Institute of International Affairs,* IX (May, 1930), pp. 288-324.

"Navies and Peace: A British View," *Foreign Affairs,* VIII (October, 1929), pp. 20-29.

"New League or no League," *International Conciliation,* No. 325 (December, 1935), pp. 589-604.

"The Outlawry of War," *Journal of the Royal Institute of International Affairs,* VII (November, 1928), pp. 361-388.

"The Place of Britain in the Collective System," *International Affairs,* XIII (September–October, 1934), pp. 622-650.

"The World Crisis of 1936," *Foreign Affairs,* XV (October, 1936), pp. 124-140.

Lothian, Philip Kerr, Marquess of, and Curtis, Lionel: *The Prevention of War.* New Haven: Published for the Institute of Politics by the Yale University Press, 1923.

MacDonald, J. Ramsay: *The Foreign Policy of the Labour Party.* London: Cecil Palmer, 1923.

"The London Naval Conference," *Journal of the Royal Institute of International Affairs,* IX (July, 1930), pp. 429-451.

"Protocol or Pact," reply to Mr. Chamberlain's address by Mr. J. Ramsay MacDonald, former British Prime Minister, April 10, 1925, *International Conciliation*, No. 212 (September, 1925), pp. 256-263.

"The Risks of Peace," *Foreign Affairs*, VIII (October, 1929), spec. supp., pp. iii-xiii.

Morrison, Herbert S.: "A New Start with the League of Nations," in *Problems of Peace*, eleventh series, *The League and the Future of the Collective System*, pp. 5-27. London: Allen & Unwin, Ltd., 1937.

Parmoor, Charles Alfred Cripps, Lord: "The Geneva Protocol," *The Contemporary Review*, CXXVII (January, 1925), pp. 1-8.

A Retrospect. London: W. Heinemann, Ltd., 1936.

Percy, Eustace, Lord: *The Responsibilities of the League*. London: Hodder and Stoughton, Ltd., 1920.

Ponsonby, Arthur: "Disarmament by Example," *Journal of the Royal Institute of International Affairs*, VII (July, 1928), pp. 225-240.

Rothermere, Harold, Viscount: *Warnings and Predictions*. London: Eyre and Spottiswoode, 1939.

Simon, Sir John: *Comments and Criticisms*. London: Hodder and Stoughton, Ltd., 1930.

Snowden, Philip, Viscount: *An Autobiography*, 2 vols. London: Nicholson and Watson, Ltd., 1934.

The Times (London), daily, 1919-1939. (Texts of speeches, resolutions, etc.)

III. TREATISES, HISTORIES, SPECIAL STUDIES

A. European Politics

Albrecht-Carrié, René: *Italy at the Paris Peace Conference*. New York: Columbia University Press, 1938.

Angell, Sir Norman: *The Defence of the Empire*. New York: D. Appleton-Century Company, Inc., 1937.

Peace with the Dictators? New York: Harper and Brothers, 1938.

Aubert, Louis: "Security: Key to French Policy," *Foreign Affairs*, XI (October, 1932), pp. 122-136.

Bainville, Jacques: *L'Angleterre et l'Empire Britannique*. Paris: Librairie Plon, 1938.

Les Conséquences Politiques de la Paix. Paris: Nouvelle Librairie Nationale, 1920.

Histoire des Deux Peuples, continuée jusqu'à Hitler. Paris: A. Fayard, 1933.

Baker, Ray S., and Dodd, William E., eds.: *The Public Papers of Woodrow Wilson:* Vols. 3-4, *The New Democracy;* Vols. 5-6, *War and Peace.* New York: Harper and Brothers, 1926.

Bardoux, Jacques: *L'Ile et L'Europe: la politique anglaise (1930-1932).* Paris: Librairie Delagrave, 1933.

Lloyd George et la France. Paris: F. Alcan, 1923.

Le Socialisme au Pouvoir: l'expérience de 1924. Paris: Firmin-Didot, 1930.

Barrès, Maurice: *Le Génie du Rhin.* Paris: Plon-Nourrit, 1921.

Les Grands Problèmes du Rhin. Paris: Librairie Plon, 1930.

La Politique Rhénane: discours parlementaires. Paris: Bloudet Gay, 1922.

Beer, Max: *L'Allemagne devant le Monde: la politique extérieure du Troisième Reich.* Paris: B. Grasset, 1935.

Béraud, Henri: *Faut-il réduire l'Angleterre en Esclavage.* Paris: Editions de la France, 1935.

Berber, Fritz: *Prinzipien der britischen Aussenpolitik.* Schriften des Deutschen Instituts für aussenpolitische Forschung und des Hamburger Instituts für Auswärtige Politik, Heft 61. Berlin: Junker und Dünnhaupt, 1939.

Beuve-Méry, H.: *Vers la plus grande Allemagne,* Centre d'Etudes de Politique Etrangère, Section d'Information, Publication No. 14. Paris: Paul Hartmann, 1939.

Bonnamour, George: *Le Rapprochement franco-allemand.* Paris: Delpeuch, 1927.

Boveri, Margret: *Mediterranean Cross-Currents.* New York: Oxford University Press, 1938.

Brinon, Ferdinand de: *France-Allemagne, 1918-1934.* Paris: B. Grasset, 1934.

Brossolette, Pierre: "Origine et éléments de la conception française 'du règlement général' de la paix en Europe," *Politique Etrangère,* II (février 1937), pp. 82-91.

Brown, Francis J.; Hodges, Charles; and Roucek, Joseph S., eds.: *Contemporary World Politics: an introduction to the problems of international relations.* New York: John Wiley & Sons, Inc., 1939.

Buell, Raymond L.: *Poland: Key to Europe.* New York: A. A. Knopf, 1939.

Bugnet, Charles: *En écoutant le maréchal Foch (1921-1929).* Paris: B. Grasset, 1929. (U. S. ed., *Foch Speaks.* New York: The Dial Press, 1926.)

Bywater, Hector: "The Changing Balance of Power in the Mediterranean," *International Affairs*, XVI (May–June, 1937), pp. 361-388.

Chaput, Rolland A.: *Disarmament in British Foreign Policy*. London: Allen & Unwin, Ltd., 1935.

Charvet, Jean Félix: *L'Influence britannique dans la S. D. N.* Paris: Librairie L. Rodstein, 1938.

La Conciliation Internationale. Bulletin, since 1919, Centre Européen de la Dotation Carnegie, Division des Relations Internationales et de l'Education.

Crane, John O.: *The Little Entente*. New York: The Macmillan Company, 1931.

Cumming, Henry H.: *Franco-British Rivalry in the Post-War Near East*. New York: Oxford University Press, 1938.

Currey, Muriel I.: *Italian Foreign Policy, 1918-1932*. London: Nicholson & Watson, Ltd., 1932.

Davis, Kathryn W.: *The Soviets at Geneva: The U.S.S.R. at the League of Nations, 1919-1933*. Geneva: Librairie Kundig, 1934.

Dawson, William H.: *Germany under the Treaty*. London: Allen & Unwin, Ltd., 1933.

Dewall, Wolf von: *Der Kampf um den Frieden: Deutschland-Frankreich in der Europäischen Politik*. Frankfurt: Frankfurter Societätsdruckerei, 1929.

Edwards, William: *British Foreign Policy from 1815 to 1933*. London: Methuen & Company, Ltd., 1934.

Einzig, Paul: *Finance and Politics*. London: Macmillan & Company, Ltd., 1932.

Eschmann, Ernst Wilhelm: *Die Aussenpolitik des Faschismus*. Berlin: Junker und Dünnhaupt, 1934.

Escholier, Raymond: *Souvenirs Parlés de Briand*. Paris: Librairie Hachette, 1932.

Fabre-Luce, Alfred: *La Crise des Alliances: essai sur les relations franco-britanniques depuis la signature de la paix (1919-1922)*. Paris: B. Grasset, 1922.

Locarno, the Reality. New York: A. A. Knopf, 1928.

Fischer, Louis: *The Soviets in World Affairs: a history of relations between the Soviet Union and the rest of the world*, 2 vols. New York: Jonathan Cape & Harrison Smith, 1930.

Foreign Affairs: an American quarterly review, Vol. I, No. 1, September, 1922—. New York: Council on Foreign Relations.

Foreign Policies of the Great Powers. Lectures arranged by the University of California Committee on International Relations. Delivered in the spring of 1939. Berkeley: University of California Press, 1939.

The Foreign Policy of the Powers. France, Germany, Great Britain, Italy, Japan, Soviet Russia, the United States, by Jules Cambon, Richard von Kühlmann, Sir Austen Chamberlain, Dino Grandi, Viscount Ishii, Karl Radek, John W. Davis. New York: Harper and Brothers for the Council on Foreign Relations, 1935.

Foreign Policy Reports, biweekly, Vol. I, No. 1, October, 1925—. New York: Foreign Policy Association.

Friedrich, Carl J.: *Foreign Policy in the Making: the search for a new balance of power.* New York: W. W. Norton & Co., Inc., 1938.

Gautier, Charles: *L'Angleterre et Nous.* Paris: B. Grasset, 1922.

Géraud, André, see Pertinax.

Glasgow, George: *MacDonald as a Diplomatist: the foreign policy of the first Labour government in Great Britain.* London: J. Cape, Ltd., 1924.

Gooch, George P.: *British Foreign Policy since the War.* Historical Association Pamphlet, No. 102. London: G. Bell and Sons, Ltd., 1936.

Grigg, Sir Edward W.: *Britain Looks at Germany.* London: Nicholson & Watson, Ltd., 1938.

The Faith of an Englishman. London: Macmillan & Company, Ltd., 1936.

Hamburger, Maurice: *Léon Bourgeois, 1851-1925: la politique radicale socialiste, la doctrine de la solidarité, l'arbitrage international et la Société des Nations.* Paris: M. Rivière, 1932.

Harper, Samuel N., ed.: *The Soviet Union and World Problems.* Lectures on the Harris Foundation, 1935. Chicago: University of Chicago Press, 1935.

Hérisson, Charles D.: *Les Nations Anglo-Saxonnes et la Paix.* Paris: Recueil Sirey, 1936.

Hoetzsch, Otto: *Germany's Domestic and Foreign Policies.* New Haven: Yale University Press, 1929.

International Affairs, bi-monthly, Vol. I, No. 1, January, 1922—. London: Royal Institute of International Affairs.

International Conciliation, monthly, No. 134, January, 1919—. New York: Carnegie Endowment for International Peace, Division of Intercourse and Education.

Jäckh, Ernst: *Deutschland, das Herz Europas.* Berlin: Deutsche Verlagsanstalt, 1928.

Der Kampf um die Deutsche Aussenpolitik. Leipzig: Liszt, 1931.

Kayser, Jacques: "France and the International Situation," *International Affairs,* XV (July–August, 1936), pp. 506-524.

"French Policy and the Reconstruction of the League," in *Problems of Peace,* twelfth series, *Geneva and the Drift to War,* pp. 161-175. London: Allen & Unwin, Ltd., 1938.

Kennedy, Aubrey L.: *Britain Faces Germany.* London: J. Cape, Ltd., 1937.

Keynes, John M.: *The Economic Consequences of the Peace.* Harcourt, Brace and Howe, 1920.

A Revision of the Treaty. New York: Harcourt, Brace and Company, 1922.

Koch-Weser, Erich: *Germany in the Post-War World.* Philadelphia: Dorrance, 1930.

Lhopital, René M.: *Foch, l'Armistice et la Paix.* Paris: Librairie Plon, 1938.

Lichtenberger, Henri: *Relations between France and Germany.* Washington: Carnegie Endowment for International Peace, 1923.

The Third Reich. Translated from the French and edited by Koppel S. Pinson. New York: Greystone Press, 1937.

Liddell Hart, Basil H.: *The Defence of Britain.* New York: Random House, 1939.

Livingstone, Dame Adelaide: *The Peace Ballot: the official history.* London: V. Gollancz, Ltd., 1935.

Macartney, Maxwell H., and Cremona, Paul: *Italy's Foreign and Colonial Policy, 1914-1937.* New York: Oxford University Press, 1938.

Machray, Robert: *The Little Entente.* New York: Richard R. Smith, 1930.

The Struggle for the Danube and the Little Entente, 1929-1938. London: Allen & Unwin, Ltd., 1938.

Madariaga, Salvador de: *Englishmen, Frenchmen, Spaniards: an essay in comparative psychology.* New York: Oxford University Press, 1928.

Maddox, William P.: *Foreign Relations in British Labour Politics.* Cambridge: Harvard University Press, 1934.

Martel, René: *La France et la Pologne.* Paris: M. Rivière, 1931.

Martelli, George: *Italy against the World.* New York: Harcourt, Brace and Company, 1938.

Martet, Jean: *Georges Clemenceau.* New York: Longmans, Green and Company, 1930.

"M. Clemenceau and the Versailles Peace Treaty," *Journal of the Royal Institute of International Affairs*, IX (November, 1930), pp. 783-800.

Maurras, Charles: *Casier Judiciaire d'Aristide Briand*. Paris: Editions du Capitole, 1931.

Les Conditions de la Victoire, 8 vols. Paris: Nouvelle Librairie Nationale, 1916-1920.

Devant l'Allemagne éternelle. Paris: Editions "A l'Etoile," 1937.

Le Mauvais Traité, de la Victoire à Locarno: chronique d'une décadence. Paris: Editions du Capitole, 1928.

Maxwell, Bertram W.: *International Relations*. New York: Thomas Y. Crowell Company, 1939.

Mermeix, *pseud.* (Gabriel Terrail): *Le Combat des Trois: notes et documents sur la Conférence de la Paix*. Fragments d'histoire, 1914-1919, VI. Paris: P. Ollendorff, 1922.

Les Négociations Secrètes et les Quatre Armistices avec pièces justificatives. Fragments d'histoire, 1914-1919, V. Paris: P. Ollendorff, 1921.

Milioukov, Paul: *La Politique extérieure des Soviets*, 2nd ed. Bibliothèque d'Etudes sur la Russie contemporaine, Tome 1. Paris: Librairie générale de droit et de jurisprudence, 1936.

Mistler, Jean, and others: *Problèmes de Politique extérieure*. Paris: F. Alcan, 1938.

Mordacq, Jean: *Le Ministère Clemenceau, Journal d'un Témoin*, 4 vols. Paris: Librairie Plon, 1930-1931.

Moss, Warner: "Britain and the Empire," in *Contemporary World Politics* (Brown, F. J., Hodges, C., Roucek, J. S., eds.), Chapter 6. New York: John Wiley & Sons, Inc., 1939.

New Fabian Research Bureau: *Labour's Foreign Policy*. Publication No. 18. London: V. Gollancz, Ltd., and the New Fabian Research Bureau, 1934.

Nicolson, Harold G.: *Curzon: The Last Phase, 1919-1925: a study in post-war diplomacy*. New York: Houghton Mifflin Company, 1934.

"Has Britain a Policy?" *Foreign Affairs*, XIV (July, 1936), pp. 549-562.

"What France Means to England," *Foreign Affairs*, XVII (January, 1939), pp. 351-361.

Ormesson, Wladimir, Comte d': *La Confiance en l'Allemagne?* Les Documents Bleus, No. 43. Paris: Librairie Gallimard, 1928.

France. New York: Longmans, Green and Company, 1939.

Pertinax, *pseud.* (André Géraud): "L'Assistance mutuelle franco-britannique," *Politique Etrangère*, II (avril, 1937), pp. 107-116.

"British Policy as Seen by a Frenchman," *Journal of the Royal Institute of International Affairs*, IX (March, 1930), pp. 154-179.

"British Vacillations," *Foreign Affairs*, XIV (July, 1936), pp. 584-597.

"France and the Anglo-German Naval Treaty," *Foreign Affairs*, XIV (October, 1935), pp. 51-61.

"French Responsibilities in Europe," *Foreign Affairs*, V (January, 1927), pp. 241-248.

"What England Means to France," *Foreign Affairs*, XVII (January, 1939), pp. 362-373.

Pinon, René: *L'Avenir de l'Entente Franco-Anglaise*. Paris: Plon-Nourrit, 1924.

La Bataille de la Ruhr, 1923. Paris: Perrin, 1923.

Chroniques du Ministère Poincaré: le redressement de la politique française. Paris: Perrin, 1923.

Politique Etrangère, bi-monthly, Vol. I, No. 1, October, 1936—. Paris: Centre d'Etudes de Politique Etrangère.

Problems of Peace. Lectures delivered at the Geneva Institute of International Relations. First Series, 1926 (Annual). London: Humphrey Milford, Oxford University Press, 1927-1931; Allen & Unwin, Ltd., 1932—.

Rathbone, Eleanor F., ed.: *The Tragedy of Abyssinia: what Britain feels and thinks and wants*. London: League of Nations Union, 1936.

Ray, Marcel: "French Foreign Policy," *International Affairs*, XI (May, 1932), pp. 297-320.

Recouly, Raymond: *Marshal Foch: his own words on many subjects*. London: T. Butterworth, Ltd., 1929.

Rheinbaben, Werner, Freiherr von: *Von Versailles zur Freiheit*. Hamburg: Hanseatische Verlagsanstalt, 1927.

Riddell, George, Lord: *Lord Riddell's Intimate Diary of the Peace Conference and After, 1918-1923*. New York: Reynal & Hitchcock, Inc., 1934.

The Road to War: being an analysis of the National Government's foreign policy. London: Published for the New Fabian Research Bureau by V. Gollancz, Ltd., 1937.

Rohde, Hans: *Italien und Frankreich in ihren politischen, militärischen und wirtschaftlichen Gegensätzen*. Berlin: Mittler, 1931.

Ronaldshay, Lawrence Dundas, Marquess of: *The Life of Lord Curzon*, 3 vols. New York: Boni & Liveright, 1928.

Royal Institute of International Affairs: *Germany and the Rhineland:* a record of the proceedings of three meetings held at Chatham House on March 18th, March 25th, and April 2nd, 1936. London: The Royal Institute of International Affairs, 1936.

Political and Strategic Interests of the United Kingdom. New York: Oxford University Press, 1939.

Schwoebel, Jean: *L'Angleterre et la Sécurité Collective.* Paris: Recueil Sirey, 1938.

Seeckt, Hans, Generaloberst von: *Deutschland zwischen West und Ost.* Hamburg: Hanseatische Verlagsanstalt, 1933.

Selsam, John P.: *The Attempts to Form an Anglo-French Alliance, 1919-1924.* Philadelphia: University of Pennsylvania Press, 1936.

Simonds, Frank H., and Emeny, Brooks: *The Great Powers in World Politics: international relations and economic nationalism,* new ed. New York: American Book Company, 1939.

Sipple, Chester E.: *British Foreign Policy since the World War.* University of Iowa, Studies in the Social Sciences, X, No. 1. Iowa City: University of Iowa, 1932.

Slocombe, George: *The Dangerous Sea: the Mediterranean and its future.* New York: The Macmillan Company, 1937.

Smogorzewski, Casimir M.: *La Politique Polonaise de la France.* Paris: Gebethner et Wolff, 1926.

Steed, Henry W.: "Locarno and British Interests," *Journal of the British Institute of International Affairs,* IV (November, 1925), pp. 286-303.

Stresemann, Gustav: *Essays and Speeches on Various Subjects.* London: T. Butterworth, Ltd., 1930.

Gustav Stresemann: his diaries, letters and papers. 2 vols. London: Macmillan & Company, Ltd., 1935-1937.

Stuart, Graham H.: "The Struggle of France for Hegemony and Security," in *Contemporary World Politics* (Brown, F. J., Hodges, C., Roucek, J. S., eds.), Chapter 7. New York: John Wiley & Sons, Inc., 1939.

Tabouis, Geneviève R.: *Perfidious Albion—Entente Cordiale.* London: T. Butterworth, Ltd., 1938.

Tirard, Paul: *La France sur le Rhin: douze années d'occupation rhénane.* Paris: Librairie Plon, 1930.

Toynbee, Arnold J., and others: "The Issues in British Foreign Policy," *International Affairs,* XVII (May–June, 1938), pp. 307-407.

Vaucher, Paul: *Post-War France.* London: T. Butterworth, Ltd., 1934.

Vaucher, Paul, and Siriex, Paul-Henri: *L'Opinion britannique, la Société des Nations et la Guerre italo-éthiopienne.* Centre d'Etudes de Politique Etrangère, Section d'Information, Publication No. 2. Paris: Paul Hartmann, 1936.

Vergnet, Paul: *La France au Rhin.* Paris: La Renaissance du Livre, 1919.

Vermeil, Edmond: *L'Allemagne et les Démocraties Occidentales: les conditions générales des relations franco-allemandes.* Paris: Publications de la Conciliation Internationale, 1931.

Vibraye, Regis de: *1935—Paix avec l'Allemagne?* Paris: Les Editions Denoël et Steele, 1934.

Vigilantes, *pseud.*: *Inquest on Peace: an analysis of the National Government's foreign policy.* London: V. Gollancz, Ltd., 1935.

Vondraček, Felix J.: *The Foreign Policy of Czechoslovakia, 1918-1935.* New York: Columbia University Press, 1937.

Willert, Sir Arthur: *Aspects of British Foreign Policy.* New Haven: Yale University Press, 1928.

What Next in Europe? New York: G. P. Putnam's Sons, 1936. (English ed., *The Frontiers of England.* London: W. Heinemann, Ltd., 1935.)

Willert, Sir Arthur, and others: *The Empire in the World.* New York: Oxford University Press, 1937.

Wirsing, Giselher: *Deutschland in der Weltpolitik.* Jena: Eugen Diederich, 1933.

Zwischeneuropa und die Deutsche Zukunft. Jena: Eugen Diederich, 1932.

World Affairs Pamphlets, No. 1, January, 1938—. New York: Foreign Policy Association.

B. International Law and Organization

Baker, Philip J. Noel: *Disarmament.* New York: Harcourt, Brace and Company, 1936.

The Geneva Protocol for the Pacific Settlement of Disputes. London: P. S. King & Son, Ltd., 1925.

Barandon, Paul: *Das System der politischen Staatsverträge seit 1918.* Handbuch des Völkerrechts, Vol. 4, Part II. Stuttgart: Verlag von W. Kohlhammer, 1937.

Le Système Juridique de la Société des Nations pour la Prévention de la Guerre. Paris: A. Pedone, 1933.

Berber, Fritz: *Sicherheit und Gerechtigkeit.* Berlin: Carl Heymanns Verlag, 1934.

Bourquin, Maurice, ed.: *Collective Security: a record of the seventh and eighth International Studies Conferences, Paris, 1934–London, 1935.* Paris: International Institute of Intellectual Co-operation, 1936.

Brück, Otto: *Les Sanctions en Droit International Public.* Paris: A. Pedone, 1933.

Brunet, René: *La Société des Nations et la France.* Paris: L. Tenin, 1921.

Djourovitch, Djoura: *Le Protocole de Genève devant l'Opinion anglaise.* Paris: Jouve, 1928.

Dunn, Frederick S.: *Peaceful Change: a study of international procedures.* New York: Council on Foreign Relations, 1937.

Eagleton, Clyde: "Bibliography on Aggression," *American Journal of International Law,* XXXIII (October, 1939), Section Two, Documents, pp. 831-843.

Engely, Giovanni: *The Politics of Naval Disarmament.* London: Williams and Norgate, Ltd., 1932.

Freytagh-Loringhoven, Axel, Baron von: "Les Ententes Régionales," Hague, Académie de Droit International, *Recueil des Cours,* Vol. 56 (1936, II), pp. 585-678.

Giovannucci, Francesco Saverio: *Locarno.* Rome: Edizione Roma, 1935.

Gonsiorowski, Miroslas: *Société des Nations et Problème de la Paix.* Paris: Rousseau, 1927.

Grigg, Sir Edward: "The Merits and Defects of the Locarno Treaty as a Guarantee of World Peace," *International Affairs,* XIV (March–April, 1935), pp. 176-197.

Guggenheim, Paul: *Der Völkerbund.* Berlin: B. G. Teubner, 1932.

Headway, monthly, Vol. I, No. 1, January, 1919. London: League of Nations Union.

Higgins, Alexander Pearce: *Studies in International Law and Relations.* Cambridge: The University Press, 1928.

Hindmarsh, Albert E.: *Force in Peace: force short of war in international relations.* Cambridge: Harvard University Press, 1933.

Hoijer, Olof: *Le Pacte de la Société des Nations: commentaire théorique et pratique.* Paris: "Editions Spes," 1926.

La Sécurité Internationale et ses Modes de Réalisation, 4 vols. Paris: Les Editions Internationales, 1930.

Howard-Ellis, Charles: *The Origin, Structure, and Working of the League of Nations.* London: Allen & Unwin, Ltd., 1928.

Kellor, Frances A.: *Security Against War*, 2 vols. New York: The Macmillan Company, 1924.

Kraemer, Fritz: *Das Verhältnis der französischen Bündnisverträge zum Völkerbundpakt und zum Pakt von Locarno; eine juristisch-politische Studie.* Frankfurter Abhandlungen zum modernen Völkerrecht, Heft 30, Leipzig: R. Noske, 1932.

League of Nations Union: Publications series (pamphlets, leaflets, etc.).

Linnebach, Karl: *Die Entmilitarisierung der Rheinlande und der Vertrag von Locarno.* Berlin: R. Hobbing, 1927.

Madariaga, Salvador de: *Disarmament.* New York: Coward-McCann, Inc., 1929.

Mandelsloh, Asche, Graf von: *Politische Pakte und völkerrechtliche Ordnung.* "Sonderdruck aus 25 Jahre Kaiser Wilhelm-Gesellschaft zur Förderung der Wissenschaften," Band III: Die Geisteswissenschaften, pp. 213-328. Berlin: J. Springer, 1937.

Margueritte, Victor: *The League Fiasco (1920-1936).* London: W. Hodge and Company, Ltd., 1936.

Marshall-Cornwall, Major-General J. H.: *Geographic Disarmament: a study in regional demilitarization.* London: Oxford University Press, 1935.

Miller, David Hunter: *The Drafting of the Covenant*, 2 vols. New York: G. P. Putnam's Sons, 1928.

My Diary at the Conference of Paris, 21 vols. New York: Privately printed, 1924.

Mitrany, David: *The Problem of International Sanctions.* New York: Oxford University Press, 1925.

Morley, Felix: *The Society of Nations: its organization and constitutional development.* Washington: The Brookings Institution, 1932.

The New Commonwealth Quarterly: a review devoted to research into problems of international justice and security, Vol. I, No. 1, April, 1935—. London: New Commonwealth Institute.

Nicolson, Harold G.: *Peacemaking, 1919.* London: Constable & Co., Ltd., 1934.

Pensa, Henri: *De Locarno au Pacte Kellogg: la politique européenne sous le triumvirat Chamberlain-Briand-Stresemann, 1925-1929.* Paris: Georges Roustan, 1929.

Raafat, Waheed: *Le Problème de la Sécurité Internationale.* Paris: A. Pedone, 1930.

Rappard, William E.: *International Relations as Viewed from Geneva.* New Haven: Yale University Press, 1925.

Ray, Jean: *Commentaire du Pacte de la Société des Nations selon la Politique et la Jurisprudence des Organes de la Société.* Paris: Recueil Sirey, 1930.

La Politique et la Jurisprudence de la Société des Nations du Début de 1930 au Début de 1931. (1er supplément au commentaire du pacte.) Paris: Recueil Sirey, 1931.

La Politique et la Jurisprudence de la Société des Nations du Début de 1931 au Début de 1932. (2e supplément au commentaire du pacte.) Paris: Recueil Sirey, 1932.

La Politique et la Jurisprudence de la Société des Nations du Début de 1932 au Début de 1933. (3e supplément au commentaire du pacte.) Paris: Recueil Sirey, 1933.

La Politique et la Jurisprudence de la Société des Nations du Début de 1933 au Début de 1935. (4e supplément au commentaire du pacte.) Paris: Recueil Sirey, 1935.

Rogge, Heinrich: *Kollektivsicherheit, Bündnispolitik, Völkerbund: Theorie der nationalen und internationalen Sicherheit.* Berlin: Junker und Dünnhaupt, 1937.

Nationale Friedenspolitik: Handbuch des Friedensproblems und seiner Wissenschaft auf der Grundlage systematischer Völkerrechtspolitik. Berlin: Junker und Dünnhaupt, 1934.

Das Revisionsproblem: Theorie der Revision als Voraussetzung einer internationalen wissenschaftlichen Aussprache über "peaceful change of status quo." Berlin: Junker und Dünnhaupt, 1937.

Royal Institute of International Affairs: *The Future of the League of Nations: the record of a series of discussions held at Chatham House.* New York: Oxford University Press, 1936.

International Sanctions. New York: Oxford University Press, 1938.

Saint-Aulaire, Auguste Felix, Comte de: *Genève contre la Paix.* Paris: Librairie Plon, 1936.

Salter, Sir J. Arthur: *Security; Can We Retrieve It?* New York: Reynal & Hitchcock, Inc., 1939.

Schücking, Walther, and Wehberg, Hans: *Die Satzung des Völkerbundes,* 2nd ed. Berlin: Verlag von Franz Vahlen, 1924.

Die Satzung des Völkerbundes, 3rd ed. Berlin: Verlag von Franz Vahlen, 1931.

Schuman, Frederick L.: *International Politics: an introduction to the western state system*, 2nd ed. New York: McGraw-Hill Book Company, Inc., 1937.

Schwendemann, Karl: *Abrüstung und Sicherheit*, 2 vols., 2nd ed. Berlin: Weidmann, 1933-1935.

Shotwell, James T.: *On the Rim of the Abyss*. New York: The Macmillan Company, 1936.

War as an Instrument of National Policy and its Renunciation in the Pact of Paris. New York: Harcourt, Brace and Company, 1929.

Sicherheit. Europäische Revue (Sonderheft), XI, Heft 11/12. Berlin: Deutsche Verlagsanstalt, 1935.

Spaight, James M.: *Pseudo-Security*. New York: Longmans, Green and Company, 1928.

Steinlein, Wilhelm: *Der Begriff des nicht herausgeforderten Angriffs in Bündnisverträgen seit 1870 und insbesondere im Locarno-Vertrag*. Frankfurter Abhandlungen zum Kriegsverhütungsrecht, Heft 5. Leipzig: R. Noske, 1927.

Strupp, Karl: *Das Werk von Locarno: eine völkerrechtlichpolitische Studie*. Berlin: W. de Gruyter, 1926.

Triepel, Heinrich: *Die Hegemonie: ein Buch von führenden Staaten*. Stuttgart: Verlag von W. Kohlhammer, 1938.

Wache, Walter: *System der Pakte: die politischen Verträge der Nachkriegszeit*. Berlin: Volk und Reich Verlag, 1938.

Webster, Charles K., and Herbert, Sydney: *The League of Nations, in Theory and Practice*. New York: Houghton Mifflin Company, 1933.

Wheeler-Bennett, John W.: *Disarmament and Security since Locarno, 1925-1931*. London: Allen & Unwin, Ltd., 1932.

Information on the Reduction of Armaments. London: Allen & Unwin, Ltd., 1925.

Information on the Renunciation of War, 1927-1928. London: Allen & Unwin, Ltd., 1928.

The Pipe Dream of Peace: the story of the collapse of disarmament. New York: W. Morrow and Company, 1935.

Wheeler-Bennett, John W., and Langermann, Frederic: *Information on the Problem of Security, 1917-1926*. London: Allen & Unwin, Ltd., 1927.

Wild, Payson S., Jr.: *Sanctions and Treaty Enforcement*. Cambridge: Harvard University Press, 1934.

Williams, Bruce S.: *State Security and the League of Nations*. Baltimore: The Johns Hopkins Press, 1927.

Williams, Roth: *The League, the Protocol, and the Empire.* London: Allen & Unwin, Ltd., 1925.

Zimmern, Alfred: *The League of Nations and the Rule of Law, 1918-1935.* London: Macmillan & Company, Ltd., 1936.

C. European History since 1918

Alexander, Frederick: *From Paris to Locarno, and After: the League of Nations and the search for security, 1919-1928.* London: J. M. Dent & Sons, Ltd., 1928.

Armstrong, Hamilton F.: *Europe between Wars?* New York: The Macmillan Company, 1934.

When There Is No Peace. New York: The Macmillan Company, 1939.

Baker, Ray S.: *Woodrow Wilson and World Settlement,* 3 vols. Garden City, New York: Doubleday, Page and Company, 1922.

Benns, Frank L.: *Europe Since 1914.* New York: F. S. Crofts and Company, 1930.

Carr, Edward H.: *International Relations Since the Peace Treaties.* London: Macmillan & Company, Ltd., 1937.

Dawes, Charles G.: *Journal as an Ambassador to Great Britain.* New York: The Macmillan Company, 1939.

A Journal of Reparations. London: Macmillan & Company, Ltd., 1939.

Dean, Vera Micheles: *Europe in Retreat.* New York: A. A. Knopf, 1939.

Dupuis, Charles: *La Politique internationale de l'Europe.* Institut de Hautes Etudes Internationales, Cours sténographié, 1931-1932. Paris: Centre Européen de la Dotation Carnegie, 1932.

Dutt, R. Palme: *World Politics, 1918-1936.* New York: Random House, 1936.

Fabre-Luce, Alfred: *Histoire secrète de la capitulation de Munich.* Paris: B. Grasset, 1938.

Gathorne-Hardy, Geoffrey M.: *A Short History of International Affairs, 1920-1938.* London: Oxford University Press, 1938.

Glasgow, George: *From Dawes to Locarno: being a critical record of an important achievement in European diplomacy, 1924-1925.* London: E. Benn, Ltd., 1926.

Hasluck, Eugene L.: *Foreign Affairs, 1919-1937.* New York: The Macmillan Company, 1938.

House, Edward M., and Seymour, Charles, eds.: *What Really Happened at Paris.* New York: C. Scribner's Sons, 1921.

Hutton, Graham: *Survey after Munich.* New York: Little, Brown and Company, 1939.

Jackson, J. Hampden: *A Short History of the World since 1918.* New York: Little, Brown and Company, 1939.

Kayser, Jacques: *Les Etats-Unis d'Europe* (*de Versailles à Locarno*). Paris: Les Editions du Monde Moderne, 1926.

King-Hall, Stephen: *Our Own Times, 1913-1934: a political and economic survey,* 2 vols. London: Nicholson and Watson, Ltd., 1934-35.

Langsam, Walter C.: *The World since 1914.* New York: The Macmillan Company, 1939.

Orton, William: *Twenty Years' Armistice, 1918-1938.* New York: Farrar & Rinehart, Inc., 1938.

Riddell, George, Lord, and others: *The Treaty of Versailles and After.* New York: Oxford University Press, 1935.

Royal Institute of International Affairs (Arnold J. Toynbee): *Survey of International Affairs, 1920-1923, 1924*— (annual). London: Oxford University Press, 1925—.

Schmitt, Bernadotte E.: *From Versailles to Munich, 1918-1938.* Public Policy Pamphlets, No. 28. Chicago: University of Chicago Press, 1938.

Schuman, Frederick L.: *Europe on the Eve: the crises of diplomacy, 1933-1939.* New York: A. A. Knopf, 1939.

Seton-Watson, Robert W.: *Britain and The Dictators: a survey of post-war British policy.* Cambridge, England: The University Press, 1938.

Munich and the Dictators. London: Methuen & Company, Ltd., 1939.

Seymour, Charles, ed.: *The Intimate Papers of Colonel House,* 4 vols. Boston: Houghton Mifflin Company, 1926-1928.

Sontag, Raymond J.: *European Diplomatic History, 1871-1932.* New York: The Century Company, 1933.

Stimson, Henry L.: *The Far Eastern Crisis: recollections and observations.* New York: Harper and Brothers, 1936.

Temperley, Harold W.: *A History of the Peace Conference of Paris,* 6 vols. London: H. Froude, Hodder & Stoughton, 1920-1924.

Toynbee, Arnold J.: *The World After the Peace Conference.* New York: Oxford University Press, 1925.

Werth, Alexander: *The Destiny of France.* London: Hamish Hamilton, 1937.

France and Munich: before and after the surrender. London: Hamish Hamilton, 1939.

Index

19TH- AND 20TH-CENTURY EUROPEAN HISTORY TITLES IN THE NORTON LIBRARY

Aron, Raymond. *On War.* N107

Aron, Raymond. *The Opium of the Intellectuals.* N106

Bloch, Marc. *Strange Defeat: A Statement of Evidence Written in 1940.* N371

Brandt, Conrad. *Stalin's Failure in China.* N352

Brinton, Crane. *The Lives of Talleyrand.* N188

Butterfield, Herbert. *The Whig Interpretation of History.* N318

Burn, W. L. *The Age of Equipoise.* N319

Calleo, David P. *Europe's Future: The Grand Alternatives.* N406

Dehio, Ludwig. *Germany and World Politics in the Twentieth Century.* N391

East, W. Gordon. *The Geography Behind History.* N419

Eyck, Erich. *Bismarck and the German Empire.* N235

Ferrero, Guglielmo. *The Reconstruction of Europe.* N208

Feis, Herbert. *Europe: The World's Banker 1870-1914.* N327

Feis, Herbert. *The Spanish Story.* N339

Feis, Herbert. *Three International Episodes:* Seen from E. A. N351

Gulick, Edward Vose. *Europe's Classical Balance of Power.* N413

Halperin, S. William. *Germany Tried Democracy.* N280

Hobsbawm, E. J. *Primitive Rebels.* N328

Langer, William L. *Our Vichy Gamble.* N379

Menéndez Pidal, Ramón. *The Spaniards in Their History.* N353

Rowse, A. L. *Appeasement.* N139

Russell, Bertrand. *Freedom versus Organization: 1814-1914.* N136

Thompson, J. M. *Louis Napoleon and the Second Empire.* N403

Whyte, A. J. *The Evolution of Modern Italy.* N298

Wolfers, Arnold. *Britain and France between Two Wars.* N343

Wolff, Robert Lee. *The Balkans in Our Time.* N395